I0121622

NORFOLK BOROUGH COURT HOUSE—MAIN STREET, NORFOLK, VA.
Built between 1791-1792 and remained in use until May 29, 1850.

Abstracts

FROM

Norfolk City Marriage Bonds

(1797-1850)

AND OTHER GENEALOGICAL DATA

༜

Compiled and Annotated

By

GEORGE HOLBERT TUCKER

༜

Illustrated With Original Block Prints

By

WORTH BAILEY

CLEARFIELD

Originally published
Virginia, 1934

Reprinted for
Clearfield Company, Inc. by
Genealogical Publishing Co., Inc.
Baltimore, Maryland
2001

International Standard Book Number: 0-8063-5115-2
Made in the United States of America

FOREWORD

The publication of these Norfolk City Marriage Bonds should prove of interest for several reasons. First, they have never been published before. Second, the transcription is most opportune, since the originals are rapidly becoming useless through neglect and disintegration. And third, since they are the most complete files of their particular kind to be found in this section of Virginia, this being due to the fact that Norfolk is the only large city of any importance in this vicinity. It is natural, therefore, in view of this fact, that one will not only find the names of Norfolk residents during the period covered, but also those of many who came here from adjoining towns, counties and states to be married.

The transcription has covered the period of over a year, during which time the compiler has endeavored in every possible way to make the copy as accurate as the records themselves. In every case, the names of the parties and their securities have been copied exactly as the clerk or the individuals in question set them down. Since the name of the bride was always written by the clerk of the court or one of his deputies, it is not possible for anyone to be absolutely certain at this late date that the name is spelled exactly as it should be. In many cases, however, notes from the parents or guardians of the bride giving their consent to the marriage, enabled the compiler to check on this particular point. Otherwise the names in question are published as they appear on the bonds. In a few instances, the writing was either so faded or so poor that it was almost impossible to make out a name. In such instances, two methods of possible elucidation were adopted. First, when the name appeared to be one of prominence, the contemporary deeds on file in the Clerk's office were consulted, or it was checked with family papers of known authenticity. If this method failed, the compiler copied it as it was written and followed it with an optional in parentheses, listing it under both headings in the index. Many names now spelled but one way were then spelled two, three or even four different ways. These have been transcribed exactly as they appear on the books and also have been listed in the index, headed however with the form in general use today or the most common form of yesterday. Our ancestors were peculiar people, orthographically speaking, and took great liberties with their i's and e's. As a final check for accuracy, the entire volume has been checked again with the original bonds before commencing the index. All typographical errors discovered in this check have been included in an errata, and may be found at the beginning of the book.

The compiler has also been fortunate in establishing the actual fact of marriage in the majority of cases. This has been done by referring to the Returns made by local ministers on marriages performed by them covering the period of the bonds. These valuable papers are still on file in the Corporation Court and besides having acted as a check on the bonds themselves, have also furnished the names of many who secured licenses elsewhere and came to Norfolk for the ceremony. In every case, these marriages have been included under the correct date with a proper note of explanation. It was during the examination of these particular papers that the compiler discovered the early burial and baptismal lists of the Rev. Robert S. Symes of Christ P. E. Church. Deeming them of sufficient interest, they have been included in this volume.

In conclusion, I should like to express my sincerest gratitude to all those whose kind help and interest have made this volume possible. My especial thanks are due: first, to W. L. Prieur, Esq., Clerk of the Corporation Court of Norfolk, and his able deputies, for having permitted me free access to all the fascinating old papers on file there in my efforts to make this book a creditable production; second, to the Librarian of the City of Norfolk and her assistants for aiding me in the research work connected with this volume in the Virginianna collection at the Public Library; third, to my friend, Miss Margaret Bilisoly, for her encouraging interest and material aid with the index, and, last, but not least, to my friend, Worth Bailey, for his helpful suggestions and the lovely block prints, designed and cut by him for this particular book in order that it might be artistically presentable.

GEORGE HOLBERT TUCKER.

TABLE OF CONTENTS

LIST OF ILLUSTRATIONS

> NOTE: Taken from an old drawing in the possession of Minton Wright
> Talbot, Esq. This old building stood on East Main Street on the
> present site of the Union Mission. It was built between 1790 and
> 1791 and remained in use until May 29, 1850, on which date, the
> Court of the City of Norfolk convened for the first time in the present
> City Hall.

> NOTE: This print was made from a sketch of the church in question dis-
> covered by the compiler on an early survey of the Borough of Nor-
> folk on file in the office of the Clerk of the Corporation Court.

These two illustrations as well as the other decorations that appear at
intervals through this book are the work of Worth Bailey and were printed
from the original blocks.

ERRATA

Page   1—Ricardson should read Richardson.
Page   5—Mrs. Hennah Manning should probably read Mrs. Hannah Manning.
Page   8—Mrs. Elizabeth Allin should probably read Mrs. Elizabeth Allen.
Page   11, 12—Rissaud should read Riffaud.
Page   32, 33—D'Antossy should read D'Anfossy.
Page   76—John Frnch should read John French.
Page   105—John D. Gordan should read John D. Gordan.
Page   124—Walter Pierce should read Walter Pearce.
Page   130—Love D. Nicholson should read Love T. Nicholson.
          William Sangan should probably read William Langan.
Page   131—Mrs. Elizabeth Frigeley should probably read Figeley.
Page   133—Richard Nottingham should read Richard C. Nottingham.
Page   134—William A. Dawley should read William W. Dawley.
          Hendred should read Hendren.
          Granberry should read Granbery.
Page   136—John Webster should read Webber.
Page   137—Corran should probably read Conan.
          Mrs. Catherine Raney should probably read Boney.
Page   141—Thomas Kellun should probably read Kellam.
Page   142—James T. Bloodgood should read James J. Bloodgood.
          Ananda M. F. Bullock should read Amanda M. F. Bullock.
Page   144—The note under May 9, 1836 should go under May 10, 1836.

INDEX

Eyer should read Eyre.

NORPOLK CITY, MARRIAGE BONDS
1791 — 1850

1797

January 7, 1797—Peter Gryndal and Miss Elenor Cutter (or Carter).
George Miller, security.

January 12, 1797—John Burket and Abby Foltz.
William Dalby, security.

January 16, 1797—Patrick Ryan and Miss Catherine Lee.
William Charles Lee, security.

January 20, 1797—Joseph Meifren (or Meissen) and Miss Kezerah Spence.
Lewis Marshall, security.

January 23, 1797—John Barns and Mrs. Sarah Bruer.
George Ricardson, security.

Note: Sarah Bruer was the widow of John Bruer.

January 25, 1797—Levin Dorsey and Miss Elizabeth Taylor.
James Dickenson, security.

February 2, 1797—James Ker and Miss Pamela Ann Golden.
Daniel Goulden, security.
Anthony Walac (or Walace), security.

February 3, 1797—John Reynolds and Miss Hannah Faulder.
James Tucker, security.

February 6, 1797—John Fuller and Miss Sarah Wood.
William (mark) Walsh, security.

February 11, 1797—Stephen Price and Miss Margaret Sly.
Seth Price, security.

February 17, 1797—Christopher Coffin and Miss Nancy Bridgers.
Edmund Warriner, security.

February 18, 1797—John Godinicus Brown and Mrs. Catherine Driscoll.
John Drinane, security.

1

February 25, 1797—John Billhouse and Miss Sally Price.

Seth Price, security.

Note: According to an annotation on this bond, John Billhouse was a Dutchman.

March 25, 1797—Edward Moseley and Miss Jennett Cock.

John Cock, security.

April 1, 1797—Charles Ratliff and Miss Delphe Sulivan.

William (mark) Grubb, security.

April 11, 1797—James Chudleigh Southwick and Mrs. Ann Naman.

John Richardson, security.

April 17, 1797—Moses Laurence and Miss Nancy Palmer.

Alexander McDonnald, security.

April 20, 1797—Barney Conly and Miss Jane Long.

John (mark) Barns, security.

April 28, 1797—Francis Hall and Miss Gilley Cooper.

Willis Cooper, security.

April 26, 1797—Andrew Leckie and Miss Mary Brokenbrough.

Francis S. Taylor, security.

Note: According to a note included with this bond Mary Brokenbrough was the niece and ward of John Brokenbrough of Tappahannock, Essex County, Virginia.

May 4, 1797—Isaac Avery and Miss Mary West.

John West, security.

May 13, 1797—Alexander Deal and Miss Isabella Johnson.

Benjamin New, security.

May 29, 1797—Samuel S. Leffingwell and Miss Louisa Whitfield.

William Whitfield, security.

June 1, 1797—William Consolvo and Sally Wright.

Richard Bailey, security.

June 5, 1797—Simeon Peck and Mrs. Lydia Ross.

Thomas Price, security.

June 5, 1797—James Allen and Mrs. Elizabeth Shelton.

John Parish, security.

June 21, 1797—Joseph Brown and Miss Margaret Humphreys.

John Cowdan, security.

June 22, 1797—George Lake and Miss Joanna Syllivan (or Sullivan).

James Struthers, security.

July 8, 1797—John Dougherty and Mrs. Elenor Regan.

William Charles Lee, security.

July 8, 1797—Job Gaskins and Miss Annis Broughton.

George Broughton, security.

July 13, 1797—Johnson Mallory and Miss Ann Boush.

Samuel Coleman, security.

Note: According to a note included with this bond Ann Boush was the daughter of Chas. S. Boush and was born February 16, 1775.

July 22, 1797—Walter Dorsett and Mrs. Isabella Mercer.

Francis Foster, security.

July 29, 1797—James Goodwin and Mrs. Hannah Wolland.

Charles (mark) Bayne, security.

August 7, 1797—Reuben Munn and Mrs. Esther Harris.

Richard Taylor, security.

August 24, 1797—John Nimmo and Miss Ann Archdeacon.

Joseph Nimmo, security.

Note: According to a note included with this bond bearing the signature of John Ingram, "Miss Nancy Archdeacon was born on the first day of January, 1776, a remarkable day for this town." This refers to the bombardment and partial burning of Norfolk by Lord Dunmore, Virginia's last Royal Governor. John Nimmo was the son of James Nimmo.

August 29, 1797—Richard McGrath and Miss Mary Scott.

Mathew Hearey, security.

September 6, 1797—Richard Payne and Miss Nancy Burkett.

George Suggs, security.

Note: According to a note included with this bond, Nancy Burkett was the sister-in-law of Abby Burkett.

September 8, 1797—John Havan and Mary Munroe.

John Logan, security.

September 9, 1797—Alexander McDannell and Mrs. Peggy Fitzpatrick.

John Richardson, security.

October 8, 1797—John Dunn and Miss Polly Billups.

George Billups, security.

October 9, 1797—Michael Mann and Mrs. Rebecca Lee.

George Murphy, security.

November 1, 1797—Benjamin Pollard and Mrs. Caroline H. Norton.

James Taylor, security.

November 4, 1797—Ebenezer Thomas and Miss Mariah Patterson. ╾╂

John Warner, security.

November 10, 1797—John Gray and Mrs. Nancy Coates.

John Abbott, security.

November 10, 1797—Henry B. FitzGerald and Miss Ann Douglass.

Francis Foster, security.

Note: According to an annotation on this bond, Ann Douglass was the niece of Ann Gow, decd.

November 15, 1797—Thomas Traill and Miss Jenny Gibson.

Margaret Burke, security.

November 15, 1797—Hance Hanson and Mrs. Jannet Conelly.

Peter Gryndal, security.

November 17, 1797—Henry Sample and Miss Dinah Bevans.

Francis Drake, security.

December 12, 1797—John Brown and Miss Elizabeth Hutchings.

Robert Boush, security.

1798

January 23, 1798—Richard Hurst and Miss Ailcey Lattimer.

John George, security.

January 27, 1798—Francis K. McNamara and Mrs. Elizabeth Haskings.

Henry B. FitzGerald, security.

January 27, 1798—Thomas Smoot and Mrs. Elizabeth Flagg.

William (mark) Dalby, security.

January 29, 1798—Jacob Grigg and Miss Mary Ann Littledike.

George Lake, security.

Note: According to a note included with this bond, Mary Ann Littledike was the daughter of Ann Godwin.

February 5, 1798—John Cowden and Mrs. Nancy Wallace.

Daniel McDorman, security.

February 13, 1798—Walter Herron and Miss Ann Plume.

James Herron, security.

Note: According to a note included with this bond, Ann Plume was the daughter of William Plume.

February 15, 1798—Joshua Brown and Miss Mima Simkins.

John Cowden, security.

February 24, 1798—James Ward and Mrs. Elizabeth Grogg.

John Murphy, security.

February 27, 1798—Lewis Williams and Mrs. Sally Young.

George Haynes, security.

March 2, 1798—William de Calbiac and Miss Mary Desbois Boissulant.

Alexander d'Onville, security.

March 15, 1798—Peter William Brown and Miss Mary Pembleton.

James Struthers, security.

March 22, 1798—Christopher Lewis and Mrs. Peggy Price.

Thomas Breshhood, security.

March 24, 1798—Isaac Bignall and Miss Harriot West.

James West, security.

Note: According to a note included with this bond Harriot West was the daughter of Thomas Wade West.

April 9, 1798—James Span and Miss Keziah Lewelling.

Abel Lewelling, security.

April 11, 1798—Thomas Moran and Miss Susanna Hoggart (or Hoggard).

Walter Herron, security.

April 11, 1798—Lemuel Langley and Mrs. Elizabeth Pearce.

John Woodside, security.

April 24, 1798—Francis Rice and Mrs. Elizabeth Wallace.

Francis Foster, security.

May 3, 1798—Robert F. Story and Miss Lucy Winston.

John McNeill, security.

May 7, 1798—James Spinks and Mrs. Sarah Robertson.

Francis Foster, security.

May 12, 1798—William Cooper and Mistress Maria Warren.

Henry Pritchard, security.

May 23, 1798—Thomas Boush and Miss Elizabeth Lewelling.

Manner Dyson, security.

May 29, 1798—Vincent Cadore and Miss Mary Autrusseau.

Paul Barrot, security.

Note: Accordng to a note included with this bond, Paul Barrot was the uncle and guardian of Mary Autrusseau.

June 4, 1798—Edward Diggs and Mrs. Susanna Wood.

Even Leggett, security.

June 6, 1798—Joel McDowel and Miss Elizabeth Hackett.

Goldsbury Hackett, security.

June 9, 1798—John Camp and Mrs. Ann Peters.

William Anderson, security.

June 14, 1798—David Black and Mrs. Eliza Stetson.

Martin Doyle, security.

June 21, 1798—Samuel Higgins and Miss Catherine Cruise.

Thomas Baker, security.

July 1, 1798—Thomas Drury and Pricilla Garrison.

Henry (mark) Turner, security.

4

July 5, 1798—Richard Shaw and Miss Peggy Kennedy.
Alexander Petrie, security.
July 13, 1798—Mathias Lukens and Ann Rose.
Francis Foster, security.
August 1, 1798—Henry Pallet and Miss Susannah Carey.
Philip Woodhouse, security.
Note: According to a note included with this bond, Susannah Carey was the daughter of Isaac Cary, decd.
August 13, 1798—John Grimes and Mrs. Polly Smith.
George Miller, security.
August 14, 1798—(Captain) Robert Hatton and Miss Sarah Wilson.
Archibald Williamson, security.
Note: Sarah Wilson was the daughter of George Wilson.
August 16, 1798—Levy Jackson and Miss Ann Braywell.
David McAllester, security.
August 21, 1798—Robert Reeves and Mrs. Ann Blanchard.
John Kinkhead, security.
August 22, 1798—James Carline and Miss Margaret Croutch.
Charles Carline, security.
September 10, 1798—Eutrope Berauld and Miss Bernardine Béon.
William Calbiac, security.
October 3, 1798—John Rourk and Mrs. Mary Ritter.
William Willoughby, security.
October 9, 1798—Ephram Kempton and Mrs. Eliza Carter.
William Baldry, security.
October 19, 1798—Flamstead Wake and Mrs. Hennah Manning.
Henry B. FitzGerald, security.
November 10, 1798—William Jones and Nancy Barrett.
John Barrett, security.
November 20, 1798—John Davis and Mrs. Alice Campbell.
James Turnbull, security.
November 21, 1798—Michael Miller and Miss Anne Abbott.
James Abbott, security.
November 24, 1798—Francois Marie Pigeon and Mrs. Euphrosine Sumonavril Monier.
James Maurice, security.
December 6, 1798—(Captain) Charles Mahon and Miss Maria Lownds.
Edmund Warriner, security.
Note: Maria Lownds was the daughter of John Lownds.
December 10, 1798—Charles Carline and Mrs. Margaret Ridley.
Samuel Brooks, security.
December 19, 1798—Benjamin Blundell and Ann Gordon.
John Mitchell, security.
Note: Ann Gordon was the daughter of William Gordon.
December 22, 1798—James Kilgrow and Sally Stockley.
Richard Lewelling, security.
Note: Sally Stockley was the sister-in-law of Richard Lewelling, the security.

1799

January 5, 1799—Jessie Lambert and Sally Newton.
Henry Durant, security.
January 5, 1799—Ebenezer Mourton and Mrs. Mary McGrath.
John McNeill, security.

5

February 7, 1799—Robert Elliott and Elizabeth Sly.

Gabriel Elliott, security.

Note: According to a note included with this bond, Eliabeth Sly was the sister of Margaret Lewis.

February 28, 1799—Noah Pritchard and Mrs. Sarah Telfair.

John Abbott, security.

March 13, 1799—Daniel Black and Mrs. Anne Harrison.

John McNeill, security.

Note: According to a note included with this bond, Daniel Black was the master of the Brig Aurora and Anne Harrison was the widow of John Harrison, decd., of Northumberland County, England.

March 18, 1799—Egbert Everts and Elizabeth McGarvey.

Chudleigh Southwick, security.

March 26, 1799—William Campbell and Miss Ann S. Dudley.

James Dickenson, security.

Note: According to the returns made by the Rev. John Glendy, the above couple were married the same day. Ann S. Dudley was the ward of James Dickenson, the security.

April 11, 1799—James Turnbull and Mrs. Ann Armstrong.

David McAllester, security.

April 27, 1799—Frederick Hennicke and Mrs. Amey Campbell.

John Barrett, security.

Note: The above couple were married April 28th by the Rev. Anthony Sale.

April 27, 1799—William Lake and Mrs. Ann E. Crawley.

Robert (mark) Spencer, security.

May 2, 1799—James Frazier and Rose Parker.

Philip Booze, security.

Note: According to an annotation on the bond, Rose Parker was the sister-in-law of Philip Booze, the security.

May 10, 1799—William Joseph Aldridge and Mrs. Dorothy Reynolds.

John Reynolds, security.

Note: The above couple were married on the same day by the Rev. John Glendy.

May 11, 1799—Joseph Smith and Mrs. Maxey Kelly.

Benjamin Potts, security.

May 15, 1799—Peter Daley and Mrs. Elizabeth Miller.

Martin Fisk, security.

Note: The above couple were married on May 18th, by the Rev. Anthony Sale.

May 21, 1799—John Wilson and Mrs. Mary Brown.

John Trimble, security.

May 22, 1799—Richard Harris and Mrs. Margaret Jenkins.

Henry Ortest, security.

May 22, 1799—Daniel Tracey and Miss Fanny Butt.

John Randall, security.

Note: The above couple were married on the same day by the Rev. John Glendy.

May 27, 1799—George Patton and Mrs. Elizabeth Boyd.

John O. Mullan, security.

Note: The above couple were married on the same day by the Rev. John Glendy. Elizabeth Boyd was the widow of George Boyd.

May 28, 1799—William Rey and Peggy Dolby.

William Dolby, security.

Note: According to an annotation on this bond, Peggy Dolby was the daughter of William Dolby, the security.

June 1, 1799—Spence Grayson and Bettsy Bowler.

Thomas Baker, security.

June 3, 1799—Lothrop Chase and Mrs. Elizabeth Warren.
William Ward, security.
June 8, 1799—William Presson and Mary Pear.
William Denney, security.
June 11, 1799—Benjamin Brown and Mrs. Susanah Langford, (widow).
Spence Grayson, security.
June 28, 1799—John Davidson and Mrs. Fanny Reid.
Daniel Stone, security.
July 18, 1799—Peter Eddy and Sarah Crues.
Peter Gryndal, security.
July 19, 1799—William Chambers and Peggy Byrne.
George Lake, security.
Note: According to a note included with this bond, Peggy Byrne was the daughter of Ann Byrne.
July 27, 1799—John Ventus and Miss Mary Fuller.
Peter (mark) Williamson, security.
Note: According to a note included with this bond, Mary Fuller was the daughter of Peter Williamson.
July 30, 1799—Martin Fisk and Miss Eliza Gilbert.
Christopher Fry, security.
Note: According to a note included with this bond, Eliza Gilbert was the daughter of Reymon Gilbert.
August 8, 1799—William Haughton and Mrs. Aphia Wallace.
John West, security.
August 14, 1799—Daniel Stone and Miss Jane Vaughn.
William Vaughn, security.
August 20, 1799—Nathaniel Brown and Fanny Short.
Richard Spencer, security.
August 28, 1799—John Tofel and Nancy Williams.
Francis Foster, security.
August 29, 1799—Richard Fryer and Miss Ann Dameron.
Thomas Newton, Jr., security.
September 28, 1799—Cuddy Dunn and Peggy Jolliffe.
Valentine Dunn, security.
September 28, 1799—Valentine Dunn and Cloe Dozier.
Cuddy Dunn, security.
October 4, 1799—Henry Durant and Mary Saunders.
John Hutchinson, security.
Note: According to a note included with this bond, Mary Saunders was the daughter of Mary Hutchinson.
October 7, 1799—Joseph Archer and Tabitha Jones.
William Grosten, security.
October 16, 1799—Alexander Wilson and Miss Mary Cunningham.
Robert Barron, security.
October 19, 1799—William Moseley and Miss Martha Whitehurst.
George Suggs, security.
October 23, 1799—John Boldery and Mrs. Elizabeth Richerson.
David McAllester, security.
October 23, 1799—Jesse Newcomb and Miss Margaret Willoughby.
John L. Willoughby, security.
Note: According to an annotation on this bond, Margaret Willoughby was the sister of John L. Willoughby, the security.

October 31, 1799—William Cammack and Miss Catherine Hutchings.
John Hutchings, security.

November 14, 1799—Edward H. Hasson and Hester Chesrae (or Chesrue).
George Chesrae (or Chesrue), security.

November 16, 1799—John Dejust and Mrs. Elizabeth Miller.
William Janson (or Johnson), security.

November 16, 1799—Joseph Fisher and Mrs. Ann Couch.
George Billups, security.

November 20, 1799—(Doctor) Alexander Whitehead and Miss Nancy Moseley.
Hillary Moseley, security.

December 10, 1799—Henry Jackson and Betsy Jackson.
Lemuel Bailey, security.

December 10, 1799—Francis Smith and Miss Ann Marsden.
John G. Marsden, security.

December 11, 1799—Joseph Sayer (or Sawyer) and Miss Sarah Wilder.
Henry Kelling, security.

Note: According to a note included with this bond, Sarah Wilder was the niece of Mary Poole.

1800

January 2, 1800—Richard Lattimer and Miss Frances Constable.
Thomas Constable, security.

January 7, 1800—Thomas Peters and Elizabeth Pebworth.
Nathaniel (mark) Anderson, security.

January 14, 1800—Robert Meeks and Mrs. Mary Tobitt.
George Lake, security.

Note: According to an annotation on this bond, Mary Tobitt was the widow of George Tobitt.

January 30, 1800—John Davis and Mrs. Sally Williams.
Thomas Haynes, security.

January 30, 1800—Nathaniel Lord and Miss Mary Blanchard.
Ferdinand Stephenson, security.

February 8, 1800—David Wright and Elizabeth Standfast.
John Reynolds, security.

February 20, 1800—Edourd Ruy and Mrs. Marie Jeanne Desmortiers.
William Bland, security.

February 26, 1800—John Ligh and Mary Irwin.
Joseph Fisher, security.

February 27, 1800—William Skipton and Mrs. Ann Campbell.
Margaret Burke, security.

March 1, 1800—Peter Holland and Rebecca Ogborne.
Richard Gibbons, security.

March 1, 1800—John Hannaford and Mrs. Elizabeth Allin.
John Turner, security.

March 7, 1800—John Turner and Martha Parish.
John Hannaford, security.

Note: According to a note included with this bond, Martha Parish was the daughter of John Parish.

March 14, 1800—William Combs and Sarah Allwood (or Attwood).
William K. Keins, security.

March 27, 1800—John Charles Niemeyer and Miss Catherine Adam.
Duncan McDonald, security.
March 29, 1800—William Williams and Catherine Booze.
Nicholas Booze, security.
April 10, 1800—James Goodwin and Miss Polly Bird.
Charles (mark) Bain, security.
April 14, 1800—Joel Cornick and Nancy Cornick.
Joseph Hodges, security.
April 22, 1800—David Knox and Mrs. Dinah Walker.
George Fritts, security.
April 29, 1800—William Webb and Miss Frances Hester.
John Richardson, security.
Note: According to a note included with this bond, Frances Hester was the niece of John George.
May 24, 1800—John Gozelin and Miss Susanna Kellar.
Thomas Divit, security.
May 24, 1800—Isaac Vaughn and Miss Sarah Camper.
John Gozelin, security.
May 30, 1800—Edward Smith and Mary Moore (or Moon).
Henry (mark) Turner, security.
May 31, 1800—Levi Johnson and Betsy Mills.
Nicholas Wilkinson, security.
June 2, 1800—William Thompson and Mary Brandon.
Joseph (mark) Hickerson, security.
June 6, 1800—Jonathan Cooke and Miss Mary Owenbread.
William (mark) Chambers, security.
June 6, 1800—Philip Nicholas Brown and Miss Eliza Kello Curle.
Robert Brough, security.
Note: According to a note included with this bond, Eliza Kello Curle was the ward of Mary Curle.
June 11, 1800—James Taylor, Jr., and Miss Sarah Newton.
Theodoric Armistead, security.
June 12, 1800—Robert Watkins and Mrs. Jennett Moseley.
Absolom Stevens, security.
Note: According to a note included with this bond, Jennett Moseley was the widow of Edward Moseley.
June 14, 1800—Dudley Crandal and Miss Elizabeth Hubbard.
Mathew Hubbard, security.
Note: According to a note included with this bond, Elizabeth Hubbard was the sister of Mathew Hubbard, the security.
June 19, 1800—William Good and Nancy Tisdale.
Richard Burke, security.
June 21, 1800—John Parker and Miss Nancy Wales.
Thomas Baker, security.
June 23, 1800—William Holt and Mrs. Polly Longest.
Joseph Hickerson, security.
Note: According to a note included with this bond, Polly Longest was the widow of William Longest.
July 18, 1800—Aaron Cottell and Ann Chapman.
William Bryan, security.
Note: According to a note included with this bond, Ann Chapman was the niece of William Bryan, the security.

August 6, 1800—Orlando Dana and Mrs. Mary Lewis.

Richard Spencer, security.

August 8, 1800—John Storse and Miss Elizabeth Wade.

John Reynolds, security.

August 20, 1800—William Montgomery and Miss Mary Carline.

Charles Carline, security.

Note: According to a note included with this bond, Mary Carline was the daughter of Charles Carline, the security.

August 23, 1800—William Dunn and Mrs. Elizabeth Elliott.

Benjamin Harrison, security.

August 24, 1800—Mathias Eastwood and Mistress Honour Bagnall.

William Sharp, security.

August 24, 1800—John Southwick and Mrs. Ann Norman.

John Richardson, security.

September 2, 1800—Severn Kellum and Mrs. Anna Harding.

Mathew Harrison, security.

September 24, 1800—Thomas Halliday and Mrs. Ann Hall.

Charles Mahon, security.

September 27, 1800—John Thomas and Miss Nancy Disher.

James Struthers, security.

Note: According to a note included with this bond, Nancy Disher was the daughter of Margaret Walker "aged 43 next March."

October 2, 1800—Bartholomew Broaders and Mrs. Sarah Connor.

Richard Good, security.

October 24, 1800—William Rickard and Christy Steward.

Quinten Clark, security.

November 1, 1800—Benjamin Hathaway and Miss Nancy Forres.

Joseph Hodges, security.

November 6, 1800—John Barns and Mrs. Susanna Roye.

Joseph Clerico, security.

November 6, 1800—Job Palmer and Miss Margaret Cummings.

James Woodside, security.

November 15, 1800—John Burcher and Miss Margaret Vickery.

Eli Vickery, security.

Note: According to a note included with this bond, Margaret Vickery was the daughter of Eli Vickery.

November 26, 1800—William Cawson and Mrs. Ann Fisher.

George Billups, security.

December 4, 1800—George Farrington and Mrs. Anna Barns.

William Dunn, security.

December 9, 1800—Francis Harvey and Mrs. Elizabeth Wilson.

Nicholas Booze, security.

Note: According to a note included with this bond, Francis Harvey was the son of .... Scott.

December 20, 1800—Charles Tyler and Miss Sally Haynes.

Thomas Haynes, security.

December 20, 1800—Joseph Repiton and Miss Margaret Helen Tanguy.

Joseph Antoine Dufort, security.

December 23, 1800—George White and Miss Amelia Metcalf.

Anthony Metcalf, security.

December 29, 1800—Calven Turner and Mrs. Catherine Flahavan.

James Turnbull, security.

1801

January 1, 1801—Nathaniel Nicholson and Miss Sally Shipp.
Samuel Shipp, security.
January 1, 1801—John Rush and Synthia Hall.
William Carson, security.
January 5, 1801—William Cox and Rosanna Owens.
Moses Myers, security.
January 6, 1801—William Nickell and Elizabeth Wright.
Richard Good, security.
January 7, 1801—Roc Brumaud and Miss Marie Lucile Reimoneng.
Peter Steven Blondell, Jr., security.
January 16, 1801—Thomas Masters and Miss Martha Griffin.
David McAllester, security.
January 17, 1801—Thomas Moody and Mourning Mathias.
Joshua Clark, security.
January 17, 1801—John Turner and Grace Benson.
David McAllester, security.
January 19, 1801—John Montgomery and Jannett Hamilton.
Charles Carline, security.
January 21, 1801—William Sharp and Miss Mary Willoughby.
John Tabb Rowsay, security.
January 22, 1801—John Hughes and Mary Channicks.
Samuel Scarlet, security.
January 24, 1801—William Butman and Isabella Hamman.
Duncan McNabb, security.
February 4, 1801—Guilliaume Vanososte and Mrs. Marie Victoire Becdelieve.
Etienne Rissaud, security.
February 6, 1801—Willam P. Pollard and Miss Hannah Peters.
William Blyth, security.
February 9, 1801—George Dashielle and Miss Prudence Williamson.
William Sharp, security.
February 17, 1801—William Moffitt and Anna Wilder.
Lothrop Chace, security.
February 22, 1801—Joshua Hughburg and Mrs. Elenor Kelly.
George Seckel, security.
February 25, 1801—James Greaves and Miss Nancy Williams.
Joseph Bowen, security.
February 26, 1801—Jeremiah Dorsey and Mrs. Elizabeth McDowell.
Robert Chapman, security.
March 4, 1801—Baylor Hill, Jr., and Miss Mary Boush.
Nathaniel Boush, security.
March 4, 1801—Joseph Bartley and Miss Polly Bailey.
Lewis Armistead, security.
Note: According to a note included with this bond, Polly Bailey was the daughter of Lemuel Bailey.
March 4, 1801—Patrick Harmanson and Miss Ann Parker.
Baylor Hill (Jr.), security.
March 8, 1801—John Dunivan and Mrs. Catherine Jackson.
Thomas FitzGerald, security.

11

March 23, 1801—John Donaghey and Mrs. Elizabeth Murphy.
Bryan Ward, security.
March 24, 1801—Robert E. Steed and Miss Frances Ramsay.
William Sharp, security.
April 2, 1801—John Moreland and Miss Susannah Heath.
George Gormly, security.
April 4, 1801—William Hasset and Miss Eliza Kennedy.
Patrick Ryan, security.
April 7, 1801—Joseph Hickerson and Mrs. Elizabeth Fletcher.
Severn (mark) Kellum, security.
April 8, 1801—John Lovell and Miss Ann Robertson.
Mathew Hawthorn, security.
April 10, 1801—James Kennedy (or Canniday) and Elizabeth Walker.
Joshua (mark) Hughsburg, security.
April 15, 1801—William Hood and Mrs. Ann Richards.
George Sidney Smith, security
April 20, 1801—Etienne Rissaud and Miss Margueritte Nouvelle Jannette
William Vanososte, security
April 25, 1801—(Captain) Edward Chamberlain and Miss Sarah Critchet.
Robert Woodside, security.
April 27, 1801—John Anderson and Miss Elizabeth Vaughn.
John C. Hedrick, security.
April 28, 1801—Henry Behenna and Miss Hayder Melson.
Peter (mark) Juro, security.
April 28, 1801—Raymond Figeroux, Jr., and Miss Louise Joseph Rei-
moneing.
Peter Stephen Blondell, security.
May 2, 1801—John Frazier and Miss Susan Carter.
Peter (mark) Grundel (or Gryndal), security.
Note: According to a note included with this bond, Susan Carter was the daugh-
ter of Peter Grundel, the security.
May 2, 1801—Patrick Quinn and Mistress Hannah Caslin.
John Cottrill, security.
May 13, 1801—Joseph Samuel (or Samuels) and Constance Talbot.
Samuel Coleman, security.
Note: According to a note included with this bond, Constance Talbot was the
ward of Samuel Coleman.
June 12, 1801—John Flowers and Miss Mary Butt.
Thomas (mark) Edwards, security.
June 18, 1801—Theodorick Armistead and Miss Martha T. Newton.
James Taylor, Jr., security.
Note: According to a note included with this bond, Martha T. Newton was the
daughter of Thomas Newton.
June 23, 1801—James P. Preston and Miss Ann Taylor.
Robert Taylor, security.
June 24, 1801—William Bennett and Miss Elizabeth Hodges.
George McIntosh, security.
Note: According to a note included with this bond, Elizabeth Hodges was the
daughter of Josiah Hodges.
June 25, 1801—William Hall and Miss Sarah Hackett.
Goldsbury Hackett, security.
June 27, 1801—Andrew Wood and Margaret Frazier.
Peter Crager, security.

July 3, 1801—Benjamin Valentine and Joanna Pinn.
Benjamin Pinn, security.
July 4, 1801—Peter Crager and Betsy Wadkins.
James Whitehurst, security.
July 11, 1801—James Murphy and Hannah Huggins.
John Tyler, security.
July 14, 1801—Henry Bingham and Mrs. Peggy Whites.
Lemuel Bailey, security.
July 15, 1801—John B. Cordis and Miss Eliza Randolph.
William Shaw, security.
July 16, 1801—James Alexander Cunningham and Miss Mary Murphy.
Joseph Samuel, security.
Note: According to a note included with this bond, Mary Murphy was the daughter of Nathaniel Murphy.
July 24, 1801—Kader Talbot and Mrs. Mariam Talbot.
William Sharp, security.
August 8, 1801—Nathan Strong and Miss Sarah Bradford.
Daniel Brian, security.
August 10, 1801—Lewis Armistead and Grace Lee.
Lemuel Bailey, security.
August 19, 1801—John B. Bonneaud and Elizabeth Barber.
James Maurice, security.
August 22, 1801—Jesse Farinholt and Mrs. Dolly Driver.
James Thompson, security.
August 25, 1801—William Kelsey Mackinder and Miss Elenor Moseley.
John Reynolds, Jr., security.
September 3, 1801—John Bainbridge and Mrs. Peggy Dozier.
Joseph Benson, security.
September 3, 1801—Thomas Greenshields and Sarah Parsons.
David Gourley, security.
September 29, 1801—John Hipkins and Miss Elizabeth Marsden.
John G. Marsden, security.
October 1, 1801—James Waldie and Miss Mary Welch.
Benjamin New, security.
October 2, 1801—Michael Lowber and Miss Elizabeth Dolby.
John Bainbridge, security.
Note: Included with this bond is the following note addressed to the clerk of the Norfolk Borough Court:
Sir: There is an intended marriage between my daughter Elizabeth Dolby, who is under age, and Mr. Michael Lowber. This is to certify, as I am obliged to embark for the West Indies before the day appointed for their marriage, that she has my free consent to marry the said Michael Lowber and this shall justify you in granting them a license in my absence.
Sept. 24th, 1801   WILLIAM DOLBY.
Teste—PETER JOHNS
    MARGARET (mark) WRAY
October 6, 1801—Joseph January and Mrs. Catherine Bryan.
Joseph Clerico, security.
October 14, 1801—William Etherton and Mrs. Catherine Irvin.
Levin McAllester, security.
October 14, 1801—John Deverux and Miss Mary Metcalf.
William Rogers, security.
Note: According to a note included with this bond, Mary Metcalf was the daughter of Anthony Metcalf.

13

October 22, 1801—John Cowper and Miss Susanna Barron.
Robert Barron, security.
October 27, 1801—John Francis and Miss Nancy Wood.
John Hannaford, security.
October 31, 1801—William Smith and Mrs. Abby Burgett (or Burgett).
Stephen Hopkins, security.
October 31, 1801—Alexander Cunningham and Miss Nancy Moseley.
George Suggs, security.
November 24, 1801—Sampson Vincent and Mrs. Mary Vruy.
Joseph Clerico, security.
November 26, 1801—James Taylor and Mrs. Frances Holley.
Thomas Orrison, security.

Note: According to an annotation on this bond, Frances Holley was the widow of William Holley.

December 5, 1801—Willis Daley and Mrs. Frankey Denny.
William Wright, security.
December 8, 1801—Joshua Walker and Miss Phebe Hayes.
Jesse Farinholt, security.
December 9, 1801—Charles Rattliff and Miss Nancy Phillips.
Benjamin Norris, security.
December 12, 1801—James Card and Miss Sally Moseley.
George Suggs, security.
December 12, 1801—Reuben Fentress and Mrs. Betsy Strand.
James Harmon, security.
December 24, 1801—Joseph Winslow and Miss Rachel Hutchinson.
John Hutchinson, security.
December 24, 1801—Daniel Sulivan and Nancy Woods.
Richard (mark) Smith, security.
December 24, 1801—James Gill (or Gell) and Mrs. Peggy Wray.
William Dolby, security.
December 24, 1801—Buller Cocke and Miss Elizabeth Barron.
Robert Barron, security.
December 26, 1801—William Harnett and Miss Affia Boush.
Bennett Boush, security.
December 26, 1801—Robert Gamble and Kitty Fuller.
Peter (mark) Wakefield, security.

1802

January 5, 1802—Joshua Guy and Miss Abby James.
James Guy, security.

Note: According to a note included with this bond, James Guy, the security, was the father of Joshua Guy and the guardian of Abby James.

January 30, 1802—Jesse Ewell and Miss Mary Cooke.
John Tabb Smith, security.
February 2, 1802—Hugh Fallon and Mrs. Elizabeth Russel.
Richard Good, security.
February 13, 1802—John West and Mrs. Rose Frazer.
Richard Good. security.
March 12, 1802—James Watson and Mrs. Mary Brown.
Richard Shaw, security.
March 22, 1802—Nathaniel Boush and Miss M. Polly Coleman.
Samuel Coleman, security.

March 23, 1802—William Evans Price and Miss Elizabeth Richard.
Joseph Mitchell, security.

April 10, 1802—Daniel Miller and Mrs. Mary Baynes.
John (mark) Barns, security.

April 12, 1802—Edmund Davey and Mrs. Catherine McBride.
Robert Smith, security.

Note: According to a note included with this bond—bearing the signature of Allen Knox—"Catherine McBride was a widow, and was married before she came to this country."

April 13, 1802—Noah Weston and Mrs. Elizabeth Archer.
Peter Lugg, security.

April 24, 1802—Edward Johnston and Miss Elizabeth Shepherd.
Robert Brough, security.

Note: According to a note included with this bond, Elizabeth Shepherd was the daughter of Elizabeth Shepherd and Soloman Shepherd, decd.

May 14, 1802—Henry Holt and Miss Ann Tunstall.
Baylor Hill, security.

May 15, 1802—William Simington and Miss Isabella Webb.
Thomas Hawthorn, security.

May 26, 1802—William Franklin and Mrs. Nancy Parker.
Simeon Peck, security.

June 14, 1802—Louis Santejau and Miss Elizabeth Gorlier.
Francis Gorlier, security.

June 24, 1802—Lewis Fort and Miss Elizabeth Coleman.
Samuel Coleman, security.

July 1, 1802—William Watson and Miss Mary Hubbard.
Mathew Hubbard, security.

July 9, 1802—Pierre Adde and Jane Bousoumat.
Honore Lelievre, security.

Note: According to a note included with this bond, Jane Bousoumat, whose name is given as Jeanne Genevive Antoinette Bakamie Bousoumat, was the daughter of Marianne Revel Bousoumat.

July 15, 1802—Littleton Waller Tazewell and Miss Ann Stratton Nivison.
Robert Oliphant, security.

Note: According to a note included with this bond, Ann Stratton Nivison was the daughter of John Nivison. Littleton Waller Tazewell was governor of Virginia from 1834 to 1836.

July 17, 1802—Turner Stevenson and Mrs. Grace Lewelling.
James Kilgrow, security.

July 24, 1802—Thomas Gamble and Mrs. Lucy Hutchings.
Richard Shaw, security.

Note: According to an annotation on this bond, Lucy Hutchings was the widow of Richard Hutchings.

August 14, 1802—James Dawley and Miss Margaret Baker.
Hance Baker, security.

September 9, 1802—Jeremiah Barton and Miss Margaret Watson.
Charles Willett, security.

September 11, 1802—James Walker and Mrs. Elizabeth Redpath.
William Bland, security.

October 26, 1802—John C. Herbert and Miss Polly Butler.
(Dr.) Peter Nestell, security.

15

October 27, 1802—William Hill and Mrs. Jane Randles.

James Whitehead, security.

Jethro Hathaway, security.

Hannah Brown, security.

November 1, 1802—Alexander Jordan and Mrs. Susanna Miles.

Augustus C. Jordan, security.

November 4, 1802—James Patterson and Mrs. Dorothy Simmons.

Richard Good, security.

November 8, 1802—Michael Miller and Mary Howes.

Michael (mark) Myler, security.

November 13, 1802—Joseph Hull and Mrs. Elizabeth Mathews (widow).

John Marr, security.

November 18, 1802—William Marsh and Miss Rachael Cruse.

Samuel Higgins, security.

Note: According to a note included with this bond, Rachael Cruse was the sister of Catherine Higgins.

November 20, 1802—Henry Scarburgh and Miss Hannah Herbert.

Thomas Scarburgh, security.

Note: According to a note included with this bond, Thomas Scarburgh, the security, was the guardian of Henry Scarburgh, and "was appointed guardian of the said Henry in the County Court of Accomac."

November 20, 1802—Edward Hudson and Pheby Reardon.

Timothy Reardon, security.

Note: The above couple were married the same day by the Rev. Michael DeLacy, pastor of the Norfolk Catholic Congregation. William Anderson and Henry Cavan are listed as witnesses.

November 24, 1802—John Burton and Nancy Fitzhugh.

John (mark) Fitzhugh, security.

November 24, 1802—Anthony Bohlken and Miss Rebecca Cuthrell.

Joyce (her mark) Cuthrell, security.

Note: According to a note included with this bond, Rebecca Cuthrell was the daughter of Joyce Cuthrell.

November 25, 1802—Samuel Howard and Mrs. Sarah Rankins.

Lawrence (mark) Butler, security.

November 27, 1802—James Piercy and Miss Mary Lee.

William Charles Lee, security.

Note: The above couple were married the same day by the Rev. Michael DeLacy, pastor of the Norfolk Catholic Congregation. William Charles Lee, Patrick Ryan and Charles Frances Lee are listed as witnesses.

December 4, 1802—Richard White and Mrs. Ann Clark.

Peter Crager, security.

December 17, 1802—James Briggs and Mrs. Margaret Langley.

David Cooper, security.

December 23, 1802—Samuel Holt and Miss Mary W. Tabb.

Nathaniel Boush, security.

December 23, 1802—Edward Roberts and Miss Elizabeth Triplett.

John Taylor, security.

December 25, 1802—John H. Cocke and Anne B. Barraud.

Robert B. Taylor, security.

Note: According to a note included with this bond, Anne B. Barraud was the daughter of Philip Barraud.

December 27, 1802—John E. Holt and Miss Clarissa Moseley.

Hillary Moseley, security.

December 30, 1802—Thomas Gamble and Lucy Hutchings.

Charles Harrison, security.

Note: According to an annotation on this bond, Lucy Hutchings was the widow of John Hutchings.

December 31, 1802—Richard Bowden and Mrs. Eliza Sohan.

Philip Henop, security.

Note: The above couple were married on January 1st, 1803, by the Rev. Michael DeLacy, pastor of the Norfolk Catholic Congregation. John Anderson, Ann Anderson and Ann Junior are listed as witnesses.

1803

January 1, 1803—Elias Highes (or Hughes) and Miss Frances Marney.

William Hughes, security.

January 1, 1803—Anthony Walke, Jr., and Miss Jane Ritson.

Thomas Ritson, security.

January 4, 1803—Meshac Wilson and Mrs. Peggy Bingham.

Lemuel Bailey, security.

January 7, 1803—Alexander Clark and Miss Helen Forbes.

Finlay Ferguson, security.

January 10, 1803—Alexis Julias Moody, Jr., and Miss Margaret Mohan.

Mary (her mark) Donavon, security.

January 15, 1803—John Boyd and Mrs. Unice Whitehead.

James (mark) Bidgood, security.

January 21, 1803—William Roser and Nancy D. Singleton.

John Singleton, security.

January 25, 1803—Goodrich Hatton and Miss Mary Hobday.

George Finch, security.

January 27, 1803—Octavus Augustus Valentine Bowen George Washington Warren Lewis Raillon, Jr., and Miss Elizabeth Myers Porter.

Nicholas Holmes, security.

Note: According to a note included with this bond, Eliabeth Myers Porter was the daughter of Elizabeth Myers Porter.

February 1, 1803—Robert Orr and Mrs. Sarah Crawford.

Nathaniel Murphy, security.

February 5, 1803—Nathaniel Anderson (a free mulatto man) and Mourning Reid (a mulatto woman).

Pliny Skipwith, security.

February 12, 1803—Charles Beale and Patsey Whitfield.

William Whitfield, security.

February 16, 1803—Nathaniel Clark and Miss Nancy Moore.

Joseph (mark) Gabriel, security.

February 15, 1803—Philip Henop and Miss Frances Shepherd.

Robert Brough, security.

Note: According to a note included with this bond, Francess Shepherd was the daughter of Elizabeth Shepherd and Soloman Shepherd, decd.

February 19, 1803—John Boyd and Elizabeth Angel.

Winefred (her mark) Angel, security.

February 23, 1803—George Parker and Peggy Floyd.

Arthur Taylor, security.

February 24, 1803—James Hagne and Mrs. Mary Obrian.

William Leake, security.

February 25, 1803—Valentine John Collier and Mrs. Elioner Brownlow.

William (mark) Williams, security.

March 1, 1803—James Anderson and Catherine Welch.

Peter (mark) Brown, security.

March 3, 1803—Pierre Morel and Miss Mary Vitoria Garsent.

Soulage (fils), security.

Note: The above couple were married the same day by the Rev. Michael DeLacy, pastor of the Norfolk Catholic Congregation. John Peter Andre, Lewis LePage, Luke Peter Moizeau and Peter Vizonneau are listed as witnesses. Mary Vitoria Garsent was the ward of Soulage (pere).

March 3, 1803—George Ott and Miss Jane Martin McIvain.

James Maurice, security.

Note: The above couple were married the same day by the Rev. Michael DeLacy, pastor of the Norfolk Catholic Congregation. Peter Andre and Mathew Cluff are listed as witnesses.

March 9, 1803—William B. Brown and Mrs. Nelly Stervant.

David Patterson, security.

March 10, 1803—John F. Hodges and Mrs. Mary J. White.

William Bennett, security

March 15, 1803—Louder Horner and Mrs. Hannah Wilson.

Benjamin White, security

March 17, 1803—Edwin Stark and Mrs. Mary Vaughn.

William Vaughn, security.

March 17, 1803—Francis O'Mara and Miss Francisca Martin.

Tristram Butler, security.

Note: The above couple were married the same day by the Rev. Michael DeLacy, pastor of the Norfolk Catholic Congregation. James Wallis and Tristram Butler are listed as witnesses.

March 29, 1803—John French and Gratia Turner.

Note: The above marriage was copied from the Catholic Register. There is no bond for the above couple in the Corporation Court.

March 31, 1803—Thomas Nolen and Priscilla Kellum.

Severn (mark) Kellum, security.

April 5, 1803—William West and Miss Nancy Johnson.

William C. Farr, security.

April 9, 1803—George Wills and Patsey Weaver (a woman of colour).

John (mark) Ventus, security.

April 21, 1803—Livy Grear and Mrs. Fanny Butler.

Peter Nestell, security.

April 26, 1803—Robert Wonahan and Mrs. Ann Burmot.

John G. Marsden, security.

April 26, 1803—James Barnet and Mrs. Sarah Esperance Eatt.

John Cunningham, security.

April 28, 1803—William Lewis and Mary Ballard.

Richard Good, security.

April 30, 1803—Ambrose Shirley and Miss Ann D. Tomkins.

Henry Brown, security.

April 30, 1803—George Washington White and Mrs. Nancy Cotrel.

Dudley Crandel, security.

May 1, 1803—Henry Brown and Miss Elizabeth Crouch.

Ambrose Shirley, security.

May 7, 1803—John Staples and Grace Wrigh.

Benjamin Hathaway, security.

May 11, 1803—Francis H. Hayer and Latsha Hunley.

Charles Mahon, security.

May 16, 1803—James Anderson and Margaret O'Rourk.
Alexander (mark) McDonald, security.
Note: The above couple were married the same day by the Rev. Michael DeLacy, pastor of the Norfolk Catholic Congregation. Edward Weld, Matilda Hogges, Brigida Madden and Edmund McGuire are listed as witnesses.

May 21, 1803—Henry Prescot and Miss Charlotte Ritter.
James Taylor, security.
Note: According to a note included with this bond, Charlotte Ritter was born in March, 1781. She was the sister of Elizabeth Ritter.

May 21, 1803—Richard Good and Mrs. Sarah Eddy.
Abraham Deacon, security.

May 26, 1803—George Halson and Miss Elizabeth Talbot Ingram.
William Ingram, security.

May 27, 1803—John Byrd and Polly McGuay.
Mathew McGuay, security.

May 30, 1803—John Davie and Mrs. Mary Barney.
William Jacobs, security.

June 1, 1803—Peter Martin and Miss Jane Branigan.
Simeon Peck, security.

June 6, 1803—Alexander Mitchell and Miss Frances Jones.
William Jones, security.

June 9, 1803—Terentius Foy and Mrs. Mary Melvin.
George (mark) Blakeley, security.
Note: The above couple was married on May 16th, by the Rev. Michael DeLacy, pastor of the Norfolk Catholic Congregation. John Donaghey and O'Mara are listed as witnesses.

June 14, 1803—Thomas Rowe and Mrs. Maryan Murphy.
Walter Stephens, security.

June 25, 1803—John E. Beale and Miss Margaret Ritter.
James Woodward, security.

July 1, 1803—Joshua Buskey and Miss Mary Jenkins.
John Freeman, security.
Note: According to a note included with this bond, Mary Jenkins was the ward of John Freeman, the security.

July 8, 1803—John Deverux and Miss Isabella Redpath.
William Atkinson, security.

July 26, 1803—James Spinks and Sophia Mackalpin.
George Grubb, security.

August 6, 1803—Samuel Edwards and Christina Dudgen.
John Randall, security.

August 8, 1803—John Harvey and Mrs. Mary Jones.
Gerrard Seymour, security.

August 26, 1803—Penuel Russell and Nancy Willis George.
Michael Crasmuck, security.

August 29, 1803—Richard Mason and Miss Mary Cochran.
Taffe O'Connor, security.
Note: According to an annotation on this bond, Mary Cochran was the ward of Taffe O'Connor, the security.

September 7, 1803—Thomas Gayner and Miss Elizabeth Johnson.
Thomas Ross, security.

September 16, 1803—Thomas Ross and Martha Watkins.
John Rice, security.

September 19, 1803—William Curran and Mrs. Mary Ann Atkins.
William Couper, security

October 5, 1803—Thomas Gayner and Mrs. Elizabeth Barrington.
Peter Crager, security.
October 20, 1803—Thomas Bark and Mrs. Hannah Horner.
Abraham Deacon, security.
October 29, 1803—John Pretlove and Miss Sally Hickerson.
William Webb, security.
November 1, 1803—Emanuel Rothery and Peggy Vilet.
John (mark) Vickers, security.
November 4, 1803—Theoderic Bland and Miss Sarah Lawson.
Charles L. Beale, security.
November 4, 1803—John Joseph Ledo and Anne Maria Malon.
Peter Vizeneau, security.
November 19, 1803—Joseph C. Maigne and Miss Ann Billups.
George Billups, security.
November 24, 1803—John Baker (a free man of colour) and Lilly Walker (a free woman of colour).
Lemuel Bailey, security.
November 25, 1803—Orran Byrd and Mrs. Sarah Lewis.
David Knox, security.
December 3, 1803—Hugh Scott and Miss Elizabeth Butt.
Reuben Coffin, security.
December 5, 1803—Edward Primrose and Elizabeth Cuthrile.
John (mark) Hale, security.
Note: According to an annotation on this bond, Elizabeth Cuthrile was the widow of John Cuthrile.
December 7, 1803—Robert Mills and Mrs. Mary Ann Denby.
James Martin, security.
December 10, 1803—John Roberts and Miss Frances McClanhan.
John (mark) Stroud, security.
December 12, 1803—John Sanford and Elizabeth Hobbs.
David Moore, security.
December 15, 1803—William Hughes and Miss Peggy James.
John West, security.
December 21, 1803—(Captain) John P. Davis and Miss Mildred Dudley Smith.
William Bennett, security.
December 27, 1803—John McPhail and Miss Mary Wilson.
George Wilson, security.
December 31, 1803—John Lamphear and Mrs. Sarah Gay.
William Iron Rae, security.

1804

January 2, 1804—Alexander Server and Miss Sarah Sannaford.
James Martin, security.
January 4, 1804—Walter Ross and Mrs. Polly Peed.
William Cooper, security.
January 19, 1804—William Small and Mrs. Lilley Wilkinson.
William Thompson, security.

January 31, 1804—(Doctor) Nehemiah Gregory and Miss Elizabeth Metcalf.

Carter B. Poindexter, security.

Note: According to a note included with this bond, Elizabeth Metcalf was the daughter of Anthony Metcalf.

February 5, 1804—Bernard Bourdain and Rosa Celestine Flac.

Note: According to the returns of the Rev. Michael DeLacy, pastor of the Norfolk Roman Catholic Congregation, the above couple were married in Norfolk on above date. Auguste Mastot, Peter Froment and Peter Terrier are listed as witnesses. There is no bond for the marriage of Bernard Bourdain and Rose Celestine Flac in the files of the Corporation Court.

February 24, 7804—John Hamlin and Miss Hannah E. Brown.

John Bramble, security.

March 1, 1804—John Hutchinson and Miss Fanny Pabeth.

William Holmes, security.

March 5, 1804—Peter Vizonneau and Miss Orphise Mariane Monye.

Lewis Lepage, security.

March 5, 1804—Morris Minahin and Mrs. Nancy Jackson.

George Grubb, securty.

March 8, 1804—Fortescue Whittle and Miss Mary Ann Davies.

William Pennock, security.

Note: According to an annotation on this bond, Mary Ann Davies was the daughter of Col. William Davies.

March 13, 1804—Overton Tiler and Sarah Gay.

John Baldrey, security.

April 5, 1804—Robert Jones Leggett and Margaret Draper.

Charles Campbell, security.

April 9, 1804—Thomas Warren and Elizabeth Dawley.

Note: According to the returns of the Rev. Benjamin Grigsby, the above couple were married on April 9th. There is no bond for the marriage of Thomas Warren and Elizabeth Dawley in the files of the Corporation Court.

April 19, 1804—Richard Bailey and Mrs. Elizabeth Rutledge.

Thomas Griffin, security.

April 26, 1804—George M. Mitchell and Miss Elizabeth Gibson Hopkins Knight.

William G. Knight, security.

April 27, 1804—Robert Munford Armistead and Ann Lee.

William Charles Lee, security.

Note: According to the returns of the Rev. Michael Delacy, pastor of the Norfolk Catholic Congregation, the above couple were married on April 28th. Wlliam Charles Lee, James Piercy, Thomas Armistead, Patrick Ryan and Charles Francis Lee are listed as witnesses.

May 3, 1804—James Milan and Jane Clark (widow).

Note: There is no bond for the above marriage in the files of the Corporation Court. It was copied from the returns made by the Rev. Michael DeLacy, pastor of the Norfolk Catholic Congregation. John Dreenan and Terentius Keenan are listed as witnesses.

May 5, 1804—America Sparrow and Fanny Rudd.

Lemuel Bailey, securty.

May 18, 1804—Mathias Ivorey and Sophia Lisburn Burne.

James Godwin, security.

Note: According to a note included with this bond, Sophia Lisburn Burne was the daughter of William Burne.

May 25, 1804—(Colonel) Larkin Smith and Mrs. Sophia Ann Toliver.

Littleton Waller Tazewell, security

May 25, 1804—Hillary Butt and Mrs. Frances Boush.

According to the returns made by the Rev. Benjamin Grigsby, the above couple were married on the above date in Princess Anne County. There is no bond for Hillary Butt and Mrs. Frances Boush in the files of the Corporation Court.

May 31, 1804—John K. Read, Jr., and Miss Sarah Maxwell.

John K. Read, Sr., security.

June 20, 1804—Cary Selden and Miss Frances Loyall.

Carter B. Poindexter, security.

June 20, 1804—Nathaniel Murphey and Miss Mary Preseorez.

John Bramble, security.

June 21, 1804—Littleton Dowty and Miss Elizabeth Clark.

John Turner, security.

Note: According to a note included with this bond, Sally Evans was the daughter of Molly Clark.

June 21, 1804—Johnson Messeck and Miss Sally Evans.

Joshua Evans, security.

Note: According to a note included with this bond, Elizabeth Clark was the ter of Joshua Evans, the security.

June 23, 1804—John Heath and Miss Ann Bains.

Robert (mark) Wilson, security.

Note: According to a note included with this bond, Ann Bains was the niece of Ann White.

July 10, 1804—John Harvey and Miss Anna Perboth.

John Hutchinson, security.

Note: According to a note included with this bond, Ann Perboth was the ward of John Hutchinson (the security) during her minority. This note also states that John Hutchinson was the brother-in-law of Anna Perboth, and a shoemaker by trade.

July 10, 1804—James Thorburn and Martha King.

Miles King, security.

July 14, 1804—Robert W. Bailey and Frances Lambard.

Benjamin Ashley, security.

Note: In a note included with this bond, certifying the age of Frances Lambard, her name is given as Fanny Wallace. Since Benjamin Ashley's name appears in this note, there can be no doubt that it refers to the above bond. Frances Lambard may have been a widow—her maiden name having been Wallace.

July 16, 1804—William Ryan and Elizabeth Nichols.

George Smith, security.

Note: In a note included with this bond, certifying the age of Eliabeth Nichols, her name is given as Nicholson.

July 28, 1804—Auguste Boisard and Louise Lacroix.

Note: There is no bond in the files of the Corporation Court for the above marriage. It was copied from the returns made by the Rev. Michael DeLacy. Lucie Balay Senebier, John Faucher, Hardy Aime Pascault and Jean Baptiste Foulon are listed as witnesses.

August 7, 1804—Joshua Hudgins and Ann Froud.

Morris (mark) Minahin, security.

August 18, 1804—Charles Wood and Mrs. Rosina Von Kalthen.

Lawrence Spencer, security.

August 21, 1804—William Hudson and Mrs. Ann Etheredge.

Thomas M. (mark) Dorman, security.

August 23, 1804—Christian Miller and Jane Isenberg.

John G. Brown, security.

September 5, 1804—Lewis M. Rivalain and Susannah Victoria Lombrage.

James Maurice, security.

September 8, 1804—William B. Suggs and Miss Elizabeth Warren.

George Suggs, security.

Note: According to a note included with this bond, Elizabeth Warren was the ward of Ann Row.

September 12, 1804—Isaiah Cooke and Fanny Davis.

John Johnson, security.

October 4, 1804—Joseph Marquis and Mrs. Nancy Parker.

George Smith, security

October 15, 1804—James Newton and Elizabeth Venters.

Benjamin Ashley, security.

Note: In a note included with this bond, certifying the age of Elizabeth Venters, her name is given as Ventis.

November 3, 1804—Adam Lindsay and Ann Harper (widow).

John Dunn, security.

November 9, 1804—John Frazer and Ann Campbell.

John Scott, security.

November 10, 1804—Daniel Desmond and Elizabeth Smith.

Peter Nestell, seccurity.

November 13, 1804—John Lewis George and Miss Flora La Breun.

Stephen Rissaud, security.

November 22, 1804—John Hunt and Mary McDonald.

John Boldry, security.

December 3, 1804—Charles Cockburn and Mary Crown.

John Davis, security.

December 11, 1804—Thomas Gatewood and Miss Ann Cunningham.

James B. Cunningham, security.

Note: According to a note included with this bond, Ann Cunningham was the daughter and ward of Eliza Cunningham.

December 15, 1804—Joseph Benthall and Frances Peed.

Lemuel Peed, security.

Note: According to an annotation on this bond, Frances Peed was the ward of Lemuel Peed, the security.

December 15, 1804—Robert Banks and Susanna Jarvis.

Edward Allmand, security.

December 18, 1804—James Massenham and Julia Shipwash.

William E. Price, security.

1805

January 4, 1805—Francis Elder and Mary Augsburgern.

James Dorsey, security.

January 5, 1805—Antonius Martin and Marci.

Note: There is no bond for the above marriage in the files of the Corporation Court. It was copied from the returns made by the Rev. Michael DeLacy, pastor of the Norfolk Catholic Congregation. John Dennis, Jacques Bell and Elizabeth Foulon are listed as witnesses.

January 9, 1805—Willoughby Jordan and Elizabeth Benstan.

John Benstan, security.

Note: Elizabeth Benstan was the daughter of John Benstan, the security.

Jaunary 15, 1805—Miles King, Jr., and Miss Rebecca Calvert.

Miles King, Sr., security.

January 19, 1805—William Gardner and Nancy Anderson (wdow).

John Winters, security.

January 24, 1805—John Green and Sarah Lucas (widow).

Richard Bailey, security.

January 24, 1805—James Hoggard and Sarah Parker.

William (mark) Yates, security.

January 30, 1805—Thomas Fountain and Miss Nancy Cox.

John Ewell, security.

January 30, 1805—Thomas Smith and Nancy Carter.

Robert Simington, security.

Note: According to an annotation on this bond, Nancy Carter was a ward of Thomas Smith.

February 9, 1805—Major Taylor and Elizabeth Love.

John Freeman, security.

February 14, 1805—Thomas Hobday and Elizabeth D. Thelaball.

Richmond Thelaball, seccurity.

February 14, 1805—Levi Tull and Elizabeth Lenard.

Maxey Keller, security.

February 14, 1805—John Mahan and Eleanor McKim.

Bryan Gormley, seccurity.

Note: The above couple were married the same day by the Rev. Michael DeLacy, pastor of the Norfolk Catholic Congregation. Bryan Gourmly and Thomas Reyly are listed as witnesses.

February 16, 1806—Joseph Granier and Miss Frances Bousoumat.

Peter Adde, security.

Note: The above couple were married the same day by the Rev. Michael DeLacy, pastor of the Norfolk Catholic Congregation. Gabriel H. Lelievre, Achilles Plunket, Peter Adde and Francis Curlier Devisles are listed as witnesses.

February 18, 1805—John Elcock and Bridget Charnick.

Elijah Jarvis, security.

February 23, 1805—James Hay and Sarah Ward.

William Ward, security.

Note: According to an annotation on this bond, Sarah Ward was the daughter of William Ward, the security.

February 25, 1805—Thomas O'Meare and Martha Wyart.

Henry Etheridge, security.

February 26, 1805—Peter Chabanet and Adelaine Roug.

John Peter Laperouse, security.

Note: The above couple were married the same day by the Rev. Michael DeLacy, pastor of the Norfolk Catholic Congregation. John Baptiste Delievre, Henry Cornalet, Peter Barrot, John Francis Dionisus, John Peter Laperouse, Gabriel Bernard, Ann John Marchant and Edward Berauld are listed as witnesses.

February 28, 1805—Edward Evans and Elizabeth Porter.

William Simington, security.

March 7, 1805—Salem Riley and Miss Sarah Grimes.

Seven Watson, security.

March 9, 1805—William Beal and Mrs. Mary Ross.

William Good, security.

March 13, 1805—William G. Camp and Anne Begg.

George W. Camp, security.

March 16, 1805—Joshua Herbert and Elizabeth Oldner.

Joshua Oldner, security.

Note: According to an annotation on this bond, Joshua Oldner was the father of Eliabzeth Oldner.

March 18, 1805—Anthony Lawson and Miss Frances Marvault.

David Cooper, security.

March 21, 1805—Thomas Praderes and Mary Pampaille.
Stephen Rissaud, security.
Note: According to a note included with this bond, Mary Pampaille was the ward of C. Novert.

March 23, 1805—Killey Giddens and Ann Jackson.
Joshua Buntin, security.

April 13, 1805—George Baynes and Miss Ann Morriss.
James Woodward, security.
Note: According to an annotation on this bond, Ann Morriss was the ward of George Baynes.

April 16, 1805—Thomas Bunting and Mrs. Ann Hodges.
Peter Lugg, security.

April 16, 1805—John Walters Allison and Mary Harris West.
John Davie, security.

April 17, 1805—Lewis Hansford and Maria Pennock.
Philip Barraud, security.
Note: According to a note included with this bond, Maria Pennock was the daughter of William Pennock.

April 22, 1805—Casper Gottlieb Diedrich and Mrs. Fanny Pierce.
William C. Farr, security.

April 24, 1805—William Harmer and Mrs. Bridget Birmingham.
Joseph Highley, security.

April 25, 1805—Jeremiah McPherson and Mildred Kelfren.
Anthony Crips, security.

April 26, 1805—George English and Mrs. Eliza Tate.
James Flowers, security.

April 27, 1805—John Hodges and Frances Warren.
John Warren, security.
Note: The above couple were married the same day by the Rev. Benjamin Grigsby, pastor of the Presbyterian Congregation.

April 27, 1805—John Farrier and Isabelle Trumble (or Trimble).
Stephen Wilson, security.
Note: The above couple were married the same day by Thomas T. Jones, a local Methodist elder.

April 30, 1805—Jacob R. Rhodes and Ann Anderson.
R. Keel, security.

May 1, 1805—William Smith and Margaret Williams.
Thomas Hobday, security.

May 4, 1805—Andrew Hutchings and Polly Mills.
Lewis Humphrey, security.

May 9, 1805—Francis Foster and Mrs. Eliza McGibon.
Charles Mahon, security.

May 17, 1805—Phineas Dana and Miss Susan Oliphant.
Stephen Parham, security.
Note: The above couple were married the same day by the Rev. Benjamin Grigsby, pastor of the Presbyterian Congregation.

May 24, 1805—Nathaniel Burgess and Mrs. Nancy Loward.
Killey Giddens, security.
Note: The above couple were married by the Rev. James Dawley. No date is given. In his report, Nancy Loward is given as Nancy Seward.

May 31, 1805—John Archer and Mary Cornick.
Solomon Steed, security.

May 31, 1805—William Fulton and Miss Ann Haley.

Reuben Coffin, security.

Note: The above couple were married the same day by Thomas T. Jones, a local Methodist elder.

June 26, 1805—Daniel Wright and Elizabeth Coody.

David McAllister, security.

Note: According to an annotation on this bond, Elizabeth Coody was the ward of David McAllister.

June 27, 1805—William Butt and Miss Esther Buntin.

Joshua Buntin, security.

oNte: According to an annotation on this bond, Esther Buntin was the daughter of Joshua Buntin, the security.

July 2, 1805—Anthony Lester and Mrs. Mary Spann.

Thomas (mark) Hutchings, security.

July 8, 1805—Ralph Johnson and Elizabeth Crager.

Obadiah (mark) Gunn, security.

July 17, 1805—John J. Cornwall and Rosannah Charnick.

Peter (mark) Jerro, security.

August 4, 1805—John Warren and Mrs. Mary M. Bennett.

William Sharp, security.

Note: The above couple were married the same day by the Rev. Benjamin Grigsby, pastor of the Presbyterian Congregation.

August 6, 1805—Peter Miles and Eleonore Drinan.

Note: There is no bond on file in the Corporation Court for the above marriage. It was copied from the returns of marriages performed by the Rev. Michael DeLacy, pastor of the Norfolk Catholic Congregation. Ann Benson, Elizabeth Foulon and Dabney Lepscomb are listed as witnesses.

August 14, 1805—William Atkinson and Mrs. Margaret Williams.

William Cadenhead, security.

August 17, 1805—Archibald Rose and Elizabeth Hickerson (widow).

Paul G. C. Jones, security.

August 26, 1805—Augustus Johnson and Miss Frances Fisher.

Dale Carr, security.

August 26, 1805—Edward S. Waddy and Miss Margaret Stratton.

William T. Stone, security.

Note: According to a note included with this bond, Margaret Stratton was the daughter of John Stratton. Edward S. Waddy and Margaret Stratton were married on August 28th, by the Rev. Benjamin Grigsby, pastor of the Presbyterian Congregation.

September 22, 1805—John Davis and Mrs. Sarah Barron.

Thomas Glenn, security.

September 2, 1805—John Moore and Mrs. Frances Butt.

John West, security.

September 23, 1805—Henry Hunt and Miss Elizabeth Philips.

Joel Hodges, security.

Note: The above couple were married by the Rev. James Dawley. No date is given. According to an annotation on the bond, Elizabeth Philips was the ward of Joel Hodges, the security.

October 6, 1805—James Stady and Miss Frances Vansant.

Rebecca (her mark) Barnaby, security.

Note: The above couple were married on October 8th by Thomas T. Jones, a local Methodist elder. In his report the bride's name is given as Francinai Vansant.

October 12, 1805—John Stublin and Mrs. Sarah Johnson.

John Turner, security.

October 26, 1805—John Campbell and Miss Mary Murden.
John Madden, security.

October 31, 1805—Thomas Balls and Miss Kitty Murphy.
Tristrim Butler, security.
Note: The above couple were married the same day by the Rev. Benjamin Grigsby, pastor of the Presbyterian Congregation.

November 9, 1805—Thomas Newton and Mrs. Margaret Poole.
Note: There is no bond for the above marriage in the files of the Corporation Court. It is copied from the returns on marriages made by the Rev. Benjamin Grigsby, pastor of the Presbyterian Congregation.

November 16, 1805—Thomas Bruswood and Miss Maria Gilbert.
Reymon Gilbert, security.

November 20, 1805—Thomas Lumsden and Miss Mary Everedge.
Benjamin New, security.

November 23, 1805—John Gilman and Lydia Tart.
John Eaton, security.
Note: The above couple were married the same day by the Rev. Benjamin Grigsby, pastor of the Presbyterian Congregation. According to an annotation on this bond, Lydia Tart was the ward of John Eaton, the security.

November 27, 1805—(Captain) Henry Bruce and Ann H. Fleming.
Alexander Cunningham, security.
Note: The above couple were married the same day by the Rev. Benjamin Grigsby, pastor of the Presbyterian Congregation.

December 13, 1805—John Reed and Miss Mary Robertson.
William Butt, security.
Note: The above couple were married by the Rev. James Dawley. No date is given for the marriage.

December 18, 1805—George Shuster and Miss Catherine Buntin.
William Butt, security.

December 21, 1805—David Maxwell and Miss Elizabeth Barrett.
Joseph Hull, security.

1806

January 2, 1806—Benjamin Grigsby and Miss Elizabeth McPherson.
John McPhail, security.
Note: According to an annotation on this bond, Elizabeth McPherson was the ward of John McPhail, the security.

January 2, 1806—John Price and Miss Sally Bignall.
James Martin, security.
Note: The above couple were married the same day by Thomas T. Jones, a local Methodist elder.

January 4, 1806—John Doll and Mrs. Elizabeth Ross.
Benjamin White, security.

January 10, 1806—William Ward and Mrs. Mary Hodges.
James Hay, security.

January 14, 1806—Redmund Gervais and Sophia Bereau.
Note: There is no bond for the above marriage in the files of the Corporation Court. It was copied from the returns of the Rev. Michael DeLacy, pastor of the Norfolk Catholic Congregation. Claud Jas. Lemasurier, Lewis Mary Bobia and John-Charles-Mary-Lewis Boutin are listed as witnesses.

January 14, 1806—George Wright and Miss Elizabeth Mahon.
Charles Mahon, security.
Note: The above couple were married on January 16th by the Rev Benjamin Grigsby, pastor of the Presbyterian Congregation. According to an annotation on this bond, Elizabeth Mahon was the daughter of Charles Mahon, the security.

January 16, 1806—Thomas Davis and Mrs. Fanny Brown.

David Gourlay, security.

January 18, 1806—George Silverthorn and Miss Margaret Steed.

James Dyson, Jr., security.

January 21, 1806—John Cochetel and Miss Sairaphine Chastelier.

John Potts, security.

Note: The above couple were married the same day by Thomas T. Jones, a local Methodist elder.

January 23, 1806—John Cooper and Miss Prudence Tatum.

James Tatum, security.

Note: According to a note included with this bond, Prudence Tatum was the daughter of James Tatum, the security.

January 24, 1806—Robert Souter and Margaret Taylor.

Note: There is no bond for this marriage in the files of the Corporation Court. It was copied from the returns of the Rev. Benjamin Grigsby, pastor of the Presbyterian Congregation.

February 12, 1806—John Williams and Miss Kitty Baynes.

George (mark) Walker, security.

February 16, 1806—William F. Stone and Miss Sarah Oldner.

Joshua Oldner, security.

February 19, 1806—Mathew FitzGerald and Miss Margaret Wood.

Mary Rowe, security.

Note: The above couple were married on February 20th ,according to the returns made by the Rev. Michael DeLacy, pastor of the Norfolk Catholic Congregation. Roger Walsh is listed as witness.

March 3, 1806—Luther Smith and Mrs. Hannah Balfour.

Joseph Dawson, security.

March 8, 1806—Wilson Oliver and Miss Abigail Hopkins.

Maximilian Herbert, security.

March 13, 1806—(Doctor) George Davis and Miss Ann Pennock.

Philip Barraud, security.

Note: According to a note included with this bond, Ann Pennock was the daughter of William Pennock.

March 13, 1806—John Jefferies and Mrs. Adeline Parkerson (or Perkerson).

Robert Simington, security.

March 14, 1806—Thomas Jennings and Miss Jane Crab.

Alexander Hayward, security.

Note: The above couple were married the same day by Thomas T. Jones, a local Methodist elder.

March 22, 1806—Edward Smith and Hannah Harris.

Henry (mark) Jackson, security.

Note: The above couple were married the same day by Thomas T. Jones, a local Methodist elder.

March 8, 1806—Stephen Decatur, Jr., and Miss Susan Wheeler.

Luke Wheeler, security.

Note: The above couple were married the same day by the Rev. Benjamin Grigsby, pastor of the Presbyterian Congregation. Susan Wheeler was the daughter of Luke Wheeler, the security.

April 3, 1806—Sampson Cofield and Mrs. Lydia Wright.

Claudius Briquet, security.

Note: The above couple were married the same day by Thomas T. Jones, a local Methodist elder.

April 10, 1806—Michael McLane and Mrs. Susanna Winters.

Joseph Marques, security.

April 12, 1806—Moses Ruth and Mrs. Sarah Wood.

John (mark) Gilman, security.

April 26, 1806—John Oliver and Miss Catherine Hackett.

Goldsbury Hackett, security.

Note: The above couple were married on the same day by Thomas T. Jones, a local Methodist elder. According to an annotation on this bond, Catherine Hackett was the daughter of Goldsbury Hackett, the security.

April 30, 1806—Peter Stocker and Mrs. Mary Cassen.

John Cochetel, security.

May 3, 1806—James Hunter and Mrs. Ann Armistead (alias) Lee.

Note: There is no bond in the files of the Corporation Court for the above marriage. It was copied from the returns of the Rev. Michael DeLacy, pastor of the Norfolk Catholic Congregation. William Hunter, James T. Huston, William Charles Lee, Ann Hunter, Catherine Ryan and Catherine Hunter are listed as witnesses.

May 8, 1806—Robert Chapman and Miss Susan Martin.

Reuben Coffin, security.

Note: The above couple were married the same day by the Rev. Benjamin Grigsby, pastor of the Presbyterian Congregation. According to a note included with this bond, Susan Martin was the ward of James W. Langley. Harriet M. Langley and Reuben Coffin witnessed this note.

May 12, 1806—Hendrick Zaal and Miss Catherine Curle.

Thomas Smith, security.

May 24, 1806—Jean Baptiste Sejourne and Miss Marie Magdaline Elizabeth Violeau.

Laurent Prin, security.

Note: The above couple were married on May 27th by the Rev. Michael DeLacy, pastor of the Norfolk Catholic Congregation. Laurent Prin, Joseph Antoni Dufort, Peter Adde, John Peter Laperouse and Vincentius Parlato are listed as witnesses. Marie Magdaline Violeau was the daughter of Rene Charles and Arnaud Violeau.

June 3, 1806—Robert Robertson and Frances Fereber.

Note: There is no bond in the files of the Corporation Court for the above marriage. It was copied from the returns of the Rev. Benjamin Grigsby, pastor of the Presbyterian Congregation.

June 3, 1806—John Palmer and Miss Martha Butt.

Wilson Butt, security.

Note: The above couple were married the same day by the Rev. Benjamin Grigsby, pastor of the Presbyterian Congregation.

June 4, 1806—Daniel Hall and Miss Sarah Slack.

Luke (mark) Doland, security.

June 10, 1806—Reuben Coffin and Miss Polly Butt.

John Randall, security.

Note: The above couple were married the same day by the Rev. Benjamin Grigsby, pastor of the Presbyterian Congregation. According to an annotation on this bond, John Randal, the security, was the guardian of Polly Butt.

June 16, 1806—Edward Brock and Mrs. Sarah Parbless.

John Brock, security.

Note: The above couple were married the same day by the Rev. Benjamin Grigsby, pastor of the Presbyterian Congregation.

June 18, 1806—Joseph Dander and Barbara Swab.

Robert Simington, security.

Note: The above couple were married the same day by the Rev. Michael DeLacy, pastor of the Norfolk Catholic Congregation. Charles Ricter and George Clingmen are listed as witnesses. According to an annotation on this bond, Barbara Swab was a servant girl of Robert Simmington, the security.

June 23, 1806—William King and Margaret Scott.

Note: The above marriage was copied from the returns of the Rev. Michael DeLacy, pastor of the Norfolk Catholic Congregation. B. Magnien, Carleton Wheeler, Francisca Beasy and Ann Kean are listed as witnesses.

June 26, 1806—Richard Herbert and Miss Selina Patience Osborne.

Maximilian Herbert, security.

July 2, 1806—Soloman Carrier and Mrs. Jane Davis.

George Fritts, security.

July 5, 1806—Thomas Roberts and Miss Mary Dear.

Nathaniel (mark) Burgess, security.

Note: The above couple were married the same day by Thomas T. Jones, a local Methodist elder.

July 17, 1806—Henry Brunet and Mrs. Sarah Read.

William Maxwell, security.

Note: The above couple were married the same day by the Rev. Benjamin Grigsby, pastor of the Presbyterian Congregation.

July 17, 1806—Henry Shields and Miss Chloe Calbert.

Sally (mark) Calbert, security.

July 31, 1806—William Millson and Miss Eliza Singleton.

John Singleton, security.

Note: According to an annotation on this bond, Eliza Singleton was the daughter of John Singleton, the security.

July 28, 1806—Spencer Gaskins and Miss Mary Cooper.

Thomas Halliday, security.

Note: According to an annotation on this bond, Mary Cooper was the ward of Thomas Halliday, the security.

August 1, 1806—Mathew Murphey and Mrs. Mary Miller.

James Barey, security.

August 4, 1806—John Connoway and Mrs. Nancy Wood.

Luke (mark) Dolen, security.

August 14, 1806—John Soddridge and Mrs. Catherine Morgan.

James Roberts, security.

August 30, 1806—Eugene Higgins and Miss Eliza Andrews.

Joseph Moran, security.

Note: The above couple were married on August 21st by the Rev. Michael DeLacy, pastor of the Norfolk Catholic Congregation. John Donaghey, Eliza Donaghey, Gasper Moran and Henrietta Piercy are listed as witnesses. According to a note included with this bond, Eliza Andrews was the daughter of Jeremiah Andrews.

August 21, 1806—William Thomas and Mrs. Mary Kirgan.

Thomas Bark, security.

August 28, 1806—Mordecai Tyler and Miss Sarah Hillen.

John (mark) Fitzhugh, securty.

Note: The above couple were married the same day by Thomas T. Jones, a local Methodist elder.

September 13, 1806—James Kilgore and Miss Peggy Elliott.

John Robbins, security.

October 2, 1806—Stephen Hopkns and Miss Ann Philips.

William Evans Price, security.

October 3, 1806—Erasmus H. Tipling and Miss Nancy Murden.

John Madden, securty.

October 4, 1806—Alexander Cherry and Miss Matilda Hodges.

Willis Cherry, security.

Note: According to a note on the back of this bond, Alexander Cherry was the son of Willis Cherry, the security. According to the same source, Matilda Hodges was the daughter of Joel Hodges.

October 8, 1806—John Owen and Miss Peggy Clarkson.

Thomas Wirt, security.

Note: The above couple were married the same day by the Rev. Benjamin Grigsby, pastor of the Presbyterian Congregation. According to an annotation on this bond, Peggy Clarkson was thirty years of age.

October 9, 1806—Joseph Middleton and Miss Ann Goff.

Francis Hall, securty.

October 16, 1806—John Peacham and Mrs. Eliza James.

Edward Weld, seccurity.

Note: The above couple were married the same day by the Rev. Benjamin Grigsby, pastor of the Presbyterian Congregation.

October 18, 1806—Michael Bentancurt and Miss Nancy Grant.

John (mark) Grant, security.

Note: According to an annotation on this bond, Nancy Grant was the daughter of John Grant, the security.

November 3, 1806—William Stephens and Hannah Cody.

Note: There is no bond for the above marriage in the files of the Corporation Court. It was copied from the returns made by the Rev. Benjamin Grigsby, pastor of the Presbyterian Congregation.

November 4, 1806—Ole Anderson and Miss Jane Trimble.

William Carson, security.

Note: The above couple were married the same day by Thomas T. Jones, a local Methodist elder.

November 8, 1806—Lars Olsen Palsey and Mrs. Sarah Grimshield.

Note: There is no bond for the above marriage in files of the Corporation Court. It was copied from the returns made by the Rev. Benjamin Grigsby, pastor of the Presbyterian Congregation.

November 14, 1806—Godt Fredrich Cook and Miss Eleanor Flood.

Anthonie Spegthoft, security.

Note: The above couple were married November 24th by the Rev. Benjamin Grigsby, pastor of the Presbyterian Congregation.

November 15, 1806—Preeson McGee and Miss Rachel Taylor.

John (mark) Taylor, security.

Note: According to an annotation on this bond, Rachel Taylor was the daughter of John Taylor, the security.

November 15, 1806—Edward Allen and Mrs. Maria W. O'Grady.

Richard L. Green, security.

Note: The above couple were married the same day by Thomas T. Jones, a local Methodist elder.

November 21, 1806—Anthony Frank and Mrs. Nancy Morris.

Joseph A. Maile (mark), security.

November 29, 1806—James Thompson and Mrs. Mary Hender.

Benjamin Ashley, security.

December 4, 1806—Terentius Keenan and Sarah Wyatt.

Note: There is no bond for the above marriage in the files of the Corporation Court. It was copied from the returns made by the Rev. Michael DeLacy, pastor of the Norfolk Catholic Congregation. Patrick and William Keenan are listed as witnesses.

December 20, 1806—Jean Joseph LeBon and Mrs. Polly Godwin.

Note: There is no bond for the above marriage in the files of the Corporation Court. It was copied from the returns made by the Rev. Benjamin Grigsby, pastor of the Presbyterian Congregation.

31

December 20, 1806—Nicholas Brandt and Mrs. Susanna McLane.

Anthonie Spegthoft, security.

Note: The above couple were married the same day by the Rev. Benjamin Grigsby, pastor of the Presbyterian Congregation.

December 23, 1806—John L. Cosby and Miss Mary White.

Thomas R. Ingram, security.

Note: According to a note included with this bond, Mary White was the ward of Thomas H. Parker.

December 24, 1806—Robert Brough and Mrs. Ann Shepherd.

Wilson Boush, security.

December 24, 1806—Jasper Moran and Miss Frances Sayer.

Eugene Higgins, security.

Note: According to a note included with this bond, Frances Sayer was the daughter of Charles Sayer.

December 24, 1806—William Stevens and Mrs. Ann Tobin.

George B. Kerr, security.

Note: The above couple were married on December 25th by the Rev. Benjamin Grigsby, pastor of the Presbyterian Congregation.

December 25, 1806—John Pray and Miss Mary Shipp.

William Jones, security.

Note: According to an annotation on this bond, Mary Shipp was the ward of William Jones, the security.

December 25, 1806—James Davis and Miss Nancy Herbert.

George Wilson, security.

Note The above couple were married on December 27th by the Rev. Benjamin Grigsby, pastor of the Presbyterian Congregation.

1807

January 3, 1807—Josiah Cole and Miss Mary Field.

James Dawley, security.

January 3, 1807—Joshua Merriken and Miss Nancy Guy.

Henry Guy, security.

Note: According to an annotation on this bond, Nancy Guy was the daughter of Henry Guy, the security.

January 8, 1807—Francis Tompkins and Sarah Cooper.

Note: There is no bond for the above marriage in the files of the Corporation Court. It was copied from the returns made by the Rev. Benjamin Grigsby, pastor of the Presbyterian Congregation.

January 10, 1807—Enoch Land and Miss Elizabeth Ward.

William Ward, security.

Note: According to an annotation on this bond, Elizabeth Ward was the daughter of William Ward, the security.

January 12, 1807—Thomas Walker and Miss Esther Cowdery.

Savage B. Cowdery, security.

Note: The above couple were married on January 17th by Thomas T. Jones, a local Methodist elder.

January 12, 1807—Giles Picot and Miss Marie Rosalie Simonet.

Patrick Ryan, security.

Note: The above couple were married the same day by the Rev. Michael DeLacy, pastor of the Norfolk Catholic Congregation. Luke Lawrence Prin, Eutrop Berauld, Baltazard Maurice Dantossy and James Delaunay are listed as witnesses.

January 14, 1807—Anthony Moffat and Miss Sarah Wirling.

Samuel Mathews, security.

Note: The above couple were married the same day by the Rev. Benjamin Grigsby, pastor of the Presbyterian Congregation. According to a note included with this bond, Sarah Wirling was the ward of Jannet Patterson.

January 19, 1807—Houstet Arnand Echevarria and Miss Polly Parrish Bains.

Henry Bains, security.

Note: According to an annotation on this bond, Polly Parrish Bains was the daughter of Henry Bains, the security.

January 21, 1807—William Gregory and Miss Mary Mathews.

Thomas Mathews, security.

January 27, 1807—Ephraim Hathaway and Miss Mary Murray.

David Murray, security.

February 5, 1807—Henry Cornick and Miss Mary Old.

John West, security.

Note: The above couple were married on February 10th by the Rev. Benjamin Grigsby, pastor of the Presbyterian Congregation.

February 12, 1807—Jeremiah Banks and Mrs. Elizabeth Bailey.

Richard H. Cocke, security.

Note: The above couple were married the same day by the Rev. Benjamin Grigsby, pastor of the Presbyterian Congregation.

February 17, 1807—Joe (a black man) and Bridget (a black woman).

Jacob (mark) Newby, security.

March 2, 1807—Duncan McPherson and Miss Louisa Gordon.

James Mitchell, security.

Note: According to an annotation on this bond, Louisa Gorden was the ward of James Mitchell, the security. Duncan McPherson and Louisa Gordon were married on March 5th by the Rev. Benjamin Grigsby, pastor of the Presbyterian Congregation.

March 6, 1807—Roger Walsh and Brigida Madden.

Note: There is no bond for the above marriage in the files of the Corporation Court. It was copied from the returns made by the Rev. Michael DeLacy, pastor of the Norfolk Catholic Congregation. No witnesses are listed.

March 11, 1807—Willis Simmons and Miss Eliza Elliott.

Peter Elliott, security.

Note: The above couple were married on March 12th by Thomas T. Jones, a local Methodist elder.

March 12, 1807—Gershom Nimmo and Mrs. Elizabeth J. Smith.

Josiah Wilson Hunter, security.

April 3, 1807—George Brumfield and Mrs. Hannah Nicolls.

Claudius Briquet, security.

Note: The above couple were married the same day by Thomas T. Jones, a local Methodist elder.

April 7, 1807—William Dye and Miss Susan Spratley.

Charles Davis, security.

Note: The above couple were married on April 9th by Thomas T. Jones, a local Methodist elder.

April 7, 1807—John Jasper and Miss Eady West.

Francis Drake, security.

April 9, 1807—Edward Seymour and Miss Mary Keeling.

William Davis, security.

Note: The above couple were married the same day by the Rev. Benjamin Grigsby, pastor of the Presbyterian Congregation. According to an annotation on this bond, Mary Keeling was the ward of Mary Keeling.

April 10, 1807—Joseph Frydie Lavialle and Miss Anne Rose Sophie D'Antossy.

Laurent Prin, security.

Note: The above couple were married the same day by the Rev. Michael DeLacy, pastor of the Norfolk Catholic Congregation. Luke Laurence Prin and Baltazard Maurice Dantosy are listed as witnesses.

April 20, 1807—John Rodgers and Mrs. Ann Markus.

John Hannaford, security.

Note: The above couple were married the same day by the Rev. Benjamin Grigsby, pastor of the Presbyterian Congregation.

April 29, 1807—William Storrs and Mary Precious (widow).

John Dunn, security.

May 2, 1807—Alexander Cunningham and Miss Elizabeth Suggs.

George Suggs, security.

Note: The above couple were married the same day by the Rev. Benjamin Grigsby, pastor of the Presbyterian Congregation.

May 4, 1807—William Willbron and Mrs. Ann Mathias.

John Pallett, security.

May 4, 1807—James Peters and Miss Tinny Johnson.

Benjamin Pinn, security.

Note: The above couple were married the same day by Thomas T. Jones, a local Methodist elder.

May 5, 1807—John Menzier and Mrs. Rachael Fisher.

William Dick, security.

Note: The above couple were married the same day by the Rev. Benjamin Grigsby, pastor of the Presbyterian Congregation.

May 16, 1807—Joshua Moore and Miss Mary Thorowgood.

James Bishop, security.

May 21, 1807—Thomas Herbert and Miss Ann Williamson.

Jonathan Williamson, security.

Note: The above couple were married the same day by the Rev. Benjamin Grigsby, pastor of the Presbyterian Congregation. According to an annotation on this bond, Ann Williamson was the daughter of Jonathan Williamson, the security.

May 25, 1807—Stephen H. Drummond and Mrs. Mary Hamilton.

David Gourley, security.

May 28, 1807—Littlebury Stainback and Miss Sarah Drummond.

Richard Drummond, security.

Note: The above couple were married the same day by the Rev. Benjamin Grigsby, pastor of the Presbyterian Congregation.

May 30, 1807—Joseph Brown and Mrs. Ann Wescot.

James Brooks, security.

Note: The above couple were married the same day by Thomas T. Jones, a local Methodist elder. According to an annotation on this bond, Ann Wescot was the widow of Major Wescot.

May 30, 1807—John Arselle and Mrs. Antoinette Augustine.

Claudius Briquet, security.

Note: The above couple were married the same day by Thomas T. Jones, a local Methodist elder.

June 1, 1807—Charles S. Fullerton and Mrs. Margaret Hudson.

John Davis, security.

June 4, 1807—Daniel Goulden and Mrs. Ann Dayton.

William Atkinson, security.

June 27, 1807—George Clark and Miss Anne Murphy.

John Murphy, security.

June 30, 1807—John Saints and Mrs. Nancy Johnson.

James Elton, security.

July 4, 1807—Peter Nelson and Miss Rebecca Goodson.

Levi Tull, security.

July 23, 1807—Matthias Precious and Miss Mary Brazil.

J. Peter Dieterich, security.

July 28, 1807—Jacob Shuster, Jr., and Miss Fanny Dyson.
James Dyson, security.

September 2, 1807—John Sharples and Miss Mary Henderson.
Edward Weld, security.

September 7, 1807—William Babbington and Miss Elizabeth Nestell.
Thomas B. Seymour, security.

September 12, 1807—William Mc. Rice and Ann Kein.

Note: There is no bond for the above marriage in the files of the Corporation Court. It was copied from the returns made by the Rev. Michael DeLacy, pastor of the Norfolk Catholic Congregation. George Davis, Margaret Mackey and Eleanor Kein are listed as witnesses.

September 27, 1807—Jonathan Dyson and Miss Sarah Hobday.
Goodrich Hatton, security.

October 1, 1807—John Gurfin and Mrs. Jane Face.
Richard Good, security.

October 5, 1807—William McGuire and Mrs. Mary Garner.
Thomas (mark) Lucas, security.

October 8, 1807—James Jarvis and Mrs. Elizabeth Peed.
Walter Ross, security.

October 24, 1807—Arthur Cooper and Mrs. Elizabeth Suggs.
John Warren, Jr., security.

October 27, 1807—James Mitchell and Mrs. Hannah Welch.
Peter Lugg, security.

October 29, 1807—William Howell and Miss Pricilla Powers.
Edward Widgen, security.

Note: According to an annotation on this bond, Pricilla Powers was the ward of Edward Widgen, the security.

October 29, 1807—Job B. Mills and Mrs. Elizabeth Storrs.
Peter Daley, security.

November 10, 1807—Thomas Holden and Mrs. Mary Watson.
Mathew Hubbard, security.

November 16, 1807—Nicholas Reeves and Miss Mary Perin.
Patrick Perin, security.

Note: According to an annotation on this bond, Mary Perin was the ward of Patrick Perin, the security.

November 14, 1807—George Nicholson and Miss Martha Ann Cooper.
David Cooper, security.

Note: According to an annotation on this bond, Martha Ann Cooper was the daughter of David Cooper, the security.

November 29, 1807—George Kells (or Kello) and Mrs. Peggy Beggy.
Smith Stringer, security.

December 1, 1807—Charles Fair and Miss Patsey Parey.
James Pate, security.

December 4, 1807—Thadeus Muncham and Miss Elizabeth Smith.
Hermon D. Beadles, security.

Note: The above couple were married the same day by the Rev. Benjamin Grigsby, pastor of the Presbyterian Congregation.

December 9, 1807—John L. Leland and Miss Mary Pusey.
George Kelly Wright, security.

December 13, 1807—(Doctor) Robert Holmes and Miss Louisa Maxwell.
William Maxwell, security.

Note: According to a note included with this bond, Louisa Maxwell was the ward of Helen Read. Louisa Maxwell was the daughter of the above mentioned Helen Read and her first husband, William Maxwell.

December 19, 1807—Benjamin Nottingham and Miss Margaret Herbert.
John Hall, security.
Note: According to a note included with this bond, Margaret Herbert was the ward of John Portlock.
December 19, 1807—Benjamin Cowling and Mrs. Mary Cooper.
John W. Henop, security.
Note: The above couple were married the same day by the Rev. Benjamin Grigsby, pastor of the Presbyterian Congregation.
December 24, 1807—William Cameron and Miss Elizabeth Forrest.
John Forrest, security.
Note: According to an annotation on this bond, Elizabeth Forrest was the ward of John Forrest, the security.
December 30, 1807—John Davie and Mrs. Mary Ferry.
Peter Nestell, security.
December 31, 1807—John Moore and Mrs. Jane Miller.
Peter Nestell, security.

1808

January 28, 1808—George Middleton and Mrs. Fanny Dixon.
Shadrack (mark) Harmon, security.
February 6, 1808—Tildsley Graham and Mrs. Jennet Watkins.
Thomas Crossley, security.
February 9, 1808—Daniel Hodges and Mrs. Kezia Wallace.
James Massingham, security.
February 13, 1808—Jonathan Cowdery and Mrs. Elizabeth Riddick.
Henry Keele, security.
February 27, 1808—Francis Moore and Mrs. Mary Millison.
Joseph Abrahams, security.
March 2, 1808—George Rowland and Miss Ann Dickson.
Henry Dickson, security.
March 2, 1808—Severn Watson and Miss Mary McClanehan.
James McKeel, security.
March 11, 1808—John Reed and Mrs. Annis Gaskins.
James McKeel, security.
March 12, 1808—William A. Armistead and Miss Joanna T. Newton.
William Sharp, security.
March 12, 1808—William Lindsay and Miss Mary Ann Newton.
Edwin Stark, security.
March 17, 1808—John Houghton and Miss Martha Poole.
Thomas Jennings, security.
March 19, 1808—Caleb Batten and Miss Elizabeth Randolph.
Adam Randolph, security.
Note: According to an annotation on this bond, Elizabeth Randolph was the daughter of Adam Randolph, the security.
April 5, 1808—Thomas Dickson and Miss Rehobonth Redmon.
Bartholomew Redmon, security.
April 7, 1808—Nathaniel Fitz and Miss Lydia Billups.
James C. Maigne, security.
April 14, 1808—John Pendred and Mrs. Mary Miller.
William Tonkin, security.
April 19, 1808—Thomas McCandlish and Miss Mary C. Peters.
Charles D. Brodie, security.
Note: According to a note included with this bond, Mary C. Peters was the daughter of Ann Camp.

April 21, 1808—John Gordon and Elizabeth Widgen.

Edward Widgen, security.

Note: According to a note included with this bond, Elizabeth Widgen was the daughter of Edward Widgen, the security.

April 26, 1808—William Pennock and Mrs. Elizabeth Reynold.

William K. Mackinder, security.

May 4, 1808—William Parrington and Miss Elizabeth Laurence.

Robert Simmington, security.

Note: According to an annotation on this bond, Elizabeth Laurence was the ward of Robert Simington, the security.

May 6, 1808—Thomas G. Broughton and Miss Ann Bell.

James Mitchell, security.

May 14, 1808—Philip Lambert and Mrs. Elizabeth Dowly.

William C. Farr, security.

Note: According to an annotation on this bond, Elizabeth Dowly was the widow of John Dowly.

May 16, 1808—Daniel R. Waddy and Miss Ann Patterson.

David Patterson, security.

Note: According to an annotation on this bond, Ann Patterson was the daughter of David Patterson, the security.

June 4, 1808—William Stewart and Miss Juliana Perry.

John Rowls, security.

July 5, 1808—Henry Dorsey and Miss Louisa Nixon.

John Shuster, security.

July 6, 1808—Miles Smelt and Miss Ann C. McKendrie.

Thomas B. Seymour, security.

Note: The above couple were married the same day by Thomas T. Jones, a local Methodist elder. According to an annotation on this bond, Ann C. McKendrie was the ward of Job B. Mills.

July 7, 1808—Charles S. Boush and Mrs. Ann Rowe.

Robert Boush, security.

July 11, 1808—Edward Turner and Miss Isabella Caffrey.

Robert Simington, security.

July 22, 1808—John Hall and Mrs. Jane Hill.

Jonathan Rogers, security.

July 23, 1808—John Lewis Arnaud and Mrs. Orphise Marie Ann Vizonneau.

James Maurice, security.

July 26, 1808—Frederick Kighley and Miss Ellen Reid.

George Reid, security.

Note: According to an annotation on this bond, Ellen Reid was the daughter of George Reid, the security.

July 27, 1808—Charles F. Toomer and Miss Maria Walsond.

Francis Butt, security.

Note: The above couple were married on July 28th by Thomas T. Jones, a local Methodist elder.

August 3, 1808—Abraham Cowper and Miss Margaret Hunt.

Joseph Hunt, security.

Note: According to an annotation on this bond, Margaret Hunt was the daughter of Joseph Hunt, the security.

August 19, 1808—John Moore and Mrs. Frances Ruggles.

Thomas Smith, security.

August 20, 1808—Rudolph Breneman and Mrs. Sarah Woodhouse.

James P. Loenes, security.

Note: The above couple were married the same day by Thomas T. Jones, a local Methodist elder.

September 3, 1808—John Gowan and Miss Mary Smith.

John Norris, security.

September 3, 1808—William W. Smith and Miss Catherine Hendre.

Chester Sully, security.

Note: According to an annotation on this bond, Catherine Hendre was the ward of Chester Sully, the security.

October 24, 1808—Lewis LePage and Rosalie Accinelly.

Note: There is no bond for the above marriage in the files of the Corporation Court. It was copied from the returns made by the Rev. Michael DeLacy, pastor of the Norfolk Catholic Congregation. Francis Gorlier, Peter Germain, Bernard Magnien and John Peter Andre are listed as witnesses.

October 26, 1808—John Smith and Miss Frances Addington.

John (mark) Heth, security.

November 3, 1808—James Wilson and Mrs. Elizabeth Boush.

Francis Butt, security.

Note: The above couple were married the same day by Thomas T. Jones, a local Methodist elder.

November 15, 1808—Casper Gottlieb Deidrich and Miss Mildred Denson.

James Grolean, security.

November 24, 1808—George Reed and Miss Mildred Henderson.

John L. Sharples, security.

November 25, 1808—L'amy Voyart and Miss Esther Morris.

George Fritts, security.

November 26, 1808—Thomas Wilson and Mrs. Martha Turner.

John Hannaford, security.

November 28, 1808—James Dewbre and Miss Euphan Watts.

Edward Boutwell, security.

Note: The above couple were married the same day by Thomas T. Jones, a local Methodist elder.

December 8, 1808—Joseph Cutchin and Miss Ann Bagnell.

Richard Fryer, security.

December 8, 1808—Thomas J. Haynes and Miss Margaret O. Bushnell.

Samuel Smith, security.

Note: According to an annotation on this bond, Margaret O. Bushnell was the ward of Samuel Smith.

December 10, 1808—John Dunston and Miss Frances Haynes.

Joel Hodges, security.

December 22, 1808—James Wales and Mrs. Amelia McPherson.

William Wood, security.

Note: According to an annotation on this bond, Amelia McPherson was the widow of James McPherson, deceased.

December 26, 1808—Charles Rattliff and Miss Charlotte Wilder.

Hermon D. Beadles, security.

December 29, 1808—John Quinn (a widower) and Mrs. Ann McDonald.

John Donaghey, security.

Note: The above couple were married the same day by the Rev. Michael DeLacy, pastor of the Norfolk Catholic Congregation. John Donaghey, John McDonald and Mary McDonald are listed as witnesses.

1809

January 5, 1809—William Ford and Mrs. Jemima Shipwash.
James Massingham, security.
January 9, 1809—Charles Campbell and Mrs. Ann Tippett.
Peter Foster, security.
January 27, 1809—James Johnston and Miss Ann Jones.
James Thompson, security.
Note: Ann Jones was the ward of the security.
January 28, 1809—John Hurt and Mrs. Mary Cooper.
George Wakefield, security.
February 2, 1809—Carter Tarrant and Mrs. Margaret Brown.
John Cooper, security.
February 2, 1809—Zebard Martin and Miss Peggy Archer.
Jacob (mark) Wingate, security.
February 11, 1809—John Roux and Miss Mary J. C. Lelievre.
Gabriel Lelievre, security.
Note: The above couple were married the same day by the Rev. Michael De-
Lacy, pastor of the Norfolk Catholic Congregation. Ann Jn. Marchant, Eu-
tropius Berauld, Peter Chabenet, Leonard Anglier, Peter Adde and Louise Mary
Lemasurier are listed as witnesses. According to an annotation on this bond,
Mary J. C. Lelievre was the daughter of Gabriel Lelievre.
February 11, 1809—Mathew Wallace and Miss Sarah Langley.
James Cox, security.
February 25, 1809—James Corsey and Miss Nancy Cross.
William Cross, security.
Note: The above couple were married on February 26th by Thomas T. Jones, a
local Methodist elder. According to an annotation on this bond, Nancy Cross
was the daughter of William Cross, the security.
March 1, 1809—Andrew J. McConnico and Miss Eliza Jordan.
Edwin Stark, security.
March 4, 1809—John Cooper and Mrs. Susanna Denby.
George Wakefield, security.
March 4, 1809—Samuel Smith, Jr., and Miss Eleanor Mansfield.
James Thomson, security.
Note: The above couple were married the same day by Thomas T. Jones, a
local Methodist elder. According to an annotation on this bond, Eleanor Mans-
field was the ward of James Thomson, the security.
March 13, 1809—George Kelly and Miss Margaret Armistead.
George Newton, seccurity.
Note: The above couple were married on March 14th by the Rev. Robert Symes,
rector of Christ P. E. Church.
March 25, 1809—Thomas Jandrell and Mrs. Rachell Menzies.
Charles Mahon, security.
April 14, 1809—David Frazer and Miss Mary Binnie.
John McPhail, security.
Note: According to an annotation on this bond, Mary Binnie was the ward of
John McPhail, the security.
May 2, 1809—Peter Germain Tetreville and Miss Louisa Maria Therese
Sejourne. Jean Baptiste Sejourne, security.
Nicholas Simon, security.
Note: The above couple were married the same day by the Rev. Michael De-
Lacy, pastor of the Norfolk Catholic Congregation. Marie Margaret Berselet,
John Simon, Jean Baptiste Sejourne, Francoise Gorlier, Peter Germain, Joseph
Antonie Dufort, Jean Francois, Jerome Violeau and John Augustus Violeau are
listed as witnesses.

May 15, 1809—William Willis and Mrs. Hannah Welsh.

George Smith, security.

Note: The above couple were married the same day by the Rev. Robert Symes, rector of Christ P. E. Church.

May 15, 1809—Richard Gore and Miss Mary Woodhouse.

Edmund McGuire, security.

May 18, 1809—John Fauquier and Mrs. Susanna Jarvis.

William Fauquier, security.

June 1, 1809—John Gilden and Miss Sally Wood.

Jane (mark) Rogerson, security.

Note: According to an annotation on this bond, Sally Wood was the daughter of Jane Rogerson, the security.

June 3, 1809—John Annatoir and Mrs. Ann Whitehurst.

Claudius Briquet, security.

Note: The above couple were married the same day by Thomas T. Jones, a local Methodist elder.

June 10, 1809—Peter Ferguson and Miss Peggy Cornick.

Soloman Steed, security.

Note: The above couple were married the same day by the Rev. Robert Symes, rector of Christ P. E. Church.

June 26, 1809—William P. Foster and Lucy Wilkinson.

Note: The above marriage was copied from the returns of the Rev. Robert S. Symes, rector of Christ P. E. Church.

July 8, 1809—William Couper and Mrs. Eleanor Clarke.

Thomas Allan, security.

July 15, 1809—Richard Good and Mrs. Ann Batterson.

Hugh McQuillin, security.

July 13, 1809—Thomas Williamson and Anne Walke.

Note: There is no bond for the above marriage in the files of the Corporation Court. It was copied from the returns of the Rev. Robert Symes, rector of Christ P. E. Church.

July 18, 1809—Joshua Herbert and Anna A. Allmand.

Note: There is no bond for the above marriage in the files of the Corporation Court. It was copied from the returns of Thomas T. Jones, a local Methodist elder.

July 22, 1809—Thomas B. Seymour and Miss Jane W. Whitney.

Johnson Mallory, security.

Note: The above couple were married the same day by the Rev. Robert Symes, rector of Christ P. E. Church.

July 26, 1809—William Grigsby Freeman and Miss Peggy English.

George Smith, security.

Note: According to an annotation on this bond, Peggy English was the ward of George Smith, the security.

August 1, 1809—Charles Swain and Miss Maria Frazer.

Andrew Wood, security.

Note: The above couple were married the same day by Thomas T. Jones, a local Methodist elder.

August 11, 1809—John N. Martin and Miss Mary McDonald.

John C. Niemeyer, security.

August 12, 1809—James C. Smith and Mrs. Aphia Harnett.

William Biddle, security.

August 19, 1809—Captain Samuel Vickery and Miss Catherine B. Boush.

John Fawn, security.

Note: According to a note included with this bond, Catherine B. Boush was the daughter of Robert Boush. The above couple were married the same day by the Rev. Robert Symes, rector of Christ P. E. Church.

August 22, 1809—Pierre Labrue and Mrs. Anne Justine Pelon.
Francois Audibert, security.
Note: The above couple were married the same day by the Rev. Michael De-Lacy, pastor of the Norfolk Catholic Congregation. No witnesses are listed.

September 1, 1809—Joel Hodges and Miss Mary Clayton.
Tildsley Graham, security.

September 9, 1809—Francis Reynolds and Mrs. Sarah Wilson.
John (mark) Reynolds, security.

September 28, 1809—John Huntley and Nancy Tucker.
Francis Drake, security.

October 26, 1809—George Newton and Miss Courtney Norton.
James Taylor, Jr., security.
Note: The above couple were married the same day by the Rev. Robert Symes, rector of Christ P. E. Church. According to an annotation on this bond, Courtney Norton was the ward of James Taylor, Jr., the security.

November 3, 1809—William Simington and Miss Sarah Murphy.
Nathaniel Murphy, security.

November 17, 1809—James Dawley and Mrs. Alice Dick.
Dennis Whitehurst, security.

November 23, 1809—John Cornick and Elizabeth Terrant Simpson.
Note: There is no bond for the above marriage in the files of the Corporation Court. It was copied from the returns of the Rev. Robert Symes, rector of Christ P. E. Church.

November 29, 1809—Stephen P. Rose and Miss Sarah Archer Gibbons.
Thomas Gibbons, security.

November 30, 1809—Drayton M. Curtis and Mary Walke.
Note: There is no bond for the above marriage in the files of the Corporation Court. It was copied from the returns of the Rev. Robert Symes, rector of Christ P. E. Church.

November 30, 1809—Daniel Desmon and Sara Morris.
Note: There is no bond for the above marriage in the files of the Corporation Court. It was copied from the returns made by the Rev. Michael DeLacy, pastor of the Norfolk Catholic Congregation. Edward Maguire and Mrs. John G. Brown are listed as witnesses.

December 2, 1809—Joseph Stripe and Miss Mary Clarke.
Richard Good, security.

December 22, 1809—Rennison Nichols and Sally Whitehurst.
John Wiles, security.

December 23, 1809—Gerard Seymour and Mrs. Mary Maye.
Thomas Lester, security.

December 28, 1809—Peter Desnoes and Mrs. Louiza Henrietta Leydier Clement.
Vincent Dallest, security.
Note: The above couple were married the same day by the Rev. Michael De-Lacy, pastor of the Norfolk Catholic Congregation. Charles Dominic Marsaud, Hue Vincent Dallest, Jos. Antonio Dufort and Paul Polycarp Pascal are listed as witnesses.

December 28, 1809—William Armistead and Elizabeth W. Booker (widow).
Note: There is no bond for the above marriage in the files of the Corporation Court. It was copied from the returns of the Rev. Robert Symes, rector of Christ P. E. Church, who adds the name Elizabeth City after the name of the bride. This may refer either to Elizabeth City, Virginia, or Elizabeth City, N. C.

1810

January 4, 1810—Edward Delany and Miss Mary Ann Nisbit.

James Dawley, security.

Note: According to an annotation on this bond, Mary Ann Nisbit was the ward of James Dawley, the security.

January 11, 1810—John C. Saunders and Miss Mary Ann Campbell.

Archibald B. Campbell, security.

Note: The above couple were married the same day by the Rev. Robert Symes, rector of Christ P. E. Church.

February 9, 1810—William Cary and Mrs. Abigail Guy.

James Reed, security.

February 12, 1810—Thomas Hume and Miss Ruth Stiger.

William M. Tanguire, security.

February 12, 1810—James Gilbert and Mrs. Sarah Boyce.

Richard L. Green, security.

Note: The above couple were married the same day by Thomas T. Jones, a local Methodist elder.

February 13, 1810—William Clarke and Miss Margaret Mitchell.

James Mitchell, security.

Note: According to an annotation on this bond, Margaret Mitchell was the daughter of James Mitchell, the security.

February 17, 1810—John Roberts and Patsey Matthias.

Note: There is no bond for the above marriage in the files of the Corporation Court. It was copied from the returns made by Thomas T. Jones, a local Methodist elder.

February 22, 1810—(Lieutenant) Edmund P. Kennedy and Miss Martha Brodie.

James R. Nimmo, security.

Note: The above couple were married the same day by the Rev. Robert Symes, rector of Christ Church. According to a note included with this bond, Martha Brodie was the daughter of Lodowick Brodie, deceased, and the ward of James Nimmo. His note was witnessed by Ann Camp and James R. Nimmo, the security.

February 22, 1810—Abel Curtis and Miss Martha Reard.

Note: The above marriage was copied from the returns of the Rev. Michael DeLacy, pastor of the Norfolk Catholic Congregation. No witnesses are listed.

February 24, 1810—Jeremiah Leecock and Miss Sally T. Jeffery.

Richard Jeffery, security.

March 3, 1810—Robert Shannon and Miss Sally James.

John Gray, security.

Note: The above couple were married the same day by Thomas T. Jones, a local Methodist elder.

March 6, 1810—Willoughby Cason and Miss Kezia King.

William (mark) Mathias, security.

Note: The above couple were married the same day by Thomas T. Jones, a local Methodist elder.

March 13, 1810—David Pierce and Margaret Martin.

Andrew Martin, security.

Note: According to an annotation on this bond, Margaret Martin was the daughter of Andrew Martin, the security.

March 14, 1810—Richard Kane and Mrs. Fanny Boush.

James (mark) Cuterel, security

March 17, 1810—John Farmer and Mrs. Elizabeth Sanford.

Richard Good, security.

Note: The above couple were married the same day by the Rev. Robert Symes rector of Christ P. E. Church.

March 19, 1810—John Whiting and Miss Elizabeth Walden.

Godfrey Cox, security.

Note: The above couple were married on March 21st by Thomas T. Jones, a local Methodist elder.

March 20, 1810—Thomas Armistead and Miss Pricilla M. Armistead.

George Kelly, security.

Note: The above couple were married the same day by the Rev. Robert Symes rector of Christ P. E. Church.

March 29, 1810—Julian Magagnos and Mrs. Dorothea Krafft.

Benjamin Pollard, security.

Note: The above couple were married the same day by the Rev. Robert Symes, rector of Christ P. E. Church.

April 21, 1810—James Jackson and Miss Elizabeth Frazer.

Godfrey Cox, security.

Note: The above couple were married on April 22nd by Thomas T. Jones, a local Methodist elder.

April 26, 1810—James Keenan and Fanna Watirs.

Note: The above marriage was copied from the returns of the Rev. Michael DeLacy, pastor of the Norfolk Catholic Congregation. John Dreenan and William Keenan are listed as witnesses.

April 30, 1810—(Lieutenant) Walter G. Anderson and Miss Mary Ann Crawford.

Nathaniel Murphy, security.

Note: According to an annotation on this bond, Ann Crawford was the ward of Nathaniel Murphy, the security. The above couple were married on May 1st by the Rev. Robert Symes, rector of Christ P. E. Church.

May 8, 1810—George Bennett and Mrs. Sarah White.

John Green, security.

Note: The above couple were married the same day by Thomas T. Jones, a local Methodist elder.

May 19, 1810—George Wilson and Miss Elizabeth Edwards.

Martha (mark) Turner, security.

Note: The above couple were married the same day by Thomas T. Jones, a local Methodist elder.

May 28, 1810—Milnor W. Peters and Miss Elizabeth Carter.

Robert McCandlish, security.

Note: The above couple were married the same day by the Rev. Robert Symes, rector of Christ P. E. Church. According to a note included with this bond, Elizabeth Carter was the ward of Robert Saunders of Williamsburg.

June 2, 1810—William Flintham and Mrs. Susan Dana.

Robert Oliphant, security.

June 6, 1810—George W. Camp and Miss Frances Willoughby.

William Sharp, security.

Note: The above couple were married the same day by the Rev. Robert Symes, rector of Christ P. E. Church. According to a note included with this bond, Frances Willoughby was the ward of Margaret Willoughby.

July 5, 1810—William Henderson Williams and Miss Polly Williams.

William (mark) Ward, security.

July 7, 1810—John W. Henop and Miss Elizabeth C. Wallace.

Johnson Mallory, security.

July 9, 1810—John Nadaux and Miss Elizabeth Lestrade.

Andre Michel, security.

Note: The above marriage was copied from the returns of the Rev. Michael DeLacy, pastor of the Norfolk Catholic Congregation. Andre Michel, Capamagy, Florentine Brette and Vincent Parlatto are listed as witnesses. Elizabeth Lestrade was the daughter of Mary Lestrade.

July 10, 1810—William T. Hunter and Miss Henrietta Louisa Andre.

James Hunter, security.

Note: The above couple were married the same day by the Rev. Robert Symes, rector of Christ P. E. Church.

July 23, 1810—Thomas M. Corby and Miss Mary Hester.

Francis Butt, security.

July 27, 1810—Lorea Fraetas and Miss Sarah Ward.

John Nash, security.

July 28, 1810—James B. Butt and Sarah Cann.

Note: There is no bond for the above marriage in the files of the Corporation Court. It was copied from the returns of the Rev. Robert Symes, rector of Christ P. E. Church, who also states that the above couple were married in Portsmouth, Virginia.

August 1, 1810—Jonas Hastings and Miss Eliza Granberry.

Willis R. Stowe, security.

Note: The above couple were married on August 2nd by the Rev. Robert Symes, rector of Christ P. E. Church. According to a note included with this bond, Eliza Granberry was the daughter of John Granberry.

August 6, 1810—James Wakeman and Mrs. Hetty Golding.

William Simington, security.

August 6, 1810—William C. Farr and Miss Barbara Cox.

Godfrey Cox, security.

Note: The above couple were married the same day by Thomas T. Jones, a local Methodist elder.

August 25, 1810—Samuel Parish and Mrs. Nancy Saints.

Godfrey Cox, security.

Note: The above couple were married the same day by Thomas T. Jones, a local Methodist elder.

October 11, 1810—Charles Grymes and Ann Butt.

David Brooks, security.

October 20, 1810—John Dunlavy and Miss Elizabeth Gardner.

Joseph Gardner, security.

Note: The above couple were married on October 26th by Thomas T. Jones, a local Methodist elder.

November 15, 1810—Alexander Bell and Miss Rachel Valentine.

John (mark) Bell, security.

December 5, 1810—Richard W. Baugh and Mrs. Serina Yarwood.

Stark Hobday, security.

Note: The above couple were married the same day by the Rev. Robert Symes, rector of Christ P. E. Church.

December 13, 1810—Richard H. Cooke and Ann H. Adams (widow).

Note: There is no bond for the above marriage in the files of the Corporation Court. It was copied from the returns of the Rev. Robert Symes, rector of Christ P. E. Church.

December 15, 1810—Joseph Spratley and Mrs. Elizabeth D. Hobday.

James Dameron, security.

Note: The above couple were married the same day by Thomas T. Jones, a local Methodist elder.

December 21, 1810—William Balsom and Miss Charlotte Brewer.

Jacques Touzard, seccurity.

December 24, 1810—Jordan Winslow and Miss Jane Needham.

George Chamberlaine, security.

Note: The above couple were married by the Rev. C. Callaway. No date is given.

December 27, 1810—Richard Hetherington and Miss Peggy Hardison.

Tildsley Graham, security.

1811

January 4, 1811—Joseph Clerico and Miss Maria Marchant.

Elijah Marchant, security.

Note: The above couple were married on January 5th by Thomas T. Jones, a local Methodist elder.

January 5, 1811—Reuben Ridley and Miss Elizabeth Shepherd.

Richard Blin, security.

Note: The above couple were married the same day by Thomas T. Jones, a local Methodist elder.

January 8, 1811—John Kinsman and Mrs. Frances Lane.

William Jackson, security.

Note: The above couple were married by the Rev. Charles Callaway. No date is given.

January 13, 1811—John C. Kellum and Miss Eleanor Jones.

C. D. Burt, security.

January 18, 1811—John Frazer and Mrs. Ann Beacham.

John Davis, security.

Note: The above couple were married on January 19th by Thomas T. Jones, a local Methodist elder.

January 18, 1811—John Peterson and Mrs. Mary Eleanor Vickers.

Richard Good, security.

January 29, 1811—George Wilson and Mrs. Sarah Brunet.

William Maxwell, security.

Note: The above couple were married the same day by the Rev. Robert Symes, rector of Christ P. E. Church.

February 1, 1811—John R. Harwood and Miss Susanna H. Gilbert.

Martin Fisk, security.

Note: The above couple were married the same day by Thomas T. Jones, a local Methodist elder.

February 14, 1811—Arthur S. Woodhouse and Miss Jane B. Woodside.

Daniel Dorney, security.

Note: The above couple were married the same day by the Rev. Robert Symes, rector of Christ P. E. Church.

February 25, 1811—Thomas Lynes and Mrs. Elizabeth Spencer.

Richard Good, security.

Note: The above couple were married on February 26th by the Rev. Robert Symes, rector of Christ P. E. Church.

February 28, 1811—James Forest and Miss Eliza Kehlmelle.

William P. Pollard, security.

March 2, 1811—Jonathan Piper and Miss Elizabeth Haywood.

Alexander Haywood, security.

Note: Included with this bond is the following paper:

I, Larkin Smith, Collector of the District of Norfolk and Portsmouth, do hereby certify that Jonathan Piper, an American seaman, aged twenty-three years or thereabouts, of the height of five feet seven inches, of a brown complexion, dark hair, blue eyes, born in Strathum in the State of New Hampshire, has this day produced to me proof in the manner directed in the Act, entitled An act for the relief and protection of American Seamen, and pursuant to the said Act, I do hereby certify that the said Jonathan Piper is a citizen of the United States of America.

March 8, 1811—Samuel Stutson and Miss Mary Thrift.

John R. Pitt, security.

March 15, 1811—Lewis Bernard and Miss Sarah Oatest.

Henry Oatest, security.

Note: The above couple were married by the Rev. Robert Symes, rector of Christ P. E. Church. No date is given.

March 17, 1811—Joseph Perkins and Miss Elizabeth Ewell.
Francis Foster, security.
March 27, 1811—James Kelsick and Henrietta Peters.
John (mark) Lewis, security.
April 1, 1811—John Dennis and Miss Eliza Morgan.
Francis Foster, security.
April 4, 1811—James Mahon and Miss Mary Crocker.
Joseph (mark) Stripe, security.
April 4, 1811—Nicholas Kennedy and Miss Sarah Miller.
John Clarke, security.
April 20, 1811—Thomas W. Hawkins and Miss Eliza Griffon.
William Cary, security.
Note: The above couple were married the same day by Thomas T. Jones, a local Methodist elder. According to a note included with this bond, Eliza Griffon was the ward of William Carey, the security.
April 20, 1811—Peleg Barstow and Miss Mary Rollins.
Francis Foster, security.
May 7, 1811—Jacob Vickery and Miss Ann W. Peters.
Thomas McCandlish, security.
Note: According to a note included with this bond, Ann Peters was the ward of Ann Camp.
May 9, 1811—William Wright and Miss Juliana Holloway.
John Pierce, security.
May 9, 1811—William Johnson and Mrs. Sally Howard.
William Wright, security.
May 29, 1811—Stephen Andrew Pater and Miss Mary White.
Absolom Stephens, security.
Note: According to a note included with this bond, Mary White was the ward of Stephen Andrew Pater.
June 3, 1811—William Stant and Mrs. Margaret Allen.
Barnaby Scully, security.
Note: The above couple were married the same day by Thomas T. Jones, a local Methodist elder.
June 5, 1811—John Davie and Mrs. Margaret Carline.
Philip (mark) Booz, security.
June 12, 1811—James Cox and Miss Elizabeth Powell.
Sarah Powell, security.
Note: According to a note included with this bond, Elizabeth Powell was the daughter of Sarah Powell, the security.
June 15, 1811—Gilbert Spilman and Miss Eleanor Evans.
George Evans, security.
Note: According to an annotation on this bond, Eleanor Evans was the daughter of George Evans, the security.
June 20, 1811—Medara Portelette and Mrs. Marianna Tietrine.
George Eberle, security.
June 21, 1811—Henry Guy and Miss Margaret Annatoy.
Nathaniel (mark) Burgess, security.
June 24, 1811—Anthony Walke, Jr., and Miss Ann Livingston.
John Livingston, security.
June 27, 1811—Pleasant Stewart and Miss Ann Turner.
Nicholas (mark) Turner, security.
Note: The couple were married on June 28th by Thomas T. Jones, a local Methodist elder.

July 2, 1811—John Black and Martha Pebworth.
Note: There is no bond for the above marriage in the files of the Corporation Court. It was copied from the returns made by Thomas T. Jones, a local Methodist elder.

July 19, 1811—Robert Darrah and Miss Unice Stewart.
William Stewart, security.
Note: According to an annotation on this bond, Unice Stewart was the daughter of William Stewart, the security.

July 21, 1811—Edmond B. Winterbotham and Miss Eliza Harding.
John Vernon, security.
Note: The above couple were married the same day by Thomas T. Jones, a local Methodist elder.

July 26, 1811—Jonathan Woodhouse and Mrs. Jane Montgomery.
Job Palmer, security.
Note: The above couple were married the same day by Thomas T. Jones, a local Methodist elder.

July 26, 1811—Berard McGuire and Miss Mary Polding.
Charles Donaldson, security.

July 29, 1811—Soloman Brant and Mrs. Jane Blackford.
Benjamin (mark) Davis, security.

July 30, 1811—Jacob Klien and Miss Esther Colegate.
George Newton, security.
Note: The above couple were married on July 31st by the Rev. Robert Symes, rector of Christ P. E. Church. According to an annotation on this bond, Esther Colegate was the ward of William B. Selden.

August 1, 1811—William Smith and Mrs. Sarah White.
Patrick Ryan, security.

August 1, 1811—Edward Chamberlaine and Miss Maria Robertson.
Henry Keele, security.
Note: The above couple were married the same day by the Rev. Robert Symes, rector of Christ P. E. Church.

August 9, 1811—Robert M. Rose and Miss Eliza Gilbert.
John H. Fosdick, security.
Note: The above couple were married the same day by the Rev. Robert Symes, rector of Christ P. E. Church.

August 10, 1811—George Joseph Richardson and Miss Ann Stroud.
John Garrow, security.
Note: The above couple were married the same day by Thomas T. Jones, a local Methodist elder.

August 19, 1811—Merideth Boldware and Mrs. Elizabeth Johnson.
Moses (mark) Rickets, security.
Note: The above couple were married the same day by Thomas T. Jones, a local Methodist elder.

August 20, 1811—William Ennis and Mrs. Mary Whiggleton.
Casper Gottleib Deidrick, security.

August 23, 1811—Peter Jansen and Mrs. Sarah Roberts.
Thomas Halliday, security.

August 27, 1811—John Carraway and Miss Martha Canby Suggs.
George Suggs, security.
Note: The above couple were married the same day by the Rev. Robert Symes, rector of Christ P. E. Church.

September 3, 1811—Edward Absolam and Miss Anne Chapman McCall.
William Edmonds, security.
Note: According to a note included with this bond, Anne McCall was the orphan of Archibald McCall.

September 13, 1811—William P. Precious and Miss Mary Hester.
Nathaniel Murphy, security.

October 12, 1811—Benjamin Frost and Mrs. Nancy Baynes.
Gersham Moore, security.

Note: The above couple were married on October 13th by the Rev. Robert Symes, rector of Christ P. E. Church.

October 17, 1811—John Whaley and Miss Rebecca Carroll.
Edward Miner, security.

October 17, 1811—Mr. Richard Bagnall and Miss Mary B. Moseley.

Note: The above marriage was copied from the returns of the Rev. Robert S. Symes, rector of Christ P. E. Church.

October 17, 1811—Thomas Scott and Susan Butt.

Note: The above marriage was copied from the returns of the Rev. Robert S. Symes, rector of Christ P. E. Church.

October 27, 1811—John T. Bodet and Mrs. Sarah Kennedy.
Samuel (mark) Parish, security.

October 21, 1811—William Sturgis and Miss Nancy Russell.
Jeremiah Smith, security.

November 7, 1811—James McMin and Miss Elizabeth Cooke.
Zacheus Ellis, security.

November 9, 1811—John S. Sharples and Mrs. Catherine Jacobs.
John K. Clark, security.

November 14, 1811—Henry Jackson and Mrs. Katy Ambler.
Bryan Gormley, security.

November 16, 1811—John H. Fosdick and Miss Mary Bell.
Thomas G. Broughton, security.

November 16, 1811—David Watson and Sophia Gleeson.
William Howell, security.

November 21, 1811—James Duncan and Miss Hannah Durant.
Thomas G. Broughton, security.

Note: According to an annotation on this bond, Hannah Durant was the ward of Thomas G. Broughton, the security.

November 28, 1811—Marcus T. C. Jordan and Miss Abby Pusey.
Andrew McConnico, security.

Note: The above couple were married the same day by Thomas T. Jones, a local Methodist elder.

November 30, 1811—Joshua Moore and Mrs. Mary Archer.
Peter Ferguson, security.

Note: The above couple were married the same day by the Rev. Robert Symes, rector of Christ P. E. Church.

November 30, 1811—Stephen Smith and Mrs. Eleanor Ornsberry.
Joseph Addington, security.

Note: The above couple were married the same day by Thomas T. Jones, a local Methodist elder.

December 5, 1811—Captain Isaac Park of Newbury Port and Eliza Miler of Gosport, Va.

Note: There is no bond for the above marriage in the files of the Corporation Court. It was copied from the returns of the Rev. Robert Symes, rector of Christ P. E. Church.

December 7, 1811—David Outlaw and Miss Harriet Swain.
Charles Swain, security.

Note: The above couple were married the same day by Thomas T. Jones, a local Methodist elder. According to an annotation on this bond, Harriet Swain was the daughter of Benjamin Swain.

December 9, 1811—John Kirkpatrick and Mrs. Susan Brent.
Michael Madden, security.

December 11, 1811—William D. Roberts and Miss Margaret Guy.
Henry Guy, security.

Note: According to an annotation on this bond, Margaret Guy was the daughter of Henry Guy, the security.

December 17, 1811—Jacob Wingate and Mrs. Fanny Middleton.
Richard Vanderberry, security.

December 19, 1811—Reuben McClenachan and Elizabeth Capps.
Samuel (mark) Kellum, security.

Note: The above couple were married on December 19th by Thomas T. Jones, a local Methodist elder.

December 21, 1811—Edward Jones and Rachael McGee (widow).

Note: There is no bond for the above marriage in the files of the Corporation Court. It was copied from the returns of the Rev. Robert Symes, rector of Christ P. E. Church.

December 28, 1811—Jonathan Williamson and Miss Eliza Hodgkin.
James Murphy, security.

Note: The above couple were married the same day by Thomas T. Jones, a local Methodist elder.

1812

January 13, 1812—William Dwyer and Mrs. Elizabeth Langley.
James Darcy, security.

Note: The above couple were married the same day by Thomas T. Jones, a local Methodist elder.

January 23, 1812—Henry Moore and Sally Nestor.

Note: There is no bond for the above marriage in the files of the Corporation Court. It was copied from the returns of the Rev. Robert Symes, rector of Christ P. E. Church.

January 25, 1812—William Langley and Sukey Langley.

Note: There is no bond for the above marriage in the files of the Corporation Court. It was copied from the returns of the Rev. Robert Symes, rector of Christ P. E. Church.

March 2, 1812—James Middleton and Miss Mary Whitlow.
Zacheus Ellis, security.

March 4, 1812—Wilson Styles and Miss Charlotte Randall.
Robert (mark) Randall, security.

Note: The above couple were married on March 5th by Thomas T. Jones, a local Methodist elder. According to an annotation on this bond, Charlotte Randall was the daughter of Robert Randall, the security.

March 10, 1812—Nathaniel Watlington, Jr., and Miss Martha Smith Pitt.
Benjamin Pitt, security.

Note: The above couple were married the same day by the Rev. Robert Symes, rector of Christ P. E. Church. According to an annotation on this bond, Martha Smith Pitt was the daughter of Benjamin Pitt, the security.

March 4, 1812—George Raincock and Rebecca Parham Louis.

Note: There is no bond for the above marriage in the files of the Corporation Court. It was copied from the returns of the Rev. Robert Symes, rector of Christ P. E. Church.

March 16, 1812—Felix Lefaucheur and Melanie Rose Decormis.
Laurent Prin, security.

Note: The above couple were married on March 19th by the Rev. Michael DeLacy, pastor of the Norfolk Catholic Congregation. Joseph Antoine Dufort is listed as witness.

March 26, 1812—Lieutenant Thomas R. Swift and Ann P. Cox.

Note: There is no bond for the above marriage in the files of the Corporation Court. It was copied from the returns of the Rev. Robert Symes, rector of Christ P. E. Church.

March 26, 1812—Mills Nicholas and Nancy Johnson (free negroes).

George (mark) Wells, security.

Note: The above couple were married the same day by the Rev. Michael De-Lacy, pastor of the Norfolk Catholic Congragtion. Wells Francis is listed as witness.

March 28, 1812—Oney S. Dameron and Miss Alice H. Herbert.

James Dawley, security.

Note: According to an annotation on this bond, Alice H. Herbert was the ward of James Dawley, the security.

March 28, 1812—James Lighton and Miss Martha Millow.

Zacheus Ellis, security.

Note: The above couple were married on March 28th by Thomas T. Jones, a local Methodist elder.

March 31, 1812—Francois Latour and Miss Marie Eugene Lestrade.

Andre Michell, security.

Note: The above couple were married April 1st by the Rev. Michael DeLacy, pastor of the Norfolk Catholic Congregation. Florentinus Brette and John Dufort are listed as witnesses. According to an annotation on this bond, Marie Eugene Lestrade was the ward of Andre Michell, the security.

April 4, 1812—(Lieutenant) Jesse D. Elliott, U. S. N., and Miss Frances Vaughn.

Daniel Stone, security.

Note: The above couple were married on April 7th by the Rev. Robert Symes, rector of Christ P. E. Church. According to an annotation on this bond, Frances Vaughn was the ward of Daniel Stone, the security.

April 9, 1812—Hugh Scott and Miss Catherine Townsend.

John Bell, security.

April 10, 1812—Nicholas Francis Seveno and Miss Marie Antoinette Pamela Roux.

John Roux, security.

Note: The above couple were married the same day by the Rev. Michael De-Lacy, pastor of the Norfolk Catholic Congregation. Marie Lemasurier and Henry Boucher are listed as witnesses.

April 14, 1812—Edward Elstob and Miss Ann Love.

James Middleton, security.

April 16, 1812—William C. Holt and Mrs. Ann C. Campbell.

Francis C. Fontaine, security.

April 17, 1812—John Burgess and Jannet Halsey.

Note: There is no bond for the above marriage in the files of the Corporation Court. It was copied from the returns made by Thomas T. Jones, a local Methodist elder.

April 18, 1812—Robert B. Stark and Miss Matty F. Lindsay.

William Lindsay, security.

Note: The above couple were married April 19th by the Rev. Robert Symes, rector of Christ P. E. Church.

May 6, 1812—John Hedrick and Miss Sarah McKendrie.

George Smith, security.

Note: The above couple were married May 7th by the Rev. Robert Symes, rector of Christ P. E. Church. According to an annotation on this bond, Sarah McKendrie was the ward of Harlow Harwood.

May 9, 1812—Malachi Oldner and Miss Elizabeth Reed.

John (mark) Reed, security.

May 14, 1812—John Garris and Miss Elizabeth Purdy.

Samuel Pierce, security.

May 20, 1812—Thomas Pierce and Margaret Miller.

Note: There is no bond for the above marriage in the files of the Corporation Court. It was copied from the returns of the Rev. Robert Symes, rector of Christ P. E. Church.

May 26, 1812—Francis Vincent and Mrs. Elizabeth Boyd.

Alexander Haywood, security.

May 30, 1812—Hugh Dougherty and Ann Orr (widow).

Note: There is no bond for the above marriage in the files of the Corporation Court. It was copied from the returns of the Rev. Robert Symes, rector of Christ P. E. Church.

June 3, 1812—James Cuthbert and Miss Frances Bragg.

Talbot Bragg, security.

Note: The above couple were married the same day by the Rev. Robert Symes, rector of Christ P. E. Church. According to an annotation on this bond, Frances Bragg was the ward of Talbot Bragg, the security.

June 4, 1812—Adam Adams and Mrs. Frances Roberts.

John Smith, security.

Note: The above couple were married the same day by Thomas T. Jones, a local Methodist elder.

June 20, 1812—Stephen Windenger and Miss Catherine Wood.

Charles D. Wood, security.

Note: The above couple were married the same day by Thomas T. Jones, a local Methodist elder. According to an annotation on this bond, Catherine Wood was the daughter of Charles D. Wood, the security.

June 20, 1812—Harmon Hanor and Mrs. Mary Banks.

Charles C. Davis, security.

June 23, 1812—William Scott and Miss Nancy Hummins.

Zacheus Ellis, security.

Note: The above couple were married the same day by Thomas T. Jones, a local Methodist elder.

July 2, 1812—Henry Keeling and Fanny Wilson.

Note: There is no bond for the above marriage in the files of the Corporation Court. It was copied from the returns of the Rev. Robert Symes, rector of Christ P. E. Church.

July 11, 1812—William Clarke and Mrs. Elizabeth Kennedy.

James Mitchell, security.

July 22, 1812—David Jones and Mrs. Eliza G. C. Ward.

Thomas (mark) Scott, security.

Note: The above couple were married on July 25th by Thomas T. Jones, a local Methodist elder. According to an annotation on this bond, Eliza G. C. Ward was the widow of Dr. S. Ward.

July 23, 1812—Hugh Pannell and Miss Courtney Pennock.

Lewis Hansford, security.

Note: The above couple were married the same day by the Rev. Robert Symes, rector of Christ P. E. Church. According to a note included with this bond, Courtney Pennock was the daughter of William Pennock.

July 28, 1812—Lewis Bertre and Mrs. Anne Lagache.

Joseph Sawyer, security.

Note: The above couple were married the same day by the Rev. Robert Symes, rector of Christ P. E. Church.

July 31, 1812—John Wales and Mrs. Elizabeth Cherry.

Patrick Perin, security.

Note: The above couple were married on August 1st by Thomas T. Jones, a local Methodist elder.

August 5, 1812—William Elliott and Mrs. Mary Toohull.

Patrick (mark) Cunningham, security.

Note: The above couple were married the same day by Thomas T. Jones, a local Methodist elder.

August 7, 1812—Lawrence Ryan and Mrs. Martha Colls.

Daniel Dorney, security.

Note: The above couple were married on August 8th by the Rev. Michael De-Lacy, pastor of the Norfolk Catholic Congregation. Edward McGuire, William Simington and Daniel Dorney are listed as witnesses.

August 13, 1812—Abraham Rogers and Mrs. Mary Mason.

Mathew Hubbard, Jr., security.

August 26, 1812—Louis Edouard Laplante and Miss Aidelle Dorson.

John M. Noblet, security.

Note: The above couple were married on August 27th by the Rev. Michael DeLacy, pastor of the Norfolk Catholic Congregation. Latour and Dufort are listed as witnesses.

August 28, 1812—Joseph Savier Margutte and Mrs. Elizabeth Wolfe.

Peter Foster, security.

September 9, 1812—Caleb Wood and Miss Lydia Capps.

Reuben McClenachan, security.

Note: The above couple were married the same day by Thomas T. Jones, a local Methodist elder.

September 17, 1812—Francis Wright and Mrs. Lucretia Woodworth.

Thomas McCandlish, security.

Note: The above couple were married the same day by the Rev. Robert Symes, rector of Christ P. E. Church.

September 25, 1812—Joseph Davis and Miss Elizabeth Perin.

James Middleton, security.

October 3, 1812—Shadrack Harmon and Mrs. Nancy Grant.

Edward Widgen, security.

Note: The above couple were married the same day by Thomas T. Jones, a local Methodist elder.

November 2, 1812—Henry Murden and Miss Sally Bains.

Henry Bains, security.

Note: The above couple were married the same day by Thomas T. Jones, a local Methodist elder. According to an annotation on this bond, Sally Bains was the daughter of Henry Bains, the security.

November 7, 1812—John Stubling and Miss Elizabeth Danson.

Jacques Touzard, security.

Note: The above couple were married the same day by the Rev. Robert Symes, rector of Christ P. E. Church.

November 16, 1812—Thomas Sneed and Miss Hetty Hedrick.

George Fritts, security.

Note: The above couple were married on November 19th by Thomas T. Jones, a local Methodist elder.

November 17, 1812—John Widgen and Mrs. Elizabeth Gordon.

Edward Widgen, security.

November 28, 1812—Benjamin Gautier and Miss Maria C. Fabre.

Peter Fabre, security.

December 15, 1812—Harrison Allmand and Miss Lucy Campbell.

Copeland Parker, security.

Note: The above couple were married the same day by the Rev. Robert Symes, rector of Christ P. E. Church.

December 17, 1812—Gregory Baylor Richards and Miss Catherine Clark.

Alexander Clark, security.

Note: The above couple were married the same day by the Rev. John Weaver.

December 22, 1812—Thomas Hankins and Miss Maria Ogbourn.
George Clark, security.
Note: The above couple were married the same day by the Rev. John Weaver.
December 22, 1812—Jacob Valentine and Elizabeth Hobday.
Note: There is no bond for the above marriage in the files of the Corporation Court. It was copied from the returns of the Rev. Robert Symes, rector of Christ P. E. Church.
December 26, 1812—Joseph Anitoir and Mrs. Mary Conndly.
John (mark) Reed, security.
December 28, 1812—Edward S. Waddy and Mrs. Sarah Bowdoin.
Thomas McCandlish, security.
Note: The above couple were married the same day by the Rev. Robert Symes, rector of Christ P. E. Church.
December 29, 1812—John B. Ogg and Miss Elizabeth Whitehurst.
Caleb Bonsal, security.
Note: According to a note included with this bond, Elizabeth Whitehurst was the daughter of Daniel Whitehurst.
December ——, 1812—Gabriel Achille and Henriette (negroes).
Note: There is no bond for the above marriage in the files of the Corporation Court. It was copied from the returns made by the Rev. Michael DeLacy, pastor of the Norfolk Catholic Congregation. No witnesses are listed.

1813

January 13, 1813—Henry Snyder and Miss Caherine Sawback.
Henry Guy, security.
Note: The above couple were married on January 14th by Thomas T. Jones, a local Methodist elder.
January 21, 1813—Edward Henry Stewart and Mary Wilcocks.
Note: There is no bond for the above marriage in the files of the Corporation Court. It was copied from the returns made by the Rev. Michael DeLacy, pastor of the Norfolk Catholic Congregation. John Cassin, Henry Henry and Richard J. Cox are listed as witnesses.
January 21, 1813—John Burcher and Lucy Kellinger (widow).
James Thomas, Jr., security.
February 2, 1813—Edward Gee and Mrs. Nancy Gorden.
Edward Elstob, security.
February 2, 1813—Thomas Scott and Miss Eliza Jones.
David Jones, security.
February 5, 1813—John T. Bowdoin and Sally Edwards Browne.
Note: There is no bond for the above marriage in the files of the Corporation Court. It was copied from the returns of the Rev. Robert Symes, rector of Christ P. E. Church.
February 6, 1813—Bassett McCoy and Miss Susan Morris.
Oney Edwards, security.
February 11, 1813—Lemuel B. Clarke and Miss Grace Turner Cleaver.
John McPhail, security.
Note: According to a note included with this bond, Grace Turner Cleaver was the daughter of John Cleaver.
February 11, 1813—Caleb Bonsal and Miss Sarah Dawley.
Earl Sturtevant, security.
February 16, 1813—Robert Mitchell and Miss Sarah Keeling.
Thomas Davis, security.
Note: The above couple were married the same day by the Rev. Robert Symes, rector of Christ P. E. Church. According to a note included with this bond, Sarah Keeling was the daughter of Mary G. Keeling.

February 18, 1813—Robert Coxell and Miss Elizabeth Mary Newell.

John J. Campbell, security.

Note: According to a note included with this bond, bearing the signature of George Young, minister of Trinity Parrish, Elizabeth Mary Newell was "the daughter of James Charles Newell and Catherine, his wife, and was baptised agreeable to the rites of the Protestant Episcopal Church in the town of Portsmouth in the State of Virginia on the twentieth day of October in the year of Our Lord One Thousand Seven Hundred and Ninety-one."

February 18, 1813—James Nimmo and Mary M. Scott.

Note: The above marriage was copied from the returns of the Rev. Robert S. Symes, rector of Christ P. E. Church.

April 3, 1813—Benjamin Bryan and Margaret O. Haynes (widow).

Note: The above marriage was copied from the returns of the Rev. Robert S. Symes, rector of Christ P. E. Church.

April ___, 1813—John Bernard and Justine (negroes).

Note: There is no bond for the above marriage in the files of the Corporation Court. It was copied from the returns of the Rev. Michael DeLacy, pastor of the Norfolk Catholic Congregation.

April 17, 1813—Robert L. Edmonds and Julia Graves.

Note: There is no bond for the above marriage in the files of the Corporation Court. It was copied from the returns of Thomas T. Jones, a local Methodist elder.

May 24, 1813—Augustine Blake and Mrs. Mary Gray.

Alexander Haywood, security.

Note: The above couple were married May 26th by the Rev. Robert Symes, rector of Christ P. E. Church.

June 3, 1813—John Riggs and Miss Susan Hederick.

John Willia, security.

Note: The above couple were married the same day by Thomas T. Jones, a local Methodist elder.

June 19, 1813—Andrew Hyle and Miss Nancy Haywood.

Alexander Haywood, security.

Note: The above couple were married the same day by Thomas T. Jones, a local Methodist elder.

July 1, 1813—John Francois (a free man of colour) and Madame Infantine (a free woman of colour).

Henry (mark) Jackson, security.

Note: The above couple were married the same day by Thomas T. Jones, a local Methodist elder.

July 30, 1813—William Deford and Mrs. Kitty A. Gamble.

Isaiah Fearing, security.

August 21, 1813—James Seal and Nancy Daugherty.

Note: There is no bond for the above marriage in the files of the Corporation Court. It was copied from the returns of the Rev. Robert Symes, rector of Christ P. E. Church.

August 26, 1813—Jacques Touzard and Miss Margaret Bantell.

Joseph Sawyer, security.

Note: The above couple were married August 28th by the Rev. Robert Symes, rector of Christ P. E. Church.

August 26, 1813—Jacob Gerhart and Miss Polly Cherry.

John Wales, security.

Note: The above couple were married August 28th by Thomas T. Jones, a local Methodist elder.

August 26, 1813—Lewis Hawke and Mrs. Jane Wells.

John G. Brown, security.

Note: The above couple were married the same day by Thomas T. Jones, a local Methodist elder.

August 31, 1813—Carl C. Lunning and Miss Esther Pebworth.

John Black, security.

Note: The above couple were married September 4th by Thomas T. Jones, a local Methodist elder.

September 6, 1813—Joel Morse and Mrs. Frances O'Meara.

John West, security.

Note: The above couple were married the same day by Thomas T. Jones, a local Methodist elder.

September 10, 1813—Winston Shiflet and Miss Mary Hatton.

John Robins, security.

Note: The above couple were married the same day by Thomas T. Jones, a local Methodist elder.

September 16, 1813—James Thompson and Miss Elizabeth Church.

James Middleton, security.

Note: The above couple were married the same day by Thomas T. Jones, a local Methodist elder.

September 25, 1813—Richard Dove and Nancy Mathias.

Note: There is no bond for the above marriage in the files of the Corporation Court. It was copied from the returns of the Rev. Robert Symes, rector of Christ P. E. Church.

October 2, 1813—James Christie and Miss Charlotte Johnson.

John Johnson, security.

Note: The above couple were married the same day by the Rev. Robert Symes, rector of Christ P. E. Church.

October 2, 1813—Samuel A. Binford and Miss Mary B. Williams.

Edward Chisman, security.

Note: The above couple were married the same day by the Rev. Robert Symes, rector of Christ P. E. Church. According to a note included with this bond, Mary B. Williams was the ward of Richard B. Servant.

October 14, 1813—Nathan Moore and Miss Mary Coddle.

William Scott, security.

October 19, 1813—Thomas Moore and Miss Sarah Petitt.

Isaac Pointer, security.

October 22, 1813—Henry Lafmyer and Miss Elizabeth Harris.

William Beakley, security.

October 23, 1813—John Gifford and Mrs. Margaret Etheredge.

James Middleton, security.

Note: The above couple were married the same day by Thomas T. Jones, a local Methodist elder.

October 27, 1813—Burwell Bassett Moseley and Miss Elizabeth Amy Boush.

Samuel Vickery, security.

Note: The above couple were married October 28th by the Rev. Robert Symes, rector of Christ P. E. Church.

November 6, 1813—John Pedamus and Miss Elizabeth Payne.

William Scott, security.

Note: The above couple were married the same day by Thomas T. Jones, a local Methodist elder.

November 8, 1813—Lyas Benson and Mrs. Alice Hornsby.

Nathaniel Moore, security.

November 13, 1813—James Johnson and Mrs. Ann Hill.

John (mark) Kirkpatrick, security.

November 13, 1813—Charles Ellis and Miss Margaret K. Nimmo.

James Nimmo, security.

November 21, 1813—Thomas Reiley and Miss Elizabeth M. Donaghey.

John Donaghey, security.

Note: The above couple were married the same day by the Rev. Michael De-Lacy, pastor of the Norfolk Catholic Congregation. John Donaghey, John Moran and Jasper Moran are listed as witnesses.

November 23, 1813—Samuel White and Miss Margaret McDougal.

Joseph Clarico, security.

Note: The above couple were married the same day by Thomas T. Jones, a local Methodist elder.

November 25, 1813—Hugh Wright and Mrs. Catherine Sheilds.

Samuel Scott, security.

Note: The above couple were married the same day by Thomas T. Jones, a local Methodist elder.

December 15, 1813—Jean Baptiste Castignet and Miss Anne Denoin.

Luc Laurent Prin, security.

Note: The above couple were married December 23rd by the Rev. Michael De-Lacy, pastor of the Norfolk Catholic Congregation.

December 15, 1813—Joseph F. Cunningham and Miss Mary Patterson.

John McPhail, security.

Note: The above couple were married December 16th by the Rev. Robert Symes, rector of Christ P. E. Church.

December 21, 1813—William Dunton and Mrs. Nancy Merrican.

Henry Guy, security.

December 24, 1813—Frederick Johnson and Miss Livy Payne.

John Paddimus, security.

Note: The above couple were married the same day by Thomas T. Jones, a local Methodist elder.

December 30, 1813—George W. Maupin and Anne Moffat.

Note: There is no bond for the above marriage in the files of the Corporation Court. It was copied from the returns of the Rev. Robert Symes, rector of Christ P. E. Church.

1814

January 27, 1814—Samuel Calvert and Miss Louisa C. Glenn.

Thomas Glenn, security.

Note: The above couple were married the same day by the Rev. Robert Grifith.

January 7, 1814—James Murray and Elizabeth Moran (widow).

Note: There is no bond for the above marriage in the files of the Corporation Court. It was copied from the returns of the Rev. Michael DeLacy, pastor of the Norfolk Catholic Congregation. Daniel Desmond and George Smith are listed as witnesses.

February 5, 1814—John Stavro and Mary Marrs.

Note: There is no bond for the above marriage in the files of the Corporation Court. It was copied from the returns of the Rev. Michael DeLacy, pastor of the Norfolk Catholic Congregation. Capt. Roux, Mrs. Foulon and Mrs. Murphy are listed as witnesses.

February 3, 1814—William Cake and Mary Mitchell.

Note: There is no bond for the above marriage in the files of the Corporation Court. It was copied from the returns made by Thomas T. Jones, a local Methodist elder.

February 23, 1814—William Fisher and Mrs. Mary Ann Leeson.

Philip (mark) Booz, security

February 26, 1814—Joseph Gordon and Mrs. Catherine Jacobs.

Adam Vanderslice, security.

Note: The above couple were married the same day by Thomas T. Jones, a local, Methodist elder.

March 10, 1814—Joseph C. Daffin and Miss Ann Townsend.

John B. Johnson, security.

Note: The above couple were married the same day by Thomas Bargea, a local Methodist minister.

March 17, 1814—Aaron Rogers and Ann Stewart (a free woman of colour).

John (mark) Jasper, security.

March 14, 1814—Orren Williams and Miss Margaret R. Connor.

Stephen Wright, security.

March 19, 1814—Frederick Golladay and Miss Jane Elizabeth Loury.

James Mickie, security.

Note: The above couple were married the same day by Thomas T. Jones, a local Methodist elder.

March 19, 1814—John Mahan and Mrs. Esther Moffit.

William J. Macknea, security.

Note: The above couple were married the same day by the Rev. Michael De-Lacy, pastor of the Norfolk Catholic Congregation. William J. Macknea is listed as witness.

March 23, 1814—John Owens and Miss Nancy Murray.

David (mark) Murray, security.

March 26, 1814—Joseph Tarman and Mrs. Sarah Ann Kennedy.

William Scott, security.

Note: The above couple were married the same day by Thomas T. Jones, a local Methodist elder.

March 28, 1814—Samuel Leech and Mary Thompson (widow).

Note: The above marriage was copied from the returns of Thomas T. Jones, a local Methodist elder.

March 31, 1814—John Quinn and Mrs. Lucy Gamble.

Note: The above couple were married on April 2nd by Thomas T. Jones, a local Methodist elder.

April 12, 1814—William Valery and Miss Nancy Tate.

John Miller, security.

Note: The above couple were married April 13th by Thomas T. Jones, a local Methodist elder.

May 16, 1814—James Rose and Mrs. Eleanor Creighton.

James Seal, security.

Note: The above couple were married the same day by Thomas T. Jones, a local Methodist elder.

May 23, 1814—Henry Brekenridge and Miss Catherine Cowan.

Thomas R. Swift, security.

Note: The above couple were married the same day by the Rev. John D. Paxton, pastor of the Presbyterian Congregation.

May 28, 1814—Robert Barret and Mrs. Patsey Wells.

James (mark) Wiles, security.

June 7, 1814—Alexander Douglas and Miss Mary Bright Lowry.

Josiah Cole, security.

Note: The above couple were married the same day by Thomas T. Jones, a local Methodist elder.

June 7, 1814—Nicholas Turner and Alice Collins.

Aaron (mark) Rogers, security.

Note: The above couple were married June 8th by Thomas T. Jones, a local Methodist elder.

June 15, 1814—William Turner and Mrs. Amy Singleton.

Nicholas (mark) Turner, security.

June 20, 1814—John A. Donnell and Miss Mary Eliza Sulliden.

William Bamberger, security.

Note: The above couple were married June 21st by the Rev. Michael DeLacy, pastor of the Norfolk Catholic Congregation.

June 25, 1814—Thomas Simmons and Miss Margaret Martin.

Jonathan Haynes, security.

June 25, 1814—John Payne and Mary Anne Lee (widow).

Note: There is no bond for the above marriage in the files of the Corporation Court. It was copied from the returns of the Rev. Robert Symes, rector of Christ P. E. Church.

June 29, 1814—Henry Walthall and Miss Eliza Jones.

Thomas Jones, security.

Note: The above couple were married on June 30th by Thomas T. Jones, a local Methodist elder.

July 13, 1814—January D. Souza and Mrs. Ellen Metcalf.

John West, security.

Note: The above couple were married the same day by Thomas Bargea, a local Methodist minister.

July 14, 1814—Lemuel Langley and Miss Elizabeth Mann.

Isham Dyer, security.

Note: The above couple were married the same day by the Rev. John D. Paxton.

July 18, 1814—William Francis and Martha Street.

Note: There is no bond for the above marriage in the files of the Corporation Court. It was copied from the returns of the Rev. Robert Symes, rector of Christ P. E. Church.

July 21, 1814—John Butler and Miss Sally Whitehurst.

Joseph (mark) Gordon, security.

July 27, 1814—John Anthony and Miss Frances Boos (or Booz).

George Eberle, security.

July 27, 1814—Francis J. Mettaner and Miss Mary Ann Eliza Marsden.

Mathew Cluff, security.

Note: The above couple were married July 29th by the Rev. Thomas Bargea, a local Methodist minister.

July 30, 1814—Thomas Crow and Mrs. Betsy Scott.

Elias Benson, security.

August 6, 1814—John Dunlavy and Miss Delilah Etheredge.

James Dyson, security.

Note: The above couple were married the same day by Thomas T. Jones, a local Methodist elder.

August 11, 1814—Samuel H. McCraw and Mrs. Ann Boush.

Jacob Shuster, security.

Note: The above couple were married the same day by Thomas Bargea, a local Methodist minister.

August 16, 1814—John Padmors and Miss Sarah Dawley.

John (mark) Dawley, security.

Note: The above couple were married the same day by Thomas T. Jones, a local Methodist elder.

August 20, 1814—Samuel Perrow and Miss Anne Hall.

George Smith, security.

Note: The above couple were married the same day by Thomas T. Jones, a local Methodist elder.

August 24, 1814—John R. Pitts and Miss Lelia Ann Dunn.

John Freeman, security.

November 1, 1814—James Thorowgood and Rebecca A. Elligood.

Note: There is no bond for the above marriage in the files of the Corporation Court. It was copied from the returns of the Rev. Robert Symes, rector of Christ P. E. Church.

November 14, 1814—Henry Wells and Miss Sarah Hall.

Isaiah Cooke, security.

Note: The above couple were married November 15th by Thomas T. Jones, a local Methodist elder.

November 22, 1814—Godfrey Cook and Miss Mourning Jackson.

James Ward, security.

Note: The above couple were married November 23rd by the Rev. Michael De-Lacy, pastor of the Norfolk Catholic Congregation. James Murray, Eliza Murray, Robert Woodly and Mrs. Stanford are listed as witnesses. According to a note included with this bond, Mourning Jackson was the sister of Catherine Stanford.

November 23, 1814—William L. Day and Miss Sarah W. Dunn.

William C. Holt, security.

Note: The above couple were married the same day by Thomas T. Jones, a local Methodist elder. According to a note included with this bond, Sarah W. Dunn was the daughter of John Dunn.

November 24, 1814—Ambrose Hamilton and Mrs. Susan Ferguson.

Thomas Hammond, security.

December 7, 1814—Henry Newsam and Mrs. Mary Pendred.

Harmon (mark) Redmon, security.

December 7, 1814—George Kelly and Miss Margaret E. Pollard.

William Sharp, security.

Note: The above couple were married December 8th by the Rev. Robert Symes, rector of Christ P. E. Church.

December 13, 1814—(Lieut.) Benjamin J. Neale and Miss Mary L. Whittle.

(Dr.) George T. Kennon, security.

Note: The above couple were married the same day by the Rev. Robert Symes, rector of Christ P. E. Church. According to a note included with this bond, Mary L. Whittle was the daughter of Conway Whittle.

December 15, 1814—James Keenan and Sara Desmond (widow).

Note: There is no bond for the above marriage in the files of the Corporation Court. It was copied from the returns of the Rev. Michael DeLacy, pastor of the Catholic Congregation. Patrick and Terentius Keenan, Bernard Mulhollan and Robert Woodly are listed as witnesses.

December 19, 1814—Henry Jackson, Jr., and Miss Kezia Mundowny.

James Wiles, security.

Note: The above couple were married the same day by Thomas T. Jones, a local Methodist elder.

December 28, 1814—John B. Duchamp and Miss Eliza Trutier.

Stephen Peillon, security.

December 29, 1814—Sharp Lightfoot and Mrs. Eliza Ann O'Donald.

James Murray, security.

December 31, 1814—James Ash (a free man of colour) and Pricilla Hall (a free woman of colour).

Nathan (mark) Mathews, security.

1815

January 11, 1815—James Dryden and Miss Charlotte Lesley.

John Lesley, security.

Note: The above couple were married January 19th by Thomas T. Jones, a local Methodist elder. According to an annotation on this bond, Charlotte Lesley was the daughter of John Lesley, the security.

January 19, 1815—James Young and Miss Martha Ritson.

James B. Cunningham, security.

Note: The above couple were married the same day by the Rev. Robert Symes, rector of Christ P. E. Church.

January 26, 1815—John Peter Mettaner and Miss Mary Woodward.

James Woodward, security.

January 31, 1815—Thomas Vaughn and Claudia Hamilton Allegood.

Note: There is no bond for the above marriage in the files of the Corporation Court. It was copied from the returns of the Rev. Robert Symes, rector of Christ P. E. Church.

February 1, 1815—John Hentz and Mrs. Frances Anthony.

George Eberle, security.

Note: The above couple were married February 2nd by John D. Paxton, pastor of the Presbyterian Congregation.

February 22, 1815—Lewis Galevin and Mrs. Mary Arjo.

George Smith, security.

Note: The above couple were married March 12th by Thomas T. Jones, a local Methodist elder.

February 23, 1815—Jacob Hess and Mrs. Mary Fisher.

Godfrey (mark) Cook, security.

February 25, 1815—Arthur Miles and Mrs. Hannah Foster.

George Smith, security.

February 28, 1815—John Jenkins and Miss Sarah Lewton.

Thomas Seaman, security.

Note: The above couple were married March 1st by Thomas T. Jones, a local Methodist elder.

March 4, 1815—Ira Cowles and Miss Jane Spratley.

Joseph Spratley, security.

Note: The above couple were married the same day by Thomas T. Jones, a local Methodist elder.

March 4, 1815—Jacob Mathiot and Miss Elizabeth Munroe.

Edward (mark) Spencer, security.

March 13, 1815—William Black and Mrs. Susan Kilpatrick.

John Karns, security.

Note: The above couple were married the same day by Thomas T. Jones, a local Methodist elder.

March 13, 1815—William Pannell and Miss Sarah C. Pennock.

Lewis Hansford, security.

Note: The above couple were married the same day by Thomas T. Jones, a local Methodist elder.

March 17, 1815—John Gay and Mrs. Nancy Mathias.

Tildsley Graham, security.

March 18, 1815—John Wayland and Mrs. Jane Garrow.

David C. Hicks, security.

March 23, 1815—John Christian Schyler and Miss Mary Pebworth.

John Black, security.

Note: The above couple were married the same day by Thomas T. Jones, a local Methodist elder.

March 28, 1815—Asa Joyce and Mrs. Mary Leach.
John L. Billups, security.

April 1, 1815—Edward Spencer and Miss Anne Saunderson.
Jacob Mathiot, security.

April 1, 1815—Richard Webb and Jane Schewt.

Note: There is no bond for the above marriage in the files of the Corporation Court. It was copied from the returns of the Rev. Robert Symes, rector of Christ P. E. Church.

April 3, 1815—Antonio Ferte and Miss Polly Stevenson.
Sebastian Aimar, security.

Note: The above couple were married the same day by Thomas T. Jones, a local Methodist elder.

April 11, 1815—George Scott and Miss Hetty Golding.
Oliver Wendell, security.

April 12, 1815—James Harvey and Nancy Sprague.
James Murray, security.

April 19, 1815—(Captain) William Lewis and Miss Frances Munford Whittle.
Fortescue Whittle, security.

Note: The above couple were married the same day by the Rev. Robert Symes, rector of Christ P. E. Church. According to a note included with this bond, Frances Munford Whittle was the daughter of Conway Whittle.

April 22, 1815—Joseph K. Boyd and Miss Catherine Scully.
Barnaby Scully, security.

Note: The above couple were married the same day by the Rev. John B. O'Brien, pastor of the Catholic Congregation of Norfolk.

April 25, 1815—David Brown and Nancy Johnson.
John (mark) Huntley, security.

Note: The above couple were married the same day by Thomas T. Jones, a local Methodist elder.

April 22, 1815—John Snyder and Miss Susan Welten.
Henry Snyder, security.

April 25, 1815—David Laws and Nancy Johnson.
John Huntley, security.

Note: The above couple were married the same day by Thomas T. Jones, a local Methodist elder.

May 1, 1815—William Potnet and Polly George.
John (mark) Jasper, security.

Note: The above couple were married the same day by Thomas T. Jones, a local Methodist elder.

May 6, 1815—William C. Henley and Miss Mary Summers.
William Summers, security.

May 8, 1815—Silas Lee and Miss Betsy May.
Elijah (mark) Cutrel, security.

Note: The above couple were married the same day by Thomas T. Jones, a local Methodist elder.

May 15, 1815—Nathan Bonney and Miss Pamela Harrison.
Henry H. Newsums, security.

May 17, 1815—John J. Stout and Miss Eliza Harding.
Thomas Harding, security.

Note: The above couple were married the same day by Thomas T. Jones, a local Methodist elder.

May 17, 1815—John Davis and Miss Lydia Osman Marshall.
Lewis Marchalle, security.

May 18, 1815—Lewis Hoak and Mrs. Elizabeth Stutson.

Arthur Denby, security.

May 18, 1815—Malichi Williamson and Miss Martha Batten.

John Barnes, security.

May 23, 1815—James McKeel and Miss Elizabeth McBride.

Henry Oatest, security.

May 28, 1815—Alexander Birch and Mrs. Patsy Wilson.

James Widgen, security.

May 27, 1815—Stephen Pellion and Miss Lucretia Accinelly.

Note: There is no bond for the above marriage in the files of the Corporation Court. It was copied from the returns of the Rev. John B. O'Brien pastor of the Catholic Congregation in Norfolk.

May 31, 1815—Joseph Timberlake and Miss Frances C. Butt.

John Capron, security.

Note: The above couple were married June 1st by the Rev. Robert Symes, rector of Christ P. E. Church. According to a note included with this bond, Frances C. Butt was the daughter of Dorcas Butt.

June 3, 1815—James Crommelin and Mrs. Margaret Smith.

William (mark) Whitehurst, security.

Note: The above couple were married the same day by Thomas T. Jones, a local Methodist elder.

June 3, 1815—John Elliott and Mrs. Ann Gee.

Joel Jones, security.

Note: The above couple were married the same day by Thomas T. Jones, a local Methodist elder.

June 5, 1815—James M. Calvin and Miss Ann H. Cornick.

Peter Nestell, security.

Note: The above couple were married the same day by Thomas T. Jones, a local Methodist elder.

June 7, 1815—Benjamin Russell and Mrs. Elizabeth Brinson.

Pennuel Russell, security.

June 8, 1815—John C. Rosson and Miss Nancy Strand.

Reuben Fentress, security.

June 9, 1815—Martin Dobb and Mrs. Pamelia Bartee.

John Marable, security.

June 13, 1815—Patton S. Philbrick and Miss Pamelia Eggleston.

Cornelius Riorden, security.

June 16, 1815—John Peek and Mrs. Maria Stone.

James McMin, security.

Note: The above couple were married the same day by Thomas T. Jones, a local Methodist elder.

June 19, 1815—Frederick Young and Miss Nancy Hodges.

Benjamin (mark) Oliver, security.

June 24, 1815—George Reilley and Miss Nancy Saunders.

Daniel (mark) Darling, security.

June 24, 1815—John L. Billups and Miss Ann Wood.

Cornelius C. Cross, security.

Note: According to a note included with this bond, Ann Wood was the daughter of Jane Rodgers.

June 27, 1815—Nathaniel D. Keeling and Martha R. Whitney.

John Keeling, security.

Note: According to a note included with this bond, Martha R. Whitney was the Ward of Thomas Seymour.

July 1, 1815—Jonathan Langley and Miss Susanna Cox.
Edwin Lee, security.

July 10, 1815—Thomas Parker and Mrs. Margaret Devaney.
Arthur Miles, security.

July 12, 1815—William DeLacy and Miss Eliza Lee.
William Charles Lee, security.

Note: The above couple were married the same day by the Rev. John B. O'Brien, pastor of the Catholic Congregation of Norfolk. The marriage was witnessed by "the families of both parties."

July 13, 1815—James Saunders and Lucy H. Lee.

Note: There is no bond for the above marriage in the files of the Corporation Court. It was copied from the returns of the Rev. Robert Symes, rector of Christ P. E. Church.

July 15, 1815—William Cooper and Mrs. Anna Jenkins Short.
Thomas L. Griffin, security.

Note: The above couple were married the same day by Thomas T. Jones, a local Methodist elder.

July 25, 1815—John Patterson and Miss Elizabeth Simmons.
William (mark) Dulton, security.

July 27, 1815—John Wiatt and Mrs. Catherine Stanford.
Elzy Burroughs, security.

August 2, 1815—Asaph Wales and Miss Eliza Osborne Butler.
Tristrim Butler, security.

Note: The above couple were married August 3rd by John D. Paxton, pastor of the Presbyterian Congregation. According to an annotation on this bond, Eliza A. O. Butler was the ward of Tristrim Butler, the security.

August 5, 1815—William Couper and Miss Mary Ann Holmes.
James Reed, security.

Note: The above couple were married the same day by Thomas T. Jones, a local Methodist elder. According to an annotation on this bond, Mary Ann Holmes was the ward of James Reed, the security.

August 5, 1815—George J. Blake and Anne Drinane.

Note: There is no bond for the above marriage in the files of the Corporation Court. It was copied from the returns of the Rev. Robert Symes, rector of Christ P. E. Church.

August 12, 1815—James Little and Miss Anna Stent.
Edmund McGuire, security.

August 25, 1815—John Williams and Mrs. Rebecca Haywood.
William C. Farr, security.

August 28, 1815—John H. Freeman and Miss Mary Wills.
Samuel White, security.

September 8, 1815—Elkanah Ballance and Miss Catherine McCleland.
Henry McCleland, security.

Note: According to a note included with this bond, Catherine McCleland was the ward of Henry McCleland, the security.

September 30, 1815—James W. Henop and Miss Frances W. Floyd.
James Willoughby, security.

Note: The above couple were married October 1st by John D. Paxton, pastor of the Presbyterian Congregation. According to a note included with this bond, Frances W. Floyd was the ward of Arthur Cooper.

October 3, 1815—Adam Lindsay and Miss Maria Wood.
Charles D. Wood, security.

Note: The above couple were married the same day by Thomas T. Jones, a local Methodist elder.

October 6, 1815—Bartley Potts and Miss Elizabeth Hurst.

John G. Hurst, security.

Note: The above couple were married the same day by Thomas T. Jones, a local Methodist elder.

October 10, 1815—Gabriel Johnson and Miss Susan Fulter.

Hubberd (mark) Sheborn, security.

Note: The above couple were married the same day by Thomas T. Jones, a local Methodist elder.

November 2, 1815—Richard H. Bell and Miss Maria Custine King.

Miles Kng ('Jr.), security.

Note: The above couple were married the same day by the Rev. Robert Symes, rector of Christ P. E. Church.

November 8, 1815—George Lindsay and Miss Ann D. Blakeley.

John R. Blakeley, security.

Note: The above couple were married the same day by Thomas T. Jones, a local Methodist elder.

November 15, 1815—John Rogers and Mrs. Elizabeth Hannaford.

James Glisan, security.

November 18, 1815—John Norton and Ann Haywood.

William Sharp, security.

Note: There is no bond for the above marriage in the files of the Corporation Court. It was copied from the returns of the Rev. Robert Symes, rector of Christ P. E. Church.

November 21, 1815—Isaac Talbot and Miss Sarah Colley.

Note: The above couple were married November 22nd by the Rev. Robert Symes, rector of Christ P. E. Church.

November 29, 1815—Park Goodall and Miss Eliza Woodhouse.

Joshua Woodhouse, security.

Note: The above couple were married the same day by Thomas T. Jones, a local Methodist elder.

Novemeber 29, 1815—John Reed and Mrs. Mary Legan.

Thomas Ross, security.

Note: The above couple were married the same day by Thomas T. Jones, a local Methodist elder.

December 2, 1815—John Merring and Mrs. Nancy Parsons.

William Gordon, security.

December 6, 1815—Major Kellum and Mrs. Nancy Antoine.

William Balsom, security.

Note: The above couple were married the same day by Thomas T. Jones, a local Methodist elder.

December 7, 1815—Jesse Whitehurst and Mrs. Lavery (a free mulatto).

Armistead (mark) Willis, security.

Note: The above couple were married the same day by Thomas T. Jones, a local Methodist elder.

December 8, 1815—Edward Hale and Miss Fanny Fontaine.

George Sears, security.

Note: The above couple were married December 10th by the Rev. Samuel K. Jennings.

December 11, 1815—James H. Pagaud and Mrs. Ruth Hume.

Thomas Constable, security.

December 18, 1815—Thomas L. McLean and Miss Elizabeth Ewell.

Jesse Ewell, security.

Note: The above couple were married the same day by the Rev. Robert Symes, rector of Christ P. E. Church.

December 23, 1815—Adam Vanderslice and Miss Eliza Washington Edmondston.

William Hale, security.

December 25, 1815—William Seymour and Miss Eliza Doyle.

George Doyle, security.

Note: The above couple were married the same day by the Rev. Robert Symes, rector of Christ P. E. Church.

December 25, 1815—George W. Gilbert and Mrs. Martha Manson.

Edward Reiley, security.

December 28, 1815—William H. Jennings and Jane Tarrant.

Note: There is no bond for the above marriage in the files of the Corporation Court. It was copied from the returns of the Rev. Robert Symes, rector of Christ P. E. Church.

1816

January 11, 1816—Thomas Constable and Mrs. Mary Coffin.

William Jennings, security.

January 11, 1816—Henry H. Dentzel and Mrs. Sarah Ricardo.

Samuel Dilworth, security.

January 24, 1816—John Riggins and Miss Lydia Townsend.

Joel Callis, security.

February 3, 1816—Jean Pierre Cholas and Marie Elizabeth (negroes).

Note: There is no bond for the above marriage in the files of the Corporation Court. It was copied from the returns of the Rev. James Lucas, pastor of the Norfolk Catholic Congregation. Jean Francois, Jean Baptiste and Gabriel Achille are listed as witnesses.

February 5, 1816—John Bluford and Miss Elizabeth Consolvo.

Claudius Briquet, security.

Note: The above couple were married the same day by Thomas T. Jones, a local Methodist elder.

February 6, 1816—Roger J. Blackburn and Charlotte Prescott (widow).

Note: There is no bond for the above marriage in the files of the Corporation Court. It was copied from the returns of the Rev. Samuel Low, rector of Christ P. E. Church.

February 7, 1816—Charles Britain and Amelia Godfred.

Note: There is no bond for the above marriage in the files of the Corporation Court. It was copied from the returns of the Rev. Robert Symes, rector of Christ P. E. Church.

February 15, 1816—David Scott and Mary Hunter Whitehurst.

Note: There is no bond for the above marriage in the files of the Corporation Court. It was copied from the returns of the Rev. Robert Symes, rector of Christ P. E. Church.

February 19, 1816—Thomas Trask and Mrs. Rebecca Simpson.

Henry H. Dentzel, security.

February 12, 1816—James Clarke and Mrs. Sally Smitchen.

James Harvey, security.

February 17, 1816—Joel Callis and Miss Eliza Mathias.

William (mark) Mathias, security.

Note: The above couple were married the same day by Thomas T. Jones, a local Methodist elder.

February 17, 1816—Stephen G. Buxton and Miss Ann Briquet.

James Buxton, security.

Note: The above couple were married the same day by Thomas T. Jones, a local Methodist elder. According to a note included with this bond, Ann Briquet was the daughter of Claudius Briquet.

February 24, 1816—Cyrus Stow and Miss Nancy Ellis.
Zacheus Ellis, security.
February 27, 1816—Edward and Mary (negroes).
Note: There is no bond for the above marriage in the files of the Corporation Court. It was copied from the returns of the Rev. James Lucas, pastor of the Norfolk Catholic Congregation. Mrs. Higgins is listed as witness.
February 29, 1816—Giles B. Cooke and Miss Sarah W. Talbot.
Charles S. Boush, security.
Note: The above couple were married the same day by the Rev. Robert Symes, rector of Christ P. E. Church.
March 1, 1816—James Hynd and Miss Ann Reid.
George Reid, security.
Note: The above couple were married March 2nd by John D. Paxton, pastor of the Presbyterian Congregation.
March 3, 1816—Uriah Hayden and Anne Dougherty (widow).
Note: There is no bond for the above marriage in the files of the Corporation Court. It was copied from the returns of the Rev. Robert Symes, rector of Christ P. E. Church.
March 16, 1816—David Milhado and Miss Lydia Warren.
John Hodges, security.
Note: The above couple were married March 17th by John D. Paxton, pastor of the Presbyterian Congregation.
March 25, 1816—Charles A. Murduck and Miss Judith Cherry.
William Bamberger, security.
Note: The above couple were married the same day by Thomas T. Jones, a local Methodist elder.
March 27, 1816—James Graves and Miss Maria Graves.
Milnor W. Peters, security.
Note: The above couple were married the same day by the Rev. Robert Symes, rector of Christ P. E. Church.
March 28, 1816—Robert Archer and Miss Frances Williamson.
James Williamson, security.
Note: The above couple were married the same day by John D. Paxton, pastor of the Presbyterian Congregation.
April 10, 1816—Henry Singleton and Miss Mary Ann Waldron Reynolds.
Benjamin Reynolds, security.
Note: The above couple were married the same day by John D. Paxton, pastor of the Presbyterian Congregation.
April 11, 1816—James Willoughby and Miss Content Ingram.
William F. Foster, security.
April 13, 1816—James Baker and Miss Jane H. Young.
Robert S. Symes, security.
Note: The above couple were married April 14th by the Rev. Robert Symes, rector of Christ P. E. Church.
April 27, 1816—Henry Woodis and Miss Ann McDonald.
William F. Hunter, security.
Note: The above couple were married the same day by the Rev. James Lucas, pastor of the Norfolk Catholic Congregation. James Hunter, William F. Hunter, L. L. Piercy and Thomas Owens are listed as witnesses.
May 10, 1816—John Shibley and Mrs. Wilhelmina Auckenbrock.
William McDaniel, security.
May 18, 1816—James Bailey and Mrs. Troy Clarke.
John (mark) Starbrow, security.
Note: The above couple were married the same day by Thomas T. Jones, a local Methodist elder.

May 18, 1816—Denward Townsend and Miss Catherine Mars.
John (mark) Starbrow, security.
Note: The above couple were married the same day by Thomas T. Jones, a local Methodist elder.

May 30, 1816—Thomas C. Keaton and Miss Isabella H. Childers.
Nathaniel Childers, security.
Note: The above couple were married the same day by Thomas T. Jones, a local Methodist elder.

June 10, 1816—William Wicker and Miss Martha Roberts.
Philmer Clark, security.

June 12 1816—John Tilford and Miss Mary Ann Slack.
Henry McDowell, security.

June 13, 1816—John D. Ghiselin and Miss Mary Dyson.
James Nimmo, security.
Note: The above couple were married the same day by John D. Paxton, pastor of the Presbyterian Congregation.

June 19, 1816—James Casteen and Miss Elizabeth Sherman.
Herbert Sherman, security.
Note: The above couple were married the same day by Thomas T. Jones, a local Methodist elder.

June 26, 1816—Timothy Houghton and Mrs. Elizabeth McMinn.
James Murray, security.

July 13, 1816—John Saunders and Miss Margaret Trainer.
John Davis, security.
Note: The above couple were married the same day by Thomas T. Jones, a local Methodist elder.

July 27, 1816—John Bartee and Miss Mary Widgen.
Coston F. Ballentine, security.
Note: The above couple were married the same day by Thomas T. Jones, a local Methodist elder.

July 30, 1816—Joseph-Francois-Henri Courreck and Miss Mary Augustine Evelina Pointier.
Honore Pointier, security.
Note: The above couple were married August 13th by the Rev. James Lucas, pastor of the Norfolk Catholic Congregation. Berauld, Benford, L. Santejau, Jas. Cochetel, A. O. Fernandes, Laurede Chaudron, Sejourne and Honore Pointier are listed as witnesses.

July 31, 1816—George T. Hall and Mary Mackie.
Note: The above marriage was copied from the returns of the Rev. Robert Symes, rector of Christ P. E. Church. According to the same source, the bond was issued in Princess Anne County.

August 9, 1816—Lewis Marshall and Mrs. Elizabeth Prince.
James Eccles, security.

August 10, 1816—John Robbins and Mrs. Mary Ann Weaver (free persons of colour).
Robert (mark) Barrett, security.

August 24, 1816—William Jennings and Miss Frances B. Keaton.
Thomas Constable, security.
Note: The above couple were married the same day by Thomas T. Jones, a local Methodist elder.

August 26, 1816—George Ross and Mrs. Nancy Catt.
Josiah Titus, security.
Note: The above couple were married the same day by Thomas T. Jones, a local Methodist elder.

August 30, 1816—Sampson Clement Vincent and Miss Marie Heloïse Pointier.

Honore Pointier, security.

Note: The above couple were married August 31st by the Rev. James Lucas, pastor of the Norfolk Catholic Congregation. Jas. Cochetel, P. Bobee, J. Courrech, L. Santejau, Honore Pointier, Berauld, Sejourne, Bonford, etc., are listed as witnesses.

October 2, 1816—William E. Williams and Miss Eliza Appleby.

Joshua Appleby, security.

Note: The above couple were married the same day by Thomas T. Jones, a local Methodist elder. Eliza Appleby was the daughter of Joshua Appleby, the security.

October 2, 1816—John Thorowgood and Elizabeth T. Mackie.

Note: There is no bond for the above marriage in the files of the Corporation Court. It was copied from the returns of the Rev. Robert Symes, rector of Christ P. E. Church.

October 5, 1816—Francis Vincent and Miss Jane Stevens.

Lorentz Haster, security.

Note: The above couple were married the same day by Thomas T. Jones, a local Methodist elder.

October 12, 1816—Edward Pannell, Jr., and Miss Amy Caroline Newton.

Francis Wright, security.

Note: The above couple were married the same day by the Rev. Samuel Low, rector of Christ P. E. Church. According to a note included with this bond, Amy Caroline Newton was the daughter of Thomas Newton.

October 18, 1816—Thomas Owens and Catherine H. Hunter.

James Hunter, security.

Note: The above couple were married the same day by the Rev. Samuel Low, rector of Christ P. E. Church.

October 22, 1816—Adam Lyon and Elizabeth Young.

John (mark) Young, security.

October 23, 1816—Thomas L. Robertson and Miss Helen Proby.

Robert E. Steed, security.

Note: The above couple were married the same day by the Rev. Samuel Low, rector of Christ P. E. Church. According to an annotation on this bond, Helen Proby was the ward of Robert E. Steed, the security.

October 24, 1816—William McDaniel and Miss Rebecca Cooke.

Isaiah Cooke, security.

November 5, 1816—Andre Dubourg and Miss Marie Henriette Virginie Delaunay.

James Delaunay, security.

Note: The above couple were married November 9th by the Rev. James Lucas, pastor of the Norfolk Catholic Congregation. J. A. Delaunay, Peillon, B. D'antossy, Lewis M. Rivalain, Le Bourdais, Francois LeBourdais, etc., are listed as witnesses.

November 16, 1816—John Fatherly and Mrs. Nancy Bishop.

William Garrow, security.

November 16, 1816—Jean Baptiste and Veronique (Sally), (negroes).

Note: There is no bond for the above marriage in the files of the Corporation Court. It was copied from the returns of the Rev. James Lucas, pastor of the Norfolk Catholic Congregation. Achille, Jean Pierre Cholas, Marie Anne L'Eveille, Francois Losier and Madame Baptiste are listed as witnesses.

November 26, 1816—Roger Jones Blackburn and Mrs. Charlotte Prescott.

Nathaniel Watlington, security.

Note: The above couple were married November 28th by the Rev. Samuel Low, rector of Christ P. E. Church.

November 30, 1816—Pierre Antoine and Marie Catherine (alias Reine), (negroes).

Note: There is no bond for the above marriage in the files of the Corporation Court. It was copied from the returns of the Rev. James Lucas, pastor of the Norfolk Catholic Congregation. Achille, Joseph Thomas, Elie Barrot, Adolphe Maurice are listed as witnesses.

December 6, 1816—Bernard Kid and Mrs. Catherine Andre.

M. Portelet, security.

Note: The above couple were married the same day by Thomas T. Jones, a local Methodist elder.

December 19, 1816—(Rev.) Samuel Low and Miss Ann Elizabeth B. Brown.

William Cammack, security.

Note: The above couple were married the same day by the Rev. William H. Hart.

December 24, 1816—Thomas Franklin and Mrs. Catherine Cooper.

Lorenzo Nicholett, security.

December 28, 1816—George Tilley and Miss Mary Buck.

William (mark) Jackson, security.

1817

January 8, 1817—George Finch and Mrs. Ann D. Roser.

John Singleton, security.

Note: The above couple were married by the Rev. John French, a local Methodist (Protestant) minister. No date is given in the return for the marriage.

January 16, 1817—Nathan Colgate Whitehead and Mrs. Elizabeth Grigsby. John McPhail, security.

Note: The above couple were married the same day by John D. Paxton, pastor of the Presbyterian Congregation.

January 16, 1817—John White and Miss Sarah Barber.

Lewis Granbery, security.

Note: The above couple were married by the Rev. John French, a local Methodist (Protestant) minister. No date for the marriage is given in his return.

January 18, 1817—Richard Etheredge and Mrs. Mary Mahone.

Isaiah Cooke, security.

January 23, 1817—Charles Harshaw and Mrs. Elizabeth E. Hoake.

William Gordon, security.

February 5, 1817—George S. Hodges and Miss Martha R. Pusey.

M. T. C. Jordan, security.

February 6, 1817—Alexander Galt and Miss Mary S. Jeffery.

Richard Jeffery, security.

Note: The above couple were married the same day by the Rev. Samuel Low, rector of Christ P. E. Church.

February 6, 1817—Thomas Bess and Miss Susan Dawley.

John (mark) Dawley, security.

Note: The above couple were married the same day by Thomas T. Jones, a local Methodist elder. According to a note included with the same bond, Susan Dawley was the daughter of John Dawley, the security.

February 13, 1817—Willis Rosson and Miss Martha Willia.

John Willia, security.

Note: The above couple were married the same day by Thomas T. Jones, a local Methodist elder.

February 18, 1817—George T. Kennon and Miss Ann M. (or N.) Boush.

Burwell B. Moseley, security.

Note: The above couple were married February 22nd by the Rev. Samuel Low, rector of Christ P. E. Church.

February 19, 1817—William Moseley and Miss Jane Stith Westwood.
Samuel Moseley, security.
Note: The above couple were married February 2th by the Rev. Samuel Low, rector of Christ P. E. Church.

February 26, 1817—Shadrack Alfriend and Miss Eliza B. Woodlief.
Richard Jeffery, security.
Note: The above couple were married February 27th by th Rev. Samuel Low, rector of Christ P. E. Church.

March 1, 1817—William B. Winckley and Miss Mary Susan Cuthbert.
Francis Wright, security.
Note: The above couple were married the same day by John D. Paxton, pastor of the Presbyterian Congregation. According to a note included with this bond, Mary Susan Cuthbert was the ward of Elzy Burroughs.

March 10, 1817—John Selden and Malana W. George.
John H. George, security.
Note: The above couple were married the same day by Thomas T. Jones, a local Methodist elder.

March 11, 1817—Michael Anderson and Mrs. Louisa McPherson.
Christopher Mason, security.

March 13, 1817—Lewis Warrington and Miss Margaret Cary King.
Miles King, security.
Note: The above couple were married the same day by the Rev. Samuel Low, rector of Christ P. E. Church.

March 20, 1817—James Barnett (or Burnett) and Miss Martha Hunter.
James Hunter, security.
Note: The above couple were married March 22nd by the Rev. Samuel Low, rector of Christ P. E. Church.

March 25, 1817—Thomas Hall and Mrs. Martha Ryan.
William Thomas, security.

April 1, 1817—Henry Smaw and Miss Sarah Fatherly.
John Fatherly, security.

April 3, 1817—Thomas W. Johnston and Miss Elizabeth Murden.
Joles Jones, security.
Note: According to a note included with this bond Elizabeth Murden was the daughter of Nancy Murden.

April 5, 1817—Francis Meneal and Mrs. Elizabeth Johnson.
Jonathan (mark) Clark, security.
Note: The above couple were married the same day by Thomas T. Jones, a local Methodist elder.

April 9, 1817—Patrick V. Perin and Mrs. Mary Cowan.
Francis Meneal, security.
Note: The above couple were married the same day by Thomas T. Jones, a local Methodist elder.

April 14, 1817—Paul Emile Chaudron and Miss Charlotte Elizabeth Francois Rose Tombarel.
Note: There is no bond for the above marriage in the files of the Corporation Court. It was copied from the returns of the Rev. James Lucas, pastor of the Norfolk Catholic Congregation.

April 24, 1817—James Cooper and Mrs. Lucretia Watts.
Reuben Fentress, security.
Note: The above couple were married by the Rev. John French, a local Methodist (Protestant) minister. No date for the ceremony is given.

April 26, 1817—James Yates and Miss Sarah Stripe.
Joseph (mark) Stripe, security.
Note: According to a note included with this bond, Sarah Stripe was the daughter of Joseph Stripe, the security.

April 29, 1817—Henry Henry and Mary Ann Cassin.
Note: There is no bond for the above marriage in the files of the Corporation Court. It was copied from the returns of the Rev. James Lucas, pastor of the Norfolk Catholic Congregation.

May 1, 1817—Thomas W. Lowry and Miss Martha B. Mallory.
Johnson Mallory, security.
Note: The above couple were married the same day by the Rev. Samuel Low, rector of Christ P. E. Church.

May 8, 1817—Robert McCandlish and Miss Ann Campbell.
Philip Barraud, security.
Note: The above couple were married the same day by the Rev. Samuel Low, rector of Christ P. E. Church.

May 14, 1817—Arthur Taylor, Jr., and Miss Anne Saunders.
John N. Gibbons, security.
Note: The above couple were married May 15th by the Rev. Samuel Low, rector of Christ P. E. Church. According to a note included with this bond, Anne Saunders was the wards of Thomas L. Robertson.

June 30, 1817—Pierre Louis and Mary (negroes).
Note: The above couple were married by the Rev. James Lucas, pastor of the Catholic Congregation. His report also states that they were the slaves of Mr. Santejau. There is no bond for the above marriage in the files of the Corporation Court.

May 21, 1817—Edward Lattimer and Miss Ann Eliza Rowe.
Richard D. Brown, security.
Note: The above couple were married May 22nd by the Rev. Mathew M. Danck. According to a note included with this bond, Ann Eliza Rowe was the daughter of William Rowe, decd., and the ward of Robert Brough.

May 27, 1817—John Bailey and Miss Sally Hall.
Daniel Seaman, security.

June 3, 1817—Pierre G. Bonford and Miss Eliza Vincent Parlato.
Frederick Vincent, security.
Note: The above couple were married June 10th by the Rev. James Lucas, pastor of the Norfolk Catholic Congregation. According to a note included with this bond, Eliza Vincent Parlato was the daughter of Vincent Parlato.

June 4 1817—Edward Valentine and Miss Susan Archer.
Robert Archer, security.
Note: The above couple were married by the Rev. John French, a local Methodist (Protestant) minister. No date is given.

June 14, 1817—Elisha Hammond and Miss Elizabeth Shannon.
Francis Magagnos, security.

June 26, 1817—William S. Keeling and Miss Harriet Jane Leslie.
William Sharp, security.
Note: The above couple were married by the Rev. Mathew M. Danck. The date for the ceremony has been torn away.

June 26, 1817—Robert Potts and Mrs. Elizabeth Patterson.
Thomas Simmons, security.
Note: The above couple were married June 30th by the Rev. James Lucas, pastor of the Norfolk Catholic Congregation.

July 3, 1817—John R. Palmer and Mrs. Ann Haywood.
William B. Newell, security.

July 5, 1817—William Cotton and Miss Susan Gains.
Henry Johnson, security.

July 10, 1817—John B. Baird and Maria Thompson.
Note: There is no bond for the above marriage in the files of the Corporation Court. It was copied from the returns of the Rev. Samuel Low, rector of Christ P. E. Church.

July 12, 1817—Christopher Snail and Miss Elizabeth Wangner.
William (mark) Whitehouse, security.
Note: The above couple were married the same day by the Rev. Mathew M. Danck.

July 17, 1817—Joshua S. Oldner and Miss Sally Webb.
William Webb, security.
Note: The above couple were married the same day by Thomas T. Jones, a local Methodist elder.

July 18, 1817—George Broughton and Miss Martha Bunting.
William Jackson, security.
Note: The above couple were married the same day by the Rev. Mathew M. Danck.

August 1, 1817—Semon Flaney and Mrs. Maria Arm.
M. (mark) Portlet, security.
Note: The above couple were married August 2nd by John D. Paxton, pastor of the Presbyterian Congregation.

August 13, 1817—George Smith and Mrs. Fanny Walters.
John Davie, security.
Note: The above couple were married August 14th by Thomas T. Jones, a local Methodist elder.

August 13, 1817—James Jollif and Lucretia A. Herbert.
Note: There is no bond for the above marriage in the files of the Corporation Court. It was copied from the returns of the Rev. Samuel Low, rectors of Christ P. E. Church.

August 18, 1817—Michael Delany and Miss Mary Ann Madden.
Michael Madden, security.
Note: The above couple were married August 19th by the Rev. James Lucas, pastor of the Norfolk Catholic Congregation.

August 19, 1817—Athel Stewart and Miss Elizabeth Black.
Elias Benson, charity.

August 25, 1817—Isaac Tyne and Charity (commonly called Charity Foster).
Benjamin Tynes, security.
Note: The above couple were married August 21st by Thomas T. Jones, a local Methodist elder.

September 6, 1817—Samuel Lindsay and Mrs. Susan Black.
Henry H. Dentzel, security.

September 24, 1817—William F. Gray and Mitty Richards Stone.
Note: There is no bond for the above marriage in the files of the Corporation Court. It was copied from the returns of the Rev. Samuel Low, rector of Christ P. E. Church. He states that the license was issued by the clerk of the Hustings Court of Fredericksburg, Va.

September 26, 1817—Robert Dunn and Miss Margaret Cavender.
James Petree, security.
Note: The above couple were married the same day by Thomas T. Jones, a local Methodist elder.

September 29, 1817—Jacob Hull and Miss Jane Collins.
John McPhail, security.
Note: The above couple were married September 30th by John D. Paxton, pastor of the Presbyterian Congregation.

September 30, 1817—Thomas Joseph and Arsene Monier (free negroes).
James Cochetel, security.
Note: The above couple were married October 11th by the Rev. James Lucas, pastor of the Norfolk Catholic Congregation.

October 2, 1817—James B. Vaughn and Miss Mary Grace Bagnall.
Richard Bagnall, security.
Note: The above couple were married the same day by the Rev. John D. Paxton, pastor of the Presbyterian Congregation. According to an annotation on this bond, Mary Grace Bagnall was the daughter of Richard Bagnall, the security.

October 8, 1817—William Couper and Miss Elizabeth Hamilton.
Michael Crosmuck, security.
Note: The above couple were married October 9th by the Rev. John D. Paxton, pastor of the Presbyterian Congregation.

October 9, 1817—James Daniel and Miss Polly Cotton.
Bernard Roux, security.

October 9, 1817—Thomas G. Peachy and Miss Sarah M. Campbell.
Philip Barraud, security.
Note: The above couple were married the same day by the Rev. Samuel Low, rector of Christ P. E. Church.

October 16, 1817—Crawley Finney and Miss Eliza Woodward.
James Woodward, security.
Note: The above couple were married the same day by the Rev. Mathew W. Danck.

October 25, 1817—Henry Pinkham and Miss Ann Blunden.
Richard Jeffery, security.
Note: The above couple were married the same day by the Rev. Samuel Low, rector of Christ P. E. Church.

October 25, 1817—Robert G. Williamson and Miss Mary Hackett.
Peter Martin, security.

October 27, 1817—William Frederick Wilson Boush and Miss Mary L. Chandler.
John A. Chandler, security.
Note: The above couple were married the same day by the Rev. Mathew W. Danck.

October 31, 1817—Louis Breville and Madame Barba Orsi Soumeillan.
Gabriel Bocciardi, security.
Note: The above couple were married November 4th by the Rev. James Lucas, pastor of the Norfolk Catholic Congregation.

November 8, 1817—Marshall Parks and Mrs. Martha S. F. S. Jordan.
David Parks, security.

November 19, 1817—Thomas Glenn and Ann Mills.
Note: There is no bond for the above marriage in the files of the Corporation Court. It was copied from the return of the Rev. Samuel Low, rector of Christ P. E. Church. According to this source, the license was issued in Norfolk County.

November 27, 1817—William Loyall and Miss Camilla Butt.
Joseph Timberlake, security.
Note: The above couple were married the same day by the Rev. Samuel Low, rector of Christ P. E. Church. Camilla Butt was the daughter of Dorcus Butt.

December 2, 1817—John Bignall and Mrs. Catherine Harman.
James West, security.

December 3, 1817—Andrew Haberfield and Mrs. Margaret Clark.
James Mitchell, security.

December 17, 1817—John Fuller and Miss Maria Butler.
William (mark) Gardner, security.
Note: According to an annotation on this bond, Maria Butler was the ward of William Gardner, the security.

December 18, 1817—John Tabb and Evalina M. Proper.
Note: There is no bond for the above marriage in the files of the Corporation Court. It was copied from the return of the Rev. Samuel Low, rector of Christ P. E. Church. From this same source we learn that the license was issued by the clerk of Gloucester County.

December 21, 1817—Richard D. Brown and Miss Ann B. Shepherd.
Thomas B. Seymour, security.
Note: The above couple were married December 24th by the Rev. Samuel Low, rector of Christ P. E. Church. According to an annotation on this bond, Thomas B. Seymour, the security, was the guardian of Ann B. Shepherd.

December 27, 1817—James Bentall and Miss Patsy White.
John Cunningham, security.

December 31, 1817—Jeremiah Leecock and Miss Sarah Williamson.
Richard Jeffery, security.
Note: The above couple were married the same day by the Rev. Samuel Low, rector of Christ P. E. Church.

1818

January 8, 1818—John G. Wilkinson and Elizabeth Keeling.
Note: There is no bond for the above marriage in the files of the Corporation Court. It was copied from the return of the Rev. Samuel Low, rector of Christ P. E. Church. According to the same source, the license was granted by the clerk of Princess Anne County.

January 8, 1818—Ethelbert Drake and Miss Mary G. Green.
Richard L. Green, security.
Note: The above couple were married the same day by the Rev. Mathew W. Danck.

January 8, 1818—John Parker and Mrs. Margaret Kellum.
John Hutchinson, security.

January 12, 1818—David Halfpenny and Mrs. Gertrude Bailey.
James Robinson, security.

January 13, 1818—Anthony H. Wheton and Mrs. Lydia Shipley.
Josiah Williams, security.

January 17, 1818—James Bailey and Miss Lucy Freeman.
Joseph Freeman, security.

January 22, 1818—William R. Hall and Miss Lucy Lewelling.
Note: There is no bond for the above marriage in the files of the Corporation Court. It was copied from the returns of the Rev. John D. Paxton, pastor of the Presbyterian Congregation.

January 22, 1818—Joseph Clarico and Miss Sarah Ann Slack.
George Ott, security.
Note: The above couple were married January 24th by John D. Paxton, pastor of the Presbyterian Congregation.

January 22, 1818—Charles Clark and Miss Diana Tatem.
George Wilson (Senr.), security.
Note: The above couple were married the same day by the Rev. John D. Paxton, pastor of the Presbyterian Congregation.

January 23, 1818—Edmund Spence and Miss Nancy Lewelling.
Joshua Lewelling, security.
Note: According to an annotation on this bond, Nancy Lewelling was the sister of Joshua Lewelling, the security.

January 27, 1818—Samuel Hibberd and Mrs. Betsey Powers.
John F. Williams, security.

January 31, 1818—Hillary W. Fentress and Miss Mary Ann Snail.
Thomas (mark) Snail, security.
Note: According to an annotation on this bond, Thomas Snail, the security, was a brother of Mary Ann Snail.

February 7, 1818—(In Norfolk)—William Burk, son of Edmund Burk and Catherine Fenessy, and Ann Maria Goodman, daughter of James Goodman and Mary Evans, decd.
Note: There is no bond for the above marriage in the files of the Corporation Court. It was copied from the returns of the Rev. James Lucas, pastor of the Norfolk Catholic Congregation. Gilo Armistead, John T. Armistead, J. Chapman and Edmund Burk are listed as witnesses.

February 7, 1818—Daniel C. Mellus and Mrs. Sarah Ann Summers.
Ebenezar (mark) Kennedy, security.
ote: The above couple were married February 9th by Thomas T. Jones, a local Methodist elder.

February 7, 1818—Ebenezar Kennedy and Mis. Catherine Townsend.
Daniel C. Mellus, security.

February 9, 1818—James Robertson and Mrs. Margaret Saunders.
Robert Johnson, security.

February 11, 1818—John R. West and Elizabeth Nelson.
Note: There is no bond for the above marriage in the files of the Corporation Court. It was copied from the returns of the Rev. Samuel Low, rector of Christ P. E. Church. According to that source the license was issued in York County, Virginia.

February 18, 1818—John Walker and Miss Maria Tatem.
Lovitt Fentress, security.
Note: The above couple were married the same day by the Rev. Mathew W. Danck. According to an annotation on this bond, Maria Tatem was the ward of Lovitt Fentress.

February 18, 1818—Guy C. Wheeler and Eliza Dulton.
Note: There is no bond for the above marriage in the files of the Corporation Court. It was copied from the returns of the Rev. Samuel Low, rector of Christ P. E. Church. According to that source, the license was issued by the clerk of Norfolk County.

February 19, 1818—Thomas Swain and Mrs. Mary Brown.
William Rogers, security.

February 26, 1818—Samuel Curtis and Mrs. Priscilla Howell.
James (mark) Gleason, security.

March 10, 1818—John P. Reilly and Alice Davis (widow).
Note: There is no bond for the above marriage in the files of the Corporation Court. It was copied from the returns of the Rev. Samuel Low, rector of Christ P. E. Church. According to that source, the license was issued by the clerk of Norfolk County.

March 21, 1818—William Willis and Miss Catherine Ogburn.
Alexander A. Martin, security.
Note: The above couple were married March 22nd by the Rev. John D. Paxton, pastor of the Norfolk Presbyterian Congregation.

March 25, 1818—Isaac R. Bagley and Miss Mary Townsend.
Joshua Moore, security.
Note: The above couple were married March 29th by Thomas T. Jones, a local Methodist elder.

March 26, 1818—(In Portsmouth). Bernard Oneil, son of Henry and Louisa Linden, and Jane Keenan, widow of James Millen.
Note: There is no bond for the above marriage in the files of the Corporation Court. It was copied from the returns of the Rev. James Lucas, pastor of the Norfolk Catholic Congregation. James Flinn and James Cooke are listed as witnesses.

March 27, 1818—David Tynes and Mrs. Patsy Godwin.
Lewis (mark) Godwin, security.

March 4, 1818—(In Norfolk). Julien Billingre, son of Jean Dominique Billingre, decd., and Rose Elizabeth Bobie, daughter of Louis Marie Bobie and Maria Magdalaine Valertin. Louis Bobie, security.

Note: The above couple were married on April 2nd by the Rev. James Lucas, pastor of the Catholic Congregation. M. J. Lemasurier, Rochas Jos. Magagnos and L. Santejau are listed as witnesses.

April 4, 1818—John Frnch and Mrs. Frances Marsden.

Robert Brough, security.

Note: The above couple were married April 5th by Thomas T. Jones, a local Methodist elder.

April 16, 1818—Robert M. Desha and Miss Frances Ann Ferebee.

Robert Robertson, security.

Note: The above couple were married the same day by the Rev. John D. Paxton, pastor of the Presbyterian Congregation.

April 20, 1818—Samuel Parker and Mrs. Susanna Hodges.

Benjamin Ashley, security.

April 28, 1818—Lewis Decormis, Jr., and Miss Sarah Ann Burroughs.

Elyz Burroughs, security.

Note: The above couple were married April 30th by the Rev. John D. Paxton, pastor of the Presbyterian Congregation.

April 30, 1818—John A. Chandler and Miss Sarah Woodward.

James Woodward, security.

April 30, 1818—Benjamin Spratley and Sarah Davis.

Note: The above marriage was copied from the returns of the Rev. James Lucas, pastor of the Norfolk Catholic Congregation.

May 18, 1818—John Herrington and Mrs. Susan Woodhouse.

James Casteen, security.

Note: The above couple were married May 23rd by Thomas T. Jones, a local Methodist elder.

May 23, 1818—(In Norfolk). John Harrison and Statia Harris (both slaves).

Note: This marriage was copied from the returns of the Rev. James Lucas, pastor of the Norfolk Catholic Congregation. Felix Bobie, Achille and others are listed as witnesses.

May 25, 1818—Robert M. Crow and Elizabeth Foster.

George M. Bain, security.

May 28, 1818—Nathaniel Wilburn and Miss Fanny Fiveash.

John Madden, security.

May 29, 1818—J. J. Jobert and Mrs. Marie Godin.

Frederick Pichot, security.

Note: The above couple were married June 4th by the Rev. James Lucas, pastor of the Norfolk Catholic Congregation. Dr. Marchant, Jn. Gorlier and Simon B. Werkmuller are listed as witnesses.

June 3, 1818—Zebulon Wade and Mrs. Mary Bland.

Daniel White, security.

June 4, 1818—William Cooper and Miss Ann Hodges.

America (mark) Walker, security.

June 6, 1818—Thomas Skinner and Miss Sarah Russell.

Thomas (mark) Russell, security.

June 18, 1818—Albert Allmand and Miss Margaret O'Grady.

William T. Nivison, security.

Note: The above couple were married the same day by the Rev. Samuel Low, rector of Christ P. E. Church. Albert Allmand was the son of Harrison Allmand.

June 24, 1818—Richard Holstead and Mrs. Jacomine N. Warren.

Edward Hudson, security.

June 27, 1818—John Kerr and Mrs. Margaret Butt.

Charles Grimes, security.

Note: The above couple were married the same day by the Rev. John D. Paxton, pastor of the Presbyterian Congregation.

June 27, 1818—William Fuller and Miss Nancy Moss.

Henry Oatest, security.

Note: The above couple were married by the Rev. William Compton, a local Methodist minister. According to an annotation on this bond, William Fuller and Nancy Moss were free persons of colour and were born free.

July 1, 1818—John Nebeker and Miss Ann Watts.

John E. Beale, security.

July 6, 1818—Frederick Lewis and Miss Ann B. Johnson.

William Sharp, security.

Note: According to a note included with this bond, Ann B. Johnson was the daughter of Capt. James Johnson.

July 7, 1818—William Benedict and Mrs. Patsy Keeling.

Joseph Lum, security.

July 9, 1818—Joel Jones and Miss Sarah Wright.

George Ott, security.

July 9, 1818—Mallory M. Todd and Miss Frances R. Dick.

Oney S. Dameron, security.

Note: The above couple were married the same day by the Rev. Willia.n Compton.

July 13, 1818—James Thompson and Miss Ellen Dornin.

Patrick Dornin, security.

Note: The above couple were married the same day by the Rev. Samuel Low, rector of Christ P. E. Church.

July 13, 1818—William Ashley and Miss Elizabeth Hewett.

Williarm Valery, security.

July 14, 1818—Lewis R. Pollard and Miss Mary Ann Gilbert.

James Gilbert, security.

Note: The above couple were married the same day by the Rev. John D. Paxton, pastor of the Presbyterian Congregation.

July 14, 1818—(In Williamsburg). William Domelly, son of Bartholomew Domelly, decd., and Lucy Oneil, and Eleanor Turner, daughter of Thomas Turner and Eliza Mavy.

Note: There is no bond for the above marriage in the files of the Corporation Court. It was copied from the returns of the Rev. James Lucas, pastor of the Norfolk Catholic Congregation. John Murphy, N. Lunis, Thomas Turner and Gordon McPhersan are listed as witnesses.

July 30, 1818—John Bain and Miss Elizabeth Swank.

John Swank, security.

Note: The above couple were married the same day by the Rev. James Lucas, pastor of the Catholic Congregation. According to his report, John Bain was the son of Samuel Bain and Elizabeth Jones, and Elizabeth Swank was the daughter of John Swank and Mary Whitman. Charles Price, S. B. Davis, Michael Fitzpatrick, Beverly Brown, Josh. Grice and others are listed as witnesses.

August 3, 1818—William Preston and Miss Hannah Gibson.

William Dickson, security.

Note: The above couple were married August 6th by the Rev. John D. Paxton, pastor of the Presbyterian Congregation. According to an annotation on this bond, William Dickson, the security, was the guardian of Hannah Gibson.

August 8, 1818—John H. Braine and Miss Helen Mahan.

Robert R. Braine, security.

Note: The above couple were married the same day by the Rev. Samuel Low, rector of Christ P. E. Church.

77

August 12, 1818—Samuel Vickery and Miss Eliza B. Prentis.

Edward S. Waddey, security.

August 12, 1818—William Taylor and Miss Mariam White.

Philip Rickards, security.

August 14, 1818—Joshua Moore and Miss Nancy Ann James.

Joshua James, security.

Note: The above couple were married the same day by the Rev. John D. Paxton, pastor of the Presbyterian Congregation.

August 15, 1818—Burwell Triplet and Miss Elizabeth Pullen.

Nehemiah Holland, security.

Note: The above couple were married August 17th by Thomas T. Jones, a local Methodist elder.

August 15, 1818—Thomas C. Dixon and Maria Simington.

Robert Simington, security.

Note: The above couple were married the same day by the Rev. John D. Paxton, pastor of the Presbyterian Congregation.

August 17, 1818—John Falvey and Mrs. Isabella Donelly.

John Connell, security.

Note: The above couple were married the same day by the Rev. James Lucas, pastor of the Norfolk Catholic Congregation. According to his report, John Falvey was the son of John Falvey and Catherine Lawlor, and Isabella Donelly's maiden name was Todd. Aug. Falvey and Gurlel are listed as witnesses.

August 24, 1818—Charles C. Lee and Miss Frances M. Butt.

Edward Latimer, security.

Note: The above couple were married August 25th by the Rev. Horatio E. Hall.

August 26, 1818—Cary W. Butt and Miss Elizabeth Woodard.

John W. Butt, security.

Note: According to a note included with this bond, John W. Butt, the security, was the guardian of Cary W. Butt. According to the same source, Elizabeth Woodard was the ward of Anna Woodard.

August 27, 1818—George Roper and Mrs. Maria O. Marshall.

Herbert C. Thompson, security.

September 1, 1818—Thomas W. Johnson and Miss Frances Wright.

Joel Jones, security.

September 2, 1818—Thomas Lowry and Miss Mary Ann Woodward.

Joseph Rickards, security.

September 2, 1818—Samuel Low and Miss Margaret Maria Sawyer.

James B. Cunningham, security.

September 4, 1818—John J. Levy and Mrs. Charlotte Murray.

Thomas J. Jones, security.

September 5, 1818—Joseph Bartholomew and Mrs. Sophia Hurtt.

Nicholas (mark) Darsonville, security.

September 8, 1818—Daniel Seaman and Mourning (free persons of colour).

Isaac Fuller, security.

September 10, 1818—Godfritt (Godfrey) Lambright and Miss Tabitha Heath.

Michael Crosmuck, security.

Note: The above couple were married the same day by the Rev. William Compton.

September 24, 1818—John Camp and Ann Steed (widow).

James Cornick, security.

Note: The above couple were married the same day by the Rev. John D. Paxton, pastor of the Presbyterian Congregation.

September 25, 1818—William Wesson and Mrs. Lucretia Cole.

Robert Moran, security.

Note: The above couple were married the same day by Thomas T. Jones, a local Methodist elder.

September 25, 1818—John Mealey and Miss Margaret Stevens.

Robert Moran, security.

September 26, 1818—William Magre and Miss Maria Butler.

Gabriel Bocciardi, security.

Note: The above couple were married September 27th by the Rev. John D. Paxton, pastor of the Presbyterian Congregation.

September 28, 1818—Thomas Cherry and Mrs. Mary Ross.

Arthur Denby, security.

October 1, 1818—James Paull and Anne Stevens.

Robert Moran, security.

October 1, 1818—James R. Wilson and Miss Margaret Wright.

George Wilson, Jr., security.

Note: According to a note included with this bond, Margaret Wright was the daughter of Stephen Wright.

October 8, 1818—Chauncey Clarke and Mrs. Sarah Bernard.

Henry Oatest, security.

Note: The above couple were married the same day by the Rev. Samuel Low, rector of Christ P. E. Church.

October 9, 1818—Miles Wood and Miss Mary Hopkins.

John Cooper, security.

October 16, 1818—William Bradley and Mrs. Susan Small.

James Paull, security.

Note: The above couple were married the same day by Thomas T. Jones, a local Methodist elder.

October 20, 1818—William Daley and Miss Ann Pinkerton.

James Barry, security.

Note: The above couple were married October 24th by the Rev. James Lucas, pastor of the Norfolk Catholic Congregation. According to the same source, William Daley was the son of Michael Daley and Catherine Coady, and Ann Pinkerton was the daughter of William Pinkerton and Ellena Huges. Jas. Barry, M. Reardon and Henry Reardon are listed as witnesses.

October 22, 1818—William Green and Mrs. Sarah Spansby.

James Paul, security.

November 3, 1818—James King and Mrs. Catherine Crossland.

Archibald Rose, security.

Note: The above couple were married the same day by Thomas T. Jones, a local Methodist elder.

November 5, 1818—Gilbert Spilman and Miss Rebecca Ferguson.

Benjamin Hatton, security.

Note: The above couple were married November 9th by the Rev. William Compton.

November 7, 1818—Jesse Wilson and Miss Nancy Slider.

Thomas (mark) Ruffin, security.

November 9, 1818—Edward L. Young and Miss Harriot H. Colley.

William Colley, security.

Note: The above couple were married November 12th by the Rev. Samuel Low, rector of Christ P. E. Church.

November 9, 1818—William Wilson and Miss Ann Beadles.

William Clarke, security.

November 12, 1818—Humberston Skipwith and Miss Sarah S. Nivison.

George T. Kennon, security.

November 14, 1818—Charles Spratley and Miss Frances Anderson.

Joseph Spratley, security.

November 14, 1818—William C. Shields and Miss Elizabeth Finch.

George Finch, security.

November 17, 1818—Abraham Dodd and Mrs. Almy Murphey.

George Irvine, security.

November 30, 1818—Jules-Florentin-Boulleaton Brette and Miss Emily Vincent Parlato.

F. Vincent, security.

Note: The above couple were married December 1st by the Rev. James Lucas, pastor of the Norfolk Catholic Congregation. According to his report, Emily Parlato was the daughter of Vincent Parlato and Marie Perede Morjo. Vincent Parlato, Rochas Germain, J. Gorlier, James Maurice and Dr. Galvin are listed as witnesses.

December 3, 1818—Francis A. Perrier and Miss Dinah Shipwash.

Jemima Shipwash, security.

Note: The above couple were married December 5th by John D. Paxton, pastor of the Presbyterian Congregation. According to a note included with this bond, Dinah Shipwash was the daughter of Mason and Jemima Shipwash.

December 3, 1818—James K. Rains and Mrs. Polly Warren.

Philip (mark) Booz, security.

December 11, 1818—William Burgess and Mrs. Patience Cherry.

William C. Oneal, security.

December 19, 1818—William Fairchild and Miss Lydia Grimes.

James Grimes, security.

December 19, 1818—George Irvine and Miss Ann Stewart.

William Brock, security.

December 19, 1818—Henry B. Walker and Miss Elizabeth Traill.

William S. Sclater, security.

Note: The above couple were married December 20th by the Rev. William Compton.

December 22, 1818—Robert S. Ferguson and Miss Jane Alice Montgomery.

Robert Brough, security.

Note: The above couple were married December 25th by the Rev. William Campton. According to a note included with this bond, Jane Alice Montgomery was the daughter of William Montgomery, "now of the city of Richmond."

December 24, 1818—Hamilton Shields and Miss Harriet Rogers.

William C. Shields, security.

Note: The above couple were married December 25th by John D. Paxton, pastor of the Presbyterian Congregation.

December 26, 1818—John Dunston and Miss Mary Gehart.

Joseph (mark) Anatoine, security.

Note: The above couple were married December 29th by the Rev. William Compton.

1819

January 1, 1819—T. Boyd and Mrs. Isabella Parks.

Note: There is no bond for the above marriage in the files of the Corporation Court. It was copied from the returns of the Rev. John D. Paxton, pastor of the Presbyterian Congregation.

January 1, 1819—David Brown and Miss Polly Budd (or Bird).

Christopher Mason, security.

January 2, 1819—John Croel and Mrs. Ann Tipling.

Richard H. Ramsey, security.

Note: The above couple were married the same day by the Rev. William Compton.

January 7, 1819—John Bassett and Miss Sarah Davis.

William Webb, security.

January 11, 1819—Michael Delany and Miss Nancy Shea.

Michael Shea, security.

Note: The above couple were married February 12th by the Rev. James Lucas, pastor of the Norfolk Catholic Congregation.

January 13, 1819—Jeremiah Hendren and Miss Sarah Griffin.

Obed Cary, security.

Note: The above couple were married January 16th by the Rev. William Compton.

February 3, 1819—George Haigh and Miss Elizabeth Carline.

George Smith, security.

Note: The above couple were married February 4th by Thomas T. Jones, a local Methodist elder.

February 18, 1819—Francis Santejau and Mrs. Ursula Romain (widow).

Hilary Denis, security.

Note: The above couple were married February 20th by the Rev. James Lucas, pastor of the Norfolk Catholic Congregation.

February 27, 1819—Tildsley Summers and Miss Huldah Hall.

William Summers, security.

Note: According to an annotation on this bond, William Summers, the security, was the father of Tildsley Summers.

March 4, 1819—James L. Piercy and Miss Sarah Gray Hunter.

James Hunter, security.

March 5, 1819—David Gourley and Mrs. Margaret Davie.

John P. Reilly, security.

Note: The above couple were married March 7th by John D. Paxton, pastor of the Presbyterian Congregation.

March 9, 1818—Abel Waite and Mrs. Margaret Hall.

Frederick Pichot, security.

March 9, 1819—John H. Bell and Miss Eliza Frances Whitehead.

John E. Holt, security.

Note: The above couple were married March 11th by John D. Paxton, pastor of the Presbyterian Congregation. According to a note included with this bond, Eliza Frances Whitehead was the daughter of Dr. Alexander Whitehead.

March 10, 1819—James Hendrick and Mrs. Polly Shearlot.

Paul (mark) Dedo or Deoto, security.

March 12, 1819—John Hatton and Miss Hester Griffin.

Obed Cary, security.

Note: The above couple were married March 20th by Thomas T. Jones, a local Methodist elder.

March 20, 1819—William Moore and Miss Rebecca Suggs.

William Trueman, security.

March 31, 1819—Mathew Washington and Mrs. Rebecca Williams.

George Smith, security.

Note: The above couple were married April 1st by Thomas T. Jones, a local Methodist elder.

April 2, 1819—William Culney and Miss Margaret Nottingham.

James Watson, security.

Note: The above couple were married April 4th by Thomas T. Jones, a local Methodist elder.

April 2, 1819—William Starke and Mrs. Hannah Crosbie.
Alexander Tunstall, security.
April 29, 1819—William D. White and Miss Frances Buxton.
William Fairchild, security.
May 17, 1819—Francis Thorowgood and Miss Sarah Manning.
George Wrightington, security.
May 22, 1819—John Webb and Mrs. Mildred R. Shackeford.
Christopher Wynn, security.
Note: The above couple were married May 25th by the Rev. James Lucas, pastor of the Norfolk Catholic Congregation.
May 25, 1819—James McGee and Mrs. Margaret Parker.
John (mark) Dawley, security.
June 3, 1819—Michael Morris and Mrs. Mary Shelar.
John Hutchinson, security.
June 2, 1819—Thomas Tally and Miss Eliza F. Archer.
Robert Archer, security.
June 12, 1819—Frederick Hamberry and Miss Elizabeth Thorowgood.
Argyle (mark) Thorowgood, security.
June 21, 1819—Edward Chappell and Miss Nancy Weston.
Sarah Ann Darah, security.
June 24, 1819—William Waggoner and Mrs. Parmelia Batisce.
George Hethcoth, security.
Note: The above couple were married the same day by Thomas T. Jones, a local Methodist elder.
June 25, 1819—Christopher Hughes and Mrs. Beky Cleaner.
Charles (mark) Smith, security.
July 1, 1819—Anthony Lyon and Mrs. Mary Rose.
Henry Caribo, security.
July 2, 1819—Jesse McClanan and Miss Nancy Cooper.
Henry H. Newsum, security.
July 2, 1819—Joseph White and Ann Scott (widow).
Susan (mark) Scott, security.
Note: The above couple were married the same day by Thomas T. Jones, a local Methodist elder.
July 3, 1819—James Dunovin and Abia Stewart.
Thomas (mark) Dawley, security.
July 31, 1819—David Roberts and Catherine Dye.
Joseph (mark) Gorden, security.
July 14, 1819—John DeBree and Miss Mary Walke Moseley.
William K. Mackinder, security.
August 3, 1819—Laurence Hayes and Mrs. Anis Jenkins.
Joshua Hodges, security.
August 4, 1819—Patrick V. Perin and Mrs. Elizabeth Myers.
John G. Brown, security.
Note: The above couple were married August 18th by Thomas T. Jones, a local Methodist elder.
August 11, 1819—Neil Green and Mrs. Jane Davenport (widow).
John Whitlock, security.
September 1, 1819—Josef Batista and Francois (free persons of colour).
John (mark) Francis, security.
September 8, 1819—Robert White and Mrs. Sally Clapper.
Archibald Rose, security.

September 15, 1819—Malachi Jones and Miss Lydia B. Hodges.
Noah Jones, security.
September 16, 1819—Daniel Cary Barraud and Mrs. Mary L. Boush.
John A. Chandler, security.
Note: The above couple were married the same day by Thomas T. Jones, a local Methodist elder.
September 18, 1819—James H. Swindells and Miss Eliza Benfield.
William Woodbridge, security.
September 18, 1819—Thomas McKenna and Miss Mary Byrd.
Thomas Sullivan, security.
September 20, 1819—James Bordwine and Mrs. Mary Seymour.
John (mark) Burgess, security.
Note: The above couple were married the same day by Thomas T. Jones, a local Methodist elder.
September 22, 1819—Joseph Benthall and Miss Fanny Snail.
Hillary Snail, security.
October 8, 1819—John Whitlock and Miss Hannah Mars.
John (mark) Stasborough, security.
October 11, 1819—Thomas Jones and Mrs. Ellen Porter.
Note: There is no bond for the above marriage in the files of the Corporation Court. It was copied from the returns of the Rev. James Lucas, pastor of the Norfolk Catholic Congregation.
October 12, 1819—Louis Bertre and Miss Susan Moore.
William Tecleod, security.
Note: The above couple were married October 13th by Thomas T. Jones, a local Methodist elder.
October 16, 1819—William Jamesson (or Jamieson) and Miss Catherine M. Rose. Charles H. Shield, security.
October 18, 1819—Charles Branda and Miss Mary Francoise Pointier.
Honore Pointier, security.
Note: The above couple were married October 20th by the Rev. James Lucas, pastor of the Norfolk Catholic Congregation.
October 21, 1819—Henry H. Shield and Miss Catherine B. Mallory.
Charles K. Mallory, security.
October 25, 1819—Charles Wray and Miss Alice Land.
Joshua (mark) Land, security.
November 2, 1819—Benjamin Towner and Miss Diana Hubbard.
John Tilford, security.
November 11, 1819—John J. Burroughs and Miss Eliza Thomson.
John French, security.
November 16, 1819—Mathew Gilbert and Miss Elizabeth Hughes.
Richard H. Ramsey, security.
December 7, 1819—Joseph Murden and Miss Marion Allan.
Alexander Jordan, security.
December 8, 1819—Luther Ripley and Mrs. Nancy Dunton.
James (mark) Gleeson, security.
December 21, 1819—Dr. Edward H. Carmichael and Miss Sarah Lindsay Taylor. Mann P. Lomax, security.
Note: According to an annotation on this bond, Sarah Lindsay Taylor was the daughter of Francis S. Taylor.
December 22, 1819—James Bailey and Miss Nancy Clemson.
Samuel (mark) Clubb, security.
Note: The above couple were married December 25th by the Rev. Horatio E. Hall.

December 22, 1819—Richard Reed and Miss Mary Bullock.

John Reed, security.

Note: The above couple were married December 25th by Thomas T. Jones, a local Methodist elder.

December 23, 1819—William Rogers and Miss Charlotte Murphy.

William Simington, security.

December 24, 1819—Thomas Moore and Miss Mary Ann Bunting.

William Jackson, security.

December 26, 1819—John Jasper and Mrs. Lucy Cooling.

Aaron (mark) Saunders, security.

December 27, 1819—George Honsen and Miss Louisa Watlington.

James Watlington, security.

December 27, 1819—John Simmons and Miss Jacomine Snail.

John (mark) Blueford, security.

December 27, 1819—J. B. Armarno and Miss Mary Ann Bennits.

Joseph Savier, security.

December 30, 1819—Charles H. Hunt and Mrs. Rachael G. Duke.

Richard Burnham, security.

1820

January 1, 1820—Richard Capron and Miss Sarah T. Galt.

Alexander Galt, security.

January 10, 1820—Daniel Keane and Miss Nora McGrath.

Daniel McGrath, security.

Note: The above couple were married the same day in Portsmouth, Virginia, by the Rev. M. Kerney, a Roman Catholic priest.

January 20, 1820—John N. Butt and Miss Caroline C. Tucker.

Horatio E. Hall, security.

Note: According to a note included with this bond, Caroline C. Tucker was the daughter of James Tucker.

January 22, 1820—William Bird (alias Le Hunt) and Elizabeth Fulgeron.

Note: The above marriage was copied from the returns of the Rev. James Lucas, pastor of the Norfolk Catholic Congregation.

January 24, 1820—Robert B. Langley and Miss Sarah Ballard.

Lemuel Langley, security.

Note: According to a note included with this bond, Sarah Ballard was the daughter of Mary Ballard.

February 1, 1820—William M. Crane and Miss Eliza King.

Miles King, security.

February 2, 1820—William O'Driscoll and Miss Johanna Sweeney.

Jeremiah Murphy, security.

Note: The above couple were married February 3rd, by the Rev. James Lucas, pastor of the Norfolk Catholic Congregation.

February 5, 1820—Alexander Clark and Miss Eleanor Hamilton.

William Couper, security.

February 15, 1820—Thomas Farrall and Mrs. Ann Lyons.

John Timbrell, security.

Note: The above couple were married the same day by Thomas T. Jones, a local Methodist elder.

March 21, 1820—Archibald Mossman and Mrs. Sarah Lambert.

Michael Crosmuck, security.

Note: The above couple were married the same day by Thomas T. Jones, a local Methodist elder.

March 22, 1820—Jesse Thompson and Miss Ann King.
William S. Lacoste, security.
March 23, 1820—John Marchant and Miss Mary McKay.
James Mitchell, security.
April 1, 1820—John Power and Miss Mary Peed.
Edmund Moroney, security.
April 2, 1820—John Stapleton and Margaret Broaderick.
Note: The above marriage was copied from the list of the Rev. M. Kerney, pastor of the Portsmouth Catholic Congregation.
April 11, 1820—Charles Moseley and Mrs. Elizabeth Vanholt.
William J. Nottingham, security.
April 15, 1820—Nathaniel Currier and Miss Mary Ann Carter.
John (mark) Bluford, security.
April 13, 1820—Asa Price and Mrs. Susan Mathews.
Joseph (mark) Lewis, security.
April 15, 1820—William Wood and Miss Mary Nicholls.
Elkanor Ballance, security.
April 22, 1820—Francis Monihan and Ann Connor.
Note: The above marriage was copied from the list of the Rev. M. Kerney, pastor of the Portsmouth Catholic Congregation.
April 24, 1820—William Vaughn and Elizabeth Savage.
John (mark) Whiting, security.
May 10, 1820—Mann Page Lomax and Elizabeth Lindsay.
Francis S. Taylor, security.
May 23, 1820—William Lewis and Miss Kezia Evans.
William Monger, security.
May 29, 1820—William Sandham and Mrs. Sarah Ann Darling.
David Gourley, security.
Note: The above couple were married May 30th, by Thomas T. Jones, a local Methodist elder.
May 31, 1820—Michael Francis and Miss Selah Willey.
John (mark) Shibley, security.
Note: The above couple were married the same day by Thomas T. Jones, a local Methodist elder.
June 8, 1820—John Rose and Miss Ann Marchant.
John Marchant, security.
Note: According to a note included with this bond, Ann Marchant was the daughter of A. Marchant and sister of John Marchant, the security.
June 16, 1820—Kader Morris and Miss Maria R. Newstep.
John Hubberd, security.
Note: The above couple were married June 29th, by Thomas T. Jones, a local Methodist elder.
June 23, 1820—William Hamby and Miss Nancy Hyslop.
Samuel R. Collins, security.
June 1, 1820—Argyle Thorogood and Miss Elkana Fisher.
Frederick Hamberry, security.
June 29, 1820—Joseph Barclay and Margaret Taulson.
Note: The above marriage was copied from the list of the Rev. M. Kerney, pastor of the Portsmouth Catholic Congregation. The marriage took place in Gosport, a suburb of Portsmouth, Va.
July 1, 1820—Ebenezer Halsom and Miss Sally Morris.
Lovemon Dudley, security.
July 1, 1820—William Gray and Miss Sarah Swoobe.
William Simington, security.

July 11, 1820—James Marno and Mrs. Frances M. Wilson.
Michael S. Wilson, security.
July 14, 1820—John Hatcher and Miss Mary Fear.
James Harvey, security.
July 15, 1820—George Hines and Mrs. Susan Cutrel.
John (mark) Burgess, security.
April 16, 1820—John Moseley and Charlotte Boss (free persons of colour).
William T. Anderson, security.
Note: The above couple were married June 20th by Thomas T. Jones, a local Methodist elder.
July 17, 1820—Spencer Drummond and Hannah A. Bailey.
Roger Quarles, security.
Note: The above couple were married July 18th by Thomas T. Jones, a local Methodist elder.
July 18, 1820—Henry Reardon and Miss Louisa A. Taney.
Samuel Lindsay, security.
July 20, 1820—John Reed and Mrs. Polly Scarlett.
James Boyle, security.
July 22, 1820—Bernard Tapley and Mrs. Ann Talley.
John L. Billups, security.
July 27, 1820—Michael Keane and Miss Mary Dodd.
John Dodd, security.
Note: The above couple were married July 29th by the Rev. James Lucas, pastor of the Norfolk Catholic Congregation.
August 15, 1820—John Steward and Mrs. Edward Smith.
James Robinson, security.
August 23, 1820—William Gardner and Grace Armistead (free Persons of colour).
Thomas (mark) Ruffin, security.
Note: The above couple were married August 24th by Thomas T. Jones, a local Methodist elder.
August 26, 1820—John G. Hammer and Mrs. Susanna Owens.
David (mark) Roberts, security.
September 16, 1820—John Walker and Mrs. Elizabeth McLaine.
John Rogers, security.
September 22, 1820—John Nichols and Mrs. Jane Skidmore.
James Robinson, security.
September 23, 1820—John Rea and Mrs. Frances Irons.
Patrick Donney, security.
September 27, 1820—Ellis Shackleford and Miss Isabella Deal.
John E. Beale, security.
October 4, 1820—Edward Archer and Miss Sarah J. Williamson.
Robert Archer, security.
Note: According to an annotation on this bond, Sarah J. Williamson was the ward of Robert Archer, the security.
October 12, 1820—Charles W. Skinner and Miss Clarissa Starke Whitehead.
William H. Watson, security.
October 13, 1820—Richard L. Robertson and Miss Olivia Knott.
Nathan Colgate Whitehead, security.
October 14, 1820—Patrick Bartlet and Miss Martha Oatest.
Henry Oatest, security.
Note: According to an annotation on this bond, Martha Oatest was the daughter of Henry Oatest, the security.

October 19, 1820—John Stroud and Miss Susan Fisher.

Wilson (mark) Walker, security.

October 26, 1820—David Duncan and Miss Martha Shirley.

John D. Christian, security.

Note: According to a note included with this bond, Martha Shirley was the daughter of Ann D. Shirley.

October 27, 1820—John Allgreen and Miss Eliza Harding.

Samuel Bobbitt, security.

October 28, 1820—John Lamote and Mrs. Mariah McDaniel.

Archibald Rose, security.

November 2, 1820—Cornelius K. Stribling and Miss Helen Maria Payne.

Moses B. Chase, security.

Note: According to a note included with this bond, Helen Maria Chase was the daughter of Mary Payne.

November 4, 1820—Edmund Brooke and Miss Ann H. Gammon.

Joel (mark) Gammon, security.

Note: According to an annotation on this bond, Ann H. Gammon was the daughter of Joel Gammon, the security.

November 6, 1820—Thomas Handy and Miss Sarah Kirby.

George W. Anderson, security.

Note: The above couple were married the same day by Thomas T. Jones, a local Methodist elder.

November 7, 1820—Lancaster Brown and Miss Anna Owens.

George Suggs, security.

November 10, 1820—Philip Farrell and Miss Mary Belmina or (Belmana).

Isaac Sherwood, security.

November 11, 1820—John Lindsay and Mrs. Elizabeth Haynes.

Note: The above marriage was copied from the list of the Rev. Charles Moseley.

November 14, 1820—James S. Garrison and Miss Eliza Glenn.

Mathew Glenn, security.

November 16, 1820—Edward Fowler Young and Mrs. Margaret Hastie.

James Maurice, Jr., security.

November 18, 1820—Thomas Hall and Miss Patsey Hamberry.

Thomas (mark) Leister, security.

November 20, 1820—Thomas Ruffin and Rebecca Francis (free persons of colour). Stephen (mark) Abel, security.

November 22, 1820—John S. Widgeon and Miss Ann E. Brushwood.

John Widgen, security.

November 23, 1820—Kennon Whiting and Miss Ann W. Mallory.

Thomas W. Lowry, security.

Note: According to a note on this bond, Ann W. Mallory was the daughter of Johnson Mallory.

November 29, 1820—George Hickith and Miss Jane Halsey.

John Burgess, security.

December 9, 1820—Elzy Burroughs and Mrs. Ann Murphey.

John Fartherny, security.

December 11, 1820—Thomas B. Jennings and Miss Mary P. Houghton.

Thomas Jennings, security.

December 11, 1820—Paul Jules Brette and Miss Marie Virginia Santejau.

Louis Santejau, security.

Note: The above couple were married December 14th by the Rev. James Lucas, pastor of the Norfolk Catholic Congregation.

December 14, 1820—Benjamin Robert and Miss Fanny May.

Louis Chazeux, srecurity.

Note: The above couple were married December 24th by Thomas T. Jones, a local Methodist elder.

December 18, 1820—Joseph Ribble and Miss Catherine Collins.

Charles Spratley, security.

December 21, 1820—John R. Rogers and Miss Mary Ann Ballard.

Robert B. Langley, security.

Note: According to a note included with this bond Mary Ann Ballard was the daughter of Mary Ballard.

December 21, 1820—Nathaniel Wilburn and Miss Sarah Leslie.

John Leslie, security.

November 23, 1820—Charles A. Grice and Eliza T. Davis (or Darrs).

Note: The above marriage was copied from the list of the Rev. Enoch Lowe, rector of Christ P. E. Church.

December 23, 1820—William Maurice and Miss Ann A. Jennings.

Thomas Jennings, Jr., security.

Note: According to an annotation on this bond, Ann A. Jennings was the sister of Thomas Jennings, Jr., the security.

December 24, 1820—William N. Ivey and Margaret Willoughby.

Note: The above marriage was copied from the list of the Rev. Enoch Lowe, rector of Christ P. E. Church.

December 26, 1820—Richard Ward and Miss Elizabeth Sterling.

James Swan, security.

December 28, 1820—John Long and Miss Mary Burchel.

Cornelius Mathews, security.

Note: The above couple were married the same day by the Rev. James Lucas, pastor of the Norfolk Catholic Congregation. According to an annotation on this bond, Mary Burchel was the ward of Cornelius Mathews, the security.

December 30, 1820—Yves Guyot and Miss Mary McNair Ritchie.

Nathaniel Ritchie, security.

Note: According to an annotation on this bond, Mary McNair Ritchie was the daughter of Nathaniel Ritchie, the security.

December 30, 1820—James Lees and Miss Sarah Lownder.

James Wattington, security.

Note: According to an annotation on this bond, Sarah Lownder was the ward of James Wattington, the security.

1821

January 2, 1821—Joseph Riley and Miss Eliza Ann Carson.

Charles Johnson, security.

January 6, 1821—Affrica Fuller and Nancy Davis (persons of colour).

Robert (mark) Armistead, security.

Note: The above couple were married the same day by Thomas T. Jones, a local Methodist elder.

January 20, 1821—Jeremiah S. Brown and Mrs. Mary Hargrove.

Joseph Winslow, security.

January 25, 1821—James Ennis and Mrs. Helen B. Mullan.

David Roberts, security.

February 17, 1821—Mann P. Hughes and Miss Elizabeth Archer.

Alexander Cunningham, security.

February 21, 1821—Charles Connell and Mrs. Diana Haywood.

John Connel, security.

March 10, 1821—Richard Coffman and Grace Harrison (free persons of colour).

Thomas (mark) Ruffin, security.

March 27, 1821—Moses H. Sargent and Maria Harriet Pierce.

William W. Pierce, security.

Note: According to an annotation on this bond, Maria Harriet Pierce was the daughter of William W. Pierce, the security.

March 30, 1821—William Morrisett and Mrs. Elizabeth Clarke.

George Stainback, security.

April 6, 1821—Thomas Mann Randolph and Miss Susan E. Brown.

Samuel Moseley, Jr., security.

Note: The above couple were married April 12th by the Rev. Enoch M. Lowe, rector of Christ P. E. Church. His report gives the name of the bride as Mary E. Brown. According to an annotation on this bond, Susan E. Brown was the ward of Philemon Gatewood.

April 12, 1821—Dickie Galt and Miss Mary Ann Fisk.

John R. Harwood, security.

April 18, 1821—John Fleming and Miss Sarah White.

James Watlington, security.

Note: According to an annotation on this bond, Sarah White was the ward of James Watlington, the security.

April 28, 1821—John Francois Meste and Miss Elizabeth Miller.

Simon (mark) Florie, security.

May 4, 1821—Norman L. Seaver and Miss Nancy M. Williams.

William C. Adams, security.

May 11, 1821—John M. Watts and Miss Ann White.

Thomas C. White, security.

Note: The above couple were married May 11th by Thomas T. Jones, a local Methodist elder.

May 28, 1821—Willis Banks and Mary Ann Kelly (persons of colour).

Simeon (mark) Smith, security.

June 7, 1821—Beverly West and Rebecca Atkinson (persons of colour).

Henry (mark) Gilmore, security.

June 9, 1821—Lewis Hoff and Miss Eliza M. Rapley.

Upton S. Fraser, security.

Note: The above couple were married June 10th by the Rev. Enoch Lowe, rector of Christ P. E. Church.

June 12, 1821—Abraham Brown and Miss Clarissa Cloit.

John W. Melder, security.

June 14, 1821—Augustine Drummond and Mary B. Travis.

Lewis Pagaud, security.

Note: According to an annotation on this bond, Mary B. Travis was the daughter of James Travis.

June 14, 1821—William Coleman and Miss Elizabeth Boss.

George (mark) Anderson, security.

Note: According to a note included with this bond, Elizabeth Boss was a native of the town of Westminster, Pennsylvania, and was between 35 and 40 years of age.

June 18, 1821—Henry Cummings and Miss Nancy Marle.

John (mark) Stavro, security.

June 30, 1821—Wilson Walker and Mrs. Ann Draghton.

William Nicholson, security.

July 2, 1821—Cornelius O'Keeffe and Miss Catherine Norcott.

Michael Keane, security.

July 7, 1821—William M. Atkinson and Miss Rebecca B. Marsden.
Philip E. Tabb, security.
July 19, 1821—John H. Cocke and Mrs. Louisa Holmes.
Robert B. Taylor, security.
Note: The above couple were married the same day by John H. Rice.
July 28, 1821—Willis Holt and Miss Rebecca Nicholson.
William Nicholson, security.
July 28, 1821—Francis Summers and Mrs. Nancy Smelly.
Daniel (mark) Culpepper, security.
August 6, 1821—Robert Davis and Miss Rebecca Patterson.
Garret Barry, security.
August 8, 1821—George Jackson and Miss Emmy Carroway.
David Ethridge, security.
August 8, 1821—David Cook and Alice Saunders.
John Lawton, security.
September 18, 1821—Elisha C. White and Miss Sarah W. Anderson.
William T. Anderson, security.
September 18, 1821—John Ferris and Ellen Gray.
James Alexander, security.
September 26, 1821—Samuel Hard and Miss Mary Hill.
John Gleason, security.
November 6, 1821—America Walker and Mrs. Jennette St. Pierre.
Thomas (mark) Ruffin, security.
November 17, 1821—William Gordon and Mrs. Ann Mairing.
John H. Dailey, security.
November 26, 1821—William S. Lacoste and Miss Ann Belson Moore.
John J. Campbell, security.
November 26, 1821—Patrick Rochford and Miss Catherine Tynon.
John O'Driscoll, security.
December 22, 1821—John Thomas and Miss Julian Dean.
Henry H. Newsum, security.
December 26, 1821—Lemuel W. Williams and Miss Ellen Walker.
John Dunston, security.

1822

January 3, 1822—Daniel Lyon and Miss Eliza Gilbert.
James Gilbert, security.
January 8, 1822—Patrick Cray and Miss Elizabeth Hargean.
Michael Keane, security.
January 9, 1822—William Hunter and Miss Sarah Sandyford.
Robert Montgomery, security.
January 11, 1822—Arthur Small and Miss Amy White.
Thomas C. White, security.
Note: The above couple were married the same day by Thomas T. Jones, a local
Methodist elder.
January 11, 1822—J. C. Allen and Miss Susan Eaton.
John H. Foster, security.
Note: According to an annotation on this bond, Susan Eaton was the ward of
Hannah M. Spence.
January 16, 1822—Magnus Johnson and Mrs. Poebe Davis.
Joses Bucknam, security.

January 17, 1822—Robert M. Rose and Miss Mary Talbot.
Giles B. Cooke, security.
Note: The above couple were married the same day by the Rev. Enoch Lowe, rector of Christ P. E. Church.
January 19, 1822—Samuel Thorp and Mrs. Elizabeth Madden (widow).
James Casteen, security.
January 31, 1822—(Colonel) Josiah Riddick and Miss Mary Louisa Riddick.
Jonathan Cowdery, security.
Note: The above couple were married the same day by the Rev. Enoch Lowe, rector of Christ P. E. Church.
February 1, 1822—William Clammitt and Miss Frances Keeling.
William S. Keeling, security.
February 1, 1822—James Ennis and Mrs. Catherine Archer (widow).
Charles Donaldson, security.
February 4, 1822—Thomas McKeel and Miss Minty Summers.
William Hunter, security.
Note: The above couple were married the same day by Thomas T. Jones, a local Methodist elder.
February 7, 1822—William Morris and Mrs. Hannah Goman (widow).
Charles Donaldson, security.
Note: The above couple were married February 12th.
February 12, 1822—John F. Bower and Miss Mary P. Brown.
Robert Farmer, security.
Note: According to a note included with this bond, Mary P. Brown was the ward of Philemon Gatewood. The above couple were married Feb. 14th by the Rev. Enoch Lowe, rector of Christ P. E. Church.
February 14, 1822—Mathew Dodd and Miss Honoria Hart.
John Dodd, security.
February 18, 1822—George Hickith and Miss Maria Stack.
Henry McDowell, security.
Note: According to an annotation on this bond, Maria Stack was the ward of Henry McDowell, the security.
February 25, 1822—George Hickith and Miss Charlotte Hill.
Thomas C. Dickson, security.
March 2, 1822—Isaac Vallance and Margaret Keeling.
William S. Keeling, security.
Note: The above couple were married the same day by the Rev. Enoch Lowe, rector of Christ P. E. Church.
March 7, 1822—William Hamilton Brown and Elizabeth Demortier.
James (mark) Wiles, security.
March 12, 1822—Ishmael Moody and Mrs. Eliza Ann Eager.
Joseph T. Allyn, security.
Note: The above couple were married March 14th by Thomas T. Jones, a local Methodist elder.
March 15, 1822—F. P. Roney and Miss Annet M. Waring.
Edwin Lee, security.
March 23, 1822—Rowland Jones and Mrs. Catherine Roberts (widow).
Richard Jenkins, security.
Note: The above couple were married the same day by Thomas T. Jones, a local Methodist elder.
March 26, 1822—Richard Nottingham and Alley Benson.
Joseph (mark) Taylor, security.
April 1, 1822—Francis Calleny and Miss Louisa Miller.
Bernard (mark) Tracey, security.

April 4, 1822—Henry Ashburn and Miss Harriet S. Anderson.

Hamilton Shields, security.

Note: The above couple were married the same day by the Rev. Enoch Lowe, rector of Christ P. E. Church.

April 9, 1822—David M. Woodson and Harriet E. Martin.

Angus Martin, security.

Note: According to an annotation on this bond, Harriet E. Martin was the daughter of Angus Martin, the security.

April 11, 1822—Robert H. Tatem and Miss Ann R. Gheselin.

Lewis R. Pollard, security.

April 18, 1822—James Smiley and Margaret Ferguson.

Angus Martin, security.

April 24, 1822—Thomas H. Williams and Miss Jane Jennings.

Thomas Jennings, security.

May 4, 1822—James Cogan and Mrs. Hannah Locke (widow).

David Cull, security.

May 9, 1822—William S. Walker and Elizabeth Harmen.

Robert Brough, security.

Note: The above couple were married the same day by the Rev. Francis Ward.

May 13, 1822—William B. Pebworth and Ann Warren.

John E. Beale, security.

Note: The above couple were married May 15th by Thomas T. Jones, a local Methodist elder.

May 15, 1822—Nicholas Wonycott and Elizabeth Walker.

William Balsom, security.

Note: The above couple were married May 16th by the Rev. Francis A. Ward.

May 20, 1822—Increase Chase and Miss Eliza Ann McGregor.

William Poyner, security.

Note: The above couple were married the same day by Thomas T. Jones, a local Methodist elder.

May 30, 1824—Richard Gatewood and Miss Eliza T. B. Cunningham.

William Sharp, security.

Note: The above couple were married the same day by the Rev. Enoch Lowe, rector of Christ P. E. Church.

June 6, 1822—John House and Miss Sarah Dunn.

Anthony Dunn, security.

Note: The above couple were married the same day by the Rev. Francis Ward.

June 28, 1822—John Nelson, Jr., and Mrs. Margaret Maria Low.

Moses B. Chase, security.

Note: The above couple were married June 30th by the Rev. Enoch Lowe, rector of Christ P. E. Church.

July 8, 1822—Samuel Farthery and Miss Susan Maria Mason.

Christopher Mason, security.

July 22, 1822—Leno Curtis and Miss Fanny North.

William (mark) Taylor, security.

Note: The above couple were married the same day by Thomas T. Jones, a local Methodist elder.

August 14, 1822—Thomas Bennett and Mrs. Ann Smelt.

Edward Delaney, security.

August 17, 1822—Abel Lewelling and Miss Mary Henley.

Benjamin Hatton, security.

August 17, 1822—Edward Daly and Mrs. Rebecca Holt.

William Nicholson, security.

August 27, 1822—William Fields and Miss Sarah Boyd.
John Patterson, security.
Note: The above couple were married the same day by Thomas T. Jones, a local Methodist elder.
August 29, 1822—George Sealey and Amy Eyer.
John (mark) Dupuy, security.
September 9, 1822—Thomas Griffin and Miss Nancy Patterson.
John Patterson, security.
September 11, 1822—Alexander P. Darragh and Eliza T. Armistead.
George Newton, security.
September 20, 1822—John R. Welker and Susan Bishop.
Frederick Myer, security.
September 23, 1822—Fowler Smith and Miss Eliza Fisher.
William Coffin, security.
September 23, 1822—Theodore Benson and Jane Smiley.
Francis Smiley, security.
October 11, 1822—John Piemont and Miss Margaret Cooper.
Samuel K. Dameron, security.
Note: According to a note included with this bond, Margaret Cooper was the daughter of Mary Ann Cooper.
October 24, 1822—John Henry and Mrs. Ruth Sandy.
James (mark) Miller, security.
Note: The above couple were married by the Rev .Francis A. Ward.
October 31, 1822—Jonathan F. Ross and Miss Matilda Glenn.
Mathew Glenn, security.
October 31, 1822—Elihu Parsons and Miss Mary Ann Cogheler.
William Rogers, security.
November 9, 1822—Robert Stantial and Sarah Handy (widow).
Francis (mark) Gantz, security.
November 21, 1822—William Noke and Catherine McMannus.
Ephraim Mills, security.
December 4, 1822—Samuel Ray and Sarah Shannon.
Thomas G. Johnson, security.
December 19, 1822—George Warderman and Sally Roberts.
Lemuel Roberts, security.
Note: The above couple were married December 22nd by the Rev. Francis A. Ward.
December 23, 1822—Michael Nocette and Salah Francis.
Ambrose Hamilton, security.
December 26, 1822—Arthur C. Denby and Miss Sarah Latham.
Frederick Hennicke, security.
Note: The above couple were married the same day by the Rev. Francis A. Ward.
December 31, 1822—William Outten and Ellen Kenan.
Samuel Trimble, security.

1823

January 3, 1823—William Hillen and Miss Elizabeth Godfrey.
Joshua Fentress, security.
Note: The above couple were married January 9th by Thomas T. Jones, a local Methodist elder.
January 10, 1823—David Briquet and Mrs. Eliza Godfrey.
Andrew Scott, security.

January 20, 1823—Francis A. Ward and Miss Mary Watkins.
Tildsley Graham, security.
Note: The above couple were married the same day by the Rev. John French, a local Methodist (Protestant) minister. According to an annotation on this bond, Mary Watkins was the ward of Tildsley Graham, the security.

January 25, 1823—Thomas K. Mayer and Miss Ann Hopkins.
James Mitchell, security.
Note: According to an annotation on this bond, Ann Hopkins was the ward of James Mitchell, the security.

January 31, 1823—Robert Mitchell and Agnes Wilson.
Robert Souter, security.

February 1, 1823—(Lieut.) William Henry Gardner and Miss Frances Jordan Marchant.
James G. Boughan, security.

February 17, 1823—John T. Swords and Jane Dickson.
James (mark) Simpson, security.

February 24, 1823—Howard Poole and Miss Harriot C. Hollier.
John Williams, security.
Note: The above couple were married by the Rev. John H. Wingfield. No date is given.

March 1, 1823—Peter O'Lemercier and Sophia Golding.
George Scott, security.

March 1, 1823—Erasmus Ballance and Miss Ann Nixon.
Jesse Mercer, security.
Note: According to an annotation on this bond, Ann Nixon was the ward of Jesse Mercer, the security.

March 3, 1823—George Davison and Miss Sarah Grimes.
William Hale, security.

March 12, 1823—Andrew Clark and Judiah South.
James A. Smith, security.

March 17, 1823—Hyacinthe Palais and Mrs. Rose Billingre.
J. M. Duperu, security.
Note: The above couple were married by the Rev. John H. Wingfield. No date is given.

April 2, 1823—Crocker Harden and Miss Frances Dameron.
James Dameron, security.
Note: According to an annotation on this bond, Frances Dameron was the ward of James Dameron, the security.

April 3, 1823—Robert Montgomery and Mrs. Elizabeth Wright.
William Hunter, security.

April 5, 1823—Benjamin Grimke (or Grimkey) and Miss Mary Augusta Barron.
James Maurice, Jr., security.
Note: According to a note included with this bond, Mary Augusta Barron was the ward of Jane E. Barron.

April 8, 1823—Isaac A. Coles and Miss Louisa G. Nivison.
Humberston Skipwith, security.
Note: The above couple were married by the Rev. John H. Wingfield. No date is given.

April 10, 1823—Shelburn Mahone and Mary Whitehurst.
William (mark) Whitehurst, security.
Note: The above couple were married April 12th by Thomas T. Jones, a local Methodist elder.

May 12, 1823—William B. Wrenn and Eliza N. Marchant.
John Marchant, security.

May 16, 1823—Dempsey Woodward and Mrs. Sally Gray.

Robert (mark) Stantial, security.

Note: The above couple were married May 24th by Thomas T. Jones, a local Methodist elder.

May 20, 1823—Henry Duesberry and Miss Catherine Swank.

Samuel Dameron, security.

Note: The above couple were married the same day by John French, a local Methodist (Protestant) minister. According to a note included with this bond, Catherine Swank was the daughter of John Swank.

May 31, 1823—John Sharpless and Mrs. Ann Campbell.

John Henry, security.

Note: The above couple were married the same day by the Rev. John French, a local Methodist (Protestant) minister.

June 5, 1823—George L. Lawton and Maria Slaghill.

John Tilford, security.

June 26, 1823—Josiah Thomas and Mrs. Jane Winslow (widow).

Robert A. Carter, security.

Note: The above couple were married by the Rev. Caleb Leach, a local Methodist (Episcopal) minister.

July 12, 1823—Richard Styles and Elizabeth Banks.

Robert (mark) Barrot, security.

July 14, 1823—D'Arcy Paul and Elizabeth S. Cooke.

Giles B. Cooke, security.

Note: The above couple were married the same day by the Rev. John French, a local Methodist (Protestant) minister.

July 16, 1823—George Rowland and Miss Sarah S. Neilson.

William Rowland, security.

Note: The above couple were married the same day by the Rev. William Wicks, rector of Christ P. E. Church.

August 8, 1823—Sherman Mitchell and Mrs. Ann Pierce (widow).

Benjamin Thomas, security.

Note: The above couple were married August 15th, by Thomas T. Jones, a local Methodist elder.

August 26, 1823—Thomas Boyd and Ann Hayden.

George Savage, security.

Note: The above couple were married August 27th by the Rev. John French, a local Methodist (Protestant) minister.

September 1, 1823—Henry H. Redman and Miss Susan F. Slack.

Joseph Clerico, security.

September 25, 1823—William H. Macfarland and Ann T. Roberts.

Archibald Taylor, security.

Note: The above couple were married the same day by the Rev. William Wicks, rector of Christ P. E. Church. According to a note included with this bond, Ann T. Roberts was the ward of John Taylor.

October 2, 1823—Luke Reed and Nancy Johnson (free persons of colour). James (mark) Johnson, security.

October 9, 1823—Elijah Goodridge and Lydia Macgregor.

Alexander Anderson, security.

October 13, 1823—William Robson and Miss Elizabeth Wood.

William Cook, security.

October 18, 1823—James Spalding and Miss Susan Hutchinson.

Thomas Williams, security.

October 20, 1823—Edward C. Mallory and Mrs. Eliza Latimer.

Note: The above couple were married October 21st by the Rev. William Wicks, rector of Christ P. E. Church.

October 25, 1823—Pablo Charcon and Miss Georgiana Hand Stuart Gilfillan.

J. C. de Figaniere e Morao, security.

November 20, 1823—James Scott and Miss Ann Ferguson.

William Rogers, security.

November 27, 1823—Samuel Butt and Miss Evelina Brown.

Samuel W. Brown, security.

Note: The above couple were married the same day by the Rev. John French, a local Methodist (Protestant) minister.

November 29, 1823—William Garrow and Miss Dorothy Suggs.

George Suggs, security.

December 6, 1823—William Miller and Miss Margaret Powell.

William Walker, security.

Note: The above couple were married the same day by Thomas T. Jones, a local Methodist elder.

December 6, 1823—John Adams and Actous Crocker.

Thomas (mark) Hall, security.

Note: The above couple were married the same day by the Rev. John French, a local Methodist (Protestant) minister.

December 13, 1823—William Webb and Mary Ann Golden.

George Scott, security.

December 16, 1823—John W. Fiveash and Mary Ann Frances Moore.

Gersham Moore, security.

Note: According to an annotation on this bond, Ann Frances Moore was the daughter of Gersham Moore, the security.

December 19, 1823—Darius Woodland and Miss Eliza Stone.

Thomas Glenn, security.

Note: The above couple were married December 19th by the Rev. William Wicks, rector of Christ P. E. Church. According to a note included with this bond, Eliza Stone was the daughter of Elizabeth Stone.

December 23, 1823—James Fertson and Betsey Wilson.

Thomas (mark) Smith, security.
Cornelius Reardon, security.

December 31, 1823—Ballance Creekmure and Miss Paulina White.

Joel Callis, security.

1824

January 3, 1824—William Beckley and Miss Maria Bridgeford.

James Dameron, security.

Note: The above couple were married by the Rev. Caleb Leach.

January 10, 1824—William Hoops and Miss Ann Morris (or Maurice).

James Murphy, security.

Note: The above couple were married by the Rev. John French, pastor of the local Methodist Protestant congregation. No date is given.

January 15, 1824—Philip Edward Tabb and Emmeline M. Allmand.

Thomas Williamson, security.

Note: The above couple were married the same day by the Rev. William Wicks, rector of Christ P. E. Church. Emmeline Allmand was the daughter of Harrison Allmand.

January 15, 1824—George Johnson and Hannah Kemp.

Thomas (mark) Ruffin, security.

Note: According to a note included with this bond, Hannah Kemp was the daughter of Hannah Bacon, a free person of colour.

96

January 16, 1824—Michael Griffin and Mrs. Sarah Simmington.
George Clark, security.
January 20, 1824—Walter F. Jones and Miss Mary Eliza Taylor.
Charles O. Handy, security.
Note: Eliza Taylor was the daughter of Richard Taylor. The above couple were married the same day by the Rev. William Wicks, rector of Christ P. E. Church.
January 26, 1824—Edward Ingram and Miss Sarah Foster.
Joseph (mark) Stripes, security.
January 28, 1824—William Johnson and Miss Mary D. Seymour.
William Seymour, security.
Note: The above couple were married the same day by the Rev. William Wicks, rector of Christ P. E. Church.
February 7, 1824—Thomas Carbry and Mrs. Jane Perry.
Elkanor Ballance, security.
February 16, 1824—John P. Vincent and Miss Ann Hughes.
James Maurice, Jr., security.
Note: According to a note included with this bond, Ann Hughes was the daughter of Elias Hughes.
February 19, 1824—Conway Whittle and Chloe Tyler.
Note: There is no bond for the above marriage in the files of the Corporation Court. It was copied from the returns of the Rev. William Wicks, rector of Christ P. E. Church.
February 26, 1824—Thomas Brushwood and Sarah Stephenson.
Edmund Spence, security.
Note: The above couple were married the same day by the Rev. John French, pastor of the local Methodist Protestant Church. According to an annotation on this bond, Sarah Stephenson was the ward of Edmund Spence, the security.
February 28, 1824—William Duncan and Mrs. Nancy Dowens (widow).
Archibald Crow, security.
March 5, 1824—Robert Diggs and Miss Kesiah Spann.
Abel Lewelling, security.
Note: The above couple were married by the Rev. Caleb Leach. According to an annotation on this bond, Kesian Spann was the ward of Abel Lewelling, the security.
March 6, 1824—Josiah Grimes and Eliza Housaur.
George Lesslie, security.
March 10, 1824—Joseph Cassin and Miss Frances B. Moseley.
Samuel Moseley, security.
Note: The above couple were married March 11th by the Rev. William Wicks, rector of Christ P. E. Church.
March 18, 1824—John Reed and Mrs. Mary Myers (widow).
Wiliam Hatfield, security.
March 27, 1824—John Owens and Mrs. Ann Hayden (widow).
Joseph K. Boyd, security.
Note: The above couple were married by the Rev. John French, a local Methodist Protestant minister.
April 1, 1824—John Flowers and Mrs. Charlotte Hickkith (widow).
Henry Etheridge, security.
April 7, 1824—David Duncan and Miss Amanda Peimont.
Robert C. Jennings, security.
Note: The above couple were married April 8th by the Rev. John French, a local Methodist Protestant minister. According to an annotation on this bond, Amanda Piedmont was the ward of Robert C. Jennings, the security.
April 22, 1824—Alexander P. Smith and Mrs. Ann S. Etheridge (widow).
Nathaniel Berry, security.

April 24, 1824—Joseph C. Maigne and Mrs. Abby Jordan (widow).
Thomas Constable, security.
April 26, 1824—George Bullock and Mary Ann Martin.
John (mark) Waterman, security.
April 29, 1824—Thomas Ruffin and Miss Margaret Gangs (free blacks).
John M. Burt, security.
May 6, 1824—John C. Jones and Miss Eliza S. Parker.
Copeland Parker, security.
Note: According to a note included with this bond, Eliza S. Parker was the daughter of Copeland Parker, the security.
May 18, 1824—Nathaniel Berry and Miss Mary Ann D. Rogers.
William Rogers, security.
May 23, 1824—William Burgen and Mrs. Sophia Hall (widow).
William Hatfield, security.
May 25, 1824—Thomas C. Williams and Mrs. Sarah Grymes (widow).
William (mark) Burgen, security.
June 2, 1824—Joel Peed and Miss Sarah Shipp.
John Shipp, security.
June 2, 1824—John Smith and Miss Sareina Thompson.
Thomas (mark) Lynch, security.
June 8, 1822—Eugene de Montelant and Celestina Lamasurier Boutin.
Note: The above marriage was copied from the list of the Rev. Enoch Lowe, rector of Christ P. E. Church.
June 14, 1824—Chauncey Clarke and Mrs. Louisa Howser.
Elias Wadlington, security.
June 30, 1824—Pinckney George and Martha C. Drew.
William D. Roberts, security.
Note: According to an annotation on this bond, Martha C. Drew was the ward of William D. Roberts, the security.
July 6, 1824—Abel Lewelling and Mrs. Sarah Wakefield (widow).
Charles L. Beale, security.
july 20, 1824—Richard Delafield and Miss Helen Summers.
Charles Gratiot, security.
July 28, 1824—Willoughby Butt and Miss Mary C. Webb.
Samuel Hodges, security.
Note: According to an annotation on this bond, Mary C. Butt was the ward of Samuel Hodges, the security.
August 3, 1824—John Campbell and Mrs. Sophia Stanwood (widow).
Giles Edwards, security.
August 11, 1824—Henry Robinson and Miss Frances M. Boush.
Aleander Tunstall, security.
Note: The above couple were married by the Rev. John H. Wingfield, rector of Trinity P. E. Church, Portsmouth, Va.
August 16, 1824—John Burchill and Mrs. Jane McAvoy (widow).
William Morris, security.
August 18, 1824—John P. Tuttle and Miss Margaretta Barron.
James D. Thorburn, security.
Note: The above couple were married by the Rev. John H. Wingfield, rector of Trinity P. E. Church, Portsmouth, Va.
August 21, 1824—David Carson and Mrs. Ann Nebeker (widow).
John Carson, security.
Note: The above couple were married by the Rev. John French, pastor of the local Methodist (Protestant) congregation.

August 25, 1824—Richard McCoy and Miss Ann Lewelling.
George Edmonds, security.
August 26, 1824—Joseph A. Freeman and Miss Margaret Jordan.
Thomas Morris, security.
August 27, 1824—Robert Reeves and Mrs. Saka Gleason (widow).
John Tilford, security.
September 1, 1824—David Glasgo Farragut and Miss Susan Caroline
Marchant. William H. Gardner, security.
Note: The above couple were married by the Rev. John H. Wingfield, rector of
Trinity P. E. Church, Portsmouth, Va.
September 4, 1824—John Ridley and Miss Mary Ann Gardner.
Joel Callis, security.
Note: The above couple were married by the Rev. Noah Davis, pastor of the
Cumberland Street Baptist Church.
September 8, 1824—Patrick Henrytta (or Hanraty and Mrs. Frances
Hutchins. Richard Hartnett, security.
October 12, 1824—James Ayres and Maria Blades.
Campbell (mark) Blades, security.
Note: Maria Blades was the daughter of Campbell Blades, the security.
October 26, 1824—Mark L. Chevers and Miss Mary D. Singleton.
John Singleton, security.
Note: The above couple were married by the Rev. John H. Wingfield, rector of
Trinity P. E. Church, Portsmouth, Va.
November 6, 1824—Henry Shettle and Mrs. Louisa Dosson.
William Denby, security.
November 9, 1824—Michael Darcy and Miss Elizabeth Gray.
John Ferris, security.
Note: The above couple were married November 16th by Thomas T. Jones, a
local Methodist elder.
November 10, 1824—Benjamin Emmerson and Miss Sarah Fauquier.
William M. Fauquier, security.
November 17, 1824—Robert S. Smith and Miss Elizabeth Bastian.
Robert Chapman, security.
Note: The above couple were married by the Rev. John H. Wingfield, rector of
Trinity P. E. Church, Portsmouth, Va.
November 18, 1824—Lemuel W. Williams and Miss Eliza Buntin.
Edward Delany, security.
Note: Eliza Buntin was the ward of Edward Delany, the security.
November 20, 1824—Philip Ashley and Miss Margaret Butt.
Francis (mark) Darling, security.
November 20, 1824—John Shenton and Miss Sarah Rouse.
George Bragg, security.
November 22, 1824—Thomas Samuel Barrott and Miss Catherine C.
Jones. John Stewart, security.
Note: The above couple were married the same day by Thomas T. Jones, a local
Methodist elder.
December 4, 1824—John Hester and Martha Biddle.
George Doyle, security.
Note: The above couple were married the same day by Thomas T. Jones, a local
Methodist elder.
December 4, 1824—Richard Anderson and Miss Mary Newton (free
blacks). Isaac Fuller, security.
Note: The above couple were married the same day by Thomas T. Jones, a local
Methodist elder.

99

December 10, 1824—William Millison and Miss Elizabeth Pool.

John (mark) Burgess, security.

Note: The above couple were married the same day by Thomas T. Jones, a local Methodist elder.

December 10, 1824—James Good and Mrs. Elizabeth Small (widow).

Edward Pritchard, security.

December 15, 1824—Nicholas Wilson Parker and Miss Frances E. Boush.

Copeland Parker, security.

Note: The above couple were married by the Rev. John H. Wingfield, rector of Trinity P. E. Church, Portsmouth, Va. Nicholas Wilson Parker was the son of Copeland Parker and Frances E. Boush was the daughter of Nathaniel Boush.

December 16, 1824—Francis S. Taylor and Jane E. C. Hackley.

John Tunis, security.

Note: The above couple were married by the Rev. John H. Wingfield, rector of Trinity P. E. Church, Portsmouth, Va. According to a note included with this bond, Jane E. C. Hackley was the daughter of Richard J. Hackley.

December 23, 1824—David Mason and Miss Mary Boggs.

Robert Bingham, security.

1825

January 1, 1825—Caleb Fisher and Miss Mahala B. Cowdry (or Cowdery).

Thomas R. Walker, security.

Note: The above couple were married January 2nd by Thomas T. Jones, a local Methodist elder.

January 27, 1825—John Allmand and Miss Mary Ann Parker.

Albert Allmand, security.

Note: The above couple were married by the Rev. John H. Wingfield, rector of Trinity P. E. Church, Portsmouth, Va. According to a note included with this bond, Mary Ann Parker was the daughter of Copeland Parker. John Allmand was the son of Harrison Allmand, and brother of Albert Allmand, the security.

February 3, 1825—William White and Miss Elizabeth Griffith.

Thomas Crane, security.

February 15, 1825—George Diemond and Miss Tabitha Heath.

William Miller, security.

February 22, 1825—James Dameron and Mary Ann Dancker.

Charles W. Dancker, security.

Note: The above couple were married the same day by the Rev. John French, pastor of the local Methodist Protestant congregation.

February 23, 1825—John Carson and Eliza Mason.

Joseph Reiley, security.

Note: According to a note included with this bond, Eliza Mason was the ward of Timothy Mason.

March 7, 1825—George Kaye and Mrs. Julia Ann Lewis.

Charles G. Carter, security.

March 8, 1825—Francis Grouchy and Miss Ann Bazin.

George Heath, security.

Note: The above couple were married by the Rev. Noah Davis, pastor of the Cumberland Street Baptist Church.

March 11, 1825—Bernard Roux and Mrs. Peggy Grolot.

John (mark) Denson, security.

March 15, 1825—John Anderson and Miss Susan Almira Moore.

James Murphy, security.

March 16, 1825—Charles D. Wood and Miss Mary Ann Ryan.

Otis Ellis, security.

March 23, 1825—Joseph B. Whitehead and Miss Rebecca Tucker.
Nathan C. Whitehead, security.
Note: According to a note included with this bond, Rebecca Tucker was the daughter of James Tucker.

April 5, 1825—John Webb and Ann Leslie.
George Leslie, security.
Note: The above couple were married the same day by the Rev. Noah Davis, pastor of the Cumberland Street Baptist Church. According to an annotation on this bond, Ann Leslie was the ward of George Leslie, the security.

April 6, 1825—William Stewart and Mrs. Eliza Clarke (widow).
George Jacobs, security.

April 8, 1825—Gideon Kilgour and Mrs. Elizabeth Potts (widow).
Abel Lewelling, security.
Note: The above couple were married April 9th by Thomas T. Jones, a local Methodist elder.

April 8, 1825—Nathaniel Anderson and Miss Nancy Gilly.
Thomas (mark) Humphreys, security.

April 9, 1825—Robert Jones and Miss Pemmy W. McCoy.
Richard W. (mark) McCoy, security.
Note: The above couple were married the same day by the Rev. Noah Davis, pastor of the Cumberland Street Baptist Church.

April 19, 1825—Richard Henry Baker and Lelia A. Barraud.
D. C. Barraud, security.
Note: According to a note included with this bond, Lelia A. Barraud was the daughter of Philip Barraud.

April 20, 1825—George W. Owens and Miss Elizabeth Stevens.
Nathaniel Berry, security.

April 28, 1825—Andrew Scott and Mrs. Sarah Fields (widow).
Clark Hitchcock, security.
Note: The above couple were married by the Rev. Thomas Crowder.

May 4, 1825—Robert Butler and Miss Otelia Voinard.
James C. Jordan, security.
Note: The above couple were married May 5th by the Rev. John French, pastor of the local Methodist Protestant congregation.

May 5, 1825—William Whitaker and Miss Sarah Tatem.
James Tatem, security.

May 10, 1825—Littleton S. Savage and Miss Mary F. Dunn.
Charles R. Bushnell, security.
Note: The above couple were married the same day by the Rev. Noah Davis, pastor of the Cumberland Street Baptist Church.

May 19, 1825—William Ready and Mrs. Mourning Crittmore (widow).
Samuel Eddens, security.

June 3, 1825—Charles W. Davis and Mrs. Gertrude Clarke.
John Stavro, security.

June 3, 1825—Henry Ferguson and Mrs. Mary G. Oram (widow).
Samuel Ray, security.
Note: The above couple were married June 4th by the Rev. John French, pastor of the Local Methodist Protestant congregation.

June 7, 1825—Henry Duesberry and Miss Sarah S. Latham.
Frederick Henikie, security.
Note: The above couple were married the same day by the Rev. John French, pastor of the local Methodist Protestant congregation.

June 18, 1825—John Welsh and Mrs. Martha Briggs (widow).
William Bryant, security.

June 20, 1825—Victor M. Randolph and Miss Augusta E. Granberry.

George T. Kennon, security.

June 30, 1825—James H. Johnston and Miss Louisa C. M. Garrison.

Mathew Glenn, Jr., security.

Note: Louisa C. M. Garrison was the daughter of Joshua Garrison.

July 1, 1825—Benjamin Ackerley and Miss Martha Grimes.

John Cason, security.

July 6, 1825—Robert Keeling and Miss Elizabeth Duesberry.

William S. Keeling, security.

Note: The above couple were married the same day by the Rev. John French, a local Methodist (Protestant) minister. According to an annotation on this bond, William S. Keeling, the security, was the guardian of Elizabeth Duesberry.

July 7, 1825—William Elliott and Mrs. Elizabeth Birds (widow).

William (mark) Fallington, security.

July 8, 1825—Davis Sloane and Miss Elizabeth Billups.

Tildsley Summers, security.

Note: The above couple were married July 9th by the Rev. John French, a local Methodist (Protestant) minister.

July 12, 1825—Eli Barrott and Miss Mary Bonnaud.

John Bonnaud, security.

July 19, 1825—Wright Cherry and Gowsadey Cherry.

Josiah Cherry, security.

July 26, 1825—James Emmerson and Miss Mary Ann Blane.

Chauncey Clarke, security.

July 26, 1825—Henry Norton and Maria Bligh (free blacks).

John M. Burt, security.

August 2, 1825—Alexander C. Newman and Miss Desdemona Foster.

Hannah (mark) Miles, security.

Note: According to an annotation on this bond, Desdemona Foster was the ward of Hannah Miles, the security.

August 2, 1825—Richard Bedell and Mrs. Catherine Jones (widow).

Thomas (mark) Crow, security.

Note: The above couple were married the same day by Thomas T. Jones, a local Methodist elder.

August 3, 1825—Robert Jones and Mrs. Susan Walker (widow).

James B. Jacobs, security.

August 11, 1825—Jeremiah M. Huntington and Mrs. Julia Ann Doneven.

James A. Smith, security.

Note: The above couple were married August 17th by the Rev. John French, pastor of the local Methodist Protestant congregation.

August 13, 1825—John Hutchings and Miss Juliann Gines.

Henry Cannon, security.

August 24, 1825—Henry Stevenson and Mrs. Elizabeth Castine (widow).

Joshua Lewelling, security.

Note: The above couple were married August 25th by the Rev. John Frnch, a local Methodist (Protestant) minister.

August 27, 1825—Benjamin Deans and Miss Elizabeth Banes.

John Riggins, security.

September 7, 1825—John Steward and Miss Ann Harvey.

Thomas Cosgrove, security.

September 21, 1825—John G. Hurst and Mrs. Fanny Sheerman.

Henry Stephenson, security.

Note: The above couple were married the same day by Thomas T. Jones, a local Methodist elder.

September 22, 1825—Charles Tonkins and Miss Elizabeth W. Wiatt.
John R. Wiatt, security.
Note: The above couple were married the same day by the Rev. Thomas Crowder.

October 11, 1825—Joseph Green and Miss Elizabeth Spratt.
Lydia Spratt, security.

October 15, 1825—Daniel Smith and Mrs. Alcy Owens (widow).
J. P. Geoffroy, security.
Note: The above couple were married the same day by the Rev. Noah Davis, pastor of the Cumberland Street Baptist Church.

October 18, 1825—Smith Shepherd and Miss Sarah M. Camp.
Horatio Cornick, security.
Note: According to a note included with this bond, Sarah M. Camp was the daughter of John Camp.

October 19, 1825—George Killinger and Miss Mary Ann Whiton (or Whiting).
John (mark) Whiting, security.
Note: The above couple were married the same day by the Rev. Noah Davis, pastor of the Cumberland Street Baptist Church.

October 20, 1825—John Banks and Mrs. Sarah Martin (widow).
James Murphy, security.
Note: The above couple were married by the Rev. Thomas Crowder.

October 20, 1825—Thomas Crane and Mrs. Hetty Sneed (widow).
William McDaniel, security.

October 22, 1825—James Ward and Mrs. Elizabeth Holton (widow).
Caleb Smith, security.
Note: The above couple were married the same day by the Rev. Noah Davis, pastor of the Cumberland Street Baptist Church.

October 26, 1825—Elie Durand and Miss Mary Antoinette Berauld.
E. Berauld, security.
Note: According to an annotation on this bond, Mary Antoinette Berauld was the daughter of E. Berauld, the security.

November 2, 1825—Joshua Lewelling and Miss Mary Lester.
Thomas Lester, security.
Note: The above couple were married by the Rev. Thomas Crowder, Jr.

November 7, 1825—Edward Carter and Mrs. Mary Ann Kite (widow).
Henry Oatest, security.

November 7, 1825—Edward O'Brien and Mrs. Mary Frutier (widow).
Edward Daley, security.
Note: The above couple were married the same day by Thomas T. Jones, a local Methodist elder.

November 10, 1825—James McCawley and Mary Eloiza Holt.
John E. Holt, security.
Note: The above couple were married the same day by the Rev. Shepard K. Kollock, pastor of the Presbyterian congregation. According to an annotation on this bond, John E. Holt, the security, was the father of Mary Eloiza Holt.

November 10, 1825—Ezra Summers and Ann Hawkins.
John Hawkins, security.
Note: According to an annotation on this bond, Ann Hawkins was the daughter of John Hawkins, the security.

November 12, 1825—John McEune and Miss Elizabeth Holmes.
John Lovely, security.

November 23, 1825—John C. Hope and Miss Mary Clarke.
Charles W. Davis, security.
Note: The above couple were married by the Rev. Noah Davis, pastor of the Cumberland Street Baptist Church.

November 24, 1825—William Williams and Miss Margaret Hitchings.

Caleb Smith, security.

November 30, 1825—Robert H. Banks and Miss Mary Ann Moore.

Joshua Moore, security.

Note: The above couple were married the same day by the Rev. Shepard K. Kollock, pastor of the Presbyterian congregation.

December 3, 1825—Smith Burcher and Miss Ann Wilkins.

Robert A. Carter, security.

Note: The above couple were married by the Rev. Thomas Crowder. According to an annotation on this bond, Ann Wilkins was the ward of Robert A. Carter, the security.

December 5, 1825—Joseph Martin and Julia Ann Barney.

Alexander Clarke, security.

Note: The above couple were married by the Rev. John H. Wingfield, rector of Trinity P. E. Church, Portsmouth, Va. According to an annotation on this bond, Julia Ann Barney was the ward of Alexander Clarke, the security.

December 6, 1825—John H. Gee and Miss Elizabeth Proper.

Walter F. Jones, security.

Note: The above couple were married by the Rev. John H. Wingfield, rector of Trinity P. E. Church, Portsmouth, Va.

December 21, 1825—Hezekiah Smaw and Miss Eliza Wrightington.

George Wrightington, security.

Note: The above couple were married by Thomas T. Jones, a local Methodist elder. Accordng to an annotation on this bond, Eliza Wrightington was the daughter of George Wrightington, the security.

December 17, 1825—Isaiah W. Baker and Miss Kesty J. Wise.

John L. Levy, security.

Note: The above couple were married by the Rev. John French, a local Methodist (Protestant) minister.

December 19, 1825—William S. Sclater, Jr., and Virginia A. Bobee.

William S. Sclater, Sr., security.

December 20, 1825—William E. Keeling and Miss Susan S. Lovett.

Thomas W. Keeling, security.

Note: The above couple were married December 26th by Shepard K. Kollock, pastor of the Presbyterian congregation. According to a note included with this bond, Susan S. Lovett was the ward of John Cornick.

1826

January 4, 1826—John T. Raymond and Miss Susan Brooke.

James Mitchell, security.

January 5, 1826—Manuel A. Santos and Miss Mary Rogers.

Nathan Colgate Whitehead, security.

Note: The above couple were married the same day by the Rev. Francis A. Ward, (Methodist).

January 14, 1826—Charles L. Cocke and Miss Ann R. Cooper.

Buller Cocke, security.

January 12, 1826—John Lewis Scholaser and Mrs. Sally Sanderford.

Henry Oatest, security.

January 18, 1826—Samuel W. Hartshorn and Miss Mary A. Warren.

George J. Ham, security.

Note: The above couple were married the same day by the Rev. Henry W. Ducachet, rector of Christ P. E. Church.

January 25, 1826—Philip J. Cohen and Miss Augusta Myers.

Samuel Etting, security.

February 22, 1826—Asa C. Saville and Miss Elizabeth Heddrick.
John Riggs, security.
February 28, 1826—William Knight and Miss Ann A. Nicolson.
John D. Gordon, security.
Note: According to a note included with this bond, Ann A. Nicholson was the ward of William N. Ivey.
February 28, 1826—James B. Sloan and Mary Ann Starrett.
William Gleason, security.
Note: The above couple were married by the Rev. Noah Davis (Baptist).
March 23, 1826—George Griffin and Miss Mary Godfrey.
Edward Williams, security.
Note: The above couple were married the same day by Thomas T. Jones, a local Methodist elder.
April 5, 1826—Henry Hopkins and Mrs. Pricilla Tyler.
Richard (mark) Etheridge, security.
April 22, 1826—Philip O'Neil and Miss Ann M. Bourk.
Redmond Bourk, security.
April 26, 1826—Doctor John P. Young and Miss Hulda E. C. Wilson.
Caleb Wilson, security.
Note: The above couple were married by the Rev. John H. Wingfield, rector of Trinity P. E. Church, Portsmouth, Va.
May 6, 1826—Ralph P. Keeling and Miss Maria Callan.
John M. Watts, security.
Note: The above couple were married the same day by Thomas T. Jones, a local Methodist elder.
May 16, 1826—Edward Ford and Mrs. Mary Lawton.
Michael Dorsey (or Darcy), security.
Note: The above couple were married May 17th by Thomas T. Jones, a local Methodist elder.
May 18, 1826—Gilbert Mester and Miss Sally Mills.
George Turner, security.
May 25, 1826—William G. Morgan and Mrs. Martha Welch.
William Chowning, security.
Note: The above couple were married by the Rev. John French (Methodist Protestant).
June 19, 1826—E. P. Ackerman and Susanna Boush.
Note: There is no bond for the above marriage in the files of the Corporation Court. It was copied from the returns of the Rev. Shepard K. Kollock (Presbyterian).
June 22, 1826—Moses Bonney and Mrs. Ann R. Branda.
Note: There is no bond for the above marriage in the files of the Corporation Court. It was copied from the returns of the Rev. Henry W. Ducachet, rector of Christ P. E. Church.
June 30, 1826—John Mahagan and Miss Jane B. Madden.
John P. Reilly, security.
June 30, 1826—Thomas Mahagan and Miss Margaret Madden.
John P. Reilly, security.
July 25, 1826—William Wilson and Miss Ann Pennywell.
William (mark) Whitehurst, security.
July 27, 1826—Jerke Gervais and Miss Ann Goodall.
Peter (mark) Fiett, security.
July 28, 1826—Thomas Duesberry and Miss Eliza Latham.
Frederick Henekie, security.
Note: The above couple were married by the Rev. Thomas Crowder.

July 31, 1826—Elijah Cooper and Mrs. Elizabeth Hawk.
Samuel Allen, security.
Note: The above couple were married by the Rev. Noah Davis (Baptist).
August 5, 1826—John Davidson and Mrs. Susan Chambers (widow).
William Chawning, security.
August 10, 1826—Hutcheson Scott and Miss Eliza Witter Senior.
David Maitland, security.
Note: The above couple were married August 10th by the Rev. Shepard K. Kollock (Presbyterian).
August 12, 1826—Thomas Drayton and Miss Ann Cullany.
James Watson, security.
Note: The above couple were married by the Rev. Thomas Crowder.
August 12, 1826—David Kincey and Miss Elizabeth Bluford.
Erasamus Capps, security.
August 12, 1826—William Hannaford and Miss Sarah Custer (or Caster).
James W. Saunders, security.
Note: The above couple were married the same day by Thomas T. Jones.
August 31, 1826—Benjamin Warwick and Mrs. Mary Anne Chrowhorn.
William Chawning, security.
September 1, 1826—James A. Graham and Miss Eliza J. Hallsey.
Joel Green, security.
Note: The above couple were married by the Rev. Noah Davis (Baptist).
September 2, 1826—Jacob Smith and Mrs. Ann D'Grouche.
James (mark) Ward, security.
September 16, 1826—John Deans and Miss Alice G. Gray.
Edward Clarke, security.
Note: The above couple were married by the Rev. Thomas Crowder.
October 16, 1826—Moses Van Levan and Miss Jane Summers.
Francis (mark) Summers, security.
October 20, 1826—Rice B. Pierce and Mrs. Amelia Britton.
Edmund (mark) Twiford, security.
Note: The above couple were married by the Rev. Thomas Crowder.
October 21, 1826—Daniel Stone and Mrs. Martha C. Carroway.
John Williams, security.
Note: The above couple were married by the Rev. Thomas Crowder.
October 23, 1826—William C. Kripgans and Miss Elizabeth Lumsden.
William D. Roberts, security.
Note: The above couple were married by the Rev. Thomas Crowder.
October 23, 1826—James Hanrahan and Miss Sarah American.
William D. Roberts, security.
Note: The above couple were married November 4th by Thomas T. Jones, a local Methodist elder.
October 23, 1826—James H. Nevin and Mrs. Amelia Brown.
Thomas Adams, security.
October 30, 1826—Giles Upham and Miss Nancy Powell.
John (mark) Archer, security.
November 1, 1826—Samuel Allen and Mrs. Emily Dozier.
William Miller, security.
November 6, 1826—Alfred Olmstead and Miss Ann W. Brown.
Samuel (mark) Butt, security.
Note: The above couple were married by the Rev. Thomas Crowder.
November 21, 1826—Bowdoin Costin and Miss Polly Elliott.
Sherdrick (mark) Travis, security.

November 29, 1826—William C. Beale and Miss Catherine Gilbert.
Charles Reid, security.
Note: The above couple were married November 30th by Thomas T. Jones, a local Methodist elder.
November 29, 1826—Edward Dunn and Mrs. Margaret Bossidnick.
Nathan S. Angell, security.
November 30, 1826—John G. Colley and Miss Elizabeth B. Harwood.
John R. Harwood, security.
Note: The above couple were married the same day by Thomas T. Jones, a local Methodist elder.
December 2, 1826—John Palmer and Mrs. Elizabeth Warren.
Caleb Bonsal, security.
December 6, 1826—William R. Burns and Mrs. Hanna Rogers (widow).
Richard Numan, security.
December 23, 1826—Thomas Wittering and Mrs. Elizabeth Robertson.
Michael Russell, security.
December 26, 1826—Stephen Legry and Mrs. Marie Cassin Stokard.
Peter F. Bobee, security.
December 28, 1826—Burton W. Davis and Miss Ann D. Davis.
John (mark) Dueon, security.
Note: The above couple were married the same day by Thomas T. Jones, a local Methodist elder.
December 28, 1826—William Godfrey and Miss Catherine Latham.
Frederick Hennicke, security.
Note: The above couple were married the same day by Thomas T. Jones, a local Methodist elder.

1827

January 1, 1827—John McDonald and Mrs. Elizabeth Goodall.
William D. Young, security.
January 10, 1827—Loren Butterfield and Miss Ailcey Woolf.
George (mark) Stewart, security.
January 11, 1827—Robert Peed and Miss Jane R. McQuillan.
Hugh McQuillan, security.
January 11, 1827—Samuel S. Lightfoot and Miss Mary F. C. Lee.
Edwin Lee, security.
Note: The above couple were married the same day by the Rev. Henry W. Ducachet, rector of Christ P. E. Church.
January 16, 1827—Christopher Owens and Mrs. Sarah Keenan.
Edward Williams, security.
January 18, 1827—William Shield and Miss Elizabeth Taylor.
Isaac Wright, security.
Note: The above couple were married January 20th by Thomas T. Jones, a local Methodist elder.
February 1, 1829—Benjamin Pollard and Eliza N. Page.
Note: There is no bond for the above marriage in the files of the Corporation Court. It was copied from the returns of the Rev. Henry W. Ducachet, rector of Christ P. E. Church. They were married according to that source in Gloucester County, Virginia.
February 5, 1827—Joseph Trowbridge and Miss Charlotte Booz (or Boos).
William Booz (or Boos), security.
Note: The above couple were married February 7th by the Rev. Henry W. Ducachet, rector of Christ P. E. Church. Charlotte Booz (or Boos) was the ward of Mary Booz (or Boos).

February 8, 1827—Josiah W. Jordan and Miss Frances M. Dawley.

William J. Darden, security.

Note: The above couple were married the same day by the Rev. Henry W. Ducachet, rector of Christ P. E. Church.

March 22, 1827—John C. Ross and Miss Lucinda Hanier.

Thomas Ferrall, security.

March 27, 1827—William Hawes and Catherine Snider.

Benjamin (mark) Warwick, security.

March 27, 1827—James Henderson and Rosalin Brooke.

Edwin Lee, security.

Note: The above couple were married the same day by the Rev. Henry W. Ducachet, rector of Christ P. E. Church.

April 2, 1827—John Dudley and Miss Eliza Ann Hoggard.

William (mark) Allen, security.

Note: The above couple were married the same day by Thomas T. Jones, a local Methodist elder.

April 11, 1827—William Adams and Mrs. Lydia Curtis (widow).

Anthony Ward, security.

April 12, 1827—Thomas F. Nixon and Miss Ellen Gleason.

John Shuster, security.

April 21, 1827—William M. Wicker and Mrs. Maria Graham (widow).

John (mark) May, security.

April 27, 1827—John E. Codd and Miss Margaret Griffin.

Jeremiah Hendren, security.

April 28, 1827—James Barry and Mrs. Charlotte Christie (widow).

George Johnson, security.

May 2, 1827—Samuel Smith and Mary Ann Cooke.

Joseph Clarico, security.

Note: The above couple were married by the Rev. R. B. C. Howell.

May 3, 1827—Alexander Cunningham and Miss Mary Armistead.

Richard L. Green, security.

Note: The above couple were married the same day by the Rev. Henry W. Ducachet, rector of Christ P. E. Church.

May 3, 1827—Thomas H. Boswell and Miss Laura Margaret Lamb.

William W. Lamb, security.

Note: The above couple were married in Petersburg, Va., by the Rev. B. A. Rice.

May 7, 1827—Peter Geboo and Miss Sarah Garrett.

Frederick (mark) Smith, security.

May 8, 1827—Ardree Bartee and Miss Mary Anna Chapman.

Robert Chapman, security.

Note: The above couple were married May 8th by Thomas T. Jones, a local Methodist elder.

May 9, 1827—Wilson Boush and Mrs. Elizabeth F. Keell.

Edwin Stark, security.

May 12, 1827—Robert Selden and Jane Slaughter.

Note: There is no bond for the above marriage in the files of the Corporation Court. It was copied from the returns of the Rev. Henry W. Ducachet, rector of Christ P. E. Church.

May 10, 1827—William D. Woodhouse and Miss Martha B. Nimmo.

James Nimmo, security.

Note: The above couple were married the same day by the Rev. Henry W. Ducachet, rector of Christ P. E. Church.

May 14, 1827—Felix Kirk and Mrs. Jane Burchill (widow).

Richard Numan, security.

May 15, 1827—Richard Hale and Miss Elizabeth Jennings.
J. Whitehead, security.

May 17, 1827—Thomas Thomas and Elizabeth Bass.
John Cassady, security.

May 17, 1827—Robert E. Eddins and Keziah Fisher.
John (mark) Stroud, security.

May 28, 1827—William Allen and Miss Laura Wilson.
Josiah Grimes, security.

May 30, 1827—John Baldrey and Mrs. Elizabeth Lewelling (widow).
Thomas C. Dixon, security.

May 31, 1827—George Holm and Mrs. Elizabeth Snail (widow).
Alfred Olmstead, security.

June 15, 1827—John Blunt and Miss Ann M. Rombough.
Benjamin Bissell, security.

June 21, 1827—Lieut. Garret J. Pendegrast and Susan V. Barron.
Note: The above marriage was copied from the returns of the Rev. Henry W. Ducachet, rector of Christ P. E. Church.

June 27, 1827—James Robinson (a free black man) and Mary Ann Reynolds (a free black woman).   George T. Kennon, security.

June 28, 1827—Richard R. Corbin and Miss Mary Mallory.
Joseph H. Robertson, security.
Note: The above couple were married the same day by the Rev. Henry W. Ducachet, rector of Christ P. E. Church.

June 29, 1827—George Harvey and Miss Mary Ann Allen McHolland.
Jeremiah Hendren, security.
Note: The above couple were married by the Rev. R. B. C. Howell (Methodist).

July 5, 1827—James Cherry and Miss Lozetta Cherry.
Josiah Cherry, security

July 7, 1827—Dempsey Walker and Miss Kizzy Whitehurst.
Stephen (mark) Sherwood, security.

July 7, 1827—Andrew Simmons and Miss Ann V. Barrott.
John Riggins, security.

July 7, 1827—Stephen Finn and Miss Elizabeth Blunt (or Blount).
James Blunt (or Blount), security.
Note: The above couple were married by the Rev. R. B. C. Howell (Methodist).

July 12, 1827—Jesse Culpepper and Miss Mary Ann Cooper.
John Cooper, security.

July 21, 1827—John Archer and Margaret Simmons.
Argyle (mark) Thorowgood, security.

August 8, 1827—Isaac Dremer and Mrs. Mary Busky (a widow).
William Bath, security.

August 9, 1827—Raymond Gervais and Miss Salvani Bremond.
Dennis Bremond, security.

August 15, 1827—Francis Thorowgood and Miss Aliph Walker.
Wilson (mark) Walker, security.

August 16, 1829—Lieut. George S. Blake and Mary Barron.
Note: There is no bond for the above marriage in the files of the Corporation Court. It was copied from the returns of the Rev. Henry W. Ducachet, rector of Christ P. E. Church, who states that the ceremony was performed by the Rev. John H. Wingfield, rector of Trinity P. E. Church, Portsmouth, Va.

August 15, 1827—Walter G. Lane and Miss Mary Ann H. Barkwell.
John E. Beale, security.
Note: The above couple were married August 16th by the Rev. Henry W. Ducachet, rector of Christ P. E. Church.

August 16, 1827—William Collins and Miss Julia Ann Hutchings.
Samuel Hutchings, security.
August 20, 1827—(Lieutenant) William M. Armstrong and Miss Adelaide Tyler.
Conway Whittle, security.
Note: The above couple were married August 21st by the Rev. Henry W. Ducachet, rector of Christ P. E. Church.
August 20, 1827—James Hill and Mrs. Mary Ann Crossgrove (widow).
James Cogan, security.
Note: The above couple were married the same day by the Rev. Henry W. Ducachet, rector of Christ P. E. Church.
August 21, 1827—William Roblin and Mrs. Mary Ann Lowry.
William (mark) Eldridge, security.
August 22, 1827—John Norris and Mrs. Sarah Huddle (widow).
Henry Johnson, security.
August 22, 1827—James Long and Miss Sulphia Dunn.
William (mark) Roblin, security.
August 25, 1827—George Churchward and Miss Antoinett Ott.
Mathew Cluff, security.
Note: According to a note included with this bond, Antoinette Ott was the daughter of George Ott.
August 28, 1827—Hiram Cady and Miss Elizabeth Anderson.
James Allums, security.
Note: The above couple were married August 30th by the Rev. Henry W. Ducachet, rector of Christ P. E. Church. Elizabeth Anderson was the ward of Rachael Anderson.
September 4, 1827—Edward Williams and Miss Jane Canby.
Jeremiah Hendren, security.
Note: The above couple were married by the Rev. R. B. C. Howell (Methodist).
September 8, 1827—John Tyler and Mrs. Sarah Green.
James B. Jacobs, security.
September 14, 1827—Angus Martin and Miss Jane Eccles.
William Sharp, security.
Note: The above couple were married the same day by the Rev. Shepard K. Kollock, pastor of the Presbyterian congregation.
September 15, 1827—John Woodhouse and Miss Sarah Scott.
Isaac Scott, presiding.
September 18, 1827—Amos Moore and Miss Kitty Gilbert.
John Gray, security.
September 18, 1827—George Reed and Miss Eliza Orr.
John K. White, security.
September 20, 1827—Samuel Pickardick (a free man of colour) and Peggy Wilson (a free woman of colour).   John Voyart, security.
Note: The above couple were married the same day by Thomas T. Jones, a local Methodist elder.
September 24, 1827—Lewis Shepherd (a free man of colour) and Louisa Costin (a free woman of colour).   Stephen (mark) Abel, security.
Note: The above couple were married the same day by Thomas T. Jones, a local Methodist elder.
September 26, 1827—Ephram B. Crickmore and Miss Ann White.
Ballance Crickmore, security.
Note: The above couple were married the same day by the Rev. James Morrison (Methodist).

September 26, 1827—John Grimestead and Mrs. Sally Rogers.
William (mark) Capps, security.
September 27, 1827—James Dunbar and Miss Ann P. Widgen.
John S. Widgen, security.
Note: The above couple were married the same day by Thomas T. Jones, a local Methodist elder.
October 3, 1827—John W. Russell and Miss Ann W. Creekmore.
John (mark) Adams, security.
November 7, 1827—Joseph H. Robertson and Mrs. Sarah J. Archer.
Thomas L. Robertson, security.
Note: The above couple were married the same day by the Rev. Henry W. Ducachet, rector of Christ P. E. Church.
October 17, 1827—Mathew McMurray and Mrs. Ruth Crosgrove.
Benjamin (mark) Warwick, security.
October 29, 1827—Henry Tilden and Mrs. Mary Ann Salmon (widow).
Robert E. Steed, security.
Note: The above couple were married the same day by the Rev. Henry W. Ducachet, rector of Christ P. E. Church.
November 1, 1827—Jonathan K. Hodges and Miss Sarah Davis.
Edward Delany, security.
November 16, 1827—Wallace Flanagan and Miss Jane Campbell.
John (mark) Norris, security.
November 23, 1827—Samuel A. Bowman and Miss Marrinetta Maigne.
John D. Ghiselin, security.
Note: The above couple were married the same day by the Rev. Shepard K. Kollock, pastor of the Presbyterian congregation.
November 29, 1827—William B. Peed and Miss Sarah H. Winslow.
Joseph Winslow, security.
December 3, 1827—Mathias H. Sawyer and Miss Ann T. Whitehurst.
Michael Griffin, security.
December 12, 1827—(Captain) Samuel Selden and Miss Sarah R. Bailey.
Nicholas Wilson Parker, security.
Note: The above couple were married the same day by the Rev. Shepard K. Kollock (Presbyterian).
December 14, 1827—James Harvey and Mrs. Lovey Allen (widow).
Josiah Parker, security.
December 17, 1827—Doctor Robert E. Taylor and Anne E. Cornick.
Note: There is no bond for the above marriage in the files of the Corporation Court. It was copied from the returns of the Rev. Shepard K. Kollock (Presbyterian).
December 19, 1827—Augustus Branda and Miss Lelia A. Burns.
James Maurice, security.
December 19, 1827—David Davis and Miss Mary Nixon.
Wilson (mark) Walker, security.
December 24, 1827—George Hammond and Ellen Warren.
John Burns, sincerity.
Note: The above couple were married by R. B. C. Howell (Methodist). Ellen Warren was the daughter of Rosini Warren.
December 26, 1827—John Haywood and Frances Angel.
John P. Reilly, security.
Note: The above couple were married by the Rev. R. B. C. Howell (Methodist).

1828

January 1, 1828—Russell L. Smith and Miss Amelia Lines.
John Hutchins, security.
Note: The above couple were married the same day by the Rev. Shepard K. Kollock (Presbyterian).

January 2, 1828—Clarke Hitchcock and Miss Florinda Dameron.
Andrew Scott, security.

January 2, 1828—Henry Allen and Miss Ellen McFall.
John T. Charlton, security.

January 9, 1828—Albert J. Garber and Miss Frances S. Hancock.
William S. Keeling, security.
Note: The above couple were married the same day by the Rev. Shepard K. Kollock (Presbyterian).

January 17, 1828—Thomas Randall and Mrs. Ann La Cheuse.
Samuel Ware, security.

January 21, 1828—Samuel H. Hartshorn and Miss Amelia Dana.
Sylvannus Hartshorn, security.
Note: The above couple were married the same day by the Rev. Shepard K. Kollock (Presbyterian).

January 26, 1828—William C. Holmes and Miss Mary Elizabeth Harris.
Charles Harris, security.
Note: The above couple were married the same day by the Rev. Shepard K. Kollock (Presbyterian).

January 30, 1828—(Lieutenant) William Green and Miss Mary P. Saunders.
Arthur Taylor, Jr., security.
Note: The above couple were married February 1st by the Rev. Henry W. Ducachet, rector of Christ P. E. Church.

February 13, 1828—William H. Redwood and Miss Louisa V. Anderson.
Leroy Anderson, security.
Note: The above couple were married the same day by the Rev. Henry W. Ducachet, rector of Christ P. E. Church.

February 20, 1828—William D. Dunbar and Mrs. Jane Ross (widow).
Jeremiah Hendren, security.
Note: The above couple were married by the Rev. R. B. C. Howell (Methodist).

February 21, 1828—Joseph Murden and Miss Mary Jane Shanks.
Henry B. Reardon, security.
Note: The above couple were married the same day by the Rev. Henry W. Ducachet, rector of Christ P. E. Church.

March 10, 1828—William O'Connell and Mrs. Elizabeth White.
John Hughes, security.

March 12, 1828—John R. Berry and Miss Prudence Hunt.
Thomas Randall, security.

March 14, 1828—Ayres Kilgrove and Miss Ann Burgess.
John Barrett, security.
Note: The above couple were married the same day by Thomas T. Jones, a local Methodist elder.

March 18, 1828—Francis Thorowgood and Mrs. Hannah Nickerson.
Frederick Hambury, security.

March 22, 1828—Richard Lee and Miss Eliza Little.
Wilson (mark) Pierce, security.

April 9, 1928—Robert Brown and Mrs. Hannah Whillock.
Samuel (mark) Phillips, security.

April 15, 1828—Nathaniel D Wootten and Miss Ann Steward.
Thomas McLean, security.
Note: The above couple were married by the Rev. R. B. C. Howell (Methodist).
April 23, 1828—George W. Duesberry and Miss Mary S. Diggs.
Elias Guy, security.
May 1, 1828—Hardy Hendren and Miss Elizabeth C. Mallory.
John Williams, security.
Note: The above couple were married the same day by Shepard K. Kollock (Presbyterian).
May 1, 1828—Charles Grymes and Miss Ann R. Holt.
John E. Holt, security.
May 3, 1828—Nathaniel Currier and Miss Eliza A. Piemont.
Thomas C. Dixon, security.
Note: The above couple were married the same day by the Rev. George W. Nolley.
June 12, 1828—Francis Butt, Jr., and Miss Mary Ann Morriss.
George W. Duesberry, security.
Note: The above couple were married the same day by the Rev. George W. Nolley.
June 19, 1828—John Hopkins and Miss Elizabeth Crowell.
Thomas Hankins, security.
June 24, 1828—Gabriel Hudgen and Mrs. Finetta Hurst (widow).
Henry Stephenson, security.
July 3, 1828—George Hastings and Miss Mary Louisa Granbery.
Henry A. T. Granbery, security.
Note: The above couple were married July 5th by the Rev. Henry W. Ducachet, rector of Christ P. E. Church.
July 7, 1828—John D. Ghiselin and Miss Catherine Ferguson.
Joshua Moore, security.
Note: The above couple were married the same day by Shepard K. Kollock, (Presbyterian).
August 1, 1828—Henry A. Fredrick and Mrs. Anna Miles.
William Morris, security.
August 4, 1828—Martin Meagher and Miss Susan Phillips.
John (mark) Starvro, security.
Note: The above couple were married by the Rev. R. B. C. Howell (Methodist).
September 17, 1828—William Stott and Miss Jane Granville.
John C. Hodges, security.
Note: The above couple were married by the Rev. R. B. C. Howell (Methodist).
September 25, 1828—James Roberts and Mrs. Mary Stripes (widow).
John T. Charlton, security.
October 2, 1828—George W. Taylor and Miss Susan A. Green.
John C. Hodges, security.
Note: The above couple were married by the Rev. R. B. C. Howell (Methodist).
October 21, 1828—Thomas Machen and Miss Elizabeth Grimes.
Josiah Grimes, security.
Note: The above couple were married by the Rev. R. B. C. Howell (Methodist).
October 23, 1828—Thomas Bailey and Miss Jane Patterson.
Thomas Griffin, security.
Note: The above couple were married by the Rev. R. B. C. Howell (Methodist).
October 28, 1828—Thomas Williams and Mrs. Ann Walker (widow).
Nathaniel Williams, security.
Note: The above couple were married by the Rev. R. B. C. Howell (Methodist).

November 4, 1828—Exun Stokes and Miss Elizabeth B. Rogers.

Manuel A. Santos, security

November 4, 1828—Andrew Scott and Miss Roxina Harden.

Nathaniel Currier, security.

Note: Thea above couple were married the same day by Thomas J. Jones, a local Methodist elder.

November 6, 1828—William Hughes and Mrs. Hannah P. Burdick.

Henry Preble, security.

November 6, 1828—Thomas Abbott and Miss Mary Richards.

Thomas (mark) Richards, security.

November 11, 1828—Simon H. Simmons and Miss Esther Stevenson.

Charles Stevenson, security.

Note: The above copule were married the same day by the Rev. George W. Nolley.

November 15, 1828—John T. Price and Miss Hannah Williams.

Thomas (mark) Swann, security.

Note: Thea above couple were married the same day by Thomas J. Jones, a local Methodist elder.

November 19, 1828—William C. Ryan and Miss Elizabeth S. Wood.

Charles D. Wood, security.

November 20, 1828—Bailey Adams and Miss Susan Hargrove.

Robert B. Stark, security.

Note: The above copule were married the same day by the Rev. George W. Nolley. Susan Hargrove was the daughter of Mary Brown.

November 21, 1828—Thomas Gibbons and Miss Susan Jones.

William Bishop, security.

December 1, 1828—James T. Allison and Miss Louisa Bland.

James Murphy, security.

Note: The above copule were married the same day by the Rev. George W. Nolley.

December 4, 1828—John James Camp and Miss Euphan E. Allmand.

Harrison Allmand, Jr., security.

Note: The above couple were married the same day by the Rev. Henry W. Ducachet, rector of Christ P. E. Church.

December 9, 1828—David Carey and Mrs. Mary Ann Bell.

Randolph (mark) Cooper, security.

December 18, 1828—James Chambers and Mrs. Eliza Smaw (widow).

Charles (mark) Holm, security.

Note: The above couple were married the same day by the Rev. R. B. C. Howell (Methodist).

December 18, 1828—Talbot G. Lester and Miss Mary Ann Pendred.

Nathaniel Currier, security.

Note: The above couple were married the same day by Thomas T. Jones, a local Methodist elder.

December 24, 1828—William Gordan and Miss Elizabeth Wright.

Benjamin (mark) Bustin, security.

Note: The above couple were married the same day by Thomas T. Jones.

December 24, 1828—Samuel Blathford (or Blackford) and Mrs. Mary Ann Moore.   John T. Charlton, security.

December 26, 1828—William M. Betts and Mrs. Patsey Fritson.

James A. Armistead, security.

December 27, 1828—James M. Adrian and Miss Eliza Ann Bryan.

James Bryan, security.

Note: The above couple were married December 29th by the Rev. George W. Nolley.

December 29, 1828—Robert Camm and Miss Catherine B. Bourk.
Redmond Bourk, security.
December 29, 1828—Robert Deane and Miss Mary Wells.
George Ellis, security.

1829

January 1, 1829—William G. Webb and Miss Charlotte S. Pendred.
Edward Webb, security.
Note: The above couple were married the same day by the Rev. B. T. Blake.
Edward Webb, the security, was the father of William G. Webb.
January 24, 1829—Abraham C. Anderson and Mrs. Eliza Lyon.
Joseph T. Allyn, security.
Note: The above couple were married the same day by Shepard K. Kollock,
(Presbyterian).
January 26, 1829—Enos Murphy and Mrs. Honoria Dodd (widow).
John Dodd, security.
January 27, 1829—James G. White and Miss Pricilla Potts.
George Irvine, security.
Note: The above couple were married January 28th by the Rev. George W.
Nolley.
January 29, 1829—Joseph Nimmo and Hannah Dickson.
Note: There is no bond for the above marriage in the files of the Corporation
Court. It was copied from the returns of the Rev. Shepard K. Kollock (Presby-
terian).
January 31, 1829—Daniel Cunningham and Miss Louisa Worrell.
David Bell, security.
February 1, 1829—Rufus K. Rogers and Miss Mary Hughes.
John Vincent, security.
Note: The above couple were married the same day by the Rev. George W.
Nolley.
February 14, 1829—Robert Dalrymple and Miss Mary Martin.
Angus Martin, security.
Note: The above couple were married the same day by the Rev. Shepard K.
Kollock (Presbyterian).
February 14, 1829—Edward Mills and Miss Susan Kelley.
Benjamin Scott, security.
Note: Thea above couple were married the same day by Thomas J. Jones, a local
Methodist elder.
February 26, 1829—Joseph F. Bobee and Miss Margaretta Hunter.
William Darragh, security.
Note: Margaretta Hunter was the ward of William Darragh, the security.
February 26, 1829—Littleton Tazewell Waller and Miss Margaretta V.
Sharp.   William W. Sharp, security.
Note: The above couple were married the same day by the Rev. Henry W.
Ducachet, rector of Christ P. E. Church.
March 7, 1829—Benjamin C. Siddons and Miss Emeline West.
Robert (mark) Scott, security.
Note: The above couple were married the same day by Thomas T. Jones, a local
Methodist elder.
March 10, 1829—Frederick Williams and Miss Louisa A. Cowling.
Thomas Jennings, Sr., security.
Note: The above couple were married the same day by the Rev. Shepard K.
Kollock (Presbyterian).

March 11, 1829—Joseph Smoot and Miss Margaret Ann M. Talbot.
George T. Kennon, security.
Note: The above couple were married March 12th by the Rev. Henry W. Ducachet, rector of Christ P. E. Church. Margaret Ann M. Talbot was the ward of Isaac Talbot.

March 14, 1829—Philip G. Brundell and Mrs. Martha Powell.
James Mitchell, security.

March 19, 1829—Samuel Coulton and Miss Lilly F. Grigsby.
Nathan Colgate Whitehead, security.
Note: The above couple were married the same day by the Rev. Shepard K. Kollock (Presbyterian).

March 23, 1829—James Higden and Miss Sarah Billings.
William Berry, security.

March 25, 1829—John T. Robinson and Mrs. Elizabeth Morris.
Isaac Scott, security.
Note: The above couple were married the same day by the Rev. R. B. C. Howell (Methodist).

April 8, 1829—William D. Seal and Miss Frances T. Gardner.
John Ridley, security.
Note: The above couple were married the same day by the Rev. R. B. C. Howell (Methodist).

April 25, 1829—William Keeling and Miss Eliza Lester.
Joshua Lewelling, security.

May 19, 1829—Miles Davis and Miss Martha R. McCarty.
Samuel Smith, security.
Note: The above couple were married the same day by the Rev. B. T. Blake.

May 27, 1829—Jesse Frizzel and Mary Ann Banthall.
Willoughby Frizzel, security.
Argyle Thorogood, security.
Note: The above couple were married June 2nd, 1829, by Thomas T. Jones, a local Methodist elder. Jesse Frizzel was the ward of Willoughby Frizzel, one of the securities.

June 24, 1829—Richard Henry Custis and Miss Keziah C. Jones.
Thomas T. Jones, security.
Note: According to a note inclosed with this bond, Keziah C. Jones was the ward of Thomas T. Jones, the security.

July 11, 1829—Josiah Dows and Miss Frances Ann Kilgrove.
Joshua Lewelling, security.
Note: The above couple were married the same day by the Rev. B. T. Blake.

July 14, 1829—William Woodward and Miss Sarah A. W. Owens.
C. H. Gist, Jr., security.
Note: The above couple were married the same day by the Rev. B. T. Blake.

July 16, 1829—Thomas Clarke and Miss Robinsonova Jennings.
William P. Vincent, security.
Note: The above couple were married the same day by the Rev. B. T. Blake.

July 28, 1829—Lewis Jones and Mrs. Ann Sumers.
William Mathias, security.

August 6, 1829—John May and Miss Mary Ann Poke.
Joshua Lewelling, security.

August 26, 1829—Griffin Barnes and Eliza Jane Whiting.
John (mark) Whiting, security.
Note: The above couple were married the same day by the Rev. R. B. C. Howell (Methodist).

August 27, 1829—John A. Jordan and Miss Kitturah G. Frith.

Josiah W. Jordan, security.

Note: According to notes included with this bond, John A. Jordan was the ward of James C. Jordan of Isle of Wight County, and Kitturah G. Frith was the ward of William Benthall of Portsmouth, Va.

August 27, 1829—John H. Butler and Miss Rebecca F. B. Camp.

William G. Camp, security.

Note: The above couple were married by the Rev. John H. Wingfield, rector of Trinity P. E. Church, Portsmouth, Va.

September 8, 1829—John Adams and Miss Sarah Newman.

Joseph G. Savier, security.

Note: The above couple were married the same day by the Rev. Henry W. Ducachet, rector of Christ P. E. Church.

September 19, 1829—Charles F. Buxenstein and Miss Federeic A. Graenacher.

Joseph G. Savier, security.

Note: The above couple were married the same day by the Rev. Henry W. Ducachet, rector of Christ P. E. Church.

September 22, 1829—George Wilson and Miss Matilda Wilson.

William Wilson, security.

Note: The above couple were married the same day by Thomas T. Jones, a local Methodist elder.

October 14, 1829—George J. Byrd and Miss Carolina V. Taylor.

James R. Wilson, security.

Note: The above couple were married by the Rev. John H. Wingfield, rector of Trinity P. E. Church, Portsmouth, Va.

October 17, 1829—John J. B. Porter and Miss Susan Lindsay.

George (mark) Wilson, security.

Note: The above couple were married the same day by Thomas T. Jones, a local Methodist elder.

October 22, 1829—Samuel or (Lemuel) Sutton and Mrs. Elizabeth Cooper.

Edwards Clarke, security.

Note: The above couple were married the same day by Thomas T. Jones, a local Methodist elder.

October 23, 1829—Elias Lankam and Miss Catherine Rogers.

Ellen (mark) McCarty, security.

October 24, 1829—William Thomas and Miss Frances Benthall.

Ambrose Dudley, security.

Note: The above couple were married the same day by the Rev. R. B. C. Howell (Methodist).

October 26, 1829—Charles Davis and Susan Gibbons.

William Bishop, security.

Note: The above couple were married the same day by Thomas T. Jones, a local Methodist elder.

October 28, 1829—John J. Clarke and Miss Maria P. Bryan.

James Bryan, security.

November 3, 1829—James Gammon and Mrs. Mary Wilson (widow).

Isaac Scott, security.

Note: The above couple were married the same day by the Rev. B. T. Blake.

November 5, 1829—Joseph Walker and Miss Martha C. Mason.

Timothy Mason, security.

Note: The above couple were married the same day by the Rev. R. B. C. Howell (Methodist).

November 5, 1829—John Simpson and Miss Elizabeth Burgess.

Henry G. Dunton, security.

Note: The above couple were married the same day by the Rev. B. T. Blake.

November 7, 1829—Samuel Davis and Mrs. Eliza Latimer.

William Dye, security.

November 10, 1829—Marcus L. Doyle and Mrs. Helen H. Gibbs.

George W. Duesberry, security.

Note: The above couple were married the same day by the Rev. B. T. Blake.

November 30, 1829—Jordan M. Marchant and Miss Juliana Stone.

Richard Crump, Jr., security.

Note: The above couple were married the same day by the Rev. Henry W. Ducachet, rector of Christ P. E. Church.

December 10, 1829—Isaac Clowes and Mrs. Susan Parker.

James McCullough, security.

Note: The above couple were married the same day by the Rev. R. B. C. Howell (Methodist).

December 15, 1829—Richard Harris Stevens and Miss Louisa Decormis.

Joseph D. Decormis, security.

Note: The above couple were married the same day by the Rev. R. B. C. Howell (Methodist).

December 18, 1829—Richard Cooper and Ann Duvel (or Davel).

John Reed, security.

December 19, 1829—John Beachem and Louisa Beat.

Joseph Simpkins, security.

December 21, 1829—William N. Whiting and Miss Mary E. Dawley.

Thomas Williamson, security.

Note: The above couple were married the same day by the Rev. Henry W. Ducachet, rector of Christ P. E. Church.

December 26, 1829—Thomas Lambert and Miss Mary Murphy.

James Murphy, security.

Note: The above couple were married the same day by the Rev. B. T. Blake.

December 31, 1829—George C. Conwell and Sarah Foreman.

Robert A. Carter, security.

1830

January 2, 1830—Joseph Cannon and Sara Revol.

Joseph Trowbridge, security.

January 12, 1830—Caleb Brooks and Miss Eliza S. Bucknam.

Joses Bucknam, security.

January 23, 1830—Mathew C. Glenn and Miss Ades Okey.

Chauncey Clarke, security.

January 25, 1830—William C. Nelson and Mrs. Ann Norton.

John Stewart, security.

January 26, 1830—John G. Colley and Miss Elizabeth K. Cornick.

Nathaniel W. Colley, security.

Note: The above couple were married the same day by the Rev. Shepard K. Kollock (Presbyterian).

February 8, 1830—William Cullen and Mrs. Ann Brown.

William Miller, security.

February 12, 1830—Godfrey Berkmire and Miss Frances Ann Kaho.

William Marrast, security.

February 13, 1830—Henry F. Harding and Miss Margaret Dickson.

Bernard Roux, security.

Note: The above couple were married the same day by the Rev. R. B. C. Howell (Methodist).

February 15, 1830—William B. Webb and Miss Mary A. Nicholson.

Willoughby Butt, security.

February 18, 1830—William Green and Miss Louisa Tidens.
Robert (mark) Brittam, security.
February 20, 1830—William Armstrong and Miss Margaret Hamilton Hellen.
Peter Y. Hellen, security.
February 26, 1830—James Dix and Mrs. Eliza Ann Hogwood.
William (mark) Willison, security.
February 27, 1830—Charles Dudley and Miss Eliza Manning.
John (mark) Manning, security.
Note: Eliza Manning was the daughter of John Manning, the security.
March 1, 1830—John Slate and Miss Mary Fetnam.
William (mark) Lewis, security.
Note: The above couple were married March 4th by Henry W. Ducachet, rector of Christ P. E. Church.
March 2, 1830—Daniel Brown and Phoebe Spencer (free persons of colour).
Swepson Whitehead, security.
March 2, 1830—Clark Lillybridge and Miss Clarissa Coffield.
William Coffield, security.
Note: The above couple were married March 4th by Henry W. Ducachet, rector of Christ P. E. Church.
March 18, 1830—William J. C. Wileman and Miss Mary Allums.
James Allums, security.
March 20, 1830—John Woodward and Bethiah Henderson.
Jane H. McCraw, security.
March 20, 1830—Thomas Butler and Mrs. Martha Ann Bartlett.
John (mark) Dixon, security.
March 20, 1830—Daniel Mace, Jr., and Miss Gertrude Errickson.
James Hart, security.
March 23, 1830—John Gormly and Miss Hannah Mitchell.
George Bramble, security.
Note: The above couple were married the same day by the Rev. R. B. C. Howell (Methodist).
March 24, 1830—Augustine Blake and Mrs. Polly Dreamer.
Charles Stephenson, security.
April 6, 1830—Henry S. Haynes and Miss Catherine D. Dickson.
Thomas Dickson, security.
Note: The above couple were married the same day by the Rev. R. B. C. Howell (Methodist). Thomas Dickson, the security, was the father of Catherine D. Dickson.
April 8, 1830—Abel Widgeon and Mrs. Betty Turnbull.
William (mark) Rippen, security.
April 9, 1830—Robert Clemmett and Mrs. Issabella Shackleford.
Elias Guy, security.
Note: The above couple were married April 11th by the Rev. Henry W. Ducachet, rector of Christ P. E. Church.
April 14, 1830—Sem Porter and Ally Cooke (free persons of colour).
James Murphy, security.
April 15, 1830—Ebenezer Barker and Miss Mary Ann Warren.
Godfrey (mark) Cook, security.
Note: The above couple were married the same day by the Rev. R. B. C. Howell (Methodist).
April 15, 1830—Robert B. Cunningham and Miss Ann H. Stark.
Robert B. Stark, security.
Note: The above couple were married the same day by the Rev. R. B. C. Howell (Methodist).

119.

April 20, 1830—Joseph W. Hall and Miss Mary Guirard.

John Guirard, security.

Note: John Guirard, the security, was the father of Mary Guirard.

April 22, 1830—James Baker and Christianna Young.

Swepson Whitehead, security.

Note: The above couple were married the same day by the Rev. Henry W. Ducachet, rector of Christ P. E. Church.

April 23, 1830—John Elliott and Miss Ann Fentress.

Reuben Fentress, security.

Note: The above couple were married April 27th by the Rev. George W. Nolley.

April 29, 1830—John W. Custis and Miss Eliza A. F. B. Drummond.

William F. Foster, security.

Note: The above couple were married the same day by the Rev. Henry W. Ducachet, rector of Christ P. E. Church. Eliza A. F. B. Drummond was the daughter of Richard Drummond.

April 30, 1830—Frederick Mayer and Miss Mary Ann Slack.

Simon B. Werkmuller, security.

Note: The above couple were married the same day by the Rev. R. B. C. Howell (Methodist).

April 30, 1830—Ferdinand Willcocks and Miss Margaret Hawke.

Richard Dove, security.

May 10, 1830—Morris Curtis and Miss Neoma North.

Leno Curtis, security.

Note: The above couple were married May 11th by the Rev. George W. Nolley.

May 22, 1830—William Albertson and Miss Bethia Crandell.

Charles Ramsay, security.

Note: The above couple were married the same day by the Rev. R. B. C. Howell (Methodist).

May 26, 1830—William Collins and Mrs. Sarah Berry.

William Winslow, security.

May 27, 1830—Lemuel Malbone and Mrs. Elizabeth McDaniel.

Isadore Smith, security.

Note: The above couple were married the same day by the Rev. George W. Nolley.

June 8, 1830—Doctor George Terrill and Miss Emily Ann Eyre.

Robert E. Taylor, security.

Note: The above couple were married June 15th in Northampton County by the Rev. Henry W. Ducachet, rector of Christ P. E. Church.

June 15, 1830—John Benston and Miss Elizabeth Hall.

John W. Russell, security.

June 26, 1830—Robert Williams and Mrs. Sarah Shelton.

Leno Curtis, security.

July 15, 1830—John Henderson and Mrs. Louisa A. Post.

Louis J. Fourniquet, security.

Note: The above couple were married the same day by the Rev. Henry W. Ducachet, rector of Christ P. E. Church.

July 19, 1830—James Andria and Mrs. Ellen Rogers.

James Mitchell, security.

July 22, 1830—John Owens and Miss Elishia Wilby.

William S. Powell, security.

July 22, 1830—William Babbington and Miss Alice H. Paguad.

John Dunston, security.

Note: The above couple were married the same day by the Rev. Henry W. Ducachet, rector of Christ P. E. Church.

July 22, 1830—Levi Walker and Margaret Dozier.
Allen (mark) Kirby, security.
August 12, 1830—Henry Marchant and Miss Rebecca Jane Poke.
John (mark) May, security.
August 12, 1830—Doctor Francis Mallory and Miss Mary Frances Wright.
Stephen Wright, security.
Note: The above couple were married the same day by the Rev. Henry W. Ducachet, rector of Christ P. E. Church.
August 26, 1830—David Williams and Miss Thurza Consolvo.
William Consolvo, security.
Note: The above couple were married the same day by the Rev. R. B. C. Howell (Methodist).
September 1, 1830—Charles Ramsay and Ellenor Cunningham.
Alexander Cunningham, security.
Note: The above couple were married the same day by the Rev. R. B. C. Howell (Methodist).
September 2, 1830—Timothy Mason and Miss Ann Eliza Maigne.
John C. Maigne, security.
Note: The above couple were married the same day by the Rev. Shepard K. Kollock (Presbyterian).
September 4, 1830—Samuel Bacon and Mary Eliza Eddens.
Robert Eddens, security.
Note: The above couple were married the same day by the Rev. George W. Nolley.
September 4, 1830—William Holms and Mrs. Lillia A. Williams.
Thomas (mark) Williams, security.
September 9, 1830—John Dyson and Frances Henop.
Swepson Whitehead, security.
September 16, 1830—Isaac Moore and Ann Leslie.
James Dunbar, security.
Note: The above couple were married the same day by the Rev. R. B. C. Howell (Methodist).
September 16, 1830—James Bevans and Rebecca Weldin.
Allen (mark) Bacchus, security.
September 25, 1830—Richard G. Baylor and Miss Catherine B. Tunstall.
Alexander Tunstall, security.
Note: According to an annotation on this bond, Richard G. Baylor was the son of Richard Baylor and the ward of John Yates of Jefferson County.
September 24, 1830—Henry Smith and Helen Jamerson.
John T. Charlton, security.
September 29, 1830—Samuel Drummond and Mrs. Mary C. Davis.
Edward Delany, security.
October 6, 1830—Frederick L. Henop and Miss Julia Dickinson.
John Williams, security.
October 14, 1830—John Brown and Mrs. Ann Criswell.
William Hale, security.
October 18, 1830—John Richardson and Mrs. Louisa Cox.
Peter Y. Hellen, security.
October 28, 1830—William Spangler and Miss Virginia Brown.
Samuel (mark) Butt, security.
Note: The above couple were married the same day by the Rev. George W. Nolley.
November 2, 1830—Stephen S. Russell and Miss Eliza Harshaw.
William Armstrong, security.

November 3, 1830—Enoch Leggett and Miss Mary Ann Keeling.
Robert Keeling, security.
Note: The above couple were married the same day by the Rev. George W. Nolley.
November 4, 1830—William Harding (or Harden) and Miss Amy Moseley.
Tildsley Summers, security.
November 4, 1830—Christian A. Stolp and Mrs. Elizabeth J. Graham.
William Hays, security.
November 4, 1830—William Snow and Mrs. Ann Maria Hallan.
Alexander Harrison, security.
November 17, 1830—John H. Roberts and Mrs. Alice Nottingham.
Henry Etheridge, security.
November 20, 1830—James Wright and Miss Martha Ann Absolam.
Note: Edward Absolam, the security, was the father of Martha Ann Absolam.
November 25, 1830—James Ferris and Sarah Gray.
James Gray, security.
December 3, 1830—John Le Sieur and Miss Eliza Godfrey.
Ann McLean, security.
December 8, 1830—William Hamilton Browne and Nancy Langley (free persons of colour).
Robert B. Langley, security.
December 9, 1830—Cader W. White and Mrs. Nancy Spence.
Thomas A. Kirstead, security.
December 8, 1830—Lemuel P. Nicholson and Miss Charlotte A. Tabb.
John Tabb, security.
December 20, 1830—William C. Camp and Miss Elizabeth F. Warren.
John Palmer, security.
December 23, 1830—Thomas F. Hatton and Miss Rebecca Hawkins.
Jeremiah Hendren, security.
December 28, 1830—Augustine R. Malicote and Miss Mary Ann Cunningham.
Alexander Cunningham, security.
Note: Alexander Cunningham was the father of Mary Ann Cunningham.
December 29, 1830—Robert Morris and Miss Elen Malane.
James (mark) O'Brien, security.
December 29, 1830—Timothy Childs and Mrs. Louisa S. Dickinson.
John S. Millson, security.

1831

January 3, 1831—Edward Gray and Miss Mary Ann Deans.
Benjamin Deans, security.
Note: Mary Ann Deans was the daughter of Benjamin Deans, the security.
January 4, 1831—Joseph Hoffman and Mrs. Jane C. Perrier.
William Nicholson, security.
Note: The above couple were married the same day by the Rev. George W. Nolley.
January 6, 1831—Henry Gardner and Miss Mary Ann Keemer.
William Burns, security.
January 7, 1831—Richard Kerry and Mrs. Sarah Butt.
John O. Taylor, security.
January 24, 1831—Benjamin K. Johnson and Miss Mary E. Moseley.
Charles Moseley, security.
January 25, 1831—John N. Walke and Miss Mary E. Land.
John Petty, Jr., security.
Note: Mary E. Land was the ward of Henry Keeling of Princess Anne County.

January 26, 1831—Daniel Lloyd and Miss Margaret Goulding.
                                            Otis Ellis, security.
January 27, 1831—James D. Fisher and Mrs. Elizabeth Brissie.
                                            John F. Whitehead, security.
Note: The above couple were married the same day by the Rev. Arthur
Cooper (Methodist). Elizabeth Brissie was the widow of Thomas M. Brissie.
January 28, 1831—John Waters and Miss Catherine Jones.
                                            William C. Camp, security.
February 2, 1831—Edward S. Pegram and Miss Sarah Raincock.
                                            George Raincock, security.
February 9, 1831—William A. Cooke and Miss Mary Wilson Sanford.
                                            Daniel Sanford, security.
February 10, 1831—John Adams and Miss Etta Emeline Filley.
                                            Chauncey Clarke, security.
Note: The above couple were married the same day by the Rev. R. B. C. Howell
(Methodist).
February 19, 1831—Owen Wallace and Miss Mary Crickmore.
                                            William F. Borum, security.
February 12, 1831—Thomas K. C. Woodhouse and Miss Sarah Ann Peters.
                                            Jacob Vickery, security.
Note: The above couple were married the same day by the Rev. Shepard K.
Kollock (Presbyterian).
February 24, 1831—Andrew Ross and Miss Ann Jennett Whitehead.
                                            Robert B. Starke, security.
Note: The above couple were married the same day by the Rev. Shepard K.
Kollock (Presbyterian). Ann Jennett Whitehead was the daughter of Ann B.
Whitehead.
February 26, 1831—James E. Wickings and Miss Elizabeth White.
                                            W. J. Hardy, security.
Note: The above couple were married the same day by the Rev. R. B. C. Howell
(Methodist).
March 1, 1831—Thomas Fleer and Miss Elizabeth Guy.
                                            Thomas Drayton, security.
March 2, 1831—Thomas S. Shepherd and Miss Ann Eliza Brown.
                                            William Shepherd, security.
Note: Ann Eliza Brown was the ward of John C. Cahoon of Nansemond County.
March 8, 1831—George M. Thompson and Miss Laura Virginia Savier.
                                            Joseph Savier, security.
Note: Laura Virginia Savier was the daughter of Joseph Savier, the security.
March 17, 1831—John Owens and Anne Wilson.
                                            James H. Jones, security.
March 19, 1831—William Betts and Miss Ann Fitnam.
                                            Christopher Fitnam, security.
March 19, 1831—Martin A. Doyle and Miss Gabriella C. W. Parsons.
                                            Hardy Hendren, security.
Note: The above couple were married the same day by the Rev. Shepard K.
Kollock (Presbyterian).
March 31, 1831—Joseph Smith and Mrs. Matilda Whitfield.
                                            James Mitchell, security.
April 2, 1831—Mathias Long and Miss Joicey Banks.
                                            John Wilson, security.
April 6, 1831—James H. Parker and Miss Catherine Satchwell.
                                            Thomas (mark) Wilburn, security.

April 20, 1831—James Low and Caroline F. Nuttall.
John F. Nuttall, security.
Note: Caroline F. Nuttall was the ward of John F. Nuttall, the security.
April 26, 1831—John Richardson and Ellen Smith.
John F. Charlton, security.
Note: The above couple were married the same day by Thomas T. Jones, a local Methodist elder.
May 2, 1831—Amos Hillman and Elizabeth Butt.
Abraham Kimball, security.
Note: The above couple were married the same day by the Rev. R. B. C. Howell (Methodist).
May 4, 1831—John Williams and Miss Martha J. Armistead.
George Newton, security.
May 12, 1831—John Harper and Miss Elizabeth Davis.
Silas Hendren, security.
May 7, 1831—Shepard K. Kollock and Miss Sarah Harris.
Harvey H. Hayes, security.
May 26, 1831—William M. Haughton and Mrs. Fanny Anne Spratley.
James H. Jones, security.
June 4, 1831—Walter Pierce and Mrs. Sarah Ann S. Clarico.
Frederick Mayer, security.
Note: The above couple were married by the Rev. William A. Smith (Methodist).
June 8, 1831—Daniel S. Doyle and Miss Sarah Godfrey.
George H. Duesberry, security.
Note: The above couple were married by the Rev. William A. Smith (Methodist).
June 13, 1831—Anthony J. McCourt and Miss Ann Ward.
William Ward, security.
June 15, 1831—John Phillips and Miss Mary Flynn.
Martin B. Meagher, security.
July 14, 1831—Thomas Davis and Mrs. Eliza Hill.
Samuel (mark) Phillips, security.
Note: The above couple were married the same day by the Rev. R. B. C. Howell (Methodist).
July 14, 1831—Joseph W. Badger and Mrs. Frances C. Latimer.
Augustus Lapelouse, security.
July 16, 1831—Frederick Smith and Mrs. Letitia Hoyer.
John Dodd, security.
Note: The above couple were married July 17th by Thomas T. Jones, a local Methodist elder.
August 3, 1831—Thomas A. Hardy and Miss Elizabeth Pierce.
William J. Hardy, security.
August 6, 1831—James Ryan and Mrs. Ellen Rogers.
James Mitchell, security.
August 6, 1831—Jeremiah Broderick and Miss Martha Gutridge.
Harold Owen, security.
August 9, 1831—John W. West and Miss Mary C. E. Holt.
Alexander Tunstall, security.
August 10, 1831—Samuel Baines and Miss Mary Miles.
Michael Keef, security.
August 18, 1831—Seth Loring and Miss Mary A. M. Dudley.
Miles H. Smith, security.
Note: The above couple were married the same day by the Rev. R. B. C. Howell (Methodist).

August 19th, 1831—Michael Keefe and Mrs. Mary Ann Gleason.
Charles Holm, security.
September 5, 1831—Obediah B. Pearson and Miss Sarah Wright.
Charles Hatcher, security.
October 5, 1831—Robert Gwinn and Miss Mary Ann Bailey.
Thomas Bailey, security.
October 27, 1831—Caleb W. Bray and Miss Sarah Moore.
John S. Widgen, security.
October 31, 1831—David C. Nicholson and Miss Martha A. T. Jones.
Thomas T. Jones, security.
Note: The above couple were married by the Rev. William A. Smith (Methodist).
Martha A. T. Jones was the daughter of Thomas T. Jones, the security.
November 4, 1831—William Smith and Miss Margaret Crickmore.
William Raleigh, security.
November 8, 1831—William L. M. Tebo and Miss Susan Harman.
James G. White, security.
Note: The above couple were married by the Rev. William A. Smith (Methodist).
November 17, 1831—Thomas T. Kempe and Miss Mary Ann Nimmo.
William N. Ghiselin, security.
November 19, 1831—William H. Harrison and Sookey (free persons of colour).
Cadjo (mark) Stevens, security.
November 24, 1831—Elisha Pendleton and Miss Eliza H. Millson.
William Millson, security.
Note: Eliza Ann H. Millson was the daughter of William Millson, the security.
November 29, 1831—William W. Hunter and Miss Jane Virginia Saunders.
John W. West, security.
Note: The above couple were married November 30th by the Rev. Henry W.
Ducachet, rector of Christ P. E. Church.
December 2, 1831—John White and Miss Susanna Dotto.
Martin Long, security.
December 3, 1831—Robert W. Bowden and Miss Ann Doyle.
George Bramble, security.
December 14, 1831—Samuel Newby and Miss Frances Starette.
James B. Sloan, security.
December 14, 1831—Jabez S. Stubbs and Miss Susan Parshley.
Angus Martin, security.
December 16, 1831—Charles Davis and Mrs. Elizabeth House.
John T. Charlton, security.
Note: The above couple were married December 17th by Thomas T. Jones.
December 20, 1831—George Keitch and Miss Charlotte Smithe.
Michael Frederick, security.
December 21, 1831—George Carter and Miss Mary S. Kellum.
John Buckley, security.
Note: The above couple were married the same day by the Rev. William A.
Smith (Methodist).
December 24, 1831—Edward Watson and Mrs. Elizabeth Stevenson.
John Riggins, security.
Note: The above couple were married by the Rev. William A. Smith (Methodist).
December 26, 1831—Caleb G. Martin and Miss Ann Bainbridge.
William (mark) Raleigh, security.
December 28, 1831—James Anderson and Mrs. Ann Eliza Ritchie.
David Bell, security.

December 29, 1831—Samuel A. Forbes and Miss Louisa C. Barkwell.

Walter G. Lane, security.

Note: The above couple were married the same day by the Rev. William A. Smith (Methodist).

1832

January 20, 1832—John Laurence and Miss Ann Eliza Seymour.

John Stewart, security.

January 28, 1832—John Neil and Miss Nancy Morgan.

Martin Long, security.

January 31, 1832—Thomas King and Miss Jane P. Hellen.

Peter Y. Hellen, security.

Note: The above couple were married the same day by Thomas T. Jones, a local Methodist elder.

January 31, 1832—George W. Topiliff and Mrs. Mahalia B. Fisher.

James B. Rogers, security.

Note: The above couple were married February 1st by Thomas T. Jones, a local Methodist elder.

February 2, 1832—Martin Kerrigan and Mrs. Jane Ervin (or Ewin).

Patrick Galagher, security.

February 2, 1832—John Phillips and Mrs. Ann Ramsay.

Abraham Kimball, security.

February 4, 1832—James Loyd and Miss Ann Shroder.

William N. Shanks, security.

Note: The above couple were married the same day by the Rev. R. B. C. Howell (Methodist).

February 6, 1832—John Alfriend and Miss Nancy R. Bailey.

Samuel (mark) Marshall, security.

February 13, 1832—Walter H. Taylor and Miss Cornelia W. Cowdery.

Jonathan Cowdery, security.

Note: The above couple were married February 14th by the Rev. Henry W. Ducachet, rector of Christ P. E. Church.

February 14, 1832—John C. O'Grady and Miss Sophia S. Proby.

Thomas L. Robertson, security.

Note: The above couple were married February 15th by the Rev. Henry W. Ducachet, rector of Christ P. E. Church.

February 15, 1832—Robert S. Bernard and Miss Nancy Broughton.

Thomas G. Broughton, security.

February 15, 1832—David Caddis and Miss Isabella Edwards.

William Edwards, security.

Note: The above couple were married the same day by the Rev. R. B. C. Howell (Methodist). Isabella Edwards was the daughter of William Edwards, the security.

February 15, 1832—Thomas Lappin and Mrs. Ann Miller.

James Cogan, security.

February 16, 1832—William R. Boswell and Miss Susannah Sterrett.

James B. Sloan, security.

Note: The above couple were married February 17th by the Rev. R. B. C. Howell (Methodist).

February 22, 1832—John C. Shepherd and Miss Frances K. Nimmo.

James R. Nimmo, security.

Note: The above couple were married February 23rd by the Rev. Henry W. Ducachet, rector of Christ P. E. Church.

February 17, 1832—Joseph Frenoi and Jane O'Gilvie (free persons of colour).

Note: There is no bond for the above marriage in the files of the Corporation Court. It was copied from the returns of the Rev. William A. Smith.

February 23, 1832—John Wickham and Miss Catherine Keefe.
David Cull, security.

February 24, 1832—Thomas Keefe and Miss Catherine Russell.
Patrick Russell, security.

February 29, 1832—John Jackson and Miss Agnes Graham.
Hugh P. Woods, security.

Note: The above couple were married March 1st by the Rev. Henry W. Ducachet, rector of Christ P. E. Church.

March 3, 1832—Benjamin Richardson and Miss Winney Carter.
George (mark) Carter, security.

March 3, 1832—Titan Rudolph and Miss Dorothy Thrift.
Henry (mark) McBride, security.

Note: The above couple were married the same day by the Rev. R. B. C. Howell (Methodist).

March 3, 1832—James Owens and Mrs. Louisa Ann Esher.
Thomas Crowder, Jr., security.

March 21, 1832—William Phillips and Miss Virginia Dixon.
Thomas B. Dixon, security.

Note: The above couple were married the same day by the Rev. William A. Smith (Methodist).

April 5, 1832—John Parry and Mrs. Mary Ann Gwinn.
Samuel Bailey, security.

April 5, 1832—James Been and Mrs. Ann Richardson.
John Garrow, security.

April 5, 1832—Thomas Keeling, Jr., and Mary Ann Seymour.

Note: The above marriage was copied from the returns of the Rev. Henry W. Ducachet, rector of Christ P. E. Church.

April 6, 1832—Andrew Talcott and Miss Hariet R. Hackley.
Charles H. Smith, security.

Note: The above couple were married April 11th by the Rev. Henry W. Ducachet, rector of Christ P. E. Church.

April 17, 1832—Joseph Wright and Miss Ann Harmon.
Lemuel Langley, security.

April 20, 1832—John Murphy and Miss Ann Clemmitt.
Robert Clemmitt, security.

Note: The above couple were married April 22nd by the Rev. Henry W. Ducachet, rector of Christ P. E. Church.

April 25, 1832—Thomas Martin and Miss Elizabeth D. Banks.
John Banks, security.

Note: The above couple were married the same day by the Rev. William A. Smith. Elizabeth D. Banks was the daughter of John Banks, the security.

May 1, 1832—William B. Thomas and Miss Elizabeth G. Fauquier.
Robert B. C. Howell, security.

Note: The above couple were married the same day by the Rev. R. B. C. Howell (Methodist). Elizabeth G. Fauquier was the daughter of Ann Fauquier.

May 2, 1832—John Weaver and Mrs. Emily Alleyn.
John (mark) Barton, security.

May 2, 1832—William Seeman and Miss Mary Manning.
John (mark) Manning, security.

Note: Mary Manning was the daughter of John Manning, the security.

May 8, 1832—Simon Laurede and Mrs. Ann Bremond.

Dennis Bremond, security.

Note: The above couple were married May 9th by the Rev. J. Van Horsigh, pastor of the Norfolk Catholic Congregation. M. O'Brien and the Rev. M. Delany are listed as witnesses.

May 9, 1832—Thomas Dewees (or Davees) and Mrs. Mary Bryant.

William H. Ripley, security.

Note: The above couple were married the same day by Thomas T. Jones, a local Methodist elder.

May 9, 1832—John B. Dods and Miss Julia Holden.

Life Holden, security.

Note: The above couple were married the same day by the Rev. Shepard K. Kollock (Presbyterian). Julia Holden was the daughter of Life Holden, the security.

May 15, 1832—John Crawley and Miss Eliza Virginia Fitzhugh.

Thomas Williamson, security.

Note: The above couple were married May 22nd by the Rev. Shepard K. Kollock (Presbyterian).

May 22, 1832—Samuel Reed and Miss Eliza Gardner.

Angus Martin, security.

May 24, 1832—John Davis and Miss Catherine Dunton.

John (mark) Roberts, security.

May 24, 1832—Thomas F. Knox, Jr., and Miss Virginia Ann Soutter.

Robert Soutter, security.

Note: The above couple were married the same day by the Rev. Shepard K. Kollock (Presbyterian).

May 24, 1832—William G. Speak and Mrs. Margaret Wilcock.

John C. Hodges, security.

May 26, 1832—Mark J. Welsh and Mrs. Eliza Menzies.

John Herrington, security.

June 4, 1832—Jeremiah Boynton and Mrs. Rebecca Marchant.

Edward O'Brien, security.

Note: The above couple were married the same day by Thomas T. Jones.

June 10, 1832—Seth March and Miss Virginia Jackson Gordon.

Robert Gordon, security.

Note: The above couple were married the same day by the Rev. R. B. C. Howell (Methodist). Virginia Jackson Gordon was the daughter of Robert Gordon, the security.

June 13, 1832—George Bailey and Miss Elizabeth White.

Samuel White, security.

Note: Elizabeth White was the daughter of Samuel White, the security.

July 10, 1832—Merchant Woodward and Miss Rachael E. Baker.

John F. Whitehurst, security.

Note: The above couple were married the same day by the Rev. R. B. C. Howell (Methodist).

July 10, 1832—William Beverridge and Mrs. Elizabeth Cason.

Charles (mark) Holm, security.

Note: The above couple were married the same day by Thomas T. Jones.

July 31, 1832—John Banks and Miss Mary Martin.

Francis Butt (Sr.), security.

Note: The above couple were married the same day by the Rev. William A. Smith (Methodist).

August 15, 1832—William Moore and Miss Margaret Benson.

James Williams, security.

Note: The above couple were married the same day by the Rev. R. B. C. Howell (Methodist).

August 21, 1832—George W. Farant and Miss Elizabeth H. Stevens.

Joseph Decormis, security.

Note: The above couple were married the same day by the Rev. R. B. C. Howell (Methodist).

August 29, 1832—John Litchfield and Mrs. Elizabeth Howell.

Gabriel (mark) Wilkinson, security.

August 29, 1832—Thomas O. Dixon and Miss Ann Elizabeth Loller Tatem. D. C. Loller, security.

Note: The above couple were married the same day by the Rev. R. B. C. Howell (Methodist).

September 10, 1832—John H. Rowland and Miss Harriet Childs.

George Rowland, security.

Note: The above couple were married by the Rev. John H. Wingfield, rector of Trinity P. E. Church, Portsmouth, Va.

September 20, 1832—Charles Tonkin and Miss Elizabeth L. Moore.

John W. Fiveash, security.

Note: The above couple were married the same day by the Rev. R. B. C. Howell (Methodist).

September 21, 1832—John Collins and Mrs. Eliza Ann Colls.

Hugh McCubbin, security.

Note: The above couple were married the same day by the Rev. R. B. C. Howell (Methodist).

September 22, 1832—Jonas Mayer and Miss Susan Ann Smith.

Anthony Nelson, security.

September 25, 1832—George Dosson and Miss Marion Wilson.

Thomas Wilson, security.

Note: The above couple were married the same day by the Rev. R. B. C. Howell (Methodist). Marion Wilson was the daughter of Thomas Wilson, the security.

October 2, 1832—William D. Simms and Miss Louisa T. Smith.

George O. Poulson, security.

Note: The above couple were married the same day by the Rev. Vernon Ethridge.

October 10, 1832—Isaac O. Peck and Miss Eliza Graves.

Samuel Cain, security.

October 11, 1832—Charles Consolvo and Miss Eliza Ann Riggins.

John Riggins, security.

October 20, 1832—William Stiron and Miss Louisa Kilgrove.

Josiah (mark) Dobbs, security.

October 29, 1832—William F. Tyler and Miss Eliza Ann Mathias.

Nathaniel Currier, security.

October 20, 1832—Lieutenant Samuel Barron and Miss Imogen Wright.

William E. Cunningham, security.

Note: The above couple were married by the Rev. John H. Wingfield, rector of Trinity P. E. Church, Portsmouth, Va.

October 30, 1832—William Richardson and Miss Lydia M. Cherry.

Silas Cherry, security.

November 6, 1832—John McLeland and Miss Georgiana A. Taylor.

George J. Byrd, security.

Note: The above couple were married November 26th by the Rev. Henry W. Ducachet, rector of Christ P. E. Church. Georgiana A. Taylor was the daughter of Arthur Taylor.

November 6, 1832—Robert E. Taylor and Miss Virginia Southgate.

Wright Southgate, security.

Note: The above couple were married November 8th by the Rev. Henry W. Ducachet, rector of Christ P. E. Church.

November 7, 1832—William Rowan and Miss Margaret Collins.

Peter O'Neil, security.

November 7, 1832—William Harvey and Miss Emily Crouch.

Francis H. Brown, security.

Note: The above couple were married the same day by the Rev. R. B. C. Howell (Methodist).

November 14, 1832—Martin Burke and Miss Matty Taylor.

Upton S. Frazier, security.

Note: The above couple were married the same day by the Rev. Henry W. Ducachet, rector of Christ P. E. Church.

November 16, 1832—Everard Hall and Mrs. Catherine Pearce.

John French, security.

Note: The above couple were married November 20th by the Rev. John French (Methodist—Protestant).

November 17, 1832—Mitchell Hall and Mary Ann Berry (free persons of colour).

James (mark) Robertson, security.

November 22, 1832—James Williamson and Miss Love D. Nicholson.

William B. Webb, security.

Note: The above couple were married the same day by the Rev. William A. Smith (Methodist).

November 28, 1832—Lewis Burcher and Elizabeth Gould (free negroes).

Josiah Thomas, security.

December 3, 1832—Samuel Scott and Miss Catherine Hall.

John Wilson, security.

Note: The above couple were married the same day by Thomas T. Jones, a local Methodist elder.

December 3, 1832—Bartholomew Ast and Miss Ann Morris.

Robert Morris, security.

December 3, 1832—Norton Reynolds and Mary Ann Atkinson (free negroes).

James Bligh, security.

December 3, 1832—James Cornick and Catherine B. Moseley.

Note: There is no bond for the above marriage in the files of the Corporation Court. It was copied from the returns of the Rev. Henry W. Ducachet, rector of Christ P. E. Church.

December 12, 1832—William Sangan and Miss Ellen Barrott.

Hugh P. Woods, security.

December 15, 1832—William H. Porter and Miss Jane Edna Marchant.

David G. Farragut, security.

Note: The above couple were married December 17th by the Rev. Henry W. Ducachet, rector of Christ P. E. Church.

December 17, 1832—Louis Augustus Lapelouse and Miss Jane E. Ward.

William Ward, security.

Note: Jane E. Ward was the daughter of Ann Ward.

December 19, 1832—William Dey and Miss Margaret Waters.

James Dameron, security.

Note: The above couple were married the same day by the Rev. R. B. C. Howell (Methodist).

December 22, 1832—John Bligh and Ellen Johnson (free negroes).

James Bligh, security.

December 24, 1832—John Dunbar and Miss Mary Ann Hawkins.
John Hawkins, security.
Note: Mary Ann Hawkins was the daughter of John Hawkins, the security.
December 26, 1832—John Stone and Miss Fanny Stone.
Daniel Stone, security.
Note: The above couple were married the same day by the Rev. Henry W. Ducachet, rector of Christ P. E. Church. Fanny Stone was the daughter of Daniel Stone, the security.
December 31, 1832—Bardon Barron and Miss Ann Elizabeth Hennery.
John Hennery, security.
Note: Ann Elizabeth Hennery was the daughter of John Hennery, the security.

1833

January 3, 1833—William Smith and Mrs. Elizabeth Shute (widow).
John (mark) Adams, security.
January 4, 1833—John Lumsden and Mrs. Elizabeth Finn.
Isaac O. Peck, security.
Note: The above couple were married the same day by the Rev. R. B. C. Howell (Methodist).
January 9, 1833—John Tunis and Miss Rebecca B. Waddey.
James Cornick, security.
Note: The above couple were married January 10th by the Rev. Henry W. Ducachet, rector of Christ P. E. Church. Rebecca B. Waddey was the daughter of Sarah E. Waddy.
January 12, 1833—William Hale and Mrs. Elizabeth Frigeley (widow).
Peter O'Neil, security.
Note: The above couple were married the same day by Thomas T. Jones, a local Methodist elder.
January 15, 1833—William A. Brooks and Mrs. Mary Bellifelt.
Isaac Clowes, security.
Note: The above couple were married the same day by the Rev. R. B. C. Howell (Methodist).
January 16, 1833—James Bligh and Elizabeth Knight (free persons of colour).
John Bligh, security.
January 17, 1833—George Cuthbert Gary and Elishea A. F. Drummond.
Note: There is no bond for the above marriage in the files of the Corporation Court. It was copied from the returns of the Rev. Henry W. Ducachet, rector of Christ P. E. Church.
January 28, 1833—John Adams and Mrs. Sarah Bassett.
Joseph Spratley, security.
February 9, 1833—Jacob R. Ashby and Miss Mary Ridley.
John Ridley, security.
Note: The above couple were married the same day by the Rev. R. B. C. Howell (Methodist).
February 9, 1833—Joseph Tonkins and Miss Julia Ann Mason.
Robert (mark) Williams, security.
Note: The above couple were married by the Rev. Jeremiah Hendren.
February 11, 1833—William Mathias and Miss Letitia Lovett.
Jesse Long, security.
February 12, 1833—Crowell Noe and Miss Mary Eliza Spaulding.
John Tabb, security.
Note: Mary Eliza Spaulding was the daughter of John Spaulding.

131

February 12, 1833—Lewis Salusbury and Miss Mary Ann Swank.

John Swank, security.

Note: The above couple were married February 13th by the Rev. R. C. C. Mowell (methodist). Mary Ann Swank was the daughter of Catherine Swank.

February 20, 1833—Samuel Parker and Miss Susan Belotte.

Shepherd Savage, security.

Note: The above couple were married the same day by the Rev. R. B. C. Howell (Methodist).

February 20, 1833—Ebenezer C. Bosworth and Miss Rebecca Glass.

Nicholas W. Parker, security.

Note: The above couple were married February 21st by the Rev. Henry W. Ducachet, rector of Christ P. E. Church.

February 25, 1833—Miles S. Cox and Mrs. Eliza M. Keeling (widow).

Keeling (mark) Sammons, security.

February 28, 1833—George H. Jones and Miss Frances Jane Raincock.

George Raincock, security.

Note: The above couple were married the same day by the Rev. Henry W. Ducachet, rector of Christ P. E. Church.

March 19, 1833—John M. Galt and Miss Ann W. Land.

Francis Mallory, security.

Note: The above couple were married the same day by the Rev. Henry W. Ducachet, rector of Christ P. E. Church. Ann W. Land was the ward of Henry Keeling.

March 28, 1833—John Loury and Miss Ann Ellen.

Christian Stolp, security.

March 30, 1833—Shepherd Savage and Miss Sarah Blow.

Samuel Parker, security.

Note: The above couple were married the same day by the Rev. R. B. C. Howell (Methodist).

March 30, 1833—Henry McBride and Miss Eliza Jones.

Absolom Thrift, security.

Note: The above couple were married the same day by the Rev. R. B. C. Howell (Methodist).

April 3, 1833—Washington Bowler and Miss Susanna Manning.

William Manning, security.

Note: The above couple were married the same day by the Rev. R. B. C. Howell (Methodist).

April 3, 1833—Thomas W. Roach and Miss Margaret A. Hodges.

John C. Hodges, security.

Note: The above couple were married the same day by the Rev. R. B. C. Howell (Methodist).

April 9, 1833—Peter O'Neil and Mrs. Charlotte Raleigh (wdow).

Samuel Hibbard, security.

April 12, 1833—John C. Saunders and Miss Mary E. McCandlish.

Jacob Vickery, security.

Note: The above couple were married April 16th by the Rev. Henry W. Ducachet, rector of Christ P. E. Church. Mary E. McCandlish was the daughtery of Mary C. McCandlish.

April 17, 1833—William Johnson and Mrs. Ann H. Pitt.

Ludelow S. Savage, security.

April 17, 1833—Joseph M. Bullock and Mrs. Mary A. Bullock.

Thomas Eccles, security.

Note: The above couple were married the same day by the Rev. R. B. C. Howell (Methodist).

April 18, 1833—Robert Blow and Susan M. Walke.
Note: There is no bond for the above marriage in the files of the Corporation Court. It was copied from the returns of the Rev. Henry W. Ducachet, rector of Christ P. E. Church, who states that the marriage was performed "in church."

April 20, 1833—Benjamin Deans and Mrs. Mary Elizabeth Armstrong.
Eyers (mark) Kilgrove, security.
Note: The above couple were married by the Rev. Jeremiah Hendren.

May 21, 1833—David M. Stokes and Miss Mary E. Nimmo.
J. H. Hoskins, security.
Note: The above couple were married the same day by the Rev. Henry W. Ducachet, rector of Christ P. E. Church. Mary E. Nimmo was the daughter of Elizabeth J. Nimmo.

May 27, 1833—James M. Brooks and Miss Susan P. Pritchard.
Robert C. Pritchard, security.

May 28, 1833—Christian Hays and Miss Elizabeth Ghiseman.
William Hays, security.

May 30, 1833—Robert Soutter, Jr., and Miss Philadelphia Campbell.
William Campbell, security.
Note: The above couple were married the same day by the Rev. Shepard K. Kollock (Presbyterian). Philadelphia Campbell was the daughter of William Campbell, the security.

May 30, 1833—Alexander Bell, Jr., and Miss Margaret Soutter.
Robert Soutter, security.
Note: The above couple were married the same day by the Rev. Shepard K. Kollock (Presbyterian). Margaret Soutter was the daughter of Robert Soutter, the security.

June 6, 1833—Richard Watson and Jane Eliza Walke.
Note: There is no bond for the above marriage in the files of the Corporation Court. It was copied from the returns of the Rev. Henry W. Ducachet, rector f Christ P. E. Church.

June 13, 1833—Willard Smith and Miss Sarah Ann Reeves.
John Tilford, security.
Note: The above couple were married the same day by the Rev. R. B. C. Howell (Methodist).

June 17, 1833—David A. Manning and Miss Frances Louisa Holt.
J. H. Hoskins, security.
Note: The above couple were married the same day by the Rev. Shepard K. Kollock (Presbyterian. Frances Louisa Holt was the daughter of Clara Holt.

June 28, 1833—John T. Charlton and Mrs. Margaret Butt.
Wright W. Cherry, security.

June 28, 1833—Robert Wright and Miss Elizabeth Jones.
Robert Burton, security.

June 29, 1833—Richard Nottingham and Mrs. Mary Thomas.
William A. Smith, security.
Note: The above couple were married by the Rev. John H. Wingfield, rector of Trinity P. E. Church, Portsmouth, Va.

July 6, 1833—Thomas A. Kirby and Miss Susan Davis.
James C. West, security.
Note: The above couple were married the same day by the Rev. R. B. C. Howell (Methodist).

July 27, 1833—Shelburne Mahone and Miss Mary Jordan.
Frederick Hambury, security.
Note: The above couple were married the same day by the Rev. R. B. C. Howell (Methodist)

August 3, 1833—Samuel O. Merwin and Miss Susan F. Chapman.
Robert Chapman, security.
Note: The above couple were married the same day by the Rev. Shepard K. Kollock (Presbyterian). Susan F. Chapman was the daughter of Robert Chapman, the security.

August 7, 1833—William A. Dawley and Mrs. Martha Ann Black.
John Dexter, security.
Note: The above couple were married the same day by the Rev. R. B. C. Howell (Methodist)

August 14, 1833—Lemuel Sutton and Mrs. Anna Wilson.
William Darragh, security.
Note: The above couple were married by the Rev. Jeremiah Hendred.

August 16, 1833—Thomas Franklin and Miss Orfa Waller.
William (mark) Smith, security.

August 24, 1833—Samuel Baines and Miss Eliza Hozier.
Robert Hozier, security.
Note: Eliza Hozier was the daughter of Robert Hozier, the security.

August 29, 1833—Abner Blanks and Miss Mary Ann Granberry.
Lewis Granberry, security.
Note: Mary Ann Granberry was the daughter of Lewis Granberry, the security.

August 30, 1833—James F. Duncan and Miss Virginia Stone.
Everard Hall, security.
Note: The above couple were married the same day by the Rev. Henry W. Ducachet, rector of Christ P. E. Church. Virginia Stone was the daughter of Elizabeth Stone.

September 3, 1833—Miles King and Miss Mary L. Fisher.
John Hodges, security.
Note: The above couple were married September 4th, "in church," by the Rev. Henry W. Ducachet, rector of Christ P. E. Church. Mary L. Fisher was the daughter of Reuben Fisher.

September 19, 1833—William S. Drummond and Miss Ann T. Foster.
Robert W. Simmington, security.
Note: The above couple were married the same day by the Rev. Henry W. Ducachet, rector of Christ P. E. Church.

September 24, 1833—Bennet Bedout and Miss Mary Scicilia Pontier.
Peter A. Adde, security.

October 2, 1833—James Drummond and Mrs. Helena Crossley.
John Lewis, security.
Note: The above couple were married the same day by the Rev. R. B. C. Howell (Methodist)

October 3, 1833—William Tucker and Miss Mary R. McCausland.
Richard Dickson, security.
Note: The above couple were married the same day by the Rev. Henry W. Ducachet, rector of Christ P. E. Church.

October 5, 1833—William Fenn Hopkins and Miss Frances Louisa Southgate.
Robert Southgate, security.
Note: The above couple were married October 6th by the Rev. Henry W. Ducachet, rector of Christ P. E. Church.

October 5, 1833—Joshua Nicholson and Miss Mary Haynor.
Harmon Hanor, security.

October 7, 1833—John Ferris and Miss Ellen A. Rodgers.
James Mitchell, security.

October 15, 1833—James R. Keating and Miss Ann Eliza Boush.
Arthur Cooper, security.

October 25, 1833—John H. Wallet and Miss Felicete Geay.

Peter Geay, security.

October 28, 1833—David Bell and Mrs. Catherine Snyder.

John Snyder, security.

October 31, 1833—Baynham Baylor and Miss Eliza F. Sharp.

William W. Sharp, security.

November 8, 1833—John Truslow and Mrs. Anna Talbot (widow).

John Barrett, security.

November 12, 1833—George Robinson and Mrs. Ann Boyd.

Angus Martin, security.

November 27, 1833—Robert T. Scott and Miss Elizabeth Granbery.

Lewis Granbery, security.

December 4, 1833—William T. Anderson and Miss Catherine J. Decker.

Silas Hendren, security.

Note: The above couple were married the same day by the Rev. R. B. C. Howell (Methodist)

December 10, 1833—Edward A. Barnes and Miss Anne Forrest.

William A. Smith, security.

Note: The above couple were married the same day by the Rev. R. B. C. Howell (Methodist). Henry B. Woodhouse of Princess Anne County was the guardian of Anne Forrest. He was appointed guardian of John Forrest, William Forrest, Anne Forrest, Ellen Forrest, Eliza Forrest and Mary Forrest, orphans of John Forrest, on May 6, 1822.

December 12, 1833—Walter Braidford and Miss Ann Finley.

George Robinson, security.

December 21, 1833—John Bonney and Elizabeth T. White.

John Ridley, security.

Note: The above couple were married the same day by the Rev. R. B. C. Howell (Methodist)

Decmber 21, 1833—Henry Tabb and Miss Eliza Cunningham.

Alexander Cunningham, security.

Note: The above couple were married December 22nd by the Rev. James Boyd (Methodist). Eliza Cunningham was the daughter of Alexander Cunningham, the security.

December 24, 1833—Charles W. Hardy and Miss Rebecca M. Pierce.

Thomas A. Hardy, security.

December 30, 1833—Charles Hebdon and Miss Lucy Ann Henry.

Charles Wray, security.

December 31, 1833—Alfred Olmstead and Mrs. Dorothea Garrow.

Charles Ramsey, security.

December 31, 1833—Harvey Beyea and Miss Margaret Egan.

Charles Mayger, security.

Note: Margaret Egan was the daughter of Lydia Egan.

1834

January 2, 1834—Robert Stewart and Miss Sarah Porter.

Thomas Wittering, security.

Note: The above couple were married the same day by the Rev. Henry W. Ducachet, rector of Christ P. E. Church.

January 4, 1834—Walter T. Brooke and Miss Olivia S. West.

Thomas B. West, security.

Note: The above couple were married January 6th, "in church," by the Rev. Henry W. Ducachet, rector of Christ P. E. Church.

January 6, 1834—Edward J. Davis and Miss Eliza A. Dryden.

Isaac Moore, security.

Note: Eliza A. Dryden was the daughter of Charlotte Dryden.

January 11, 1834—John Dickson and Miss Mary Eliza Hipkins.

James T. Hipkins, security.

Note: The above couple were married January 13th, "in church," by the Rev. Henry W. Ducachet, rector of Christ P. E. Church. Mary Eliza Hipkins was the daughter of Eliza Hipkins.

January 16, 1834—Fitz Allen Deas and Miss Levinia H. Randolph.

William H. Kennon, security.

Note: The above couple were married January 19th by the Rev. Henry W. Ducachet, rector of Christ P. E. Church. Levinia H. Randolph was the daughter of Benamin Randolph.

January 22, 1834—Isaac M. Smith and Miss Catherine H. D. Coxell.

Thomas Hankins, security.

Note: The above couple were married January 23rd by the Rev. Henry W. Ducachet, rector of Christ P. E. Church. Catherine H. D. Coxell was the daughter of Eliza M. Coxell.

January 24, 1834—Alexandre Feret and Mrs. Ann Vincent.

John Williams, security.

January 27, 1834—William B. Taylor and Miss Nancy J. Hudgin.

Isma Wyatt, security.

January 28, 1834—John Thomas and Miss Lucy Oliver.

Thomas Turner, security.

January 30, 1834—William Hogwood and Miss Tabitha Grendall.

John Dozier, security.

Note: The above couple were married the same day by the Rev. R. B. C. Howell (Methodist)

February 3, 1834—Edward F. Dayton and Mrs. Sarah Fairbanks.

Angus Martin, security.

February 7, 1834—William Taylor and Miss Frances Nimmo.

William J. Holmes, security.

Note: The above couple were married the same day by the Rev. R. B. C. Howell (Methodist)

February 14, 1834—Jesse Jones and Miss Jane Philbrick.

Henry McBride, security.

February 14, 1834—William McDonald and Miss Caroline Jones.

Mary Ann Gunn, security.

Note: The above couple were married February 15th by Thomas T. Jones, a local Methodist elder.

February 20, 1834—Pascal Schisano and Miss Mary C. Decous.

Lewis Santejau, security.

February 21, 1834—John Webster and Miss Lucy Ann P. Dots.

Peter Y. Hellen, security.

February 21, 1834—Hugh McCubbin and Mrs. Ann Munn.

John Langan, security.

Note: The above couple were married the same day by the Rev. R. B. C. Howell

February 25, 1834—John Miller and Mrs. Catherine Mullin.

William (mark) McDonald, security.

March 5, 1834—Daniel Baines and Miss Alice Robins.

Silas (mark) Sanford, security.

April 12, 1834—Lewis E. Rogers and Miss Mary Seymour.

Jonathan K. Hodges, security.

Note: The above couple were married the same day by the Rev. R. B. C. Howell

April 17, 1834—Jonathan Russell and Miss Barbara Bradshaw.

Benjamin F. Connor, security.

Note: The above couple were married the same day by Thomas T. Jones, a local Methodist elder.

April 26, 1834—Thomas Conner and Mrs. Sarah Ann Jeffers.

William Miller, security.

April 30, 1834—John H. Morcin and Miss Sarah A. Fitz.

John C. Maigne, security.

Note: Sarah A. Fitz was the daughter of Lydia Fitz.

May 5, 1834—William B. Corran and Miss Louisa A. Madden.

John T. Corran, security.

May 15, 1834—William Haynes and Mrs. Margaret Brown.

Joshua Moore, security.

Note: The above couple were married the same day by the Rev. R. B. C. Howell (Methodist).

May 20, 1834—Thomas B. Beaton and Miss Ann E. Coxell.

Henry H. Dentzell, security.

Note: The above couple were married the same day by the Rev. William A. Smith (Methodist).

May 29, 1834—Charles Lewis Bruce and Miss Mary Ann Ferebe.

Enoch (mark) Ferebe, security.

Note: The above couple were married the same day by the Rev. William A. Swith (Methodist).

June 3, 1834—Henry W. Munson and Miss Almira P. Angell.

Nathan S. Angell, security.

Note: Almira P. Angell was the daughter of Nathan S. Angell, the security.

June 4, 1834—Philip St. George Cocke and Sally E. Courtney Bowdoin.

Note: The above marriage was copied from the returns of the Rev. Henry W. Ducachet, rector of Christ P. E. Church.

June 11, 1834—Christopher Hubbard and Miss Eliza Ann Hodges.

Alexander W. Jones, security.

June 25, 1834—Edward Chamberlin, Jr., and Miss Ann A. McConnico.

Andrew McConnico, security.

July 1, 1834—Samuel Bryan and Mrs. Mary Ann Maddox.

John Webster, security

Note: The above couple were married the same day by the Rev. R. B. C. Howell (Methodist).

July 2, 1834—Gabriel G. Williamson and Miss Elizabeth A. Gatewood.

Thomas Gatewood, security.

July 2, 1834—Laurence Armstrong and Mrs. Catherine Raney.

Thomas (mark) Brown, security.

July 15, 1834—John Ramsay and Miss Mary Jones.

John Ridley, security.

July 15, 1834—John Petty, Jr., and Miss Mary E. Calvert.

William Roberts, securiy.

July 21, 1834—Benjamin J. Taylor and Miss Rebecca Peterson.

Alexander Banks, security.

August 4, 1834—William Robertson and Miss Mary Jane Perry.

James (mark) Blount, security.

August 5, 1834—William Hays and Miss Margaret Dorean.

John M. Wolfe, security.

August 7, 1834—Robert Diggs and Mrs. Eliza Stout.

Bernard Roux, security.

August 9, 1834—William P. Wilson and Miss Ellen Hill.

Alfred Lacave, security.

August 20, 1834—James A. Woodward and Miss Elizabeth V. Tumlinson.

Lewis Salusbury, security.

September 3, 1834—Mathew Butler and Miss Catherine Collins.

Jeremiah Sullivan, security.

September 3, 1834—Turner H. Southall and Miss Alice Ann Wright.

William H. Day, security.

September 9, 1834—John Watson and Miss Rebecca Smith.

Samuel Bryant, security.

September 20, 1834—Stephen Fisher and Miss Caroline Baker.

Thomas Griffin, security

September 20, 1834—Edward W. Hardy and Mrs. Ann Eliza Shipp.

James Williamson, security

September 20, 1834—William Raleigh and Mrs. Bridget Burke.

David Cull, security

September 25, 1834—Daniel Quinn and Mrs. Mary Ann Massey.

James Trenor, security.

October 2, 1834—Dougald McPhail and Miss Adeline Harris.

Charles F. Harris, security.

October 6, 1834—James Ferguson and Miss Caroline G. Milhado.

Richard Watson, security.

October 8, 1834—Joseph Capps and Miss Susan A. Moseley.

Andrew Scott, security.

Note: Susan A. Moseley was the daughter of Martha Moseley.

October 12, 1834—Thomas B. Phillips and Miss Fanny Webb.

Wiloughby Butt, security.

October 15, 1834—Thomas Rooke and Miss Isabella Traill.

Henry B. C. Walker, security.

October 16, 1834—George W. Mitchell and Miss Jane Hill.

Augustus (mark) Sikes, security

Note: The above couple were married the same day by the Rev. R. B. C. Howell (Methodist).

October 20, 1834—Richard Courtney and Miss Lydia W. Poyner.

Mary Poyner (or Payner), security.

Note: The above couple were married the same day by Thomas T. Jones, a local Methodist elder.

November 1, 1834—Lemuel Sutton and Miss Martha Sparks.

Sterling S. Armistead, security.

November 6, 1834—Ransome Dibble and Miss Mary Ann D. Knight.

William Knight, security.

Note: Mary Ann Knight was the daughter of William Knight, the security.

November 8, 1834—Nathaniel Hosier and Mrs. Ann Ballance.

George W. Ashbee, security.

Note: The above couple were married the same day by Thomas T. Jones, a local Methodist elder.

November 12, 1834—Robert L. Cays and Miss Catherine E. Babbington.

William Babbington, security.

Note: Catherine E. Babbington was the daughter of William Babbington, the security.

November 22, 1834—William J. Chapman and Miss Mary Tabb Talbot.

John Southgate, security.

December 1, 1834—William A. Crane and Miss Margaret P. Fitzhugh.
Fowler Smith, security.
December 2, 1834—James Walters and Miss Georgiana V. Martin.
A. A. Martin, security.
Note: Georgiana V. Martin was the daughter of A. A. Martin, the security.
December 12, 1834—Machen Picket and Miss Eliza B. Fisher.
William B. Fisher, security.
December 11, 1834—Nelson Cory and Miss Ann W. Hanor.
Harmon Hanor, security.
December 13, 1834—John W. Holmes and Miss Eliza Fentress.
William Y. Milliner, security.
December 16, 1834—George Hays and Miss Amy Woodis.
Christian Hays, security.
December 17, 1834—William S. Prime and Miss Ann S. Moseley.
James C. Malbon, security.
December 17, 1834—James Cannon and Miss Louisa Stone.
Thomas C. Floyd, security.
December 20, 1834—Alexander Robertson and Miss Nancy Williamson.
Charles S. Holm, security.
December 24, 1834—Andrew Stevens and Miss Louisa Hill.
William Thompson, security.
December 25, 1834—Isaac J. Wilkins and Miss Mary Catherine Nicholson.
John Lewis, security.
December 26, 1834—William H. Stewart and Mrs. Sarah Fleming.
William McAllester, security.
December 31, 1834—William Ashley and Miss Jane E. Mitchell.
James Mitchell, security.

1835

January 6, 1835—Wilson Williamson and Miss Nancy James.
Henry James, security.
Note: Nancy James was the orphan of Edward James and the ward of Henry James, the security, who was appointed her guardian by the Princess Anne County Court June 1, 1829.
January 12, 1835—Thomas Leech and Mrs. Ann McConkey.
Wilson B. Morgan, security.
July 12, 1835—Simon S. Stubbs and Miss Elizabeth O. Shepherd.
Thomas S. Shepherd, security.
Note: Elizabeth O. Shepherd was the daughter of William Shepherd.
January 12, 1835—John Long and Mrs. Fanny Williams.
William Howard, security.
Note: The above couple were married the same day by Thomas T. Jones, a local Methodist elder.
January 22, 1835—John Blake Lining Marsden and Miss Margaret E. Nimmo.
John French, security.
January 24, 1835—John Callis and Miss Ann Elizabeth Richardson.
John Richardson, security.
January 28, 1835—William Hope and Miss Mary Ann Fitton.
Nathaniel Palmer, security.
January 28, 1835—Augustus Sykes and Miss Eliza Frances Murden.
George (mark) Greenwood, security.

January 31, 1835—Darius King and Phoebe Ann Moseley (free persons of colour). Tazewell Taylor, security.

February 4, 1835—John G. H. Hatton and Miss Isabella Woodward.
Alexandre Feret, security.

February 5, 1835—Eugene J. Higgins and Miss Juliet Hutchings.
William Francis, security.

Note: Juliet Hutchings was the daughter of Martha Hutchings.

February 12, 1835—Andrew Anderson and Mrs. Mary Ann Barker.
Peter O'Neil, security.

February 11, 1835—Hervey Sawyer and Miss Eliza Ann Booth.
Edmund C. Robinson, security.

February 11, 1835—William B. Campbell and Mrs. Mary Peel.
Joel Parr, security.

February 12, 1835—Thomas Cary and Mrs. Mary G. Vaughn.
William D. Bagnall, security.

February 14, 1835—Joseph Murden and Miss Laura Sanford.
Daniel Sanford, security.

February 19, 1835—John Russell and Miss Susan Mathiet.
Robert Mathews, security.

Note: The above couple were married by the Rev. Jeremiah Hendren.

February 26, 1835—William Ahern and Miss Jane Ann Johnson.
James Barry, security.

March 18, 1835—Joseph Ellis and Mrs. Mary Ann Keefe.
Charles S. Holm, security.

Note: The above couple were married by the Rev. Jeremiah Hendren.

March 25, 1835—William Wilson and Mrs. Matilda Smith.
James Balfour, security.

March 26, 1835—Asa B. Cheatham and Miss Eliza Cooper.
James Cherry, security.

Note: The above couple were married the same day by the Rev. Jeremiah Hendren.

April 2, 1835—Dennis Vermillion and Miss Averella Bonney.
John G. Colley, security.

Note: Averella Bonney was the daughter of Moses Bonney.

April 4, 1835—Gideon White and Mrs. Jaka Keeling.
Solomon (mark) Wallace, security.

Note: The above couple were married by the Rev. Jeremiah Hendren.

April 13, 1835—Samuel Brown and Miss Mary Eliza Consolvo.
John Riggins, security.

April 15, 1835—James Warren and Mrs. Harriet Keeling.
D. D. Simmons, security.

April 16, 1835—Elisha H. Newcomb and Miss Virginia Ann Young.
James Marsden Smith, security.

April 20, 1835—Arthur Sinclair and Miss Lelia J. Dawley.
Robert Robertson, security.

Note: The above couple were married by the Rev. John H. Wingfield, rector of Trinity P. E. Church, Portsmouth, Va.

April 21, 1835—S. J. Foley and Miss Martha A. Schleiker.
John A. Roberts, security.

Note: Martha A. Schleiker was the daughter of Hannah O'Neil.

April 22, 1835—Midshipman Oliver S. Glisson and Miss Pamelia A. T. Parker. Nicholas Wilson Parker, security.

Note: Miss Pamella A. T. Parker was the daughter of Copeland Parker (died 1830) and Diana Robinson (Hall) Parker.

April 25, 1835—George Dyson and Miss Sarah Bourk.

Redmond Bourk, security.

Note: Sarah Bourk was the daughter of Redmond Bourk, the security.

April 29, 1835—Peter M. Flannagan and Miss Frances S. Boush.

Lemuel Peed, security.

May 7, 1835—David Barron and Miss Mary Turner.

Thomas (mark) Kellun, security.

May 9, 1835—William D. Bagnall and Miss Elizabeth D. Stark.

Robert B. Stark, security.

Note: Elizabeth D. Stark was the daughter of Eliza W. Stark.

May 12, 1835—Charles H. Poor and Miss Mattie L. Stark.

Robert B. Stark, security.

Note: The above couple were married the same day by the Rev. William A. Smith (Methodist).

May 28, 1835—Robert Randolph and Miss Mary Louisa Cunningham.

William E. Cunningham, security.

Note: The above couple were married by the Rev. John H. Wingfield, rector of Trinity P. E. Church, Portsmouth, Va.

June 1, 1835—William Vaughn and Miss Mary Hall.

James Hall, security.

June 8, 1835—Elijah Sperry and Miss Mary Ann Sumter.

Thomas Dunbar, security.

Note: The above couple were married the same day by Thomas T. Jones, a local Methodist elder.

June 15, 1835—William P. Hall and Miss Virginia Miners.

Charles S. Holm, security.

June 20, 1835—Thomas D. Toy and Miss A. A. Rogers.

Manuel A. Santos, security.

June 26, 1835—Soloman Hodges and Sarah C. Tatem.

Edward Davis, security.

Note: The above couple were married by the Rev. Jeremiah Hendren.

July 2, 1835—Thomas Ferguson and Ellen Wilson.

John Harvey, security.

July 7, 1835—James Butler and Mary A. Bryant.

Joseph Kelley, security.

July 9, 1835—William Urquhart and Mrs. Margaret Charlton.

Charles Lyne, security.

Note: The above couple were married the Rev. J. D. Mathews.

July 18, 1835—Jordan Robinson and Eliza Ann Barry.

James Barry, security.

July 18, 1835—William New and Ann Eliza Warren.

John Alfriend, security.

Note: The above couple were married the same day by Thomas T. Jones, a local Methodist elder.

August 12, 1835—William Mason and Nancy Balentine.

Joseph Robinson, security.

August 26, 1835—Francis Silva Campos and Miss Corinne Pigeon.

E. Pigeon, security.

August 29, 1835—John Vangover and and Mrs. Ann McLean.

Elias Guy, security.

Note: The above couple were married August 30th by the Rev. J. D. Mathews.

September 2, 1835—Joseph T. A. Boyle and Miss Anna Maria Mc-
Candlish. John T. Saunders, security.
Note: The above couple were married the same day by the Rev. John H. Wingfield, rector of Trinity P. E. Church, Portsmouth, Va. Anna Maria McCandlish
was the daughter of Mary C. McCandlish.

September 21, 1835—Josiah Wills and Miss Margaret M. Walsh.
Aaron Milhado, security.
Note: The above couple were married September 22nd by the Rev. Aleander
Histelberger, pastor of the Norfolk Catholic Congregation. Aaron Milhado, Cath-
erine, Susan and Mary Moran are listed as witnesses. Margaret M. Walsh was the
daughter of Margaret Walsh.

October 1, 1835—James T. Bloodgood and Miss Ellen Bonsal.
Caleb Bonsal, security.
Note: The above couple were married the same day by the Rev. J. D. Mathews.

October 7, 1835—Ebenezer Corby and Miss Susan W. Edwards.
Overton W. Edwards, security.

October 8, 1835—Captain James Holmes and Mrs. Elizabeth Stansbury
Ryan. Alexander M. Cunningham, security.
Note: The above couple were married October 14th by the Rev. Alexander
Histelberger, pastor of the Norfolk Catholic Congregation. Captain Sutton F.
Southgate and Amanda Billups are listed as witnesses.

October 19, 1835—Charles G. Williams and Miss Georgette Augusta Ott.
Mathew Cluff, security.
Note: The above couple were married the same day by the Rev. John H. Wing-
field, rector of Trinity P. E. Church, Portsmouth, Va.

October 19, 1835—Joseph Hall and Miss Mary Ann Warren.
Richard (mark) Jones, security.

October 19, 1835—Joseph C. Addington and Mrs. Frances Dyson.
Arthur Cooper, security.

October 22, 1835—Thomas Eccles and Ananda M. F. Bullock.
Joseph M. Bullock, security.

October 24, 1835—Benjamin W. Bedell and Miss Elizabeth Rolph.
William McEllroy, security.

October 22, 1835—James H. North and Miss Emily Klein.
James Ogilvie, security.
Note: The above couple were married October 28th by the Rev. John H. Wing-
field, rector of Trinity P. E. Church, Portsmouth, Va.

November 9, 1835—Overton W. Edwards and Mrs. Ann O'Neil.
Ebenezer Corby, security.
Note: The above couple were married the same day by the Rev. Alexander
Histelberger, pastor of the Norfolk Catholic Congregation. M. Burk, Mrs. Camm
and Oyson are listed as witnesses.

November 14, 1835—William Dawley and Mary Fuller (free persons of
colour). Ebenezer Bryant, security.

November 21, 1935—John Ball and Fanny Disher.
Levi Wisner, security.
Note: The above couple were married by the Rev. Jeremiah Hendren.

November 23, 1835—Jesse Whitehurst and Miss Sarah Jane Hatton.
Esther Hatton, security.

December 24, 1835—John Dixon and Miss Margaret Ann Walker.
Elias Guy, security.
Note: The above couple were married by the Rev. Jeremiah Hendren.

December 26, 1835—Jacob Sturges and Mrs. Sarah Norris.
John H. Roberts, security.

December 21. 1835—John Ayres and Miss Betsy Ann Capps.

Thomas Braithwaite, security.

Note: The above couple were married December 24th by the Rev. William A. Smith (Methodist).

December 30, 1835—Henry B. Bagnall and Miss Sarah H. Vaughn.

William Selden, security.

Note: The above couple were married the same day by the Rev. John H. Wingfield, rector of Trinity P. E. Church, Portsmouth, Va.

December 31, 1835—John Lockley and Martha Murray (free persons of colour).

Mitchell Hall, security.

1836

January 4, 1836—Thomas C. Bissell and Miss Mary Ann L. Frith.

William R. Bissell, security.

Note: The above couple were married January 6th by the Rev. J. D. Mathews.

January 16, 1836—James Gray and Jane J. Jones.

James Doland, security.

January 16, 1836—William Thompson and Miss Mary Ann Hermoine.

Thomas (mark) Benston, security.

Note: The above couple were married the same day by Thomas T. Jones, a local Methodist elder.

January 26, 1836—Richard M. Bagnall and Miss Maria M. Nimmo.

Aaron Milhado, security.

Note: Maria M. Nimmo was the daughter of Mary Ann Nimmo.

January 26, 1836—John Ashcroft and Mrs. Susan Lawrence (widow).

Thomas Archer, security.

Note: The above couple were married the same day by the Rev. John H. Wingfield, rector of Trinity P. E. Church, Portsmouth, Va.

January 28, 1836—James Williamson and Mrs. Adeline W. Denby.

William D. Delany, security.

February 1, 1836—Henry B. Reardon and Miss Eliza B. Manning.

Edward Fitzgerald, security.

Note: The above couple were married February 2nd by the Rev. Alexander Histelberger, pastor of the Norfolk Catholic Congregation. W. DeLacy, J. M. Smith and Mary Fitzgerald are listed as witnesses.

February 1, 1836—Joseph C. Addington, Jr., and Miss Virginia Harwood.

William H. Addington, security.

Note: The above couple were married the same day by the Rev. William A. Smith (Methodist).

February 1, 1836—Patrick Russell and Miss Adeline Dey.

John N. Hall, security.

Note: The above couple were married February 2nd by the Rev. Alexander Histelberger, pastor of the Norfolk Catholic Congregation. John Hall and Miss Virginia Keele are listed as witnesses. Adeline Dey was the daughter of Sarah W. Brunett.

February 9, 1836—John Lindsay and Miss Susanna Dosson.

John Bowles, security.

February 15, 1835—Zacharia Smith and Mrs. Charlotte Murphy (widow).

Jeremiah M. Huntington, security.

March 1, 1836—George Groner and Mrs. Elizabeth M. Coxell.

Valentine Lomb, security.

March 2, 1836—Robert J. Weston and Miss Ann Eliza Benthall.

Nathaniel McCoy, security.

March 5, 1836—Thomas Hughlett and Miss Lucy L. Edwards.
William Lee Edwards, security.
March 5, 1836—John Gardner and Mrs. Ann Eliza Wheeler.
David Caddis, security.
Note: The above couple were married the same day by Thomas T. Jones, a local Methodist elder.
March 17, 1836—Lewis A. Bianchini and Miss Martha Ann Moss.
Francis S. Campos, security.
March 17, 1836—Ralph Lawrence and Mrs. Caroline Johnson (widow).
Daniel Smith, security.
March 19, 1836—Mathew Boney Crandle and Miss Mary Ann S. Mitchell.
Shelburn Mahone, security.
March 21, 1836—Hezekiah Smith and Miss Eliza Ann Bucknam.
Michael Griffin, security.
Note: Eliza Ann Bucknam was the daughter of Joses Bucknam.
March 23, 1836—Nicholas O. Thompson and Miss Lucy Ann Barnes.
Shelburn Mahone, security.
March 29, 1836—Godfrey Dowdy and Miss Eliza Isham.
John Fisher, security.
March 30, 1836—Richard Taylor and Miss Harriet Strong.
William Anderson, security.
Note: The above couple were married by the Rev. D. L. Doggitt.
April 11, 1836—Major Maclanan and Mrs. Elizabeth Heath.
Smith Capps, security.
April 15, 1836—Horatio Cornick and Miss Eliza W. B. Hunter.
James Cornick, security.
April 27, 1836—Nathaniel McCoy and Miss Elizabeth Brown.
Lemuel (mark) Fentress, security.
May 9, 1836—Stephen C. Weston and Miss Sarah Frances Ferebee.
Note: The above couple were married May 12th by the Rev. J. D. Mathews. Elizabeth H. Clarke was the daughter of Alexander Clarke, Sr., the security.
May 10, 1836—Cincinatus W. Newton and Miss Martha T. Newton.
John Williams, security.
Note: The above couple were married May 11th by the Rev. John H. Wingfield, rector of Trinity P. E. Church, Portsmouth, Va.
May 10, 1836—Gaston C. Lecompte and Miss Mary Hartshorn.
Sylvanus Hartshorn, security.
Note: The above couple were married the same day by the Rev. J. D. Mathews. Mary Hartshorn was the daughter of Sylvanus Hartshorn, the security.
May 11, 1836—James Smiley and Miss Elizabeth H. Clarke.
Alexander Clarke, Sr., security.
May 14, 1836—Crowther Morton and Mrs. Mary Poiner.
John Hicks, security.
Note: The above couple were married May 15th by the Rev. J. D. Mathews.
May 26, 1836—William Fugitt and Miss Jane Dosson.
John Williamson, security.
Note: The above couple were married by the Rev. D. L. Doggitt.
June 6, 1836—Thomas Franklin and Miss Elizabeth Jones.
John (mark) Dexter, security.
July 1, 1836—William M. Bigelow and Miss Margaret C. Dye.
Edward J. Kilgrove, security.
Note: The above couple were married by the Rev. D. L. Doggitt.

July 9, 1836—Otaway H. Berryman and Miss Sarah Frances Hipkins.
John Dickson, security.
Note: The above couple were married July 10th (Sunday) by the Rev. William V. Bowers.

July 13, 1836—Joseph Lawrence and Mrs. Mary Warburton.
Charles B. Kelly, security.

July 14, 1836—James Farmer and Miss Ann Murray.
John Odenhal, security.
Note: The above couple were married by the Rev. D. L. Doggitt.

July 28, 1836—Samuel H. Revel and Miss Isabella Hardy.
G. Harvey, security.

July 30, 1836—William A. Tufts and Miss Martha M. Tabb.
Thomas C. Tabb, security.

August 3, 1836—George W. Camp and Miss Elizabeth B. Armistead.
Samuel Barron, security.
Note: The above couple were married the same day by the Rev. M. P. Parks, rector of Christ P. E. Church.

August 6, 1836—Thomas Freeman Boothby and Miss Eunice Avery.
Joseph T. Allyn, security.
Note: The above couple were married August 7th by the Rev. J. D. Mathews.

August 16, 1836—Samuel Wheeler and Miss Mary Ann McKnight.
Lloyd Wright, security.

August 24, 1836—William H. Barrett and Miss Elizabeth Hay.
Thomas Dunbar, security.

September 1, 1836—Charles Evans and Miss Susan White.
Edward (mark) Valentine, security.

September 16, 1836—Nathaniel Hill and Miss Mary Whitehurst.
William Henley, security.

September 19, 1836—Mr. William Roberts and Miss Anzoletta Kempe.
Note: There is no bond for the above marriage in the files of the Corporation Court. It was copied from the returns of the Rev. M. P. Parks, rector of Christ P. E. Church.

September 20, 1836—George Knoller and Mrs. Mary Lee.
Miles S. Cox, security.

September 22, 1836—William S. Wright and Miss Susan V. Lee.
Samuel L. Lightfoot, security.
Note: The above couple were married the same day by the Rev. M. P. Parks, rector of Christ P. E. Church. Susan V. Lee was the daughter of Ann L. Lee.

September 30, 1836—Edward J. Kilgrove and Miss Sarah Grimes.
Josiah Grimes, security.

October 5, 1836—Isaac Rose and Mrs. Adeline Murray (widow).
Thomas B. White, security.
Note: The above couple were married the same day by the Rev. M. P. Parks, rector of Christ P. E. Church.

October 13, 1836—Aaron Milhado and Miss Mary Ann Hunter.
James F. Hunter, security.

October 15, 1836—Samuel Harwood and Mrs. Eleanor Nickson (widow).
Henry W. Frankland, security.

October 22, 1836—George Watson and Gloriana Maigne.
Joseph C. Maigne, security.
Note: The above couple were married October 23rd by the Rev. J. D. Mathews.

October 29, 1836—Joseph Fontier and Miss Mary Ann Ward.
                                    Augustus Lapelouse, security.
Note: The above couple were married the same day by the Rev. Alexander
Histelberger, pastor of the Norfolk Catholic Congregation. Mr. Bogue and E.
Russel are listed as witnesses.

November 2, 1836—Thomas Griffin and Miss Frances Stone.
                                    Joseph Cannon, security.
November 19, 1836—Richard Walke and Miss Mary D. Talbot.
                                    Isaac Talbot, security.
Note: The above couple were married November 22nd by the Rev. M. P. Parks,
rector of Christ P. E. Church.

November 25, 1836—John Walker and Miss Margaret A. T. Haynes.
                                    Thomas C. Tabb, security.
November 30, 1836—Leroy M. Lee and Miss Virginia Addington.
                                    Joseph C. Addington, security.
Note: The above couple were married by the Rev. D. S. Doggitt. Virginia Ad-
dington was the daughter of Joseph C. Addington, the security.

December 6, 1836—George T. Carraway and Miss Virginia Frances Steed.
                                    James M. Steed, security.
Note: The above couple were married the same day by the Rev. M. P. Parks,
rector of Christ P. E. Church.

December 12, 1836—John O'Brien and Mrs. Sarah Savage.
                                    David Wagan, security.
Note: The above couple were married the same day by the Rev. Alexander
Histelberger, pastor of the Norfolk Catholic Congregation. David Morgan and
Catherine Barry are listed as witnesses.

December 17, 1836—Joseph Hobday and Miss Mary White.
                                    Jesse Brownley, security.
December 19, 1836—Joseph Mary and Miss Margaret Edwards.
                                    James (mark) Howes, security.
December 20, 1836—David Ricks and Hilly Tobias Johnson (free
negroes).   William Haynes, security.
December 26, 1836—William H. Bucknam and Miss Susan W. Henry.
                                    John Henry, security.
Note: The above couple were married the same day by the Rev. M. P. Parks,
rector of Christ P. E. Church.

1837

January 5, 1837—Joseph H. Robertson and Miss Virginia F. G. Taylor.
                                    Thomas L. Robertson, security.
January 5, 1837—Ferdinand Reiger and Miss Charlotte Hafner.
                                    Andrew Schroder, security.
Note: The above couple were married the same day by the Rev. Alexander
Histelberger, pastor of the Norfolk Catholic Congregation. Mr. and Mrs. Harold
are listed as witnesses.

January 10, 1837—Stephen L. Temple and Miss Nancy Bailey.
                                    Samuel Bailey, security.
Note: Nancy Bailey was the daughter of Samuel Bailey, the security.

January 13, 1837—Leonidas L. Smith and Miss Mary E. McPhail.
                                    John McPhail; security.
Note: The above couple were married the same day by the Rev. Arestides S.
Smith.

January 28, 1837—John Hardison and Miss Jane M. Childs.
                                    William W. Childs, security.

February 3, 1837—Jesse Dawley and Sookey (free persons of colour).
Arthur Cooper, security.
February 7, 1837—Robert Cauthorn and Mrs. Elizabeth Hanberry.
George A. Barrom, security.
Note: The above couple were married the same day by the Rev. Joseph S. Baker.
February 8, 1837—John N. Hall and Miss Elizabeth Guy.
Elias Guy, security.
Note: The above couple were married February 9th by the Rev. J. D. Mathews. Elizabeth Guy was the daughter of Elias Guy, the security.
February 8, 1837—Benjamin Harris and Miss Sarah Elizabeth Walters.
James Gordon, Jr., security.
Note: The above couple were married the same day by the Rev. M. P. Parks, rector of Christ P. E. Church. Sarah Elizabeth Walters was the daughter of B. B. Walters.
February 9, 1837—Joseph Coster and Miss Frances Martin.
Joseph Mary, Jr., security.
Note: Frances Martin was the daughter of Nancy Mary, the wife of Joseph Mary, Sr.
February 14, 1837—James F. Henderson and Miss Jane E. Stone.
John Peters, security.
Note: Jane E. Stone was the daughter of Daniel Stone.
February 22, 1837—James House and Miss Mary E. Dawley.
Peter Nelson, security.
March 23, 1837—Thomas Robinson and Susan Crossley.
Hugh (mark) Smith, security.
Note: The above couple were married the same day by the Rev. Joseph T. Baker. Susan Crossley was the daughter of "Eleanor Drummond, late Crossley."
March 28, 137—Richard D. Burruss and Miss Hannah Frances Cake.
James Mitchell, security.
April 4, 1837—William H. Hallet and Miss Eliza Ann Dixon.
Thomas C. Dixon, security.
Note: Eliza Ann Dixon was the daughter of Thomas C. Dixon, the security. The above couple were married the same day by the Rev. J. D. Mathews.
April 5, 1837—William C. Veale and Miss Gertrude F. Stavro.
Robert Brown, security.
Note: The above couple were married April 6th by the Rev. Alexander Histelberger, pastor of the Norfolk Catholic Congregation. Mrs. Maher, Mrs. Barron and Mr. Davis are listed as witnesses. Gertrude F. Stavro was the daughter of Mary Stavro.
April 8, 137—Phillip B. Murdock and Mrs. Margaret Spence.
Henry Snoke, security.
April 14, 1837—John Kelly and Miss Betty Johnson.
Thomas (mark) Ferguson, security.
April 26, 1837—John Spence and Miss Polly Stokes.
John (mark) Knights, security.
April 27, 1837—George (slave of Mr. J. Decormis) and Ann Eliza (slave of Miss Sayer).
Note: There is no bond for the above marriage in the files of the Corporation Court. It was copied from the returns of the Rev. Alexander Histelberger, pastor of the Norfolk Catholic Congregation. J. Scott, Mary Louisa and Rebecca (evidently slaves) are listed as witnesses.
May 4, 1837—Howard Watkins and Mrs. Mary Hughes.
Richard C. Northington, security.
Note: The above couple were married by the Rev. David L. Doggitt.

May 4, 1837—William Manning, Jr., and Miss Catherine Winingder.

Alexander Ryan, security.

Note: The above couple were married the same day by the Rev. Alexander Histelberger, pastor of the Norfolk Catholic Congregation. Lt. Hodges, A. N. Ryan and Elizabeth Frost are listed as witnesses.

May 10, 1837—Thomas H. Williamson and Miss Louisa Garnett.

John Peters, security.

Note: The above couple were married the same day by the Rev. M. P. Parks, rector of Christ P. E. Church. Louisa Garnett was the daughter of William Garnett.

May 12, 1837—Thomas G. Broughton, Jr., and Miss Jane Soutter.

Robert S. Bernard, security.

Note: The above couple were married the same day by the Rev. J. D. Mathews.

May 13, 1837—Mirwin E. Jeffries and Ada Warren (free persons of colour).

John M. Mirwin, security.

May 17, 1837—Henry Snoke and Mrs. Isabella Curtis.

James (mark) House, security.

Note: The above couple were married the same day by the Rev. Joseph L. Baker.

May 22, 1837—Nicholas Devereux and Miss Eliza Ann Russell.

Thomas Archer, security.

Note: The above couple were married the same day by the Rev. Alexander Histelberger, pastor of the Norfolk Catholic Congregation. William Griffin and Mary Wickham are listed as witnesses.

May 25, 1837—William H. Hunter and Miss Eliza Frances Wallace.

William Walke, security.

Note: The above couple were married the same day by the Rev. M. P. Parks, rector of Christ P. E. Church. Eliza Frances Wallace was the daughter of Catherine Portlock.

June 2, 1837—John H. Cole and Miss Ann M. Norton.

George (mark) Cooper, security.

June 7, 1837—John Rawls and Miss Lucy Ann Jackson.

James Jackson, secur,ity.

Note: The above couple were married by the Rev. David L. Doggitt. Lucy Ann Jackson was the daughter of James Jackson, the security.

June 14, 1837—Walter Blake and Miss Ann S. Izard.

Marshall Parks, security.

June 22, 1837—Richard Richardson and Miss Mary Wrightington.

George Wrightington, security.

Note: Mary Wrightington was the daughter of George Wrightington, the security.

July 11, 1837—Joseph Wofford and Sarah Jane Mulhollan.

Bernard Mulhollan, security.

Note: The above couple were married the same day by the Rev. Alexander Histelberger, pastor of the Norfolk Catholic Congregation. Mr. and Mrs. Broughton and Thomas Newton are listed as witnesses.

July 20, 1837—Thomas A. Dornin, U. S. N., and Mrs. Anne M. Thorburn.

Edward T. Dunn, security.

Note: The above couple were married July 26th by the Rev. John H. Wingfield, rector of Trinity P. E. Church, Portsmouth, Va.

August 4, 1837—Edward Lowman and Miss Sophia Skilman.

John (mark) Ellers, security.

Note: The above couple were married August 5th by Thomas T. Jones, a local Methodist elder.

August 9, 1837—John W. Davis and Miss Temperance Ann Harrison.
Aaron Milhado, security.
Note: The above couple were married the same day by the Rev. Joseph L. Baker.
John W. Davis was the son of Charles W. Davis and Temperance Ann Harrison
was the daughter of Catherine Harrison.

August 10, 1837—Bartlett Watts and Anne Eliza Insley (free persons of colour).
David Cary, security.
Note: The above couple were married August 12th by Thomas T. Jones, a local Methodist elder.

August 14, 1837—Frederick W. Jones and Mrs. Mary C. Wildman.
Thomas Eccles, security.
Note: The above couple were married the same day by the Rev. Alexander Histelberger, pastor of the Norfolk Catholic Congregation. Mr. Savier and Miss Lapin are listed as witnesses.

August 15, 1837—Edward W. Moore and Miss Mary A. O. Tabb.
Thomas C. Tabb, security.
Note: The above couple were married by the Rev. David L. Doggitt.

August 17, 1837—John Farmer and Mrs. Lydia Courtney.
Miles Butcher, security.
Note: The above couple were married August 19th by Thomas T. Jones, a local Methodist elder.

August 22, 1837—William S. Forest and Miss Mary J. Constable.
Alexander A. Martin, security.
Note: The above couple were married by the Rev. David L. Doggitt.

September 9, 1837—John Ney and Miss Ann S. Spaulding.
John Spaulding, security.

September 13, 1837—Thomas H. Wellons and Miss Harriet Whiting.
John (mark) Whiting, security.

August 23, 1837—William Brown and Miss Jane Steele.
William Robinson, security.

September 1, 1837—George Cooper and Miss Caroline Miles.
Francis (mark) Ponce, security.

September 30, 1837—A. M. Rockwell and Miss Elizabeth Manning.
William Manning, security.

October 6, 1837—William Spady and Mrs. Nancy Watson.
James Spady, security.
Note: The above couple were married the same day by Thomas T. Jones, a local Methodist elder.

Otcober 7, 1837—Lemuel Fentress and Mrs. Margaret Herrington.
Nathaniel McCoy, security.

October 14, 1837—J. P. Putegnat and Miss Eliza Butt.
William B. Cowan, security.

October 16, 1837—Lewis C. Jordan and Mrs. Charlotte Haward (or Howard)
Charles Jordan, security.
Note: The above couple were married the same day by the Rev. J. D. Mathews.

October 18, 1837—Paul J. Balas and Miss Amy M. Barnes.
John J. Barnes, security.

October 26, 1837—William C. Barnes and Mrs. Sarah Ann Savage.
Samuel Parker, security.

November 1, 1837—Wilson B. Lorey and Miss Pamela A. Delany.
Charles Henley, security.
Note: The above couple were married by the Rev. David L. Doggett. Wilson B. Lorey was the son of N. Lorey and Pamela A. Delany was the daughter of Edward Delany.

November 4, 1837—Daniel D. French and Miss Elizabeth E. Foster.
William F. Foster, security.
Note: The above couple were married November 5th by the Rev. M. P. Parks, rector of Christ P. E. Church.

November 14, 1837—Finlay F. Ferguson and Miss Elizabeth Gibson.
John D. Ghiselin, security.
Note: The above couple were married the same day by the Rev. J. D. Mathews.

November 14, 1837—Robert C. Gwathmey and Miss Emily S. Smith.
John L. Saunders, security.
Note: The above couple were married November 16th by the Aev. M. P. Parks, rector of Christ P. E. Church.

November 20, 1837—James Marsden Smith and Miss Anne W. Williamson.
John G. Williamson, security.
Note: The above couple were married November 21st by the Rev. M. P. Parks rector of Christ P. E. Church.

November 21, 1837—William Titimas and Miss Mary Ann Nunnery.
Henry (mark) Deckerson, security.

November 25, 1837—William E. Stark and Miss Elizabeth W. Wilson.
William E. Cunningham, security.
Note: The above couple were married November 30th by the Rev. Thomas Atkinson, a Protestant Episcopal minister officiating for the Rev. M. P. Parks, rector of Christ P. E. Church.

November 30, 1837—Samuel Veale and Miss Mary Jenkins.
William Pool, security.
Note: The above couple were married by the Rev. David L. Doggett.

November 30, 1837—Nathaniel Nash and Miss Frances Martin.
Alexander A. Martin, security.
Note: The above couple were married by the Rev. David L. Doggett.

December 6, 1837—Joseph Kelly and Mrs. Elizabeth Vail.
George Hammond, security.

December 7, 1837—Joseph P. Fernandez and Miss Nancy Manning.
William Leeman, security.

December 7, 1837—James Shannahan and Miss Elizabeth Dunlavy.
James Watters, security.
Note: The above couple were married by the Rev. David L. Doggett.

December 9, 1837—James L. Le Compte and Miss Anna Werckmuller.
H. T. Werckmuller, security.

December 11, 1837—Nathaniel B. Peed and Miss Mary Jane Winslow.
Nathaniel Currier, security.
Note: The above couple were married by the Rev. David L. Doggitt.

December 20, 1837—James Spady and Miss Margaret Melson.
William (mark) Spady, security.
Note: The above couple were married the same day by Thomas T. Jones, a local Methodist elder.

December 21, 1837—Samuel Wallace and Miss Mary Ann Crossley.
Eleanor Drummond, security.
Note: Mary Ann Crossley was the daughter of Eleanor Drummond, the security, "late Crossley."

December 23, 1837—Francis O. Robertson and Miss Caroline T. Lee.
Samuel S. Lightfoot, security.
Note: The above couple were married December 24th by the Rev. M. P. Parks, rector of Christ P. E. Church.

December 26, 1837—John S. Charles and Miss Mary A. Busby.
John W. Keeling, security.
Note: The above couple were married by the Rev. David L. Doggett.

December 28, 1837—William Smith and Mrs. Virginia A. Carlotte.
William Armstrong, security.

1838

January 1, 1838—Hartwell J. Chandler and Miss Martha A. G. Hendren.
Jeremiah Hendren, security.
January 3, 1838—John McMahon and Mrs. Mary Bullifunt.
Charles (mark) Evans, security.
January 10, 1838—Samuel Hall and Miss Margaret Hynd.
James Hynd, security.
Note: Margaret Hynd was the daughter of James Hynd, the security.
January 11, 183—Abel Davis and Miss Eliza Whitehurst.
Francis Butt, Jr., security.
January 29, 1838—Joseph Tatem and Miss H. F. Douglas.
Cary Fentress, security.
February 3, 1838—Levi Anderson and Mrs. Susan Stroud.
Smith Capps, security.
March 1, 1838—Reuben B. Moody and Miss Mary Ann Goodson.
Edward J. Kilgrove, security.
February 7, 1838—Josiah Nelson and Miss Elizabeth Manning.
Joseph Decormis, security.
February 10, 1838—Jesse W. Duxey and Miss Rebecca F. Alford.
Benjamin W. Alford, security.
March 7, 1837—John LeRoy Berry and Miss Ann Eliza Addington.
Joseph C. Addington, security.
Note: Ann Eliza Addington was the daughter of Joseph C. Addington, the security.
March 26, 1838—John Fitzhugh and Miss Margaret Simmons.
Charles L. Holm, security.
Note: Margaret Simmons was the daughter of Jacamine Simmons.
April 5, 1838—Michael Moran and Mrs. Isabella Snokes.
Thomas Etheredge, security.
Note: The above couple were married the same day by Thomas T. Jones, a local Methodist elder.
April 16, 1838—Lewis Dutton and Miss Jane Cooper.
Nathaniel Currier, security.
Note: The above couple were married the same day by Thomas T. Jones, a local Methodist elder.
April 26, 1838—Abraham Mace and Miss Mahaly Dawley.
William W. Dawley, security.
May 4, 1838—William E. Douglas and Miss Elizabeth Wicker.
Joshua B. Swain, security.
May 7, 1838—James King and Miss Catherine Holt.
William Holt, security.
May 8, 1838—Charles H. Beale and Miss Maria Harwood.
Thomas G. Clinton, security.
May 12, 138—James Montgomery and Eliza Morey.
William W. Dawley, security.
May 21, 1838—William Weidemeyer and Miss Eliza Murphy.
Mary Murphy, security.
Note: Eliza Murphy was the daughter of Mary Murphy, the security.

May 29, 1838—George Bottirell and Miss Mary Perguson (or Ferguson).
George Smith, security.
June 1, 1838—John Benston and Miss Harriet Durfey.
Henry (mark) Bolton, security.
June 4, 1838—Lieutenant John R. Tucker and Miss Virginia Webb.
J. E. Duncan, security.
Note: Miss Virginia Webb was the daughter of Thomas F. Webb.
June 8, 1838—Thomas G. Clayton and Miss Virginia Bailey.
Robert B. Thompson, security.
June 14, 1838—Alexander Jarrot and Nancy Fuller (free persons of
colour).
John (mark) Fuller, security.
Note: The above couple were married the same day by Thomas T. Jones, a local
Methodist elder.
June 19, 1838—Henry Brock and Miss Eliza J. Spratley.
Joseph Bunkley, security.
June 26, 1838—Peter Fuller and Nancy Harrison (free persons of colour).
Thomas C. Moore, security.
June 29, 1838—Joseph P. Anderson and Miss Margaret S. Redmon.
James Baker, security.
July 2, 1838—Thomas Butler and Miss Christian A. R. Foreman.
George W. Colier, security.
Note: The above couple were married the same day by Thomas T. Jones, a local
Methodist elder.
July 10, 1838—John A. Bixby and Mrs. Eliza Ann Smith.
Joses Bucknam, security.
Note: The above couple were married the same day by the Rev. John D.
Mathews.
July 12, 1838—Ezekiel Hinton and Miss Laurena Dawley.
John (mark) Roberts, security.
Note: The above couple were married the same day by Thomas T. Jones, a local
Methodist elder.
July 23, 1838—Gabriel Haneck and Mrs. Amelia Langley.
Samuel J. Wheeler, security.
August 11, 1838—Henry Harris and Elizabeth Itchings.
James (mark) Oase, security.
August 8, 1838—William P. Burnham and Miss Anna Maria Moore.
William B. Davidson, security.
August 14, 1838—Thomas Shaw and Miss Mary C. Clarke.
Thomas Chaney, security.
Note: The above couple were married the same day by Thomas T. Jones, a local
Methodist elder.
August 16, 1838—John Starr and Miss Lucretia Simpson.
John Drewer, security.
August 22, 1838—Joseph Ferrat and Miss Catherine Geay.
Peter Geay, security.
Note: Catherine Geay was the daughter of Peter Geay, the security.
August 28, 1838—John J. Thompkins and Miss Mary L. Broughton.
John Hardison, security.
September 1, 1838—Jesse Smith and Miss Elizabeth Mason.
Elizabeth (mark) Mason, security.
Note: Elizabeth Mason was the daughter of Elizabeth Mason, the security.
September 15, 1838—Jackson L. Ray and Miss Mary West.
John Henington, security.

October 1, 1838—Harmon Hanor and Mrs. Elizabeth Oldner.
Francis (mark) Thorowgood, security.

Note: The above couple were married the same day by the Rev. George W. Nolley.

October 6, 1838—John A. McDowell and Mrs. Eleanor Drummond.
John P. Geoffroy, security.

October 15, 1838—Charles K. King and Miss Erin C. Moran.
James Francis, security.

Note: The above couple were married October 16th by the Rev. Alexander Histelberger, pastor of the Norfolk Catholic Congregation. Miles King, E. Reilly and Mary Fitzgerald are listed as witnesses.

October 15, 1838—Henry Handy and Mrs. Isabella Disher.
John Parker, security.

Note: The above couple were married the same day by Thomas T. Jones, a local Methodist elder.

October 18, 1838—William Archer and Miss Mary Diana Denby.
William Denby, security.

Note: Mary Diana Denby was the daughter of William Denby, the security.

October 27, 1838—Josiah Dobbs and Miss Christiana Whitehurst.
James Heath, security.

November 1, 1838—Eleazer Stillman and Miss Adelia Manning.
Isaac Warren, security.

November 5, 1838—James Snyder and Miss Margaret F. Spence.
David Bell, security.

November 7, 1838—John C. Henley and Miss Margaret Ose.
Thomas Haughton, security.

November 8, 1838—John Billups and Miss Susan Eddins.
John Morris, security.

Note: The above couple were married the same day by the Rev. John Morris (Methodist).

December 1, 1838—Philip H. Masi and Miss Helena M. Werkmuller.
James Gordon, Jr., security.

Note: The above couple were married December 2nd by the Rex. Alexander Histelberger, pastor of the Norfolk Catholic Congregation. Dr. Andrews and Eliose Lepage are listed as witnesses.

December 1, 1838—Timothy Kirk and Miss Nancy C. Swain.
James Jackson, security.

Note: The above couple were married December 4th by the Rev. Alexander Histelberger, pastor of the Norfolk Catholic Congregation. William Whitlock and E. Fisher are listed as witnesses.

December 10, 1838—Godlip Mayer and Miss Louisa J. Henry.
John Henry, security.

Note: The above couple were married the same day by the Rev. John D. Mathews. Louisa J. Henry was the daughter of John Henry, the security.

November 19, 1838—Jacob B. Dunston and Miss Mary H. Pray.
John Dunston, security.

December 1, 1838—Nathaniel Palmer and Mrs. Mary F. Savage.
Andrew D. Wattles, security.

December 17, 1838—David Dey and Mrs. Mary Dameron.
William Dey, security.

December 22, 1838—James B. Murphey and Miss Margaret Oakham.
William N. McDole, security.

December 24, 1838—Henry Moore and Miss Ann W. Vickery.
Jacob Vickery, security.

1839

January 25, 1839—William McDole and Miss Pamelia Puzey.

Jesse Jones, security.

January 26, 1839—Benjamin Murphy and Miss Virginia Clarke.

John A. Edwards, security.

January 30, 1839—John Nelson and Mrs. Sarah Wilkinson.

William Tatem, security.

February 6, 1839—Richard Doyle and Miss Mary Quinn.

Richard Rowan (or Rohan), security.

Note: The above couple were married February 7th by the Rev. Alexander Histelberger, pastor of the Norfolk Catholic Congregation. Mrs. Quinn, Mr. Commons and Mrs. Langan are listed as witnesses.

March 29, 1839—Edwin L. Ferris and Mrs. Pennie Cretia.

George Barrows, security.

February 12, 1839—Thomas Reilly and Miss Harriet Webb.

John E. Doyle, security.

Note: Harriet Webb was the daughter of Thomas T. Webb.

January 23, 1839—Thomas Fisher and Miss Virginia Stott.

Thomas (mark) White, security.

Note: Virginia Stott was the daughter of Sukey Stott.

January 23, 1839—John Murphy and Mrs. Jane Woodhouse.

James Murphy, security.

February 27, 1839—William Beane and Miss Susan Belote.

William Garnett, security.

March 18, 1839—William H. Hyson and Mrs. Mary Nicholson.

Harmon Hanor, security.

Note: The above couple were married the same day by the Rev. George W. Nolley.

April 2, 1839—Edward P. Tabb and Miss Anne Elizabeth Robertson.

Joseph H. Robertson, security.

Note: Anna Eliza Robertson was the daughter of Helen Robertson.

April 4, 1839—John S. Holmes and Miss Mary Eliza Hendren.

John Ridley, security.

Note: Miss Mary Eliza Hendren was the daughter of Jeremiah Hendren.

April 8, 1839—John Hipkins and Miss Matilda Hutchings.

George Reid, Jr., security.

Note: Matilda Hutchings was the daughter of Martha Hutchings.

April 11, 1839—George W. Munson and Miss Ann E. Angell.

N. S. Angell, security.

Note: Ann E. Angell was the daughter of N. S. Angell, the security.

April 24, 1839—Walter de Lacy and Miss Catherine A. D. Moran.

William Moseley, security.

Note: The above couple were married April 25th by the Rev. Alexander Histelberger, pastor of the Norfolk Catholic Congregation. Drs. Moseley and Santos and Susan Moran are listed as witnesses.

May 1, 1839—Thomas Franklin and Mrs. Elizabeth Myers.

Andrew Anderson, security.

May 1, 1839—Ebenezer Thompson and Miss Sarah Ann Bassett.

John Adams, security.

Note: Sarah Ann Bassett was the daughter of Sarah Adams.

May 31, 1839—William Maxwell and Miss Mary F. Robertson.

Cornelius K. Stribling, security.

July 6, 1839—James Barden and Miss Mary Frances Crosby.

John Quinn, security.

Note: The above couple were married the same day by the Rev. Alexander Histelberger, pastor of the Norfolk Catholic Congregation. Mrs. Fisher and J. Quinn are listed as witnesses.

July 6, 1839—Samuel Owen and Mrs. Rachel Busky.

James Mason, security.

July 9, 1839—John Joseph Anderson and Mrs. Amanda Brooks.

John Powers, security.

July 10, 1839—Richard Rohan and Miss Eliza Cooper.

John Quinn, security.

Note: The above couple were married the same day by the Rev. Alexander Histelberger, pastor of the Norfolk Catholic Congregation. Mr. Cooper and Mrs. Stavro are listed as witnesses.

July 10, 1839—Charles H. Rowland and Miss Mary W. Sharp.

George W. Camp, security.

July 13, 1839—John Woodward and Miss Frances Flanagan.

Moses Shipp, security.

July 20, 1839—Simon Stone and Miss Amelia White.

George H. Pierce, security.

August 1, 1839—James Cornick and Mrs. Clarissa B. Scott.

John Williams, security.

August 29, 1839—Robert J. Barrot and Miss Lydia L. Flanagan.

John Woodward, security.

September 2, 1839—Abraham Kimball and Miss Fanny Clarke.

Mary Short, security.

September 2, 1839—James L. Henderson and Miss Sarah Williamson.

Charles McIntosh, security.

Note: Sarah Williamson was the daughter of Thomas Williamson.

September 5, 1839—Hugh McDonald and Mrs. Mary Measels (widow).

Richard Nunan, security.

September 12, 1839—David Lawrence and Mrs. Margaret Ames.

William W. Delastatious, security.

September 17, 1839—John D. Brown and Miss Mary V. Manning.

Peter Wagner, security.

Note: Mary V. Manning was the daughter of Elizabeth Melvin.

October 3, 1839—James H. Merton and Miss Eliza Ann Binns.

John Carlon, security.

October 8, 1839—William W. Spence and Miss Mary A. C. Winkley.

George Reid, security.

Note: The above couple were married the same day by the Rev. John D. Mathews.

October 7, 1839—William Roberts and Miss Elizabeth Ferebe.

John Petty, security.

Note: The above couple were married October 8th by the Rev. John D. Mathews.

October 12, 1839—Francis Lacoste and Miss Matilda Smith.

Rose Frank, security.

October 14, 1839—Henry Bright and Miss Harriet White.

William Williams, security.

October 17, 1839—William V. Robertson and Miss Mary Ann Rhea.

Daniel Rhea, Jr., security.

Note: Mary Ann Rhea was the daughter of Daniel Rhea, Sr.

October 23, 1839—Carter L. Pearman and Miss Martha P. Owin.

Charles E. Owin, security.

Note: Martha P. Owin was the daughter of Charles E. Owin, the security.

October 31, 1839—Thomas Eldridge and Mrs. Elizabeth Hale.

C. Hiram Moon, security.

October 31, 1839—Dr. Armistead T. M. Cooke and Miss Margaret Hoggard.

Mordecai Cooke, Jr., security.

Note: The above couple were married the same day by the Rev. John H. Wingfield, rector of Trinity P. E. Church, Portsmouth, Va.

November 2, 1839—Richard Evans and Miss Jane M. Bissell.

Benjamin Bissell, security.

Note: The above couple were married the same day by the Rev. John David Mathews.

November 5, 1839—Thomas G. Baylor and Miss Margaret E. Cooke.

Richard G. Baylor, security.

Note: Margaret E. Cooke was the daughter of Giles B. Cooke.

November 11, 1839—Antonio Silvia and Mrs. Martha Ahern.

Francis (mark) Lewis, security.

November 12, 1839—Hiram Moon and Mrs. Christine Allen.

Thomas Eldridge, security.

November 13, 1839—James B. Burns and Miss Mary Ann Hedman.

Charles Ray, security.

Note: The above couple were married the same day by the Rev. John David Mathews.

November 28, 1839—David Wright and Miss Mary Ann Lewis.

Thomas M. Martin, security.

December 2, 1839—George Warner and Miss Susan Goulder.

George Mervine, security.

December 7, 1839—William A. Lowell and Miss Esther A. Ricardo.

Henry H. Dentzell, security.

Note: The above couple were married the same day by the Rev. George W. Nolley.

December 14, 1839—P. P. Learned and Miss Virginia S. Davis.

William Davis, security.

Note: The above couple were married December 15th by the Rev. John David Mathews.

December 26, 1839—John R. Knewstep and Mrs. Mary Kempe.

Robert H. Burton, security.

1840

January 2, 1840—William W. Davis and Miss Eliza Ann Pendred.

Francis Butt,, Jr., security.

January 2, 1840—John A. Fisher and Miss Margaret Shroeder.

John M. Wolfe, security.

January 10, 1840—Mark Beaumont and Mrs. Mary Ann Miles.

James (mark) Moffatt, security.

January 9, 1840—Lewis Jones and Mrs. Elizabeth Parsons.

William H. Edwards, security.

January 17, 1840—Benjamin Benson and Pricilla Durfey.

William R. Floyd, security.

January 18, 1840—Henry W. Bleeker and Harriet J. Williams.

John Jones, security.

January 30, 1840—Edward Scribner and Miss Louisa Lumsden.
David W. Glass, security.
Note: The above couple were married the same day by the Rev. Alexander Histelberger, pastor of the Norfolk Catholic Congregation. John Quinn, R. Doyle, and E. Fisher are listed as witnesses.
January 30, 1840—John M. Pullen and Miss Margaret Herman (or Harman).
Joseph Wright, security.
Note: The above couple were married the same day by the Rev. George W. Nolley.
February 4, 1840—Nicholas Doley and Mrs. Ann Eliza Gardner.
Thomas (mark) Smith, security.
February 12, 1840—Ralph G. Parsons and Miss Mary E. Holt.
William Holt, security.
February 20, 1840—Samuel Erskine and Mrs. Catherine Keeffee.
Hugh Keiger, security.
February 25, 1840—Frederick W. Southgate and Miss Angelina E. Dickson.
William E. Cunningham, security.
February 25, 1840—Peter S. March and Miss Laura M. Ott.
Charles G. Williams, security.
February 28, 1840—Wilson Bute (or Butt) and Eliza Ann Hawkins.
Jeremiah Hendren, security.
March 31, 1840—George E. Brooke and Miss Eliza Jordan.
Joseph C. Maigne, security.
Note: The above couple were married April 1st by the Rev. J. D. Mathews.
April 4, 1840—Steward Whitehurst and Miss Eliza Hebden.
Robert (mark) Cain, security.
April 7, 1840—Thomas A. Dawley and Miss Mary A. Chase.
Richard (mark) Chase, security.
Note: The above couple were married the same day by Thomas T. Jones, a local Methodist elder.
April 30, 1840—Thomas Penny and Miss Charlotte Smith.
David W. Glass, security.
May 6, 1840—William H. Lockwood and Miss Sarah A. Ballance.
Elkaner Ballance, security.
Note: The above couple were married the same day by the Rev. Joseph B. Breed. Sarah A. Ballance was the daughter of Elkaner Ballance.
May 7, 1840—Ryland Capps and Melissa M. Henley.
Charles Henley, security.
Note: The above couple were married in Northampton County by the Rev. Thomas Taylor.
May 7, 1840—James C. Ewell and Sarah A. Williams.
Ryland Capps, security.
Note: Sarah A. Williams was the daughter of Sarah Williams.
May 11, 1840—James Woodhouse (of Petersburg) and Miss Susan Gilbert Harwood.
Joseph Nash, security.
Note: Susan Gilbert Harwood was the daughter of Susan H. Harwood.
May 12, 1840—William S. Camp and Miss Heloise Lepage.
Aaron Milhado, security.
May 21, 1840—Darrell Darby and Miss Charlotte O. Garnett.
William H. Garnett, security.
May 30, 1840—Henry Reed and Miss Martha Bright.
S. Mahone, security.
Note: The above couple were married June 2nd by the Rev. Joseph B. Breed.

May 4, 1840—William McCloud and Miss Ann Etheridge.

Thomas Etheridge, security.

Note: The above couple were married the same day by Thomas T. Jones, a local Methodist elder.

June 11, 1840—Robert M. Bain and Miss Mary A. Sively.

John Hope, security.

June 25, 1840—Thomas M. Martin and Miss Jane Lewis.

William B. Fugitt, security.

July 1, 1840—William A. T. Fleming and Miss Diodemia F. G. Henley.

William Henley, security.

Note: Diodemia F. G. Henley was the daughter of William Henley, the security.

July 16, 1840—Robert Addison and Elizabeth Buskey.

George Wood, security.

August 12, 1840—Benjamin Pollard and Mrs. Eliza B. Vickery.

William Loyall, security.

August 12, 1840—Edward Hampton and Catherine (free persons of colour).

James Gilbert, security.

August 12, 1840—Edward P. Irish and Miss Elizabeth Harris.

John Thomas, security.

August 12, 1840—Manuel De Murchia and Miss Frances M. Vincent.

Nicholas Beauclair, security.

Note: The above couple were married August 16th by the Rev. Alexander Histelberger, pastor of the Norfolk Catholic Congregation. Mr. and Mrs. Beuclair and Mrs. Fitzgerald are listed as witnesses. Francis M. Vincent was the adopted daughter of Nicholas Beauclair.

August 13, 1840—James Jackson and Miss Hannah T. Angell.

N. S. Angell, security.

Note: Hannah T. Angell was the daughter of N. S. Angell the security.

August 18, 1840—Thomas Stout and Miss Mary S. Dixon.

Thomas B. Dixon, security.

Note: Mary S. Dixon was the daughter of Thomas B. Dixon, the security.

August 18, 1840—John F. Thorowgood and Miss Mary R. Fentress.

Cary Fentress, security.

Note: The above couple were married the same day by the Rev. John David Mathews. Mary R. Fentress was the orphan of Lovitt Fentress.

September 2, 1840—John E. Simpson and Miss Virginia Hope.

George Kerby, security.

Note: Virginia Hope was the daughter of John Hope. The above couple were married September 3rd by the Rev. Joseph B. Breed.

October 1, 1840—John W. Green and Miss Martha F. Winslow.

William Winslow, security.

Note: Martha F. Winslow was the daughter of Rachel Winslow.

October 1, 1840—William E. Clarke and Miss Rebecca Raincock.

Samuel W. Paul, security.

Note: Rebecca Raincock was the daughter of George Raincock.

October 6, 1840—Charles H. Sheild and Miss Mary D. Watson.

John Williams, security.

October 14, 1840—George W. Cowdery and Miss Emily Southgate.

William E. Cunningham, security.

Note: Emily Southgate was the daughter of John Southgate.

October 27, 1840—John Gaylard and Miss Sarah A. Whitlock.

Robert Brown, security.

Note: The above couple were married the same day by the Rev. Alexander Histelberger, pastor of the Norfolk Catholic Congregation. Dr. Simmons and Mrs. Veale ar listed as witnesses.

November 4, 1840—George Cross and Mrs. Elizabeth Kelly.
Isaac (mark) Warren, security.
November 6, 1840—James Kelly and Miss Penny Spruel.
Thomas (mark) Benston, security.
November 7, 1840—John W. Weston and Miss Caroline Smith.
James Kelly, security.
November 7, 1840—George Krafft and Mrs. Wilhelmina Mayer.
Louis Graenacher, security.
November 9, 1840—William Robinson and Miss Alice O. Jennings.
N. Whiting, security.
November 16, 1840—Lorenzo Parsons and Ann W. Land.
Enoch Land, security.
Note: Ann W. Land was the daughter of Enoch Land, the security.
November 19, 1840—William Thomas Voss and Miss Harriet A. Sykes.
Francis H. Browne, security.
November 23, 1840—James D. Johnson and Miss Martha Everard Parker.
Nicholas Wilson Parker, security.
Note: Martha Everard Parker was the daughter of Copeland and Diana Robinson
(Hall) Parker, and the half-sister of the security.
November 28, 1840—Thomas Jennings and Miss Rachel Chives.
Edmund P. James, security.
November 30, 1840—Jacob B. Morse and Miss Mary Ann Southgate.
Walter Herron Taylor, security.
Note: Mary Ann Southgate was the daughter of John Southgate.
December 10, 1840—George W. Codwise and Mrs. Carolina Virginia Byrd.
George Wilson, security.
December 11, 1840—William H. Wells (or Wills) and Miss Elizabeth
Ann Simpson   John E. Simpson, security.
Note: The above couple were married December 12th by the Rev. Joseph B.
Breed.
December 14, 1840—James Sclater and Miss Jane Haskins.
Miles Cary, security.
Note: The above couple were married December 15th by the Rev. Joseph B.
Breed.
December 18, 1840—William V. Montague and Mrs. Esther Hatton.
Jeremiah Hendren, security.
December 21, 1840—George Bramble and Miss Margaret W. Beale.
John Williams, security.
December 23, 1840—David Hathaway and Miss Sarah Robinson.
James L. Hathaway, security.
Note: The above couple were married December 24th by Thomas T. Jones, a
local Methodist elder. Sarah Robinson was the daughter of Mary Hutchings.

1841

January 6, 1841—William B. Wood and Miss Elizabeth Small.
William Wood, security.
Note: The above couple were married the same day by the Rev. Joseph B.
Breed.
January 14, 1841—James W. Gibbons and Miss Catherine Flynn.
Henry Tudor, security.
Note: The above couple were married the same day by the Rev. Joseph B.
Breed.

January 14, 1841—William Smelly and Miss Eliza Disher.

James Dennis, security.

Note: The above couple were married January 15th by the Rev. Joseph H. Breed.

January 26, 1841—Willoughby Nichols and Miss Eliza Webb.

Samuel Williamson, security.

January 26, 1841—Peter Brown and Miss Margaret Sickles.

Philip Palmer, security.

Note: Margaret Sickles was the daughter of Elizabeth Sickles.

January 26, 1841—John Allen and Mrs. Frances Stone.

Edmund (mark) Foster, security.

January 30, 1841—Thomas Lowery and Miss Sarah Ann Shreives.

Timothy B. Scott, security.

February 1, 1841—William Stevens and Miss Ann E. R. Burnham.

John Ridley, security.

Note: The above couple were married the same day by the Rev. Joseph B. Breed.

February 10, 1841—Russell Bell and Miss Mary Elizabeth Herman.

Charles K. King, security.

Note: The above couple were married the same day by the Rev. Thomas Crowder, Jr. Elizabeth Herman was the daughter of Henry Herman.

February 10, 1841—James Sweeney and Miss Elizabeth A. Fatherly.

Thomas (mark) Fartherly, security.

Note: Elizabeth A. Fartherly was the daughter of Ann Fartherly.

February 15, 1841—Peter Moore and Mrs. Sarah Kinsley.

Edmund (mark) Foster, security.

February 23, 1841—Wilson W. Williams and Miss Agnes Needham.

John Jones, security.

Note: The above couple were married the same day by the Rev. Joseph B. Breed. Agnes Needham was the daughter of Joseph Needham, decd., of Elizabeth City County.

February 24, 1841—William Spangler and Miss Amanda T. Hopkins.

Isaac Spangler, security.

March 3, 1841—William Smith and Mrs. Louisa Beauchamp.

William H. Edwards, security.

March 4, 1841—John O. Butler and Miss Frances C. Smith.

Soloman W. Smith, security.

Note: The above couple were married the same day by the Rev. John David Mathews.

March 4, 1841—John H. Sale and Miss Lucy L. Frost.

J. B. Minton, security.

Note: The above couple were married the same day by the Rev. John David Mathews.

March 17, 1841—Caleb W. Litchfield and Miss Elizabeth Fisher.

Richard B. Fisher, security.

Note: The above couple were married the same day by the Rev. Thomas Crowder, Jr. Elizabeth Fisher was the daughter of Richard B. Fisher, the security.

March 18, 1841—James Barcraft and Mrs. Margaret A. Spady.

Edmund P. James, security.

March 19, 1841—John Harding and Miss Frances Lovett.

Robert Allen, security.

Note: The above couple were married the same day by the Rev. Thomas Crowder, Jr.

March 26, 1841—William C. Barnes and Miss Lydia Ann Bailey.
William Beane, security.

Note: The above couple were married the same day by the Rev. Thomas Crowder, Jr.

March 31, 1841—Lewis Smith and Miss Martha Martain.
Gibson P. Ellis, security.

Note: The above couple were married the same day by the Rev. Joseph B. Breed.

April 3, 1841—Robert Carnal and Miss Lydia Dambey.
John Webber, security.

April 5, 1841—John Clements and Miss Harriet J. Spriggs.
Richard Jones, security.

April 7, 1841—Jeremiah Fuller and Miss Elizabeth Turner.
Joseph Taylor, security.

April 19, 1841—Ignatius Higgins and Miss Jane C. Drummond.
John E. Doyle, security.

Note: The above couple were married April 20th by the Rev. Alexander Histelberger, pastor of the Norfolk Catholic Congregation. Misses Doyle and Hunter and Mrs. Higgins are listed as witnesses. Jane C. Drummond was the daughter of Mrs. H. A. Drummond.

April 21, 1841—Andrew B. Hendren and Miss Mary D. Haynes.
William Haynes, security.

April 27, 1841—James F. Hunter and Miss Sarah Ann Woodis.
John E. Doyle, security.

March 13, 1841—Miles P. Burcher and Miss Mary Ann White.
Richard White, security.

Note: The above couple were married the same day by the Rev. Thomas Crowder, Jr. Mary Ann White was the daughter of Richard White, the security.

May 17, 1841—George Whiteman and Mrs. Amelia Evanstall.
Henry Jones, security.

Note: The above couple were married May 18th by the Rev. Joseph B. Breed.

May 27, 1841—Nicholas Cleary and Miss Eliza D. Reilley.
John E. Doyle, security.

Note: The above couple were married May 29th by the Rev. Alexander Histelberger, pastor of the Norfolk Catholic Congregation. Misses Webb, Fitzgerald and Doyle are listed as witnesses.

June 1, 1841—Eleazer Stillman and Miss Abigail Spence.
Margaret (mark) Spence, security.

Note: Abigail Spence was the daughter of Margaret Spence, the security.

June 1, 1841—Manuel Anthony Santos and Miss Eliza D. Ackerman.
Thomas D. Toy, security.

Note: The above couple were married the same day by the Rev. Joseph B. Breed.

June 1, 1841—John M. Hough and Miss Anna Eliza Roberts.
William D. Roberts, security.

Note: The above couple were married October 21st by the Rev. Upton Beall.

June 2, 1841—James A. S. Clarke and Mrs. Harriet B. McArthur.
Thomas Eccles, security.

Note: The above couple were married June 3rd by the Rev. Joseph B. Breed.

June 8, 1841—Charles Burruss and Miss Mary Jane Cake.
Richard D. Burruss, security.

June 16, 1841—James M. Lockert and Miss Margaret E. Pollard.
Benjamin Pollard, security.

Note: The above couple were married the same day by the Rev. Upton Beall.

June 29, 1841—Edward Kenney and Miss Emily Jane Dozier.

Thomas Haggnes, security.

June 19, 1841—Lawson Diggs and Mary Manuel (free negroes).

William Warrick, security.

June 25, 1841—Henry H. Newsum and Miss Evelina G. Murdock.

John Dunston, security.

Note: The above couple were married the same day by the Rev. Upton Beall, rector of Christ P. E. Church.

June 28, 1841—Thomas Carter and Miss Elizabeth Kelly.

Richard Jones, security.

July 3, 1841—Gilbert H. Bryson and Miss Margaret A. Lappin.

Thomas Eccles, seccurity.

Note: The above couple were married the same day by the Rev. Joseph B. Breed.

July 5, 1841—William H. Turner and Miss Susan E. Boush.

William B. Thomas, security.

Note: Susan E. Boush was the daughter of Sarah E. Boush.

July 7, 1841—Samuel Watts and Miss Louisa A. Langley.

Winchester Watts, security.

Note: The above couple were married the same day by the Rev. John H. Wingfield, rector of Trinity P. E. Church, Portsmouth, Va.

July 7, 1841—James P. Harrison and Miss Ann J. Cunningham.

Samuel Watts, security.

Note: The above couple were married by the Rev. Thomas Crowder, Jr. Ann J. Cunningham was the daughter of Joseph F. Cunningham.

July 14, 1841—Hillary Cone and Miss Jane Graham.

James Collins, security.

July 27, 1841—John B. Hunt and Miss Mary C. H. Sheild.

James H. Sheild, security.

July 29, 1841—John Gibbs and Miss Eliza Wheeler.

John (mark) Marsden, security.

August 12, 1841—William Henry Garnett and Miss Mary Ann Wilson.

James D. Wilson, security.

Note: The above couple were married the same day by the Rev. Upton Beall, rector of Christ P. E. Church.

September 2, 1841—William Parker and Miss Nancy Bailey.

Samuel Bailey, security.

September 7, 1841—William Stakes and Miss Martha Cone.

James (mark) Cone, security.

Note: Martha Cone was the daughter of James Cone, the security.

September 14, 1841—Edwin H. Delk and Miss Sarah Ann Esher.

John B. Hardy, security.

Note: The above couple were married the same day by the Rev. Thomas Crowder, Jr. Sarah Ann Esher was the daughter of Louisa A. Owens wife of James Owens.

September 30, 1841—John L. Shrives and Miss Sally Barcraft.

Timothy B. Scott, security.

September 30, 1841—Henry Barrett and Miss Sarah Harwood.

Samuel Harwood, security.

Note: Sarah Harwood was the daughter of Samuel Harwood, the security.

September 7, 1841—John H. Snider and Miss Julia Ann Minton.

John Gibbs, security.

October 12, 1841—Samuel H. Hodges and Miss Emily Nash.
Charles S. Allmand, security.
Note: The above couple were married the same day by the Rev. Thomas Crowder, Jr.
October 19, 1841—William A. Wayne and Miss Georgiana Wilson.
Edward T. Dunn, security.
Note: The above couple were married October 21st by the Rev. Upton Beall. Georgiana Wilson was the daughter of George Wilson.
October 20, 1841—James Devine and Miss Elizabeth Doyle.
Hugh P. Woods, security.
October 21, 1841—William D. Roberts and Mrs. Eliza Diggs.
Thomas B. Dixon, security.
Note: The above couple were married the same day by the Rev. Joseph B. Breed.
October 26, 1841—John E. Doyle and Miss Mary J. Fitzgerald.
George Reid, security.
Note: The above couple were married the same day by the Rev. Alexander Histelberger, pastor of the Norfolk Catholic Congregation. George Reid and C. Reardon are listed as witnesses.
November 2, 1841—James N. Goldsborough and Miss Mary E. Kennedy.
Edmund Pendleton Kennedy, security.
Note: The above couple were married the same day by the Rev. Upton Beall, rector of Christ P. E. Church. Edmund Pendleton Kennedy was the father of Mary E. Kennedy.
November 3, 1841—Richard Lucien Page and Miss Sarah Alexina Taylor.
Walter Herron Taylor, security.
Note: The above couple were married November 4th by the Rev. Upton Beall, rector of Christ P. E. Church. Richard Lucien Page was the son of William Byrd and Ann (Lee) Page of Clarke County, Virginia, and Sarah Alexina Taylor was the daughter of Richard and Eliza (Calvert) Taylor of Norfolk, Virginia.
November 10, 1841—Nathaniel R. Jones and Miss Virginia A. Wright.
Thomas B. West, security.
Note: The above couple were married November 11th by the Rev. Upton Beall, rector of Christ P. E. Church. Virginia Wright was the daughter of Stephen Wright.
November 16, 1841—Joshua Reed and Miss Mary Ann Ball.
John Ball, security.
November 18, 1841—Michael Born and Miss Caroline Myers.
John Wilson, security.
Note: The above couple were married the same day by the Rev. Thomas Crowder, Jr.
November 24, 1841—William M. Whitlock and Miss Mary Ann Moore.
Peter Moore, security.
Note: The above couple were married the same day by the Rev. Alexander Histbelerger, pastor of the Norfolk Catholic Congregation. Mrs. Brown and Mr. and Mrs. Cotton are listed as witnesses. Mary Ann Moore was the daughter of Peter Moore, the security.
November 25, 1841—John H. Williams and Miss Maria Burdick.
James Baker, security.
November 29, 1841—William T. Wingfield and Miss Jane Eliza Ribble.
William Insell, security.
Note: The above couple were married November 30th by the Rev. Alexander Histelberger pastor of the Norfolk Catholic Congregation. Mr. Ribble, Hull and family are listed as witnesses. Jane Eliza Ribble was the daughter of Joseph Ribble.
December 4, 1841—John D. Johnson and Nancy Boss (free persons of colour).
Harrison (mark) Minton, security.

December 6, 1841—Jacob Vickery, Jr., and Miss Margaret J. Saunders.

Jacob Vickery, security.

Note: The above couple were married December 7th by the Rev. Upton Beall, rector of Christ P. E. Church.

December 7, 1841—Thomas O. Young and Miss Martha A. Lester.

George Kneller, security.

Note: The above couple were married the same day by the Rev. Thomas Crowder, Jr.

December 10, 1841—Henry Dickerson and Miss Mary Mitchell.

James Alexander, security.

Note: The above couple were married the same day by the Rev. Joseph B. Breed.

December 15, 1841—Sterling T. Oliver and Miss Mary J. Carr.

John Whitehurst, security.

Note: The above couple were married the same day by the Rev. Thomas Crowder, Jr. Mary J. Carr was the daughter of Elizabeth Carr.

December 16, 1841—Elie Cutherell and Miss Sarah Anatoir.

Thomas Fleer, security.

Note: The above couple were married the same day by the Rev. Joseph B. Breed.

December 22, 1841—Christopher Hogan and Mrs. Harriet T. Wilson.

William D. Roberts, security.

Note: The above couple were married the same day by the Rev. Alexander Histelberger, pastor of the Norfolk Catholic Congregation. Mrs. Warren Harris and Mrs. Warren are listed as witnesses.

December 22, 1841—George Felthouse and Miss Susan Ripple.

William Creighton, security.

December 23, 1841—John J. Woodbridge and Miss Ann E. Shraeder.

E. F. Stephens, security.

Note: The above couple were married the same day by the Rev. Thomas Crowder, Jr.

December 24, 1841—Moses F. Murden and Miss Sarah Ann Watts.

John M. Watts, security.

Note: The above couple were married the same day by the Rev. Thomas Crowder, Jr. Sarah Ann Watts was the daughter of John M. Watts, the security.

December 27, 1841—Thomas R. Ingram and Miss Margaret D. Drewry.

Jacob Hunter, security.

Note: Margaret D. Drewry was the daughter of Mathias Drewry.

December 29, 1841—William Reid and Miss Sylvia E. Mahone.

Shelburn Mahone, security.

Note: The above couple were married December 30th by the Rev. Joseph B. Breed. Shelborn Mahone was the father of Sylvia E. Mahone.

1842

January 1, 1842—John J. Joyce and Miss Ann Quinn.

Richard Doyle, security.

Note: The above couple were married January 2nd by the Rev. Alexander Histelberger, pastor of the Norfolk Congregation. Mrs. Quinn and Mr. Murphy are listed as witnesses.

January 6, 1842—James Worden and Mrs. Catherine Free.

Edward Clearwater, security.

January 11, 1842—John Fisher and Miss Emily Flanagan.

Benjamin F. Flanagan, security.

Note: The above couple were married the same day by the Rev. Thomas Crowder, Jr.

January 11, 1842—Thomas White and Miss Mary K. Abdel.
Joseph B. Minton, security.
Note: The above couple were married the same day by the Rev. Thomas Crowder, Jr.

January 18, 1842—Edward Clearwater and Charlotte Smith.
Leon (mark) Prior, security.

January 18, 1842—John Adams and Miss Martha Rook.
James Lewelling, security.
Note: Martha Rook was the orphan of Thomas Rook.

January 25, 1842—Elijah Gardner Wells and Miss Elizabeth Hall.
Nicholas O. Thompson, security.
Note: The above couple were married the same day by the Rev. Thomas Crowder, Jr.

February 12, 1842—Jacob Thom and Mary Ann Shore.
John Rowe, security.

February 24, 1842—Elzie F. Stephens and Mrs. Sarah Stewart.
James B. Burns, security.
Note: The above couple were married the same day by the Rev. Thomas Crowder, Jr.

March 1, 1842—James G. McPheeters and Miss Susan Thorowgood.
Joshua Moore, security.

March 2, 1842—David Matthias and Miss Margaret Collins.
John Collins, security.

March 9, 1842—John Batiste and Miss Harriet Armistead.
Gabriel (mark) Manax, security.

March 23, 1842—James R. Nichols and Miss Martha Ann Bean.
George Nolan, security.

March 28, 1842—William Thompson and Miss Martha F. Luning.
George W. Randolph, security.
Note: The above couple were married the same day by the Rev. Thomas Crowder, Jr.

April 7, 1842—Charles J. Bowker and Miss Pricilla Ann Miller.
James B. Burns, security.

April 19, 1842—Walter Marr and Miss Harriet Josephine Ayres.
William (mark) Urquhart, security.

April 22, 1842—John A. Darling and Miss Margaet Frances Black.
Edward G. Fitzgibbon, security.

May 2, 1842—George Corbey and Mrs. Mary Mardeen (or Mardan).
John Power, security.

May 3, 1842—Joseph F. Battley and Miss Catherine Dixon.
James H. Reed, security.

May 4, 1842—Edward Payne and Mrs. Elizabeth O'Gilvie.
Edward P. Irish, security.

May 26, 1842—George W. Gage and Miss Susan Pines.
Robert (mark) Wilkins, security.
Note: The above couple were married the same day by the Rev. Thomas Crowder, Jr.

June 22, 1842—John Shipp and Mrs. Hester Rudder.
David (mark) Hosier, security.

June 23, 1842—Robert B. Bain and Miss Mary White.
William Pritchet, security.

June 23, 1842—Andrew J. Balcomb and Miss Sidney Simons.
John Nash, security.

June 25, 1842—John Robert Birch and Miss Martha Jane Sturtevant.

William Sturtevant, security.

June 27, 1842—William Boos and Mrs. Sarah Oldner.

Harmon Hanor, security.

June 29, 1842—John Lane and Miss Ann Thorowgood.

Eleany Thorowgood, security.

Note: Ann Thorowgood was the daughter of Eleany Thorowgood, the security.

June 29, 1842—Henry Welton and Mrs. Elizabeth Banks.

John Sutton, security.

July 1, 1842—John B. Collins and Miss Elizabeth G. Mears.

Edmund (mark) Foster, security.

Note: The above couple were married the same day by the Rev. Thomas Crowder, Jr.

July 6, 1842—John Perkins and Cecelia (free negroes).

David (mark) Boon, security.

July 19, 1842—Michael Hendren and Mrs. Sarah Woodhouse.

John (mark) Wilkins, security.

Note: The above couple were married the same day by the Rev. Thomas Crowder, Jr.

July 28, 1842—Edward Balentine and Miss Louisa A. Lovitt.

Edwin Butt, security.

Note: At a Quarter Session of the Court in Princess Anne County, held in November, 1841, John Peters was appointed guardian of William David, Louisa and Nancy Lovitt, orphans of Thomas Lovitt, decd.

July 28, 1842—James F. Wiatt and Miss Elizabeth A. McCann.

Francis C. Wiatt, security.

August 8, 1842—Charles Springer and Mrs. Charlotte Clearwater.

John S. Vincent, security.

August 11, 1842—Lovitt B. Whitehurst and Miss Mary L. Lovitt.

Newton H. Capps, security.

Note: On May 4th, 1840, Mary L. Lovitt, the orphan of Daniel Lovitt of Princess Anne County, chose Charles Henley for her guardian. The above couple were married the same day by the Rev. Thomas Crowder, Jr.

August 11, 1842—Philip H. Simpson and Miss Eliza Angell.

John Hope, security.

Note: The above couple were married the same day by the Rev. Alexander Histelberger, pastor of the Norfolk Catholic Congregation. John Hope, Mr. Wilson and Margaret A. Stervant are listed as witnesses.

August 11, 1842—William J. Lester and Miss Rora Jackson.

David B. Park, security.

August 12, 1842—Jacob J. Ackerman and Miss Susan McCrory.

James Allen, security.

August 29, 1842—St. George Lambert and Miss Eliza Ann Shipp.

Frances (mark) Shipp, security.

August 30, 1842—Charles Caffie and Miss Sarah S. Huttleston.

George (mark) Lewelling, security.

Note: The above couple were married the same day by the Rev. Thomas Crowder, Jr.

September 5, 1842—George Deane and Miss Mary Johnson.

Joseph W. Hall, security.

September 6, 1842—John Taylor and Miss Sarah Jane Rogers.

William Rogers, Jr., security.

Note: The above couple were married the same day by the Rev. Thomas Crowder, Jr.

September 7, 1842—James House and Mrs. Susan Meagher.
William (mark) Jones, security.
September 8, 1842—Manuel Borges and Miss Averilla Diggs.
Joseph Lacoste, security.
Note: The above couple were married the same day by the Rev. Alexander His-
telberger, pastor of the Norfolk Catholic Congregation. Joseph Lacoste and wife
and Joseph Mary are listed as witnesses.
September 15, 1842—Henry B. Mathiot and Miss Eliza Mathiot.
S. N. Botsford.
Note: Eliza Mathiot was the daughter of Elizabeth Mathiot.
September 15, 1842—William H. Doggett and Miss Virginia A. Keele.
Thomas Constable, security.
September 20, 1842—Eber Shaw and Mrs. Ann Uzzell.
Robert L. Bernard, security.
September 29, 1842—William Willis and Miss Mary Wilkins.
John (mark) Wilkins, security.
October 3, 1842—Charles B. Scripture and Miss Elizabeth F. Wright.
Eugene N. Bobie, security.
October 4, 1842—John B. Price and Miss Elizabeth Beshaw.
George (mark) Lewelling, security.
October 4, 1842—Samuel Frost and Miss Elizabeth Hutchingson.
Andrew Scott, security.
Note: The above couple were married the same day by the Rev. Thomas Crow-
der, Jr.
October 15, 1842—Peter H. Seaman and Miss Jane Edwards.
George Deane, security.
October 17, 1842—George F. Anderson and Miss Sarah H. McPhail.
Andrew Reid, security.
Note: The above couple were married October 18th by the Rev. James Stratton,
a Portsmouth Presbyterian minister.
October 17, 1842—Joseph Nash and Miss Evelina Harwood.
Charles H. Beale, security.
Note: The above couple were married the same day by the Rev. Thomas Crow-
der, Jr. Evelina Harwood was the daughter of Susan H. Harwood.
October 20, 1842—R. E. Manson and Miss Sophia A. Smith.
J. Marsden Smith, security.
Note: The above couple were married the same day by the Rev. Upton Beall,
rector of Christ P. E. Church.
October 22, 1842—John Burgess and Mrs. Eliza Smith.
George (mark) Lewelling, security.
Note: The above couple were married the same day by the Rev. Alexander His-
telberger, pastor of the Norfolk Catholic Congregation. George Lewelling, Jane
Kyle and Dr. Santos are listed as witnesses.
October 24, 1842—Leo Stoeser and Mrs. Sylvia Jarvais (or Gervais).
Maximilian Bremen, security.
Note: The above couple were married the same day by the Rev. Alexander His-
telberger, pastor of the Norfolk Catholic Congregation. Dr. E. Caspare and Mr.
Laurede are listed as witnesses.
October 26, 1842—James Ashton and Miss Mary Burchell.
John S. Vincent, security.
October 27, 1842—Samuel B. Chapman and Mrs. Catherine D. Haynes.
Sewall Goodridge, security.

October 28, 1842—William Jamieson and Mrs. Elizabeth Wittering.

Hezekiah Whitehurst, security.

Note: The above couple were married the same day by the Rev. Thomas Crowder, Jr.

November 1, 1842—John Dixon and Miss Susan Grant.

Josiah (mark) Deans, security.

November 1, 1842—Edward T. Dunn and Miss Louisa Klein.

James H. North, security.

Note: The above couple were married the same day by the Rev. Upton Beall, rector of Christ P. E. Church.

November 8, 1842—Patrick McCarrick and Mrs. Margaret Rohan.

Patrick Gallagher, security.

Note: The above couple were married the same day by the Rev. Alexander Histelberger, pastor of the Norfolk Catholic Congregation. Captain Henderson, P. Gallagher, Mr. Cull and Mrs. Mullane are listed as witnesses.

November 9, 1842—Edmund Taylor and Betsey Hollowell (free negroes).

Bartlett (mark) Watts, security.

November 9, 1842—Jackson Broaddus Wood and Miss Caroline A. Barnes.

John S. Salusbury, security.

Note: The above couple were married the same day by the Rev. E. G. Robinson.

November 14, 1842—Robert W. Hargrove and Miss Margaret Kustard.

Thomas Turner, security.

November 23, 1842—Michael McConaghy and Mrs. Catherine Erskine.

Bartholomew Brady, security.

November 15, 1842—William P. Sturtevant and Miss Mary Jane Bell.

Henry Tudor, security.

November 24, 1842—Joseph W. Randolph and Miss Honoria M. Tucker.

John R. Tucker, security.

Note: The above couple were married November 26th by the Rev. Alexander Histelberger, pastor of the Norfolk Catholic Congregation. T. Reilly, Sr., and family, Mrs. Jackson, Miss Randolph and the Misses Maurice and Broughton are listed as witnesses.

December 5, 1842—Benjamin Mitchell and Miss Ann F. Smith.

John Burgess, security.

December 23, 1842—James Woodhouse and Miss Fanny Salmons.

Moses Henley, security.

December 24, 1842—Benjamin Hill and Miss Martha Cooper.

Henry Hill, security.

December 27, 1842—Henry Gallagher and Miss Mary Murphy.

George Jones, security.

December 31, 1842—John Farmer and Mrs. Ann Jackson.

Joel E. Parr, security.

December 31, 1842—John Dunston and Miss Sarah Roberts.

William D. Roberts, security.

Note: The above couple were married January 1st, 1843, by the Rev. Upton Beall, rector of Christ P. E. Church. Sarah Roberts was the daughter of William D. Roberts, the security.

1843

January 3, 1843—Randolph D. Holt and Miss Ann Heath.

George A. Barrom, security.

January 9, 1843—John Sikes and Miss Lydia Stewart.

Jesse M. Caffee, security.

January 11, 1843—Thomas Evans and Miss Margaret Burk.

Joseph Kehoe, security.

Note: Margaret Burk was the daughter of Bridget Raleigh.

January 11, 1843—Orlando Windsor and Miss Catherine Ann Hall.

Alexander P. Taylor, security.

Note: The above couple were married January 12th by the Rev. Upton Beall, rector of Christ P. E. Church.

January 19, 1843—Charles W. Orton and Mrs. Sarah Bonney.

Dennis H. Dawley, security.

January 21, 1843—John B. Rooke and Mrs. Amelia Ann Warthall.

Henry Tudor, security.

January 26, 1843—Josiah T. Jones and Mrs. Margaret E. Wilson.

Charles Burruss, security.

January 27, 1843—William Falmark and Mrs. Maria Graves.

Lemuel K. Holmes, security.

February 7, 1843—John L. Ring and Miss Emily J. Starke.

Robert B. Cunningham, security.

Note: The above couple were married the same day by the Rev. Upton Beall, rector of Christ P. E. Church. Emily J. Starke was the orphan of Robert B. Starke.

February 13, 1843—Francis B. Edmonds and Mrs. Catherine E. Kays.

John Adams, security.

February 15, 1843—Soloman W. Spratt and Miss Mary Gardner.

Francis H. Browne, security.

February 16, 1843—James Givins and Mary Antoinette Burt (free persons of colour).   Henry H. Dentzell, security.

February 18, 1843—Edward Fitzgibbon and Miss Ann Wood.

William Tunbridge, security.

Note: The above couple were married the same day by the Rev. Alexander Histelberger, pastor of the Norfolk Catholic Congregation. Mr. and Mrs. Tunbridge are listed as witnesses.

February 23, 1843—John D. James and Miss Mary F. Fentress.

William H. Murphey, security.

February 27, 1843—Joseph H. Hall and Miss Catherine Pinner.

William Smith, security.

March 4, 1843—James Eustis and Miss Susan Bolton.

George Manns, security.

Note: The above couple were married the same day by the Rev. Mr. Robinson, pastor of the Cumberland Street Baptist Church. Susan Bolton was the daughter of Elizabeth Bolton.

March 8, 1843—Levi Westray and Mrs. Rebecca W. Herman.

Edward S. Pegram, security.

March 21, 1843—Edward Seymour and Miss Ann Eliza Piemont.

William Hawkins, security.

Note: The above couple were married March 22nd by the Rev. E. G. Robinson. Ann Eliza Piemont was the daughter of Margaret Piemont.

March 31. 1843—Charles Brown and Miss Julia Ann Hester Vail.

George Cross, security.

Note: The above couple were married the same day by the Rev. Alexander Histelberger, pastor of the Norfolk Catholic Congregation. George Cross and Margart Commons are listed as witnesses.

April 14, 1843—Thomas H. Cary and Miss Isabella Moir.

William H. Perry, security.

April 24, 1843—Robert D. Howard and Miss Lucy Chapman.
Horace H. Simco, security.
April 25, 1843—William McBlair and Miss Virginia Myers.
Alexander M. Pennock, security.
Note: Virginia Myers was the daughter of Louisa Myers.
April 26, 1843—James H. Jones and Mrs. Elizabeth Lilliston.
Edward Haigh, security.
April 27, 1843—Fitch Burwell and Miss Anna Maria Chapman.
S. O. Merwin, eecurity.
April 29, 1843—George Terry Sinclair and Miss Mary Thompson.
Arthur Sinclair, security.
Note: The above couple were married May 2nd by the Rev. Upton Beall, rector of Christ P. E. Church. Mary Thompson was the daughter of William H. Thompson. ....
May 2, 1843—Francis M. Armistead and Miss Frances Virginia Ann Edwards.
Oscar E. Edwards, security.
May 5, 1843—Charles Graham and Mrs. Mary Ann Anderson.
Richard Doyle, security.
May 11, 1843—Mathias Clarke and Miss Margaret Hill.
Nathaniel Lord, security.
May 15, 1843—Joseph Kehoe and Miss Susan M. Pallett.
John Herrington, security.
Note: The above couple were married May 16th by the Rev. Alexander Histelberger, pastor of the Norfolk Catholic Congregation. M. P. Woodhouse and Pricilla Cornick are listed as witnesses.
May 17, 1843—John Knight and Miss Mary Ann Whittle.
Henry (mark) Dickerson, security.
May 22, 1843—(Doctor) Henry C. Holt and Miss Susan Jane Jackson.
Henry B. Reardon, security.
Note: The above couple were married May 23rd by the Rev. Alexander Histelberger, pastor of the Norfolk Catholic Congregation. Messrs. Henry B. Reardon, T. Reilly, Jr., and Mr. Reilly are listed as witnesses.
May 23, 1843—William H. Clegg and Louisa (free mulattos).
Jack Morris, security.
May 24, 1843—Henry Murden and Miss Sarah Corbell.
Machriste Sykes, security.
May 29, 1843—John Purcell and Miss Martha M. Webb.
Thomas T. Webb, security.
Note: The above couple were married the same day by the Rev. Alexander Histelberger, pastor of the Norfolk Catholic Congregation. Charles W. Purcell, Miss Hopkins and Miss Purcell are listed as witnesses. Martha M. Webb was the daughter of Thomas T. Webb, the security.
June 27, 1843—Reese Taylor and Miss Virginia Clarico.
James A. H. Pearce, security.
June 28, 1843—Charles White and Mrs. Sarah Ann Cunningham.
Michael McConaghey, security.
July 1, 1843—Ruel V. Barlow and Miss Jane Smith.
John Wayland, security.
July 5, 1843—Nathaniel Lord and Mrs. Penelope Farris.
Frederick Le Baron, security.
July 5. 1843—Lewis Jones and Mrs. Lavinia Sutherland.
Rosa (mark) Frank, security.
July 8, 1843—William Godfrey and Miss Sarah Jordan.
William (mark) Reid, security.

July 17, 1843—John S. Salusbury and Miss Virginia Bartee.
John Burns, Jr., security.
Note: The above couple were married the same day by the Rev. E. G. Robinson.
July 22, 1843—James Buchanan and Miss Amelia Ann Scott.
Obediah (mark) Scott, security.
July 24, 1843—Carter Braxton Poindexter and Miss Mary E. Whitehead.
William C. Whitehead, security.
July 27, 1843—Edmund Thompson and Mrs. Susan Mills.
Miles D. Taylor, security.
August 30, 1843—James Cobbett and Miss Joanna Hudgins.
Timothy Donoghue, security.
August 31, 1843—James Flynn and Miss Margaret Cummings.
Joseph Kelly, security.
Note: The above couple were married the same day by the Rev. Alexander Histelberger, pastor of the Norfolk Catholic Congregation. Joseph Kelly, Sarah A. Flynn and Richard Doyle are listed as witnesses.
September 2, 1843—William H. Ferguson and Miss Jane Lappin.
Thomas Eccles, security.
September 8, 1843—Henry Powell and Miss Lucinda Walke.
John Weyland, security.
September 9, 1843—Cornelius Forbes and Miss Sarah Savage.
Richard D. Burruss, security.
Note: Sarah Savage was the daughter of Mary F. Palmer.
September 11, 1843—Henry Powell and Miss Lucinda Morriss.
Robert Bellamy, security.
September 18, 1843—George Granling and Miss Clarissa Wols.
Lewis (mark) Peters, security.
September 26, 1843—Andrew Stevens and Miss Henrietta Armistead.
John Gibbs, security.
September 27, 1843—William J. Holmes and Miss Gertrude Hendren.
Michael Hendren, security.
Note: Gertrude Hendren was the daughter of Michael Hendren, the security.
October 4, 1843—Charles T. Pope and Miss Victoria Werkmuller.
Philip H. Masi, security.
Note: The above couple were married the same day by the Rev. Alexander Histelberger, pastor of the Norfolk Catholic Congregation. A. Branda, the Misses Hartshorne, Bonford, Crisby and Mrs. Lecompte are listed as witnesses.
October 12, 1843—Thomas Gould and Mrs. Lucy Ann Hebdon.
James Duffy, security.
October 12, 1843—William H. Johnson and Miss Martha E. Reilly.
Joseph Reilly, security.
October 18, 1843—John Caphart and Miss Elizabeth Spratt.
Soloman W. Spratt, security.
October 19, 1843—Joaquin Baito and Miss Margaret Greenwood.
Martin Greenwood, security.
Note: Margaret Greenwood was the daughter of Martin Greenwood, the security.
October 19, 1843—John B. Whitehead and Miss Emily A. Herman.
Nathan C. Whitehead, security.
October 25, 1843—Barneto Garcia and Mrs. Catherine Guthrie.
Charles Graham, security.
November 1, 1843—Adolphus H. Pickerell and Miss Mary E. Watkins.
George W. Butts, security.
Note: Mary E. Watkins was the daughter of Howard Watkins.

171

November 11, 1843—Armistead T. M. Cooke and Miss Mary Louisa Todd.
Merit M. R. Todd, security.
Note: The above couple were married November 13th by the Rev. Upton Beall, rector of Christ P. E. Church.

November 23, 1843—John C. Weston and Miss Jane O. Parks.
Nicholas Wilson Parker, security.
Note: The above couple were married the same day by the Rev. Upton Beall, rector of Christ P. E. Church.

November 28, 1843—William C. Simmington and Mrs. Elizabeth S. Watkins.
Michael Griffin, security.

November 28, 1843—Horace Drury and Miss Margaret C. Dodd.
John Dodd, security.
Note: The above couple were married the same day by the Rev. Alexander Histelberger, pastor of the Norfolk Catholic Congregation. Thomas Dodd, W. Delacy and Mrs. Harris are listed as witnesses.

November 29, 1843—Batson Murden and Miss Elizabeth Jane Bonney.
Jonathan Bonney, security.

November 30, 1843—Charles H. Drummond and Miss Courtney H. Pannell.
William Pannell, security.
Note: The above couple were married the same day by the Rev. Upton Beall, rector of Christ P. E. Church.

December 5, 1843—Read Gordon and Miss Matilda Skinner.
John Bonsal, security.

December 12, 1843—Benjamin McCoy and Miss Elizabeth Styron.
Josiah Grimes, security.
Note: Elizabeth Styron was the daughter of Nancy Styron.

December 18, 1843—Thurmer Hoggard and Miss Elizabeth F. Cornick.
James Cornick, security.
Note: The above couple were married December 21st by the Rev. John H. Wingfield, rector of Trinity P. E. Church, Portsmouth, Va.

December 23, 1843—George Robins and Mrs. Susan Franies Redman.
James Baker, security.

December 25, 1843—George E. Belote and Miss Susan Wood.
William Bean, security.

December 26, 1843—David Glasgo Farragut and Miss Virginia D. Loyall.
William Loyall, security.
Note: The above couple were married the same day by the Rev. Upton Beall, rector of Christ P. E. Church.

December 28, 1843—Edward White and Martha Berry (free negroes).
Mitchell Hall, security.

December 28, 1843—William T. Morris and Miss Mary A. Morris.
Bennett (mark) Quick, security.

1844

January 3, 1844—Ephriam E. Hathaway and Miss Mary Sammons.
David M. Hathaway, security.

January 11, 1844—Marmaduke Savage and Miss Elizabeth Harrison.
Bardon Burrow, security.

February 10, 1844—John Malon and Miss Maria Ann Miller.
William Loper, security.

February 15, 1844—Alexander P. Taylor and Miss Eliza Francis.

William Francis, Jr., security.

Note: The above couple were married the same day by the Rev. Upton Beall, rector of Christ P. E. Church.

February 15, 1844—John Quinn and Miss Elizabeth Ann Rhea.

Robert (mark) Rhea, security.

Note: The above couple were married the same day by the Rev. Alexander Histelberger, pastor of the Norfolk Catholic Congregation. William Lewellyn, Richard Doyle, Catherine Miller and Dr. Glass are listed as witnesses.

February 17, 1844—Thomas Quirk and Mrs. Hannah West.

James Baker, security.

February 19, 1844—Nathaniel Currier and Miss Lucinda Mary D. Lee.

John W. Thomas, security.

February 28, 1844—James N. Wofford and Miss Mary D. T. Cocke.

Thomas J. Cocke, security.

March 2, 1844—John Dens and Miss Henrietta Sykes.

James H. Ransone, security.

March 5, 1844—Reuben A. Howard and Miss Mary Frances Howlett.

Horace H. Simcoe, security.

March 6, 1844—William A. James and Miss Harriet Rogers.

Robert O. James, security.

Note: The above couple were married March 7th by the Rev. John H. M. Williams.

March 19, 1844—Francis A. Johnston and Miss Elizabeth Ann Barnes.

William C. Barnes, security.

March 19, 1844—Patrick Murray and Miss Jane Adaline Cutrill.

James Allen, security.

Note: The above couple were married March 21st by the Rev. Upton Beall, rector of Christ P. E. Church.

April 3, 1844—William H. Cline and Miss Margaret Darling.

Benjamin A. Morris, security.

April 8, 1844—Charles Lanson and Mrs. Mary Ann Dodd.

Thomas (mark) Penny, security.

April 8, 1844—William Rowe and Miss Elizabeth Crew.

Horace Simcoe, security.

April 11, 1844—James Holland and Miss Dolly Dredge.

Phineas Williams, security.

April 11, 1844—William H. Lewelling and Miss Jane E. Doland.

James Doland, security.

Note: The above couple were married the same day by the Rev. Alexander Histelberger, pastor of the Norfolk Catholic Congregation. John Holmes and Sarah A. Ferris are listed as witnesses. Jane Doland was the daughter of James Doland, the security.

April 20, 1844—John J. Fisher and Mrs. Rebecca Haynes.

Augustus Sykes, security.

April 20, 1844—Stephen Denby and Miss Virginia Fitz.

William Denby, security.

Note: Stephen Denby was the son of William Denby, the security.

May 11, 1844—Bartley Watts and Martha A. Newton (free negroes).

John W. Thomas, security.

May 16, 1844—Michael Hanson and Mrs. Mary Thompson.

William (mark) Urquhart, security.

May 30, 1844—Edward Earle and Mrs. Susan Taylor.

John Hargrove, security.

June 6, 1844—James E. Tyson and Mrs. Emily Tomlinson.
Augustus Sykes, security.
June 7, 1844—Stacy Flanagan and Mrs. Susan M. Hoyt.
Edward Scribner, security.
June 20, 1844—William C. Veal and Miss Prudence Capps.
John (mark) West, security.
June 26, 1844—John H. Roberts and Mrs. Maria Fillmark.
Marcus A. Fairchild, security.
July 1, 1844—Mordecai Cooke, Jr., and Miss Sarah C. Klein.
Armistead T. M. Cooke, security.
Note: The above couple were married the same day by the Rev. Upton Beall, rector of Christ P. E. Church.
July 3, 1844—John J. Young and Miss Anna B. Lacoste.
Joseph Kelly, security.
Note: The above couple were married July 4th by the Rev. Alexander Histelberger, pastor of the Catholic Congregation. John Lappin, Mrs. Laurete, Jane M. Ferguson and Mrs. Cotton are listed as witnesses.
July 8, 1844—Benjamin A. Morris and Miss Elizabeth Berry.
Charles H. Graham, security.
July 5, 1844—George Manns and Miss Ann Eliza Henghings.
John Ehrbeck, security.
Note: The above couple were married July 7, 1844, by the Rev. John H. M. Williams.
July 10, 1844—William Rosson and Miss Sarah Ann Hill.
John (mark) West, security.
July 15, 1844—Edward Freeman and Miss Mary Ann Butt.
William H. Steady, security.
August 3, 1844—Francisco Cardona and Miss Frances Marshall.
Jonah Deanes, security.
August 6, 1844—James Ross and Miss Mary Ann Bailey.
Samuel Bailey, security.
Note: Mary Ann Bailey was the daughter of Samuel Bailey, the security.
August 26, 1844—William O'Connell and Miss Virginia A. Marchant.
Joseph W. Malbon, security.
Note: The above couple were married August 27th by the Rev. Alexander Histelberger, pastor of the Norfolk Catholic Congregation. James Tulane and Catherine McKegay are listed as witnesses.
August 27, 1844—George Walters and Miss Fadamy Cox.
F. A. Sibley, security.
August 27, 1844—William Price and Miss Elizabeth Cone.
George (mark) Lewelling, security.
September 17, 1844—Andrew Stortz and Miss Lucinda Ann Goulder.
John Houseman, security.
September 21, 1844—James Smith and Mrs. Cynthia Bonney.
John Lane, security.
September 25, 1844—James H. Bowyer and Miss Agnes M. K. Lamb.
William Wilson Lamb, security.
Note: The above couple were married the same day by the Rev. L. L. Smith.
October 2, 1844—Mathew W. Kemp and Mrs. Mary G. Cary.
Richard M. Bagnall, security.
Note: The above couple were married October 3rd by the Rev. John H. Wingfield, rector of Trinity P. E. Church, Portsmouth, Va.

October 5, 1844—Elisha T. Pearson and Miss Martha E. Broughton.

William Denby, security.

Note: The above couple were married October 6th by the Rev. E. G. Robinson.

October 16, 1844—William Sayre and Miss Fanny Blow Todd.

James Marsden Smith, security.

October 23, 1844—Erasmus Jones and Miss Lucinda Hill.

Henry Hill, security.

Note: Lucinda Hill was the daughter of Henry Hill, the security.

October 30, 1844—Stephen A. McCreecy and Miss Mary Bassett Stark.

William D. Bagnall, security.

Note: The above couple were married the same day by the Rev. Upton Beall, rector of Christ P. E. Church.

October 31, 1844—Thomas E. Sale and Miss Mary E. Frost.

John H. Sale, security.

October 31, 1844—John Holmes and Miss Sarah A. Ferris.

James Doland, security.

Note: The above couple were married the same day by the Rev. Alexander Histelberger, pastor of the Norfolk Catholic Congregation. James Little, Mary A. Leighton and the Misses Hall and Lewelling are listed as witnesses.

October 31, 1844—William Brock and Miss Ann Moore.

Horatio Moore, security.

Note: The above couple were married December 6th by the Rev. Thomas Crowder, Jr.

November 11, 1844—(Doctor) William B. Sinclair and Miss Lucy F. R. Jones. Joseph H. Robertson, security.

Note: The above couple were married November 12th by the Rev. Upton Beall, rector of Christ P. E. Church. Lucy F. R. Jones was the daughter of Mary E. Jones.

November 13, 1844—George Smith and Mrs. Ellen Hammond.

Henry Welton, security.

November 14, 1844—Littleton Waller Tazewell, Jr., and Mrs. Sarah E. Harris. Lloyd W. Williams, security.

Note: The above couple were married the same day by the Rev. J. H. Wingfield, rector of Trinity P. E. Church, Portsmouth, Va.

November 27, 1844—James H. Ransone and Miss Elizabeth W. Lawson.

William Knight, security.

November 28, 1844—Henry Bohm and Miss Susan Lewis.

Thomas M. Martin, security.

Note: The above couple were married November 28th by the Rev. E. G. Robinson. Susan Lewis was the orphan of John Lewis and ward of Thomas Peck, who was appointed her guardian January 26, 1837, by the Court of Elizabeth City County.

November 28, 1844—George Ramsay and Miss Eliza Dolby.

Henry A. Dolby, security.

November 30, 1844—Samuel Forrest and Miss Anna Maria Henderson.

J. M. Watson, security.

December 5, 1844—Zachariah Sykes and Miss Ann Wilkins.

James H. Jones, security.

Note: The above couple were married December 7th by the Rev. Upton Beall, rector of Christ P. E. Church.

December 12, 1844—Willis J. C. Moody and Miss Helen M. Hynd.

James Hynd, security.

Note: The above couple were married the same day by the Rev. E. G. Robinson.

December 16, 1844—Caleb Groves and Miss Harriet Cutherell.
Francis A. Johnston, security.
December 16, 1844—Robert S. Robinson and Miss Adelia W. Oldner.
John C. Guy, security.
Note: The above couple were married the same day by the Rev. Alexander Histelberger, pastor of the Norfolk Catholic Congregation. Mrs. Oldner, Dr. Gramer and the Misses Eliza, Harriet and Adel Johnson are listed as witnesses.
December 19, 1844—Edward W. Carpenter and Miss Susan C. Wilkinson.
William M. Armstrong, security.
Note: The above couple were married the same day by the Rev. Upton Beall, rector of Christ P. E. Church.
December 23, 1844—Cornelius T. Gordon and Miss Sarah E. Duesberry.
Frederick Henicke, security.
Note: Sarah E. Duesberry was the daughter of Thomas Duesberry.
December 24, 1844—George Harrington and Mrs. Rosanna Davis.
Daniel R. Johnson, security.
December 26, 1844—Francis Timberlake and Mrs. Nancy Phillips.
James Flyn, security.
Note: The above couple were married the same day by the Rev. Alexander Histelberger, pastor of the Norfolk Catholic Congregation. Mr. Flynn and Mrs. Brown are listed as witnesses.
December 28, 1844—Joseph Arguimbo and Miss Mary Virginia Hammond.
George Cross, security.

1845

January 2, 1845—Edward Mathews and Miss Hannah Whitehurst.
George A. Barrom, security.
Note: The above couple were married the same day by the Rev. E. G. Robinson.
January 8, 1845—Augustus Branda and Miss Euphemia French.
Nathaniel Currier, security.
Note: The above couple were married the same day by the Rev. Alexander Histelberger, pastor of the Norfolk Catholic Congregation. Adolphus Maurice, Maria French, Dr. Andrews and Mrs. F. Branda are listed as witnesses.
January 8, 1845—William T. Winslow and Mrs. Sarah Ann Pritchard.
Lemuel Peed, security.
Note: The above couple were married January 8th by the Rev. Edward Wadsworth (Methodist).
January 9, 1845—John Hughes and Miss Martha Cooper.
John H. Williams, security.
Note: The above couple were married the same day by the Rev. Upton Beall, rector of Christ P. E. Church.
January 11, 1845—Reuben Fentress and Mrs. Mary Loring.
Peter F. Schlieker, security.
Note: The above couple were married January 12th by the Rev. Edward Wadsworth (Methodist).
January 15, 1845—John C. Wilkins and Miss Mary Eliza Brooks.
William Willis, security.
Note: The above couple were married January 16th by the Rev. E. G. Robinson, security. Mary Eliza Brooks was the daughter of Eliza S. Brooks.
January 18, 1845—William Knight and Miss Susan H. Wilson.
John Burgess, security.
January 23, 1845—Thomas C. Bissell and Miss Sarah C. Milhado.
Thomas J. Cornick, security.
Note: The above couple were married the same day by the Rev. Upton Beall, rector of Christ P. E. Church.

January 27, 1845—Mathew Morresay and Miss Elizabeth Redding.
Jacob Fullington, security.
January 27, 1845—William McLean and Miss Mary Bonfante.
Charles Brown, security.
Note: The above couple were married January 28th by the Rev. Upton Beall, rector of Christ P. E. Church.
January 28, 1845—Nathaniel Cotton and Miss Ellen Delany.
John (mark) Cotton, security.
January 28, 1845—Thomas H. Beveredge and Miss Margaret Beckley (or Buckley).
Joseph Cannon, security.
Note: The above couple were married February 3rd by the Rev. E. G. Robinson. Margaret Beckley (or Buckley) was the daughter of Marion Beckley (or Buckley).
January 29, 1845—John Thomas Martin and Mrs. Jeanett Broughton.
William C. Veale, security.
January 31, 1845—Thomas Anson and Mrs. Mary A. Bullock.
Thomas Eccles, security.
Note: The above couple were married February 2nd by the Rev. E. G. Robinson.
February 7, 1845—Stacy Hardy and Miss Ann Booker.
John Houseman, security.
February 19, 1845—John H. Borum and Miss Sarah Jane Bucknam.
Joses Bucknam, security.
Note: Sarah Jane Bucknam was the daughter of Joses Bucknam, the security.
March 12, 1845—Thomas Nelson and Miss Margaret Core (or Cori).
John W. Vaughn, security.
Note: The above couple were married the same day by the Rev. Edward Wadsworth.
March 15, 1845—Ezekiel Davis and Miss Elizabeth Rudder.
Henry (mark) Rudder, security
March 18, 1845—Job Jakeman and Mrs. Mary Ann Dolt.
William H. Barrett, security.
Note: The above couple were married the same day by the Rev. E. G. Robinson.
March 20, 1845—William P. Grifith and Miss Georgianna Keeling.
William Day, security.
Note: The above couple were married the same day by the Rev. Edward Wadsworth. Georgianna Keeling was the daughter of Elizabeth A. Keeling.
March 27, 1845—Edward Johnston and Miss Eliza Jane Bayne.
James L. Belto, security.
Note: The above couple were married the same day by the Rev. E. G. Robinson. Eliza Jane Bayne was the daughter of Lilly Bayne.
March 27, 1845—James Cherry and Miss Anna Maria Bayne.
James L. Belto, security.
Note: The above couple were married the same day by the Rev. E. G. Robinson. Anna Maria Bayne was the daughter of Lilly Bayne.
March 27, 1845—William Kirby and Miss Ann Maria Balfour.
William C. Barron, security.
Note: The above couple were married the same day by the Rev. Edward Wadsworth.
March 28, 1845—Henry Tullock and Miss Elizabeth M. Woods.
William L. Lacoste, security.
Note: The above couple were married the same day by the Rev. Alexander Histelberger, pastor of the Norfolk Catholic Congregation. William Glennan and Mary Woods are listed as witnesses.

April 2, 1845—Tom Tynes and Minerva Tynes (free negroes).
James (mark) Achille, security.
April 3, 1845—Luther R. Gibson and Miss Emily Rolland.
Joseph B. Minton, security.
April 9, 1845—John Bartee and Mrs. Ellen Hodges.
William Vaughn, security.
Note: The above couple were married the same day by the Rev. E. G. Robinson.
April 17, 1845—Junius Adams and Mrs. Mary S. Richardson.
Samuel Rulon, security.
April 23, 1845—Robert West and Miss Lydia Parr.
Lemuel (mark) Gregory, security.
May 7, 1845—Charles Dennison and Miss Ellen E. Kulings (or Hulings).
Lloyd W. Williams, security.
May 7, 1845—John Falconer and Miss Charlotte L. Soutter.
Andrew Reid, security.
May 8, 1845—Levin Y. Winder and Miss Annie E. Decormis.
Joseph Decormis, security.
Note: The above couple were married the same day by the Rev. J. P. Scott, pastor of the Hampton Baptist Church.
May 23, 1845—Thomas Huttleston and Miss Pricilla L. B. Henley.
William Henley, security.
Note: The above couple were married May 24th by the Rev. William McGee. Pricilla L. B. Henley was the daughter of William Henley, the security.
May 28, 1845—Robert Childry and Mrs. Elizabeth Butt.
Anthony Nelson, security.
June 7, 1845—Thomas Bishaw and Miss Margaret Wilkins.
Zachariah Sykes, security.
June 17, 1845—Peter Fonto and Miss Martha Ann Butt.
Josiah Deans, security.
July 13, 1845—Edward L. Leroy and Miss Mary Jane Livesay.
Joshua Livesay, security.
Note: Mary Jane Livesay was the daughter of Joshua Livesay.
August 6, 1845—Edward Alexander Paul and Indianna Adelia Smith.
William H. Browne, security.
Note: Indianna Adelia Smith was the daughter of Fowler Smith.
August 7, 1845—Miles D. Taylor and Miss Melvina Miller.
Charles S. Manning, security.
Note: Melvina Miller was the daughter of Margaret Miller.
August 7, 1845—Willis Bass (a man of Indian descent) and Miss Mary Ann Lowry.   Cornelius Ironmonger, security.
August 9, 1845—Edward George and Mrs. Ann Eliza Hanse.
William H. Ferguson, security.
August 30, 1845—William H. Dammeron and Miss Sarah E. Shipp.
George Blow, security.
Note: The above couple were married the same day by the Rev. Edward Wadsworth.
September 2, 1845—William C. Stone and Miss Nancy E. Land.
John (mark) West, security.
September 10, 1845—John McWilliams and Miss Emeline Reilly.
Joseph C. Reilly, security.
September 13, 1845—John C. Richards and Miss Eliza Miller.
George W. Woodward, security.

September 26, 1845—James E. Field and Miss Jane Barlow.
George (mark) Scott, security.
September 27, 1845—William Hewson and Miss Martha Minter.
John H. Snider, security.
October 1, 1845—William Davis and Miss Virginia Rowe.
Stacey Flanagan, security.
October 2, 1845—William H. Murphy and Miss Elizabeth F. Van Gover.
John Van Gover, security.
October 8, 1845—Timothy B. Stott and Mrs. Margaret K. Heath.
Thomas (mark) Lowery, security.
October 9, 1845—George Sharp and Miss Mary Owens.
John Houseman, security.
October 15, 1845—John Tinges and Mrs. Ann Alfriend.
William Johnson, security.
October 20, 1845—Walter James Doyle and Miss Celestia E. Reardon.
William Hipkins, security.
Note: The above couple were married October 21st by the Rev. Alexander Histelberger, pastor of the Norfolk Catholic Congregation. William Fitzgerald, Thomas Reardon, Louisa Reardon and Emily Fitzgerald are listed as witnesses.
October 22, 1845—Jacob Zeilin and Miss Virginia Freeman.
William G. Freeman, security.
Note: The above couple were married by the Rev. L. L. Smith. Virginia Freeman, the security.
October 29, 1845—James F. Thorowgood and Miss Rachel Parker Copes.
Edward Hurst, security.
Note: The above couple were married October 29th by the Rev. Edward Wadsworth. Rachel Parker Copes was the daughter of Elizabeth Copes.
October 29, 1845—Benjamin F. Britt and Mrs. Rachael Jennings.
Soloman W. Spratt, security.
Note: The above couple were married the same day by the Rev. William McGee.
November 1, 1845—Edward L. Young and Miss Ann Cornick West.
Thomas B. West, security.
Note: The above couple were married the same day by the Rev. Upton Beall, rector of Christ P. E. Church.
November 10, 1845—Edward Walker and Miss Rosetta Forbes.
Henry (mark) Dickerson, security.
November 18, 1845—Henry Burgess and Miss Caroline Virginia Flanagan.
Benjamin F. Flanagan, security.
Note: The above couple were married the same day by the Rev. Edward Wadsworth.
November 26, 1845—Esau Pickerell and Miss Virginia E. Davis.
Arthur Cooper, security.
Note: The above couple were married November 27th by the Rev. Edward Wadsworth.
December 3, 1845—Babel Taylor and Miss Lovey Ann Sykes.
John (mark) Sykes, security.
Note: The above couple were married December 4th by the Rev. Edward Wadsworth.
December 8, 1845—Samuel Marsh and Miss Mary E. Wilkinson.
Moses P. Robertson, security.
Note: The above couple were married the same day by the Rev. Upton Beall, rector of Christ P. E. Church.

December 11, 1845—Thomas J. Cornick and Miss Margaret F. Cornick.

James Cornick, security.

Note: Margaret F. Cornick was the daughter of James Cornick, the security.

December 16, 1845—Richard D. Cutts and Miss Martha J. Hackley.

George Blow, Jr., security.

Note: The above couple were married the same day by the Rev. Upton Beall, rector of Christ P. E. Church. Martha J. Hackley was the daughter of Harriet Hackley.

December 19, 1845—John B. Dey and Miss Ellen Anna Clarke.

James Smiley, security.

December 23, 1845—Charles Phillips and Miss Harriet M. O'Gilvie.

Charles Wheeler, security.

Note: Harriet M. O'Gilvie was the daughter of Elizabeth Payne.

December 23, 1845—William Glennan and Miss Mary Woods.

Henry Tullock, security.

Note: The above couple were married the same day by the Rev. Alexander Histelberger, pastor of the Norfolk Catholic Congregation. Michael Glennan and Mrs. E. Tullock are listed as witnesses.

December 24, 1845—John Walker and Miss Margaret Millar.

William Wilson Lamb, security.

Note: The above couple were married December 24th by the Rev. Edward Wadsworth.

1846

January 1, 1846—John Hill and Miss Ann Maria Craver.

George Groner, security.

Note: The above couple were married January 2nd by the Rev. Edward Wadsworth.

January 5, 1846—Caleb Dudley and Miss Emma Heath.

Johnson Dudley, security.

January 6, 1846—Sheldon T. Burton and Miss Louisa E. Rudder.

Jonathan K. Rudder, security.

January 12, 1846—John Conrad and Miss Mahala Mace.

Robert Hayes, security.

January 13, 1846—Jose Arguinano and Miss Martha Anna Hyser.

Joaquin Bayto, security.

January 17, 1846—Joseph J. Dukes and Miss Sabra Hollowell.

William F. Long, security.

January 20, 1846—Elisha R. Johnson and Mrs. Julia A. Browne.

George Cross, security.

Note: The above couple were married January 22nd by the Rev. Alexander Histelberger, pastor of the Norfolk Catholic Congregation. Charles Wheeler and Sarah Ann Flyn are listed as witnesses.

January 22, 1846—Alexander Galt and Miss Mary Anne Raincock.

Edward S. Pegram, security.

Note: The above couple were married January 22nd by the Rev. Upton Beall, rector of Christ P. E. Church.

January 24, 1846—William J. Phillips and Miss Eliza Jane Shorter.

Peter Shorter, security.

Note: The above couple were married January 26th by the Rev. Edward Wadsworth. Eliza Jane Shorter was the daughter of Peter Shorter, the security.

Januay 27, 1846—Charles Cooke and Peachy Baretta (free negroes).

John (mark) Fuller, security.

January 28, 1846—William B. Canfield and Miss Mary Virginia Decormis.
Edward Decormis, security.
February 2, 1846—Andrew J. Capps and Miss Dorcus Murrell.
Dennis H. Dawley, security.
February 5, 1846—James Ferris and Miss Maria Carroll.
David Cull, security.

Note: The above couple were married the same day by the Rev. Alexander His-telberger, pastor of the Norfolk Catholic Congregation. Mr. Cull, Mr. and Mrs. McCarrick, Miss Burt and Miss French are listed as witnesses.

February 6, 1846—William L. Roach and Miss Anna Dugan.
Orsemus Bannor, security.
February 7, 1846—Henry Downes and Mrs. Balinda Willmot.
William Sparrow, security.
February 9, 1846—William B. Haynes and Miss Virginia Shepherd.
Benjamin Emerson, security.

Note: Virginia Shepherd was the daughter of Sarah M. C. Shepherd. The above couple were married February 10th by the Rev. Upton Beall.

February 12, 1846—John A. Cook and Miss Ellen Stone.
John (mark) Allen, security.

Note: The above couple were married the same day by the Rev. Upton Beall, rector of Christ P. E. Church. Ellen Stone was the daughter of Frances Stone.

February 17, 1846—Thomas Brooks and Miss Mary C. Johnson.
John M. Foster. security.
February 18, 1846—Charles H. Guild and Miss Susan A. Thayer.
James Little, security.

Note: Susan A. Thayer was the daughter of C. Thayer.

February 19. 1846—Peter Powell and Miss Jane Eliza Jackson.
William Jackson, Jr., security.

Note: The above couple were married the same day by the Rev. Edward Wads-worth. Jane' Eliza Jackson was the daughter of William Jackson, Jr.

February 20, 1846—William Graham and Miss Virginia Dozier.
Thomas (mark) Graham, security.

Note: Virginia Dozier was the daughter of Cader Dozier.

February 25, 1846—William B. Burnham and Miss Anna S. Hynd.
James Hynd, security.
February 25, 1846—John H. Haskell and Miss Crawford Reid.
Andrew Reid, security.
February 25, 1846—Franklin G. Moore and Miss Harriet M. Fentress.
Cary Fentress, security.

Note: The above couple were married the same day by the Rev. Edward Wads-worth.

March 5, 1846—Josiah Clift and Miss Emeline Watts.
John Watts, security.

Note: Emeline Watts was the daughter of John Watts, the security.

March 9, 1846—William A. Smith and Miss Eliza Godfrey.
Daniel R. Jackson, security.
March 14, 1846—John W. Comstock and Jerusha Simms.
James Baker, security.

Note: The above couple were married March 15th by the Rev. Upton Beall, rector of Christ P. E. Church.

March 17, 1846—John J. Lowry and Miss Louisa Ann Hallman.
Samuel Hallman. security.

Note: The above couple were married March 18th by the Rev. Edward Wads-worth. Louisa Ann Hallman was the daughter of Samuel Hallman, the security.

March 19, 1846—Lewis Holloway and Miss Susan Tunnell.

Thomas Davis. security.

Note: The above couple were married the same day by the Rev. Upton Beall, rector of Christ P. E. Church.

March 23, 1846—Joseph DeMercier and Miss Amelia Jordan.

Nicholas Beauclair, security.

March 26, 1846—Thomas F. Roundey and Miss Mary E. C. Fentress.

Lemual (mark) Fentress, security.

Note: Mary E. C. Fentress was the daughter of Lemuel Fentress, the security.

April 2, 1846—(Doctor) Richard C. Perkins and Miss Martha M. Sheild.

Richard H. Sheild, security.

Note: Martha M. Sheild was the daughter of Martha Sheild.

April 7, 1846—Moses Mayer and Miss Bette Sarlonis.

Jacob Umstadter, security.

April 13, 1846—James Diggs and Miss Mary Ann Langley.

Gabriel (mark) Manox, security.

Note: The above couple were married the same day by the Rev. Edward Wadsworth.

April 14, 1846—Hunter Woodis and Miss Louisa E. Reardon.

Henry B. Reardon, security.

Note: The above couple were married the same day by the Rev. Alexander Histelberger, pastor of the Norfolk Catholic Congregation. J. F. Hunter and the Misses Robinson, Emily Fitzgerald and Margaret Reardon are listed as witnesses.

April 14, 1846—Nathaniel Hill and Miss Amelia Perry.

William Tebo, security.

Note: The above couple were married April 18th by the Rev. Edward Wadsworth.

April 15, 1846—Frances Dawes, Jr., and Miss Mary A. V. Bluford.

George W. Bluford, security.

May 7, 1846—Dennis Kennedy (U. S. A. O. P.) and Mrs. Margaret Watters.

Patrick McCarrick, security.

Note: The above couple were married the same day by the Rev. Alexander Histelberger, pastor of the Norfolk Catholic Congregation. Mrs. Barrot and Mrs. M. F. Branda are listed as witnesses.

May 7, 1846—Jacob Smith and Miss Jane H. Whitehurst.

A. S. Dozier, security.

Note: The above couple were married the same day by the Rev. Edward Wadsworth.

May 14, 1846—Robert J. McCandlish and Miss Ann W. Sheild.

James M. McCandlish, security.

Note: The above couple were married the same day by the Rev. Upton Beall, rector of Christ P. E. Church.

May 27, 1846—John Randall Hayner and Miss Eliza Louisa Smith.

Alexander M. Pennock, security.

Note: The above couple were married the same day by the Rev. Upton Beall, rector of Christ P. E. Church. Eliza Louisa Smith was the daughter of Charles Smith.

May 28, 1846—William B. Kirwin and Miss Sarah Ann Shorter.

Peter Shorter, security.

Note: Sarah Ann Shorter was the daughter of Peter Shorter, the security.

June 1, 1846—Elijah Knox and Miss Louisiana Taylor.

George W. Snyder, security.

June 2, 1846—William H. Broughton and Miss Amelia D. Hartshorn.

Sylvanus Hartshorn, security.

June 4, 1846—Soloman Spratt and Miss Eliza Cutrell.
James H. Jones, security.
Note: Eliza Cutrell was the daughter of Harriet Cutrell.
June 10, 1846—Henry Irwin and Miss Cornelia G. Whitehead.
Nathan C. Whitehead, security.
June 16, 1846—William Quick and Miss Harriet Fentress.
John D. James, security.
July 20, 1846—David Crocker and Miss Mary Young.
Stephen Fisher, security.
Note: The above couple were married the same day by the Rev. Stephen Fisher.
July 28, 1846—John N. Wilkinson and Miss Martha Elizabeth Bissell.
Benjamin Bissell, security.
Note: Martha Elizabeth Bissell was the daughter of Benjamin Bissell, the security.
August 26, 1846—George Blow, Jr., and Miss Elizabeth Allmand.
Tazewell Taylor, security.
Note: The above couple were married the same day by the Rev. Upton Beall, rector of Christ P. E. Church. Elizabeth Allmand was the daughter of Albert (died 1831) and Margaret O'Grady Allmand.
September 19, 1846—William Parkerson and Mrs. Rebecca Mellson.
S. Reynolds, security.
October 1, 1846—Benjamin F. Anderson and Miss Mary F. Gilbert.
F. A. Sibley, security.
Note: Mary F. Gilbert was the daughter of Elizabeth Gilbert.
October 1, 1846—Alexander M. Pennock and Miss Margaret Loyall.
Monroe Kelly, security.
Note: The above couple were married the same day by the Rev. Upton Beall, rector of Christ P. E. Church.
October 5, 1846—(Captain) James C. Ryan and Miss Ann Eliza Holmes.
Robert Marsh, ecurity.
Note: The above couple were married the same day by the Rev. Alexander Histelberger, pastor of the Norfolk Catholic Congregation. Captain Marsh, La. Helmes and Margaret Simmons are listed as witnesses.
October 10, 1846—James Willis and Mrs. Margaret H. Armstrong.
Henry Thompson, security.
October 14, 1846—Henry F. Thompson and Miss Mary Elizabeth Meagher.
James (mark) House, security.
Note: The above couple were married the same day by the Rev. Alexander Histelberger, pastor of the Norfolk Catholic Congregation. John Kelly and Hannah Stavro ar listed as witnesses.
October 20, 1846—Erasmus T. Hayner and Miss Charlotte C. Swain.
Sewall Goodridge, security.
October 20, 1846—Carter P. Johnson and Miss Anne L. Forrest.
Samuel Forrest, security.
October 29, 1846—Richard B. Grinalds and Miss Mary Frances Ballance.
Elkaner Ballance, security.
November 4, 1846—James Jordan and Miss Lydia Holmes.
Shelbon Mahone, security.
November 24, 1846—Francis R. Allen and Miss Harriet F. Seymour.
James S. Gaskins, security.
Note: The above couple were married the same day by the Rev. Thomas Crowder, Jr.
November 25, 1846—Jim Tynes (of Rose) and Creasy Whitfield (free negroes).
John Perkins, security.

183

November 26, 1846—Samuel S. Dawes and Miss Mary Jane Seymour.

William Doyle, security.

Note: The above couple were married November 29th by the Rev. Upton Beall, rector of Christ P. E. Church.

Novembre 26, 1846—John W. Williams and Mrs. Charlotte Springer.

William (mark) Urquhart, security.

December 1, 1846—Benjamin C. Gray and Miss Susan E. Reid.

Charles Reid, security.

Note: Susan E. Reid was the daughter of Charles Reid, the security.

December 2, 1846—William P. Ashley and Miss Virginia D. Guy.

Elias Guy, security.

Note: Virginia D. Guy was the daughter of Elias Guy, the security.

December 8, 1846—Charles S. Allmand and Miss Sarah C. Croel.

John H. Stout, security.

Note: The above couple were married the same day by the Rev. Thomas Crowder, Jr.

December 9, 1846—Robert Frost and Miss Lorina Mathias.

David Mathias, security.

December 9, 1846—John S. Vaughn (of Richmond) and Miss S. E. E. Brunet.

J. B. Minten, security.

December 16, 1846—William Church and Miss Mary Elizabeth Lines.

William Greenwood, security.

December 23, 1846—John W. Keeling and Mrs. Mary Ann D. Berry.

Nathaniel Currier, security.

Note: The above couple were married the same day by the Rev. Thomas Crowder, Jr.

December 24, 1846—Anthony Nelson and Miss Mary Frances Summers.

Ezra T. Summers, security.

Note: Mary Frances Summers was the daughter of Ezra T. Summers, the security.

December 31, 1846—William Hartman and Mrs. Katy Rose.

James (mark) Hollan, security.

Note: The above couple were married the same day by the Rev. Upton Beall, rector of Christ P. E. Church.

1847

January 13, 1847—Edward P. Grifith and Miss Mary Eliza Beale.

William P. Grifith, security.

Note: The above couple were married by the Rev. H. B. Cowles. Mary Eliza Beale was the daughter of Catherine C. Beale.

January 14, 1847—Dennis H. Dawley and Miss Mary Ann McCann.

Andrew J. Capps, security.

Note: The above couple were married the same day by the Rev. Alexander Histelger. Mrs. Cutherel, Mrs. Franch and Mrs. Palmer are listed as witnesses.

January 20, 1847—James Tatem and Miss Ann F. Etheredge.

William P. Sparrow, security.

January 21, 1847—John Burke and Mrs. Margaret Culpepper.

Andrew (mark) Brice, security.

January 28, 1847—Robert V. Montague and Miss Elizabeth Robinson.

Andrew Simmons, security.

Note: Robert V. Montague was the son of W. V. Montague and Elizabeth Robinson was the ward of Enoch Lance.

January 28, 1847—John A. McLean and Miss Margaret F. Guy.

Elias Guy, security.

Note: Margaret F. Guy was the daughter of Elias Guy, the security.

January 28, 1847—William T. White and Miss Anne Pebworth.
William Taylor, security.
January 28, 1847—John Mathews and Mrs. Martha Allen.
William (mark) Masling, security.
February 12, 1847—Thomas Walker and Miss Emily Belote.
James E. Oakley, security.
February 15, 1847—Peter Conner and Miss Frances Etheredge.
James Tremayne, security.
February 15, 1847—(Doctor) Jerome B. Jones and Miss Mary Watters.
James Watters, security.
Note: The above couple were married the same day by the Rev. H. B. Cowles.
February 16, 1847—James Johnson (widower) and Mrs. Elizabeth Lewis.
Charles Hitchcock, security.
February 20, 1847—George Prysough and Mrs. Elizabeth Merchant.
William Hewson, security.
March 1, 1847—John T. Griffin and Miss Elizabeth S. Howell.
John Hammer, security.
Note: Elizabeth S. Howell was the daughter of Mary Howell.
March 3, 1847—William N. Blow and Miss Lavinia Cargill.
George Blow, Jr., security.
March 15, 1847—Jean Anthim Lefebvre and Miss Mary Elizabeth Simms.
James Baker, security.
March 17, 1847—Thomas D. Wallace and Mrs. Elizabeth S. Jones.
John A. McLean, security.
Note: The above couple were married the same day by the Rev. H. B. Cowles.
March 20, 1847—Charles James Calcutt and Miss Rosanna Hammon.
Benjamin A. Morris, security.
Note: The above couple were married the same day by the Rev. Alexander His-
telberger, pastor of the Norfolk Catholic Congregation. William Trumper, Mrs.
Elizabeth Ann Land and William H. Starr are listed as witnesses.
March 20, 1847—William Trumper and Mrs. Elizabeth Ann Land.
William H. Starr, security.
March 25, 1847—John R. Hathaway and Miss Ann Eliza Kirby.
George Kirby, security.
Note: Ann Eliza Kirby was the daughter of George Kirby, the security.
March 27, 1847—George W. Dill and Miss Ann Curtis.
William Howard, security.
April 1, 1847—John O. Moore and Miss Lydia Caroline Ballance.
Elkanah Ballance, security.
Note: The above couple were married the same day by the Rev. H. B. Cowles.
April 3, 1847—John Wyman and Miss Susan Wood.
David Wright, security.
Note: The above couple were married the same day by the Rev. H. B. Cowles.
April 8, 1847—Samuel B. Clarke and Miss Elizabeth J. Barcraft.
Job Rulon, security.
Note: The above couple were married the same day by the Rev. H. B. Cowles.
Elizabeth Barcraft was the daughter of James Barcraft.
April 8, 1847—Isaac O. Gardner and Miss Sarah Ann Cason.
Joseph Cason, security.
April 15, 1847—John Hammer and Miss Julia Turner.
Thomas Turner, security.
Note: Julia Turner was the daughter of Thomas Turner, the security. The
above couple were married the same day by the Rev. H. B. Cowles.

185

April 15, 1847—Benjamin Armer and Miss Rebecca Welch.

James Harrison, security.

Note: Rebecca Welch was the daughter of Sarah Welch.

April 21, 1847—John B. Newman and Miss Savilla Gale.

William K. Powell, security.

Note: The above couple were married the same day by the Rev. H. B. Cowles. Savilla Gale was the ward of Henry Tynes of Isle of Wight County.

April 24, 1847—Johnson Austin and Ardele (free negroes).

John (mark) Machins, security.

April 26, 1847—Jeremiah Land and Miss Sarah Ann Adylott.

William A. Dozier, security.

May 6, 1847—George Touzard and Miss Elizabeth Frances Murphey.

James (mark) Murphey, security.

Note: Elizabeth Frances Murphey was the daughter of James Murphey, the security.

May 13, 1847—Thomas Stokes and Miss Anne Cutherell.

Elie Cutherell, security.

May 15, 1847—William Boggs and Miss Sarah Rudder.

James (mark) Sweeney, security.

May 17, 1847—Job Rulon and Miss Ellen Barcraft.

William Steele, security.

Note: The above couple were married May 18th by the Rev. H. B. Cowles.

May 18, 1847—Augustus B. Cooke and Miss Sarah Langley.

Armistead T. M. Cooke, security.

Note: The above couple were married the same day by the Rev. H. B. Cowles. Sarah Langley was the daughter of Sarah Langley.

May 24, 1847—Samuel C. Elliott and Miss Agnes H. Coxell.

Isaac M. Smith, security.

Note: The above couple were married the same day by the Rev. H. B. Cowles.

June 16, 1847—William M. Page and Miss Media Ann Johnson.

Andrew Stokes, security.

June 16, 1847—John Waterfield and Miss Charlotte Cannon.

William C. Stone, security.

July 6, 1847—Abram F. Leonard and Miss Virginia Talbot.

George J. Halson, security.

Note: Virginia Talbot was the daughter of Diana Talbot.

July 7, 1847—Robert G. Preston and Mrs. Rebecca F. Doxey.

John C. Rogers, security.

July 20, 1847—Augustus M. Vaughn and Miss Mary L. Armistead.

John P. Leigh, security.

Note: The above couple were married the same day by the Rev. George D. Cummins, rector of Christ P. E. Church.

July 27, 1847—Horsburgh Zabriskie and Miss Virginia Hartshorn.

Sylvanus Hartshorn, security.

Note: Virginia Hartshorn was the daughter of Sylvanus Hartshorn, the security.

August 3, 1847—George Izer and Miss Mary Frances Watts.

John Watts, security.

Note: The above couple were married the same day by the Rev. H. B. Cowles. Mary Frances Watts was the daughter of John Watts, the security.

August 7, 1847—William F. Long and Mrs. Mary Ann Hamilton.

Wilson S. Pepper, security.

August 12, 1847—Moses A. Regensburg and Mrs. Rike Wollef.

Moses Mayer, security.

August 13, 1847—Thomas Finley and Miss Mary Cherry.

James R. Nichols, security.

August 24, 1847—Michael Cordona and Miss Martha Ann Foster.

John (mark) Dixon, security.

August 28, 1847—John E. Etheredge and Miss Mary Ann Howell.

Thomas C. Burroughs, security.

September 7, 1847—Edward Watson and Miss Elkanor Frances Thorowgood

John Lane, security.

Note: The above couple were married the same day by the Rev. H. B. Cowles.
Elkanor Frances Thorowgood was the daughter of Eleany A. Thorowgood.

September 7, 1847—William R. Obear and Miss Eliza Davis.

Elisha R. Johnson, security.

September 13, 1847—Joseph Davis and Miss Jemima Cutherell.

Thomas Stokes, security.

Note: The above couple were married the same day by the Rev. H. B. Cowles.

September 16, 1847—Otway C. Barnes and Miss Mary Richardson.

William W. Childs, security.

September 21, 1847—William H. Henderson and Miss Lucy Thomas.

William F. Long, security.

September 25, 1847—Caleb Dudley and Miss Ann Jones.

Clarke Hitchcock, security.

Note: The above couple were married the same day by the Rev. George D.
Cummins, rector of Christ P. E. Church. Ann Jones was the daughter of Pemma
Jones.

October 5, 1847—Augustus Winslow and Miss Elizabeth Ann Watts.

John Watts, security.

October 6, 1847—Edward Delany and Miss Amanda E. Hodges.

William D. Delany, security.

Note: The above couple were married October 7th by the Rev. H. B. Cowles.

October 6, 1847—Edmund Bradford and Miss Ann E. Tazewell.

Mathew P. Waller, security.

Note: The above couple were married October 7th by the Rev. George D. Cummins, rector of Christ P. E. Church.

October 6, 1847—Benjamin Davis and Miss Sarah Cutherill.

Elie Cutherill, security.

October 8, 1847—David F. Keeling and Miss Sarah Ann Johnston.

John R. Langley, security.

Note: Sarah Ann Johnston was the daughter of John H. Johnston.

October 12, 1847—N. G. Roberts and Miss Mary A. E. Hunt.

George L. Crow, security.

Note: Mary A. E. Hunt was the daughter of Eiza A. Owen.

October 13, 1847—David P. Williams and Miss Mary F. Haynes.

Henry F. Thompson, security.

October 19, 1847—Richard H. Applewhaite and Miss Mary Frances
Thrift.

Stephen W. Thrift, security.

Note: The above couple were married the same day by the Rev. H. B. Cowles.

October 28, 1847—Michael Rigney and Miss Jane Sykes.

William (mark) Voss, security.

November 1, 1847—Jacob Irvin and Mrs. Eliza Marshall.

Harrison (mark) Winfree, security

November 3, 1847—John Harris and Miss Mary Elizabeth Diggs.

William P. Burnham, security.

Note: Mary Elizabeth Diggs was the daughter of Ann S. Diggs.

November 4, 1847—Henry Coleman and Mrs. Nancy Anderson.

William Hess, security.

November 8, 1847—William W. Gregory and Miss Ellen V. S. Upshur.

Peter P. Mayo, security.

November 10, 1847—Henry O. Blenis and Miss Mary Anne Radcliff.

John Hatter, security.

November 10, 1847—John H. McCrackin and Miss Mary R. Weaver.

Henry O'Blenis, security.

November 13, 1847—Henry Pegler and Miss Catherine Rowe.

John H. McCrackin, security.

November 15, 1847—William Sutton and Miss Catherine Follen.

Charles H. Guild, security.

November 17, 1847—Charles Thomas Burgess and Miss Elenora E. Johnson.

William H. Johnson, security.

November 18, 1847—Thomas James and Miss Ann Eliza Stevenson.

Robert O. James, security.

November 18, 1847—James A. H. Pearce and Miss Eliza Bell Broughton.

George W. Sheffield, security.

' Note: The above couple were married by the Rev. James Stratton, a Portsmouth Presbyterian minister.

November 25, 1847—Joseph Bailey and Miss Mary Ann Wicker.

William H. Henderson, security.

November 25, 1847—Thomas Boult and Mary Jane P. Pigg.

William D. Delany, security.

November 25, 1847—John B. Gronewall and Miss Mary Virginia Davis.

Edward Wynne, security.

December 2, 1847—John S. White and Miss Mary Ann Dolt.

Job Jakeman, security.

Note: Mary Ann Dolt was the daughter of "Mary Ann Jakeman, formerly Mary Doldt.

December 7, 1847—Howard T. Hall and Miss Didemma Capps.

Ryland Capps, security.

Note: Didemma Capps was the orphan of Caleb Capps of Princess Anne County and the ward of Ryland Capps, the security.

December 8, 1847—Thomas B. Whiting and Miss Hannah Bassett Stark.

William D. Bagnall, security.

Note: The above couple were married the same day by the Rev. George D. Cummins, rector of Christ P. E. Church. In his list the name of the bride is given as Harriet Bassett Stark.

December 9, 1847—Edward Wynn and Miss Mary Woods.

Michael Glennan, security.

Note: The above couple were married December 10th by the Rev. Alexander Histelberger, pastor of the Norfolk Catholic Congregation. Michael Glennan and Margaret Numan are listed as witnesses.

December 11, 1847—Archibald Smith and Mrs. Elizabeth Davis.

John J. Thompkins, security.

December 16, 1847—William H. Maurice and Miss Elizabeth J. Ball.

Joshua D. Reed, security.

December 17, 1847—Rolland Loomis and Mrs. Sneeny Newburn.

Thomas Myers, security.

Note: The above couple were married the same day by the Rev. H. B. Cowles.

December 18, 1847—William C. Tarrant and Miss Rebecca Frances Balsom.

William Balsom, security.

Note: Rebecca Frances Balsom was the daughter of William Balsom.

December 22, 1847—James Helsen and Mrs. Martha Ann Hewson.
John H. Snider, security.
December 23, 1847—George Washington Wood and Miss Sarah Frances Whitehurst.
A. S. Dozier, security.
December 27, 1847—John Keys and Miss Elizabeth Callamber.
Isaac W. Turner, security.
Note: The above couple were married the same day by the Rev. H. B. Cowles. Elizabeth Callamber was the daughter of Elizabeth B. Callamber.
December 28, 1847—John B. Stavro and Miss Eliza A. Barker.
Henry Cotten, security.
Note: The above couple were married December 30th by the Rev. Alexander Histelberger, pastor of the Norfolk Catholic Congregation. George and Hannah Stavro are listed as witnesses.

1848

January 1, 1848—Frank Kemp and Mary Catherine Roney (free negroes).
Maximilian Herbert, security.
January 11, 1848—William S. Camp and Miss Mary E. Bonsal.
George Reid, security.
Note: The above couple were married January 13th by the Rev. George D. Cummins, rector of Christ P. E. Church.
January 12, 1848—James Foster and Miss Mary Ellen Dennis.
Wilson (mark) Johnson, security.
Note: The above couple were married January 13th by Stephen S. Barrett, a local Christian elder.
January 13, 1848—Willis Calvin Rawls and Mrs. Alaphair Dennis.
William H. Howe, security.
Note: The above couple were married January 13th by Stephen S. Barrett, a local Christian elder.
January 14, 1848—Clement Hill and Miss Catherine Keeling.
William Brown, security.
Note: Clement Hill was the son of Henry Hill.
January 17, 1848—Edward Patterson and Miss Virginia Mahoney.
Shelburne Mahone, security.
January 17, 1848—Hezekiah Williams and Mrs. Hannah Skinner.
Edward A. Latimer, security.
January 17, 1848—John C. Pemberton and Miss Martha O. Thompson.
William E. Cunningham, security.
Note: The above couple were married January 18th by the Rev. George D. Cummins, rector of Christ P. E. Church.
January 17, 1848—George Fallon and Miss Hannah Nunan.
Richard Nunan, security.
Note: Hannah Nunan was the daughter of Richard Nunan, the security.
February 1, 1848—Simon Stone and Miss Jane A. Dodd.
Thomas A. Dodd, security.
Note: The above couple were married the same day by the Rev. Alexander Histelberger, pastor of the Norfolk Catholic Congregation. John, Thomas and Eliza Dodd are listed as witnesses.
February 2, 1848—Robert Clarke and Miss Ann Grimstead.
Joseph Hall, security.
February 3, 1848—Charles Lewey and Miss Ann Warren.
John (mark) Warren, security.
February 7, 1848—John Myers and Miss Elizabeth Richardson.
William W. Childs, security.

February 9, 1848—Michael McCabe and Miss Elizabeth Evans.

Richard Nunan, security.

Note: The above couple were married the same day by the Rev. Alexander Histelberger, pastor of the Norfolk Catholic Congregation. Brian Carvanagh and Mary Boyle are listed as witnesses.

February 14, 1848—George W. Stavro and Miss Jane A. E. Lappin.

Benjamin A. Morris, security.

Note: The above couple were married February 16th by the Rev. Alexander Histelberger, pastor of the Norfolk Catholic Congregation. John Stavro and R. Hefton are listed as witnesses.

February 15, 1848—Robert W. Jackson and Miss Mary A. A. Mears.

John B. Collins, security.

February 16, 1848—John Collins and Miss Lilly Weston.

Robert (mark) West, security.

February 24, 1848—Mathew P. Waller and Miss Mary Tazewell.

George J. Halson, security.

Note: The above couple were married the same day by the Rev. George D. Cummins, rector of Christ P. E. Church.

March 2, 1848—William W. Childs and Miss Mary Ann Rogers.

William C. Diggs, security.

March 8, 1848—William R. Steel and Miss Martha Ann Rulon.

Samuel Rulon, security.

Note: Martha Ann Rulon was the daughter of Samuel Rulon.

March 6, 1848—Michael Newman and Miss Elizabeth Diggs.

William Forrest, security.

March 14, 1848—John E. Purdie and Mrs. Elizabeth S. Holmes.

James H. Jones, security.

Note: The above couple were married the same day by the Rev. William McGee.

March 15, 1848—Jonathan Gove (or Gore) and Mrs. Elizabeth Simpson.

S. O. Merwin, security.

March 20, 1848—John A. Higgins and Miss Margaret T. DeBree.

David F. Keeling, security.

Note: The above couple were married the same day by the Rev. Alexander Histelberger, pastor of the Norfolk Catholic Congregation. H. B. Reardon and Fitzgerald are listed as witnesses.

March 30, 1848—Richard E. Riddick and Miss Mary Eliza Lyon.

Thomas O. Dixon, security.

April 4, 1848—A. A. Gwaltney and Miss Margaret Thayer.

Collin Thayer, security.

Note: The above couple were married by the Rev. James S. Gwaltney of Sussex County. Margaret Thayer was the daughter of Collin Thayer, the security.

April 11, 1848—John Allen and Miss Ann Diggs.

Gabriel (mark) Mannox, security.

April 17, 1848—Littleton T. Waller and Miss Elizabeth C. Robertson.

Harrison Robertson, security.

April 27, 1848—William H. Goodson and Miss Bathsheba A. Murphey.

John J. Murphey, security.

Note: The above couple were married the same day by the Rev. James D. Couling of Portsmouth, Va.

May 2, 1848—(Doctor) Henry Selden and Miss Mary E. Ludlow.

George J. Halson, security.

Note: The above couple were married May 3rd by the Rev. George D. Cummins.

May 6, 1848—George Sharp and Mrs. Harriet Williamson.

Samuel (mark) Kidd, security.

May 16, 1848—Charles H. Gerkin and Frances M. DeMurcia.

Note: There is no bond for the above marriage in the files of the Corporation Court. It was copied from the returns of the Rev. George D Cummins, rector of Christ P. E. Church.

May 17, 1848—John N. Baird and Miss Virginia T. Wathall.

E. C. Robinson, security.

May 17, 1848—C. F. Greenwood and Miss Mary Elizabeth Griffin.

John Griffin, security.

Note: Mary Elizabeth Griffin was the daughter of John Griffin, the security.

May 25, 1848—John Fuller and Nancy Brown (free negroes).

John (mark) Williams, security.

May 16, 1848—Henry C. Hardy and Miss Huldah E. Dozier.

John B. Hardy, security.

Note: Huldah E. Dozier was the daughter of Lydia Dozier.

May 16, 1848—C. R. Hendrickson and Miss Ellen F. Dwight.

Thomas D. Toy, security.

May 31, 1848—John S. Whittle and Miss Sarah Ann Southgate.

James H. North, security.

Note: The above couple were married June 1st by the Rev. George D. Cummins, rector of Christ P. E. Church.

June 5, 1848—James Weithman and Mrs. Susan Taylor.

Jesse Dudley, security.

June 6, 1848—George R. Wilson and Miss Claudia Sharp.

William W. Sharp, security.

Note: The above couple were married June 7th by the Rev. George D. Cummins, rector of Christ P. E. Church.

June 6, 1848—Joseph W. Pugh and Miss Mary Louisa Young.

Miles S. Cox, security.

June 12, 1848—Benjamin F. Bailey and Miss Sarah Shackleford.

Robert Clemmitt, security.

Note: The above couple were married June 13th by the Rev. George D. Cummins, rector of Christ P. E. Church.

June 19, 1848—William S. Beers and Miss Lelia Ann Currier.

Nathaniel Currier, security.

Note: Lelia Ann Currier was the daughter of Nathaniel Currier, the security.

June 20, 1848—John T. Slater and Miss Mary C. Trible.

Benjamin Brown, security.

Note: Mary C. Trible was the daughter of Mary Anne Trible.

June 24, 1848—Robert A. Currier and Miss Frances A. Lee.

Nathaniel B. Lee, security.

June 27, 1848—Henry Newman and Miss Mary Ann Milby.

John H. Knewstep, security.

July 5, 1848—John J. Cannon and Miss Mary E. Bryan.

James Bryan, security.

Note: Mary E. Bryan was the daughter of James Bryan, the security.

July 11, 1848—Merit Powell and Mrs. Louisa Summerson.

Enoch Insley, security.

Note: The above couple were married the same day by the Rev. Thomas Bradshaw.

July 12, 1848—Slaughter Sykes and Miss Jane Hay.

William J. Hay, security.

August 3, 1848—John Williams and Miss Sophia Bray.

Zebedee Harper, security.

August 24, 1848—Willis Plummer and Miss Virginia Smith.

John Burgess, security.

Note: The above couple were married the same day by the Rev. William McGee.

September 7, 1848—James Price and Mrs. Elizabeth Hilling.

Robert (mark) Addison, security.

September 11, 1848—Calthorpe Howard and Miss Arlethia L. Jordan.

Henry Howard, security.

Note: Calthrope Howard was the son of Henry Howard, the security, and Arlethia L. Jordan was the daughter of Jamima Jordan.

September 11, 1848—George Bowzer and Frances A. Cotton (free negroes).

Munroe Madison Ricks, security.

September 14, 1848—John Wilson and Miss Mary Ann Haggerty.

Thomas (mark) Penny, security.

September 20, 1848—William G. Mooney and Miss Sarah Ann Shipp.

John (mark) Shipp, security.

Note: Sarah Ann Shipp was the daughter of John Shipp, the security.

September 22, 1848—Thomas D. Hall and Mrs. Elizabeth C. Collins.

Thomas (mark) Dixon, security.

October 2, 1848—Thomas Stout and Miss Louisa Ann Ashley.

William P. Ashley, security.

October 4, 1848—James Williams and Miss Elizabeth Harrison.

Edward Freshwater, security.

October 11, 1848—Charles Jordan and Miss Martha Ann Wilson.

John D. Gordan, security.

October 12, 1848—John Daniels and Miss Malinda Davis.

John G. Sibley, security.

Note: The above couple were married the same day by the Rev. William McGee.

October 16, 1848—James W. Gaskins and Miss Louisa J. Chamberlain.

James Chamberlain, the security.

Note: Louisa J. Chamberlain was the daughter of James Chamberlaine, the security.

October 17, 1848—(Doctor) Robert W. Rose and Miss Elizabeth T. Parker.

James P. Wright, security.

Note: The above couple were married October 18th by the Rev. George D. Cummins, rector of Christ P. E. Church. Elizabeth T. Parker was the daughter of Nicholas Wilson Parker, who was in turn the son of Copeland Parker and Ann Sinclair.

October 18, 1848—Edward Lloyd Winder and Miss Helen M. Thorburn.

James R. Harrison, security.

October 21, 1848—Dennis Gorman and Miss Sarah P. Cornick.

Thomas Eccles, security.

Note: The above couple were married the same day by the Rev. Alexander Histelberger, pastor of the Norfolk Catholic Congregation. Mr. Eccles and Miss Cornick are listed as witnesses.

October 23, 1848—Jacob Brice and Mrs. Susan Blake.

James Little, security.

Note: The above couple were married the same day by the Rev. Alexander Histelberger, pastor of the Norfolk Catholic Congregation. Mrs. Duffy and Margaret Finchet are listed as witnesses.

October 25, 1848—Joseph Taylor and Miss Anna Jane Broadrick.

Abel (mark) Widgen, security.

Note: The above couple were married the same day by the Rev. William McGee.

October 30, 1848—William H. Quinn and Miss Eliza Fletcher.

John McCargood, security.

November 11, 1848—Christopher C. Hope and Miss Emily Frances Dennis.
Samuel Dennis, security.
Note: Emily Frances Dennis was the daughter of Samuel Dennis, the security. The above couple were married the same day by the Rev. William McGee.

November 17, 1848—Richard W. Fisher and Miss Elizabeth Diggs.
Thomas Eccles, security.

November 30, 1848—George Simpson and Miss Ann Belote.
James (mark) Williams, security.

December 2, 1848—Jacob E. Myers and Miss Henrietta Brimline.
William Woodward, security.

December 5, 1848—Henry E. Irby and Miss Mary Ann Walker.
Christopher Tompkins, security.
Note: The above couple were married December 7th by the Rev. William McGee.

December 11, 1848—Henry Gibbons and Miss Margaret Susan Pratt.
George W. Oast, security.
Note: Margaret Susan Pratt was the daughter of Margaret Susan Pratt.

December 13, 1848—James Francis Hodges and Miss Elizabeth Ann Heath.
Jonathan K. Hodges, security.
Note: The above couple were married December 14th by the Rev. John E. Edwards. James Francis Hodges was the son of Jonathan K. Hodges, the security.

December 13, 1848—William H. Griffin and Miss Margaret F. Mears.
John B. Collins, security.
Note: The above couple were married December 14th by the Rev. John E. Edwards.

December 18, 1848—William J. Moore and Miss Camilla A. Allyn.
Joseph T. Allyn, security.
Note: Camilla T. Allyn was the daughter of Joseph T. Allyn, the security.

December 19, 1848—Herbert M. Marcus and Miss Mary Ann Emerson.
William F. Emerson, security.

December 21, 1848—Samuel A. Tweedy and Miss Eliza C. Lappin.
Thomas Eccles, security.

December 22, 1848—William A. Taylor and Miss Lucy Jane Turner.
Thomas Turner, security.
Note: The above couple were married December 25th by the Rev. John E. Edwards. Lucy Jane Turner was the daughter of Thomas Turner, the security.

December 23, 1848—Ward Millerson and Mrs. Elizabeth Howell.
William L. Shepherd, security.

December 28, 1848—Benjamin P. Owen and Miss Mary Walker.
William Ferguson, security.
Note: The above couple were married the same day by the Rev. John E. Edwards.

1849

January 1, 1849—William Reid and Miss Rebecca Ward.
Peter P. Mayo, security.

January 11, 1849—George W. Whitley and Miss Frances L. Murphy.
John J. Murphy, security.
Note: The above couple were married the same day by the Rev. John E. Edwards.

January 11, 1849—George A. G. Scott and Miss Anna Whiting.
John (mark) Whiting, security.
wards. Anna Whiting was the daughter of John Whiting, the security.

January 13, 1849—Andrew Smith and Miss Martha Murphy.

Nathan C. Whitehead, security.

Note: Married January 14th by the Rev. John E. Edwards.

January 15, 1849—Hamilton C. Brite and Miss Martha McCoy.

Francis Butt, Jr., security.

January 23, 1849—William Hess and Miss Elizabeth Toxey.

Timothy Green, security.

Note: The above couple were married the same day by the Rev. Arthur Cooper.

January 24, 1849—John D. Ghiselin, Jr., and Miss Elizabeth A. Pollard.

William J. Moore, security.

January 30, 1849—Jacob Karcher and Miss Rosina Heller.

Francis Trudewind, security.

January 31, 1849—James Smith and Mrs. Margaret Spence.

Eleazar Stillman, security.

February 1, 1849—Daniel D. Simmons and Mrs. Martha Skinner.

Henry C. Hardy, security.

February 4, 1849—James Butler and Mrs. Catherine Myers.

John Jones, security.

February 3, 1849—Marshall J. Smith and Miss Mary M. Taylor.

Moses P. Robertson, security.

Note: The above couple were married February 5th by the Rev. George D. Cummins, rector of Christ P. E. Church.

February 5, 1849—Nathaniel Taylor and Miss Harriet Ann Peet.

William Peet, security.

Note: The above couple were married February 6th by the Rev. Reuben Jones. Harriet Peet was the daughter of William Peet, the security.

February 7, 1849—Joshua Hall and Miss Nancy Britt.

Richard F. Wilson, security.

February 15, 1849—John S. Murphy and Miss Abigail P. Loring.

William (mark) Johnson, security.

Note: The above couple were married the same day by the Rev. John E. Edwards.

February 15, 1849—William Wright and Miss Elizabeth Ann Bonney.

Jesse M. Caffee, security.

February 22, 1849—John T. Powell and Miss Matilda Clarke.

William (mark) Powell, security.

February 24, 1849—George Martin and Miss Caroline Murden.

Robert Jones, security.

February 28, 1849—John R. Ludlow and Miss Martha M. Jamieson.

Calvert Walke, security.

Note: The above couple were married March 1st by the Rev. George D. Cummins, rector of Christ P. E. Church.

March 13, 1849—Conrad Lingner and Miss Elizabeth Preeschern.

William Greenwood, security.

Note: The above couple were married the same day by the Rev. John E. Edwards.

March 14, 1849—Robert J. Barrett and Miss Martha Pricilla Butt.

John J. Butt, security.

Note: The above couple were married March 15th by the Rev. Reuben Jones.

March 14, 1849—John Orfillia and Mrs. Clarissa Growling.

Joaquin Bayto, security.

Note: The above couple were married March 15th by the Rev. Alexander Histelberger, pastor of the Norfolk Catholic Congregation. Rosa and Mary Frank are listed as witnesses.

March 23, 1849—Robert Kean and Miss Ann Mellon.

James Doherty, security.

Note: The above couple were married the same day by the Rev. Alexander Histelberger, pastor of the Norfolk Catholic Congregation. James Daugherty and Catherine McGee are listed as witnesses.

March 28, 1849—William Rawlins and Miss Sarah Cooke.

James (mark) Holland, security.

March 28, 1849—Philip Ruffin and Sarah Ann Talbot.

John W. Thomas, security.

March 31, 1849—William Doughty and Miss Drucilla Cherry.

Patrick (mark) McCann, security.

April 1, 1849—John J. Thompkins and Miss Harriet L. Bailey.

William H. Murphey, security.

Note: The above couple were married April 5th by the Rev. John E. Edwards.

April 7, 1849—Joseph W. Hall and Mrs. Martha Ann Warden.

George W. Snyder, security.

April 11, 1849—Joseph Wilhelm and Miss Lydia Frances Morse.

Anthony L. Barnes, security.

Note: The above couple were married the same day by the Rev. Reuben Jones. Lydia Frances Morse was the ward of Anthony L. Barnes, the security, who was appointed her guardian by the Court of Princess Anne County November 4, 1839, upon the death of her father Jesse Morse. Lydia Frances Morse also had a brother named Charles Morse.

April 17, 1849—Moses P. Robertson and Miss Elizabeth T. Jones.

Walter H. Taylor, security.

Note: The above couple were married April 18th by the Rev. George D. Cummins, rector of Christ P. E. Church.

April 17, 1849—Thomas C. Burroughs and Miss Mary A. Whitehurst.

Francis E. Price, security.

Note: The above couple were married April 18th by the Rev. Reuben Jones.

April 19, 1849—James Dennis and Miss Elizabeth Goodson.

Pleasant H. Dixon, security.

May 1, 1849—Joseph J. Edwards and Miss Louisa G. Esher.

Thomas F. Owens, security.

May 1, 1849—John Hayman and Miss Elizabeth Ann McCoy.

Thomas D. Wallace, security.

Note: The above couple were married the same day by the Rev. John E. Edwards. Elizabeth Ann McCoy was the daughter of Catherine McCoy.

May 3, 1849—Daniel Francis and Miss Mary Ann Lappin.

Benjamin Morris, security.

Note: The above couple were married the same day by the Rev. Alexander Histelberger, pastor of the Norfolk Catholic Congregation. Mh. Morgan and Mary A. McCarty are listed as witnesses.

May 8, 1849—Henry F. Woodhouse and Miss Georgiana M. Chandler.

John H. Nash, security.

May 17, 1849—Thomas Jenkins and Miss Joyce Callis.

William (mark) Graham, security.

Note: Married the same day by the Rev. John E. Edwards.

May 23, 1849—William H. Lowring and Miss Virginia Ann Belote.

James L. Belote, security.

Note: The above couple were married May 24th by the Rev. John E. Edwards. Virginia Ann Belote was the daughter of James L. Belote, the security.

May 30, 1849—Benjamin Gale and Miss Sarah Daniel.

Moses Quarles, security.

Note: The above couple were married May 31st by the Rev. John E. Edwards.

June 2, 1849—Henry Kayton and Miss Gilly Hersburg.

Morris Hess, security.

June 4, 1849—William Michigan and Miss Sarah Virginia Oldner.

James B. Dyer, security.

Note: The above couple were married June 7th by the Rev. John E. Edwards.

June 9, 1849—Ackey White and Rachael White (free persons of colour).

John W. Thomas, security.

June 14, 1849—Jeremiah Fentress and Miss Barbara Frances Fentress.

Jesse Dudley, security.

Note: Married the same day by the Rev. John E. Edwards.

June 19, 1849—George Cooke and Georgiana Armistead (free negroes).

William Boos, security.

Note: The above couple were married June 20th by the Rev. Reuben Jones.

June 21, 1849—Tedford B. Oyler and Miss Elizabeth Cuthrill.

Soloman W. Spratt, security.

Note: The above couple were married the same day by the Rev. John E. Edwards. Elizabeth Cuthrill was the daughter of Harriet Cuthrill.

June 23, 1849—William G. Ferguson and Miss Sarah E. Small.

Arthur A. Small, security.

Note: The above couple were married June 26th by the Rev. John E. Edwards. Sarah E. Small was the daughter of Amy Small.

June 25, 1849—James B. Thurston and Miss Sarah Ann Owen.

Pearson Owen, security.

Note: The above couple were married June 26th by the Rev. John E. Edwards.

June 28, 1849—William J. Brooks and Miss Sarah J. Stayten.

John Hayman, security.

June 28, 1849—Joseph Boush, Jr., and Sarah Bell (free negroes).

William J. Holmes, security.

Note: The above couple were married the same day by the Rev. John E. Edwards

June 30, 1849—Thomas G. Griffin and Miss Sarah Jane Wood.

Robert J. Wood, security.

July 6, 1849—Micajah Morgan and Mrs. Nancy Powers.

John Quinn, security.

July 7, 1849—James Raymond and Miss Susan N. Thurston.

Nathaniel Williams, security.

Note: The above couple were married July 8th by the Rev. John E. Edwards.

July 9, 1849—Robert Hosier and Miss Jane B. Thompson.

John (mark) Wood, security.

Note: The above couple were married July 10th by the Rev. John E. Edwards.

July 21, 1849—William J. Harris and Miss Virginia Montgomery.

Robert Montgomery, security.

Note: The above couple were married the same day by the Rev. Reuben Jones. Virginia Montgomery was the daughter of Robert Montgomery, the security.

July 24, 1849—David White and Jenny Bell (free persons of colour).

Philip Palmer, security.

July 26, 1849—Francis Shermadine and Miss Elizabeth Wood.

Archibald (mark) Smith, security.

Note: Elizabeth Wood was the daughter of Sarah Jane Wood.

August 1, 1849—Ralph Dixon and Miss Jaquemine Maye.

Joseph L. Maye, security.

August 13, 1849—Robert Searles and Mrs. Ellen Langan.

Thomas A. Dodd, security.

Note: The above couple were married the same day by the Rev. Alexander Histelberger, pastor of the Norfolk Catholic Congregation.

August 16, 1849—William A. Bangs and Mrs. Elizabeth Overman.
James Luckey, security.
August 16, 1849—John G. Bohannan and Miss Laura L. Daniel.
Gideon L. Lamb, security.
August 22, 1849—William Roberts and Miss Ann Miller.
George W. Miller, security.
August 30, 1849—James D. Hanbury and Miss Sarah A. Reid.
John W. Reid, security.
September 4, 1849—John Barnett and Miss Hannah Cecelia Stavro.
Thomas Kevill, security.
Note: The above couple were married September 5th by the Rev. Alexander
Histelberger, pastor of the Norfolk Catholic Congregation. Thomas Kevill and
Eliza Stavro are listed as witnesses. Hanna Cecelia Stavra was the daughter of
Mary F. Cotton.
September 11, 1849—Zedee Westwood and Mrs. Mary Hathaway.
James Woodhouse, security.
September 13, 1849—Terry Boush and Mary Elizabeth Wilkinson (free
persons of colour). Elizabeth (mark) Hancock, security.
September 20, 1849—William Henry Coker and Mrs. Martha Ann Seneca.
Thomas Turner, security.
September 24, 1849—John W. Edmonds and Miss Ann Maria Shuttle.
John (mark) Wood, security.
October 2, 1849—John A. Mayer and Miss Nancy W. Jones.
Thomas A. Mayer, security.
Note: John A. Mayer was the son of Thomas A. Mayer and Nancy W. Jones
was the daughter of Benjamin Jones.
October 11, 1849—Thomas J. Maurice and Miss Martha Ann Langley.
George L. Crow, security.
October 16, 1849—George W. Bartley and Miss Caroline A. Wolf.
Theophilus Miller, security.
Note: Caroline A. Wolf was the daughter of John M. Wolf.
October 16, 1849—Anthony Bargamin and Miss Maria Therese Guyot.
Yves Guyot, security.
Note: The above couple were married the same day by the Rev. Alexander
Histelberger, pastor of the Norfolk Catholic Congregation. V. Bargamin and
Mary Wickham are listed as witnesses.
October 16, 1849—Thomas Spratt and Miss Martha Jane Gregory.
Isaac (mark) Gregory, security.
October 18, 1849—Thomas James Hicks and Miss Frances Manning.
James Luckey, security.
October 29, 1849—John Benton and Miss Mary Bartee.
Jacob G. Decker, security.
October 29, 1849—William C. Yeaton and Miss Mary Frances DuVal.
George W. Cowdery, security.
Note: The above couple were married October 30th by the Rev. George D.
Cummins, rector of Christ P. E. Church.
October 29, 1849—Allan Morrison and Miss Eliza Crozier.
William Greenwood, security.
October 30, 1849—Tully Flanagan and Miss Nancy Harris.
William (mark) Broughton, security.
Note: According to a note included with this bond, Nancy Harris was the
daughter of Elias and Polly Harris was born May 30, 1822.
November 1, 1849—Edmund Shepherd and Delia A. Webb.
Note: Copied from the returns of the Rev. George D. Cummins.

November 5, 1849—John Thomas Martin and Miss Sarah Louisa Hodges.
William A. Coker, security.

November 5, 1849—John M. Brooke and Miss Elizabeth S. Garnett.
William H. Garnett, security.

Note: The above couple were married November 6th by the Rev. George D. Cummins, rector of Christ P. C. Church.

November 8, 1849—Joseph Edmonds and Miss Mary Mason.
John Whitehurst, security.

November 29, 1849—George Stayler, Jr. and Miss Virginia Creakmore.
John Carlon, security.

November 29, 1849—Edward Wallace and Miss Ann Sykes.
Henry Cotton, security.

Note: The above couple were married the same day by the Rev. Alexander Histelberger, pastor of the Norfolk Catholic Congregation. Mrs. Cotton and Eliza Stavro are listed as witnesses.

December 3, 1849—Charles F. McIntosh and Miss Isabella D. Thorburn.
Anthony W. McIntosh, security.

December 4, 1849—John Fuller and Paulina Henley (free persons of colour).
James (mark) Kemp, security.

December 10, 1849—David Duke and Miss Elizabeth L. Land.
Lorenzo Parsons, security.

December 10, 1849—John G. Peake and Miss Agnes Elizabeth Everett.
Arthur T. Harper, security.

Note: Agnes Elizabeth Everett was the daughter of Nancy Everett.

December 19, 1849—Samuel Wilkinson and Miss Elizabeth J. Heath.
P. L. Belote, security.

December 20, 1849—William B. Wood and Miss Rebecca Weymouth.
James Burgess, security.

December 20, 1849—William Brewer and Mrs. Margaret Bailey.
Moses Hudgen, security.

December 20, 1849—James W. Gilbert and Miss Nancy Edwards.
Thomas W. Gilbert, security.

December 20, 1849—William Pannell and E. Fletcher.

Note: The above marriage was copied from the returns of the Rev. George D. Cummins, rector of Christ P. C. Church.

December 21, 1849—Enoch Phelps and Miss Mary Ann Holland.
George Stavro, security.

December 22, 1849—John Banks and Hannah Williams (free persons of colour).
James (mark) Holland, security.

December 24, 1849—Richard J. Rogers and Miss Ellen Owen.
John M. Webb, security.

December 24, 1849—Robert Berry and Miss Mary Jane Land.
William H. Coker, security.

December 24, 1849—Thomas C. Wright and Miss Frances Ann Angel.
Thomas Angel, security.

Note: Frances Ann Angel was the daughter of Thomas Angel, the security.

December 31, 1849—William H. Buck and Miss Mary Jane Spaulding.
Croel Noe, security.

Note: The above couple were married January 1st, 1850, by the Rev. Alexander Histelberger, pastor of the Norfolk Catholic Congregation. John and Catherine Ney and Miss Noe are listed as witnesses.

1 8 5 0

January 3, 1850—William E. Sykes and Miss Zina Mathais.
Peter E. Frost, security.
January 3, 1850—John Wood and Miss Christina Elizabeth Hayman.
James Wood, security.
Note: Christina Hayman was the daughter of Rosetta Hayman.
January 4, 1850—Soloman Unger and Miss Emma Blogg.
Nathan Baum, security.
January 7, 1850—James Cherry and Miss Mary Eliza Butt.
Josiah Deane, security.
January 9, 1849—C. Johan (or Topan) Follen (or Foller) and Miss Jane
Bohm.   James (mark) Hays, security.
January 10, 1850—Aldridge Hall and Miss Mary Eliza Moore.
Arthur T. Harper, security.
Note: Mary Eliza Moore was the daughter of Bartlet Moore.
January 12, 1850—Edward F. Murfee and Miss Josephine V. Carnes.
Joseph Carnes, security.
Note: Josephine V. Carnes was the daughter of Joseph Carnes, the security.
January 14, 1850—William S. Spratley and Miss Mary J. Delany.
William D. Delany, security.
January 15, 1850—George W. Widgen and Elizabeth Jane Hawkins.
Thomas Dunbar, security.
January 16, 1850—Robert W. Davis and Miss Georgianna Raincock.
Edward S. Pegram, security.
Note: The above couple were married the same day by the Rev. George D.
Cummins, rector of Christ P. C. Church.
January 24, 1850—Benjamin A. Barrom and Miss Maria Susan James.
George A. Barrom, security.
Note: Maria Susan James was the daughter of Ann James.
January 31, 1850—Humphrey Davis and Miss Elizabeth Miller.
Joseph Miller, security.
Note: Elizabeth Miller was the daughter of Joseph Miller, the security.
February 11, 1850—Simon Simon and Miss Adelheit Ratshield.
Aaron A. Goldsmith, security.
February 12, 1850—James Watters and Miss Alice A. Delany.
William D. Delany, security.
February 13, 1850—Francis R. Allen and Miss Julianna Dunston Rob-
erts.   William Drew Roberts, security.
Note: Julianna Dunston Roberts was the daughter of William Drew Roberts, the
security.
February 19, 1850—Richard Blow and Miss Laura Jane Dunbar.
William D. Dunbar, security.
February 21, 1850—Daniel Wadsworth and Miss Sarah E. Alford.
Benjamin W. Alford, security.
February 25, 1850—Samuel Cunningham and Mrs. Jane Hogg.
John J. Thompkins, security.
March 4, 1850—James L. Belote and Mrs. Frances Flanagan.
William H. Turner, security.
March 5, 1850—Thomas R. Gray and Miss Elizabeth Owens.
Richard Tooley, security.
March 7, 1850—Francis E. Price and Miss Lucy Ann Martin.
Thomas G. Burroughs, security.

March 7, 1850—William Durfey and Mrs. Jane Cowles.

John (mark) Benson, security.

March 23, 1850—William Sherman and Mrs. Margaret Whitehead.

William Hess, security.

March 29, 1850—Jesse T. Ewell and Miss Elizabeth Van Dalia Face.

James Bennett, security.

Note: Elizabeth Van Dalia Face was the daughter of Catherine Bennett.

April 6, 1850—Samuel Cooper and Miss Mary Ann Oast.

William Godfrey, security.

April 10, 1850—Charles Doleman and Mrs. Nancy Linsey.

Charles A. Merrio, security.

April 10, 1850—William H. Face and Miss Sarah E. Dunbar.

John T. Dunbar, security.

April 18, 1850—Erasmus Lovett and Miss Virginia Dennis.

George Washington Smith, security.

April 18, 1850—Joseph R. Small and Miss Eliza E. Burt.

Augustus Branda, security.

April 25, 1850—Boswell T. Camp and Miss Caroline J. Martin.

Alexander W. Martin, security.

Note: Caroline J. Martin was the daughter of Alexander Martin.

April 25, 1850—Elias R. Newman and Miss Eliza Ricketts.

Henry Fitzgerald, security.

April 25, 1850—Luke McKenny and Miss Sarah R. James.

Robert O. James, security.

Note: Sarah R. James was the daughter of the security.

May 7, 1850—Lewis A. Powers and Mrs. Sarah Ann Beazley.

Thomas Spratt, security.

May 2, 1850—William Harcourt and Miss Mary Ellen Betts.

William M. Betts, security.

May 2, 1850—James N. Sawyer and Mrs. Sophia Thornton.

Joseph Gerald, security.

May 9, 1850—William N. Godwin and Miss Elizabeth S. Vickhouse.

Patrick H. Cutchin, security.

May 11, 1850—Francis Jordan and Eliza Givens (free persons of colour).

James Robinson, security.

May 16, 1850—William H. Fletcher and Miss Virginia Hambury.

Francis Underhill, security.

May 23, 1850—Valentine Perkins and Miss Mary Jane Currier.

Nathaniel Currier, security.

May 23, 1850—Thomas Stokes and Miss Frances Derrah.

Levi (mark) Howard, security.

May 29, 1850—John E. Robinson and Miss Sarah Millerson.

William Brooks, security.

May 30, 1850—N. W. Paynter and Miss Eliza S. Davidson.

Duncan Robertson, security.

Note: The above couple were married "in St. Paul's" by the Rev. William M. Jackson.

June 3, 1850—John S. Taylor and Miss Virginia Williamson.

Robert B. Tunstall, security.

June 4, 1850—George Smith and Miss Mary Ann Gregory.

George (mark) Miller, security.

June 6, 1850—Charles H. Mathews and Mrs. Catherine T. Snyder.
Peter F. Schleiker, security.
Note: The above couple were married the same day by the Rev. Alexander Histelberger, pastor of the Norfolk Catholic Congregation. Mrs. Watson and Bridget Bary are listed as witnesses.
June 12, 1850—Samuel B. Laylor and Mrs. Ann D. Powell.
William K. Powell, security.
June 13, 1850—Elijah L. Etheridge and Mrs. Margaret Cooley.
Isaac (mark) Mordecai, security.
June 13, 1850—William Hamilton and Lydia Mingo (free negroes).
Peter (mark) Wilson, security.
June 14, 1850—Bernard Kayton and Esther Kneip.
Abraham Kayton, security.
June 20, 1850—James Williams and Miss Mary F. Ransone.
James H. Ransone, security.
June 25, 1850—William Wallace and Mrs. Frances Dudley.
Jesse (mark) Speed, security.
June 27, 1850—William Broughton and Mrs. Penny Sawyer.
William Ward, security.
Note: At this time the present marriage license system went into effect. No securities were required from then on.
July 1, 1850—Adolphus H. Jacqueneau and Miss Susan H. Selden.
Note: Susan H. Selden was the daughter of John Selden.
July 1, 1850—Thomas Ribby and Mrs. Bridget Malony.
Note: The above couple were married the same day by the Rev. Alexander Histelberger, pastor of the Norfolk Catholic Congregation.
July 1, 1850—John W. Harwood and Miss Elizabeth J. Moore.
Note: Elizabeth Moore was the daughter of Peter Moore.
July 3, 1850—Thomas Kevill and Miss Augusta Lavinia Shields.
Note: The above couple were married the same day by the Rev. Alexander Histelberger, pastor of the Norfolk Catholic Congregation.
July 3, 1850—Thomas Patton and Miss Mary Kavanaugh.
Note: Mary Kavanaugh was the daughter of Thomas Kavanaugh. The above couple were married the same day by the Rev. Alexander Histleberger.
July 9, 1850—Benjamin Whitehurst and Miss Lovey Cooper.
July 10, 1850—William E. Hodges and Miss Eliza Butt.
July 15, 1850—William R. S. Faulkner and Miss Catherine E. Davis.
July 16, 1850—William G. Burchett and Miss Sarah J. Skinner.
July 16, 1850—Samuel Totten and Miss Sarah Snell.
July 18, 1850—James Diggs and Miss Frances Callis.
July 25, 1850—Smith Murrell and Miss Elizabeth Cooke.
July 30, 1850—Alonzo Sanburn and Elizabeth Powell.
July 31, 1850—Judson R. Pettes and Miss Mary Jane Casey.
Note: Mary Jane Casey was the daughter of Graham Casey.
August 2, 1850—Julius H. Knop and Miss Louisa Brandt.
August 3, 1850—Peter Lent and Miss Annette Meaghers.
Note: Annette Meaghers was the daughter of Susan Howes.
August 6, 1850—Joseph Levy and Miss Henrietta King.
August 7, 1850—Joseph Dudley and Miss Virginia Ann Dennis.
Note: Virginia Ann Dennis was the daughter of James Dennis.
August 8, 1850—William Grieve and Miss Margaret R. Crane.
August 10, 1850—James Buskey and Miss Indianna Edwards.
August 13, 1850—William W. Banks and Miss Caroline Virginia Henley.
Note: Caroline Henley was the daughter of William Henley.

August 15, 1850—James B. Burns and Mrs. Margaret Lawrence.
August 17, 1850—Drew Anderson and Miss Ellen Sawyer.
August 26, 1850—Otto Zwissler and Miss Mary Fessler.
August 29, 1850—Joseph Wilkinson and Miss Virginia Watkins.
September 4, 1850—(Rev.) C. Coleman Hoffman and Miss Virginia H. Hale.
September 4, 1850—William Godfrey and Miss Margaret Susan Williams.
September 6, 1850—Andrew Sweeney and Mrs. Caroline Augusta Smith.
September 10, 1850—George T. Mills and Miss Ann D. Hall.
September 12, 1850—Mills Mathews and Miss Elizabeth Gregory.
    Note: Elizabeth Gregory was the daughter of Isaac Gregory.
September 14, 1850—Charles Antonio Santos and Miss Virginia Diana Todd.
September 14, 1850—John H. Johnson and Miss Laurina Ann Davis.
September 16, 1850—Jesse H. Sikes and Miss Amanda W. Pierce.
    Note: Amanda Pierce was the daughter of Elizabeth F. Pierce.
September 21, 1850—William Robinson (widower) and Mrs. Elizabeth Belote.
September 23, 1850—Tarleton H. Woodson and Miss Elizabeth A. Hopkins.
September 26, 1850—Albert Adam and Miss Mary Proescher.
October 3, 1850—Henry S. Harrison and Miss Elizabeth W. Anson.
October 14, 1850—Samuel R. Borum and Miss Eliza S. Stevenson.
October 16, 1850—Francis Rourk (Rorgie or Rorquie) and Miss Elizabeth Ferrarr.
October 16, 1850—Robert Gale and Miss Mary Catherine Jakeman.
    Note: Mary Catherine Jakeman was the daughter of Job Jakeman.
October 16, 1850—John C. Wood and Miss Elizabeth A. Weymouth.
October 21, 1850—Nicholas M. Pierson and Mrs. Elizabeth Land.
November 5, 1850—John Smith and Polly Holloway (free negroes)
November 14, 1850—James R. Bagley and Miss Rebecca Pollard.
November 18, 1850—James H. Powell and Miss Martha E. Oast.
November 19, 1850—Lewis E. Myers and Miss Sarah Nathans.
November 21, 1850—Mr. Francis Murden and Miss Mary Capehart.
November 25, 1850—John Fisher and Mrs. Mary Ann Counsels.
November 25, 1850—Samuel V. Turner and Miss Elizabeth J. Elliott.
November 29, 1850—Jeremiah Fentress and Miss Sarah Kemp.
November 30, 1850—William Graham and Miss Elizabeth N. Shield.
November 30, 1850—Alexander Powell and Miss Ann Simmons.
December 4, 1850—Edgar L. Brockett and Miss Georgiana C. Seymour.
December 12, 1850—George Lewelling and Mrs. Jane Parr.
December 12, 1850—William H. Granbery and Miss Ann Eliza Gornto.
    Note: Ann Eliza Gornto was the daughter of James Gornto.
December 12, 1850—John B. Foster and Miss Martha A. Oliver.
December 16, 1850—Leonidas L. Smith and Miss Sarah Jane Stewart.
December 17, 1850—William E. Sykes and Miss Julia A. B. Carr.
December 24, 1850—John F. Minter and Miss Amanda Malvina Sexton.
December 24, 1850—Nelson R. Gray and Miss Octavia Billups.
December 26, 1850—Nathaniel S. Walker and Miss Mary Jane Murphy.
December 30, 1850—Emanuel Dunford and Miss Sarah Harrison.
December 30, 1850—William C. Smith and Miss Mary P. Cocke.

CHRIST CHURCH—CHURCH STREET, NORFOLK, VA.

(Cornerstone laid St. John's Day, June 24, 1800. Consecrated by Bishop James Madison.
Destroyed by fire March 9, 1827)

Baptismal Record (1809-1816) Kept By the Rev. Robert Symes, Rector of Christ P. E. Church

————o————

1809

Nathaniel, son of Nathaniel and Polly Boush.
Baptized February 15th, 1809.
John Frederick, son of John and Sarah Dixon.
Baptized February 19th, 1809.
John Hambleton, son of George and Ann Rowland.
Baptized February 19th, 1809.
John Cornick, son of John and Elizabeth Shepherd.
Baptized March 5th, 1809.
Martha Brodie, daughter of William T. and Mary Ann Nimmo.
Baptized March 12th, 1809.
Thomas Decatur, son of James and Sarah Taylor.
Baptized March 15th, 1809; born November 2nd, 1808.
Thomas Newton, son of William and Johanna Armistead.
Baptized March 15th, 1809.
William Reuben, son of William and M. A. Lindsay.
Baptized March 15th, 1809.
Mary, daughter of William and Anne Jones.
Baptized April 30th, 1809.
Richard, son of Edward and Sax. Watson.
Baptized May 1, 1809.
Aaron, son of David and El. Milhado.
Baptized May 1, 1809.
Henry Poindexter, daughter of Nehemiah and Elizabeth Gregory.
Baptized May 8, 1809.
William Eyre, son of Robert B. and Anne Taylor.
Baptized May 11, 1809; born February 18, 1809.
Leliana, daughter of Arch. and Frances Bans.
Baptized May 12, 1809; born April 19, 1809.
Thomas, son of Samuel and Harriot Matthews.
Baptized May 25, 1809; born December 12, 1808.
William, son of William and Margaret Davies.
Baptized May 28, 1809; born May 3, 1809.
Susan Emery, daughter of John and Anne Camp.
Baptized July 2, 1809; born July 14, 1808.
Join Jordan, son of Jno. and Frances Emery.
Baptized July 27; born March 6, 1803.
Anne Eliza, daughter of Thomas and Mary McCandlish.
Baptized September 17; born August 27, 1809.
Margaretta Virginia, daughter of William and Mary Sharp.
Baptized September 17; born August 13, 1809.
William Oldner, son of William and Anne Etheredge.
Baptized September 24, 1809.
Juliana, daughter of John and Elizabeth Stone.
Baptized September 24, 1809; born September 22, 1809.

William, son of Robert E. and Fanny Steed.
> Baptized October 5, 1809; born September 4, 1809.

Caius Mutins, son of John and Anne Nimmo.
> Baptized October 29, 1809; born September 24, 1809.

Martha Eliza, daughter of William and Anne Steven.
> Baptized November 5, 1809; born October 7, 1809.

Margaret Anne Tyler, daughter of Thomas J. and Margaret O. Haynes.
> Baptized December 17, 1809; born November, 1809.

Charles Alexander, son of Charles and Sally Tyler.
> Baptized December 24, 1809; born November, 1804.

William Francis, son of Charles and Sally Tyler.
> Baptized December 24, 1809; born January 29, 1809.

Armistead, son of George and Eliz. W. Booker.
> Baptized December 28, 1809; born October 15, 1806.

John Sclater, son of Rich and Eliz. Booker.
> Baptized December 28, 1809; born September 28, 1808.

Catherine Lowly, daughter of William Sheldon and M. Holinsclater.
> Baptized December 30, 1809; born August 10, 1809.

Sarah Maria Whiting, daughter of Robert and Sarah Cowne.
> Baptized December 30, 1809; born December 6, 1803.

1810

Tabitha Herbert.
> Baptized January 11, 1810.

Margaret (Herbert) (?).
> Baptized January 11, 1810.

Thomas Whiddon, son of Thomas and Anne Gatewood.
> Baptized March 4, 1810; born February 1, 1810.

George, son of George and Margaret Kelly.
> Baptized May 1, 1810; born *dead*.

Francis Henry, son of George and Ann Brown.
> Baptized May 20, 1810; born April 8, 1810.

John Henry, son of John and Margaret Bramble.
> Baptized May 20, 1810; born April 8, 1810.

George Anthony, son of George and Amelia White.
> Baptized May 21, 1810; born December 1, 1809.

Maria Sclater, daughter of Moss and Mildred Armistead.
> Baptized May 21, 1810; born April 3, 1809.

Conway Davis, son of Fortescue and Mary Ann Whittle.
> Baptized December 31, 1809; born March 10, 1809.

Elizabeth Jane, daughter of William M. and Susanna Christian.
> Baptized May 26, 1810; born February 29, 1808.

Henry William, son of Josua and Ann Aphea Herbert.
> Baptized May 31, 1810; born May 2, 1810.

John Phripp Reid, son of Johnson and Sarah Stone.
> Baptized May 4, 1810; born April 10, 1809.

Smallwood, son of William and Eliza Thomson.
> Baptized July 1, 1810; born May 24, 1810.

Mary Ann, daughter of William Lowery (Elizabeth City).
> Baptized July 20; born March 27, 1810.

Henry B. Drisdale.
> Baptized August 12, 1810; born April 1, 1809.

Carolina Henrietta, daughter of George and Cowdery Newton.
> Baptized September 2, 1810; born August 30, 1810.

Harriot, daughter of William Dale and Frances Woodhouse.
> Baptized September 23, 1810; born November 14, 1809.

William Francis, son of Francis and Frances McClanahan.
> Baptized September 23, 1810; born October 2, 1808.

Susannah Stewart, daughter of John S. and Amy Lovett.
> Baptized September 23, 1810; born August 20, 1807.

Elizabeth Melson, daughter of Henry and Adair Behanna.
> Baptized September 29; born January 1, 1809.

Benjamin Franklin, son of Thadeus and Elizabeth McClanchan Bowman.
> Baptized October 12; born February 10, 1810.

Margaret, daughter of Henry M. and .... Armistead.
> Baptized October 14th, 1810.

George William, son of George and Ann Rowland.
> Baptized October 22; born October 5, 1810.

Josua Oldner, son of William and Ann Nicholson.
> Baptized October 22; born August 27, 1810.

Walter Herron, son of Richard and Elizabeth Taylor.
> Baptized October 23; born October 1, 1809.

Louisianna, daughter of Edwd. and Margaret Waddey.
> Baptized December 27; born October 25, 1810.

1811

William Henry, son of Francis and Ann Smith.
> Baptized January 15; born September 25, 1808.

Catherine Horseley, daughter of Francis and Ann Smith.
> Baptized January 15; born December 14, 1809.

Robert Reade, son of Robert S. and Charlotte Symes.
> Baptized January 24; born January 20, 1810.

Harriot Curl, daughter of Simon and Ann Hollier.
> Baptized February 10, 1810.

Julia Armistead, daughter of Simon and Ann Hollier.
> Baptized February 10, 1810.

Carey Hansford, son of Thomas and Amy Blanchard.
> Baptized February 10; born October 8, 1805.

Amy Georgianna, daughter of Thomas and Amy Blanchard.
> Baptized February 10; born August 28, 1807.

Theodore Armistead, son of Thomas and Amy Blanchard.
> Baptized February 10; born October 9, 1810.

Horatius Upshaw, son of John and Eliza Hipkins.
> Baptized February 17; born March 7, 1809.

John, son of John and Eliza Hipkins.
> Baptized February 17; born January 21, 1811.

Frederick Joseph, son of Julian and Dorothea Magagnos.
> Baptized March 7; born February 9, 1811.

Nathaniel, son of Salter and Nancy Colley.
> Baptized January 21; born December 11, 1802.

Mary Willoughby, daughter of Salter and Nancy Colley.
Baptized January 21; born December, 1805.
Leonora, daughter of Salter and Nancy Colley.
Baptized January 21; born December, 1808.
William Price, son of Thomas and Ann Williamson.
Baptized March 18; born July 26, 1810.
Mary Frances, daughter of Jacob and Sarah Valentine.
Baptized March 26; born March 3, 1811.
Littleton Waller Tazewell, son of Fortescue and Mary Ann Whittle.
Baptized April 7; born December 7, 1810.
Emille Eliza, daughter of James and Emilia Delauney.
Baptized April 7; born November 20, 1810.
Frederick Milcah, daughter of William T. and Henrietta Hunter.
Baptized June 2; born May 15, 1811.
Martha Jones Rivery, daughter of William M. and Susanna Christian.
Baptized June 10; born April 19, 1811.
David, son of John and Margaret Hershall.
Baptized July 15; born May 8, 1811.
Rose Lemasurier Celestine, daughter of Lewis and Margaret Boutin.
Baptized July 20; born January 17, 1807.
Augustus, son of Raymond and Sophia Gervais.
Baptized July 20; born February 20, 1807.
John Amedee, son of Raymond and Sophia Gervais.
Baptized July 20; born October 16, 1810.
Merritt Moore, son of Merritt M. and Ann Hartwell Robinson.
Baptized July 26; born February 20, 1811.
Eliza Frances, daughter of William and Mary Sharp.
Baptized August 4; born July 2, 1811.
John Thompson, son of William and Mary Clark.
Baptized August 4; born May 13, 1811.
Richard Archer, son of William and Ann Stevens.
Baptized August 18; born July 25, 1811.
Adeline, daughter of John and .... West.
Baptized September 14; born August 31, 1811.
Nathaniel, son of Nathaniel and Sarah Strong.
Baptized September 14; born June 25, 1811.
John Carr Calvert, son of Richard and Eliza Taylor.
Baptized September 22; born August 31, 1811.
Eliza, daughter of G. W. and Frances Camp.
Baptized September 27; born September 22, 1811.
Henrietta, daughter of George and Courtney Newton.
Baptized September 30; born September 29, 1811.
Juliana, daughter of John and Eliza Stone.
Baptized October 13; born June 10, 1811.

Copeland Leopold Parker, son of William and Ann Pierce Parker Cooper.
Baptized October 20; born March 8, 1811.
Mary Talbot, daughter of Fred. and Helen Kighley.
Baptized October 21; born September 3, 1811.
James, son of Geo. and Elizabeth Reid.
Baptized October 21; born March 30, 1811.

Sarah Ann, daughter of Milnor W. and Elizabeth Peters.
Baptized October 20; born February 27, 1811.
Elizabeth Lydia, daughter of John and Frances Hodges.
Baptized October 27; born October 2, 1811.
William Augustine, son of William Taylor and Sarah Taylor.
Baptized November 4; born June 1, 1811.
Alexander, son of Samuel and Hannah B. Moseley.
Baptized November 22; born November 17, 1811.
Richard Evers, son of William L. and Judith Lee.
Baptized December 8; born July 11, 1811.
Mary Taylor, daughter of Enoch and Mary Sawyer of Camden County, North Carolina.
Baptized December 11; born October 31, 1797.
William Edmund, son of James and Penelope Cunningham.
Baptized December 11; born February 18, 1803.
Mary Ann Dandridge, daughter of the Rev. George and Margaret Young.
Baptized December 12; born November 16, 1797.
George Wentworth, son of George and Sarah Wilson.
Baptized December 26; born October 24, 1811.
Julia Carolina, daughter of Thomas and Elizabeth Willock.
Baptized December 31; born December 31, 1809.

1812

Rose Hannah, daughter of John and Sarah Dickson.
Baptized January 1; born November 2, 1811.
Mary Walke, daughter of Thomas and Anne Williamson.
Baptized January 15; born December 18, 1811.
William Augustine, son of Thomas and Mary C. McCandlish.
Baptized February 2; born August 3, 1811.
Benjamin Franklin, son of Adam and Mary Ann Miller Cornick.
Baptized February 11; born September 6, 1811.
Virginia, daughter of John and Ann Camp.
Baptized February 26; born March 24, 1811.
Ann Augusta, daughter of Thomas and Ann Dulton.
Baptized March 4; born April 11, 1811.
Ann Belfield, daughter of John E. and Clara Holt.
Baptized March 14th; born March 1, 1812.
Elandia Cattell, daughter of Henry and Margaret Hastie.
Baptized March 19; born February 19, 1812.
Mulryne Hamilton, child of Henry and Margaret Hastie.
Baptized March 19; born February 19, 1812.
William Noy, son of George and Elizabeth Balfour.
Baptized March 19; born February 12, 1812.
Thomas Colgate, son of George and Elizabeth Balfour.
Baptized March 19; born February 12, 1812.
Richard Henrye, son of James and Margaret Louisa Maurice.
Baptized March 29; born March 4, 1812.
Henry Robert, son of Arthur S. and Jane Woodhouse.
Baptized March 31; born December 29, 1811.

Thomas Jefferson, son of Lemuel and Mary Cornick.
Baptized March 31; born November 16, 1810.
Elizabeth Grayson, daughter of Wm. Langley and Mary Grayson Keeling.
Baptized March 31; born August 8, 1812.
Mary Ann, daughter of William Langley and Mary Grayson Keeling.
Baptized March 31; born 1811 (or 1804).
Henry Hill, son of John and Frances Woodhouse.
Baptized March 31; born January 20, 1804.
William Moseley, son of John T. and Eliza Keeling.
Baptized March 31; born June 8, 1811.
James, son of William and Margaret Davis.
Baptized April 5th; born March 7, 1812.
William Edmund, son of Francis S. and Ann Taylor.
Baptized April 5; born April 18, 1811.
Virginia Elizabeth, daughter of Francis S. and Ann Taylor.
Baptized April 5; born December 3, 1809.
Robert Adam, son of William and Mary Ann Lindsay.
Baptized April 16; born April 8, 1812.
Theodoric Fawn Archer, son of Thomas and Pricilla M. Armistead.
Baptized April 19; born March 30, 1812.
Virginia Thomas, daughter of Augustine and Ann Moore.
Baptized April 19; born December 10, 1809.
Peggy Amelia, daughter of Casper Gottelieb and Amelia Diedrich.
Baptized April 26; born March 18, 1812.
William Pennock, son of George O. and Ann T. Davis.
Baptized May 20; born November 29, 1811.
Catherine Drummond, daughter of Thomas and Rehoboth Keel Dixson.
Baptized May 24; born March 23, 1812.
Mary Sharp, daughter of Robert S. and Charlotte Symes.
Baptized May 30; born May 29, 1812.
Littleton Waller Tazewell, son of Larkin and Ann Sophia Smith.
Baptized June 8; born November 18, 1811.
William Miles, son of William Part. and Lucy Foster.
Baptized June 10; born December 1, 1811.
Lucretia Allmand, daughter of Joshua and Anne Aphia Herbert.
Baptized July 21; born May 24, 1812.
William Francis, son of Johnson and Ann W. Mallory.
Baptized July 21; born November 6, 1810.
John Stowe Hastings, son of John and Susanna B. Granberry.
Baptized August 2; born September 27, 1811.
Edward, son of Mark and Isabella McNay.
Baptized August 2; born November 15, 1809.
George Prestman, son of John and Frances P. Southgate.
Baptized May 27th; born November 30, 1811.
James Christopher, son of John and Sally Davis.
Baptized August 9th; born February 3, 1810.
Louisa Hope, daughter of John and Sally Davis.
Baptized August 9; born May 8, 1812.
Robert Boush, son of Samuel and Catherine Vickery.
Baptized August 25; born July 27, 1812.

Sarah Ann, daughter of Littleton Waller and Ann Stratton Tazewell.
  Baptized September 15; born August 26, 1812.
Dennis, son of Caleb and Abier McCoy.
  Baptized December 2; born August 14, 1812.
Martha Tucker, daughter of George and Courtney Newton.
  Baptized December 13; born November 14, 1812.
Tazewell, son of James and Sarah Taylor.
  Baptized December 13; born January 30, 1810.
William Edward, son of William and Susanna Armistead.
  Baptized December 13; born September 11, 1811.
Robert Perrin, son of Harrison and Mary Allmand.
  Baptized December 15; born April 28, 1810.
Anne Blaws Barraud, daughter of John Hartwell and Anne Blaws Cocke.
  Baptized December 26; born December 10, 1811.
Rebecca Frances Begg, daughter of William G. and Anne Camp.
  Baptized December 27; born August 27, 1810.
Washington, son of William G. and Anne Camp.
  Baptized December 27; born November 30, 1812.
William Thorowgood, son of Wm. Thorowgood and Mary Anne Nimmo.
  Baptized December 27; born November 2, 1812.

1813

Eliza Ann Frances Bayley, daughter of Richard and Anne Drummond.
  Baptized January 5; born May 3, 1812.
Parniel Montague, son of Henry and Martha Oatest.
  Baptized February 3; born December 12, 1812.
George Prior, son of Henry and Martha Oatest.
  Baptized February 3; born December 12, 1812.
William Pennock, son of Lewis and Maria Hansford.
  Baptized February 11; born January 14, 1813.
Sarah Beddinger, daughter of Seth B. and Margaret R. Foster.
  Baptized February 15; born January 16, 1813.
Richard Causton, son of David and Anne Murray.
  Baptized February 19; born January 8, 1809.
Anne, daughter of David and Anne Murray.
  Baptized February 19; born September 15, 1811.
Josiah Wilson, son of Josiah and Margaret Hunter.
  Baptized February 19; born November 22, 1809.
Eliza, daughter of William and Parmelia Couper.
  Baptized February 23; born September 27, 1812.
Josephine, daughter of Julian and Dorothea Magagnos.
  Baptized February 25; born January 30, 1813.
Francis Henney, son of Francis and Anne Smith.
  Baptized March 21; born October 18, 1812.
Lydia Riche, daughter of Thomas R. and Anne Swift.
  Baptized March 21; born March 12, 1813.
Robert, son of Henry and Jane Dickson.
  Baptized April 8; born December 31, 1812.

Charles Henry, son of George and Anne Rowland.
>Baptized April 8; born March 9, 1813.
Martha Presburg, daughter of Walter G. and Mary Ann Anderson.
>Baptized April 12; born March 22, 1811.
George, son of George and Elizabeth T. Halson.
>Baptized April 18; born September 21, 1812.
John Granberry, son of Jonas and Eliza Hastings.
>Baptized April 18; born December 13, 1812.
Edward, son of Edward and Maria Chamberlain.
>Baptized April 26; born October 9, 1812.
Elizabeth Gordon, daughter of Edward and Sarah Carr Watson.
>Baptized May 20; born August 24, 1811.
Anne Carr, daughter of Edward and Sarah Carr Watson.
>Baptized May 20; born April 18, 1813.
William, son of James B. and Susanna H. Vaughn.
>Baptized May 23; born December 6, 1812.
Mary Wrighington, baptized June 1st, born dead.
Margaret Eliza, daughter of James R. and Eliza Nimmo.
>Baptized June 6; born May 7, 1813.
Charlotte Butler, daughter of Richard and Lucy Fisher.
>Baptized June 13; born February 3, 1812.
William Francis, son of Jonathan and Jane Wood.
>Baptized June 25th; born May 31, 1813.
Laura Margaret, daughter of William Boswell and Margaret Stuart Lamb.
>Baptized July 2; born January 7, 1808.
George Elliott, son of William Boswell and Margaret Stuart Lamb.
>Baptized July 2; born December 22, 1810.
Richard, son of William Boswell and Margaret Stuart Lamb.
>Baptized July 2; born February 22, 1813.
Lelianne Imogen, daughter of Dennis and Mary Diana Dawley.
>Baptized July 4; born April 4, 1813.
Anne Tucker, daughter of Hugh and Courtney Pannell.
>Baptized July 14; born June 3, 1813.
William Peter, son of Richard and Anne Jeffery.
>Baptized August 1; born July 14, 1813.
Robert Warren, son of John and Frances Hodges.
>Baptized August 16; born July 27, 1813.
Sarah Anne Lewis, daughter of William C. and Anne S. Holt.
>Baptized August 22; born March 25, 1813.
Joshua Nicholson, son of Maximilian and Lucretia Herbert.
>Baptized September 27; born April 17, 1813.
William Peter, son of Peter and Louisa Maria Kerrison.
>Baptized September 27; born March 7, 1813.
Anne Thomas, daughter of Patrick and Anne Harmanson.
>Baptized October 1; born November 4, 1811.
Virginia, daughter of Capt. John Maxwell.
>Baptized October 27; born dead.
William, son of Lawrence and Sally Pollacy.
>Baptized November 14; born June 2, 1813.
Mary Eliza, daughter of David and Elizabeth Milhado.
>Baptized November 21; born October 21, 1813.

Cephalie Olivia, daughter of James and Emily Delauney.
Baptized November 29; born July 30, 1812.
Edward, son of Edward S. and Sarah Waddey.
Baptized December 5; born November 7, 1813.
James Henrietta Francis, son of James and Frances Cuthbert.
Baptized December 11; born July 3, 1813.
Charles Henry Allen Harvey, son of Edward P. and Martha Kennedy.
Baptized December 16; born December 17, 1810.
Edmund Archer Champlin Fawn, son of Edward P. and Martha Kennedy.
Baptized December 16; born January 6, 1813.
George Washington, son of Robert E. and Fanny Steed.
Baptized December 25; born December 19, 1813.
Mary Eliza, daughter of Thomas and Mary McCandlish.
Baptized December 28; born April 26, 1813.
James Frances, son of William F. and Henrietta L. Hunter.
Baptized December 31; born January 1, 1813.
Frederick William, son of John and Frances P. Southgate.
Baptized October 24; born September 24, 1813.

1814

Mary Anne, daughter of George and Rebecca Parham Raincock.
Baptized January 6; born December 3, 1812.
Thomas, son of Thomas and Rehoboth K. Dickson.
Baptized February 1; born January 9, 1814.
Loyd Jones, son of Benjamin and Margaret Bryan.
Baptized February 13; born January 12, 1814.
Eliza Anne, daughter of Henry and Anne Browne.
Baptized February 14; born October 13, 1805.
Mary Susan, daughter of Henry and Anne Browne.
Baptized February 14; born January 22, 1807.
Margaret, daughter of Henry and Anne Browne.
Baptized February 14; born July 22, 1809.
Hannah Edwards, daughter of Henry and Anne Browne.
Baptized February 14; born July 25, 1811.
Thomas Henry, son of Henry and Anne Browne.
Baptized February 14; born July 15, 1813.
Anne Eliza, daughter of George A. and Anne Browne.
Baptized February 14; born September 1, 1811.
Sarah Willoughby, daughter of George A. and Anne Brown.
Baptized February 14; born November 8, 1813.
Edward Lewis, son of Patrick and Anne Harmanson.
Baptized March 6; born May 31, 1807.
Virginia, daughter of Patrick and Anne Harmanson.
Baptized March 6; born October 13, 1810.
Frances Susan, daughter of Patrick and Anne Harmanson.
Baptized March 6; born October 24, 1813.
Anne Herron, daughter of Robert B. and Matty Stark.
Baptized March 22; born March 6, 1813.
Martha, daughter of William and Mary Anne Linsey (Lindsay).
Baptized March 26; born May 5, 1813.

George, son of Thomas and Catherine Balls.
Baptized March 29; born December 11, 1811.
Richard, son of Thomas and Catherine Balls.
Baptized March 29; born April 24, 1813.
John Cowell, son of William and Anne Stevens.
Baptized April 1; born July 22, 1813.
Elizabeth Margaret, daughter of William and Suckey Langley.
Baptized April 3; born June 28, 1813.
Mary Emmott, daughter of Arthur and Mary Taylor.
Baptized April 6; born June 11, 1800.
Caroline Virginia, daughter of Authur and Mary Taylor.
Baptized April 6; born September 25, 1811.
Georgiana Alexander, daughter of Arthur and Mary Taylor.
Baptized April 6; born August 2, 1813.
Margaret Anne Miriam, daughter of Kader and Miriam Talbot.
Baptized April 17; born March 31, 1811.
Margaret Ellis, daughter of John and Margaret Bramble.
Baptized April 17; born September 12, 1813.
David Handwroy, son of George and Elizabeth H. Balfour.
Baptized April 17; born November 8, 1813.
Sarah, daughter of George and Rebecca Parham Raincock.
Baptized April 24; born February 24, 1813.
George Washington, son of George W. and Frances Camp.
Baptized May 1; born May 1, 1813.
Louisa Maxwell, son of George and Sarah Wilson.
Baptized May 31; born September 21, 1813.
Virginia, daughter of John and Elizabeth Stone.
Baptized June 23; born June 21, 1813.
William Leigh, son of Robert S. and Charlotte Symes.
Baptized June 23; Born June 22, 1813.
Edgar Haynes, son of William and Margaret Davis.
Baptized June 29; born June 29, 1814.
Sophia Anne, daughter of Francis and Anne Smith.
Baptized July 9; born February 18, 1814.
Jane, daughter of Jonathan and Jane Wood.
Baptized July 12; born July 7, 1814.
Julia Thomas, daughter of Charles and Eliza Donaldson.
Baptized July 19; born November 9, 1813.
James Madison, son of Lemuel and Mary Cornick.
Baptized June 6; born February 20 (or 23), 1813.
Julia Francis, son of Julian and Dorothea Magagnos.
Baptized August 20; born August 2, 1814.
Felle, child of Caleb and Abiah McCoy.
Baptized August 21; born June 12, 1814.
Elizabeth, daughter of William and Elizabeth Stokes.
Baptized August 21; born March 24, 1814.
Mary Willoughby, daughter of William and Mary Sharp.
Baptized September 11; born August 17, 1814.
Eliza Anne, daughter of William and Elizabeth Simmons.
Baptized October 29; born March 27, 1814.

Warren, son of John and Frances Hodges.
> Baptized November 13; born October 22, 1814.
Eleanor Sarah, daughter of John and Sarah Dickson.
> Baptized November 27; born June 29, 1813.
Frances Keeling, daughter of William Thorogood and Mary Anne Nimmo.
> Baptized December 4; born October 29, 1814.
Alexander Moseley, son of William and Elizabeth Pennock.
> Baptized December 15; born October 1, 1814.
Thomas Hoomes, son of Thomas and Ann McClanaghan McCauley Williamson.
> Baptized December 30; born August 30, 1813.

1815

Mary Eliza, daughter of John and Eliza Hipkins.
> Baptized January 1; born January 21, 1813.
Sarah Frances, daughter of John and Eliza Hipkins.
> Baptized January 1; born December 9, 1814.
Julia Imogen Young, daughter of James and Anne M. Baker.
> Baptized March 12; born August 21, 1814.
Sarah McCollock, daughter of Hugh and Courtney Pannell.
> Baptized March 13; born January 25, 1815.
John Samuel, son of Fortesque and Mary Whittle.
> Baptized April 19; born April 18, 1813.
Virginia Frances Gilliat, daughter of Richard and Mary Taylor.
> Baptized April 20; born March 18, 1814.
William Henry, son of William T. and Henrietta Hunter.
> Baptized April 30; Born November 15, 1814.
Richard Woodlief, son of Richard and Anne Jeffery.
> Baptized May 7; born March 13, 1815.
Matty Lindsey, daughter of Robert B. and Matty Starke.
> Baptized June 7; born April 25, 1815.
Frances Louisa, daughter of Wright and Anne Southgate.
> Baptized June 10; born October 20, 1810.
Robert, son of Wright and Anne Southgate.
> Baptized June 10; born February 27, 1812.
Virginia, daughter of Wright and Anne Southgate.
> Baptized June 10; born August 10, 1814.
Wentworth Willis, son of Thomas and Margaret Pierce.
> Baptized June 10; born March 8, 1815.
Lelianne, daughter of John and Elizabeth Stone.
> Baptized June 17; born May 29, 1815.
Anne Maria Whiddon, daughter of Thomas and Mary C. McCandlish.
> Baptized June 28; born June 1, 1815.
Andrew Jackson, son of Lemuel and Mary Cornick.
> Baptized July 5; born June 19, 1815.
Camilla Carolina, daughter of James and Emile Delauney.
> Baptized July 6; born December 28, 1814.
John Samuel, son of Daniel and Mary Sandford.
> Baptized August 13; born March 24, 1810.
Laura Virginia, daughter of Daniel and Mary Sandford.
> Baptized August 13; born January 23, 1813.

Daniel, son of Daniel and Mary Sandford.
Baptized August 13; born June 9, 1815.
Wilson Tyler, son of John and Sally Davis.
Baptized August 20; born July 21, 1815.
Sarah Virginia, daughter of Maximilian and Lucretia Herbert.
Baptized August 31; born August 17, 1815.
Frances Jane, daughter of George and Rebecca Raincock.
Baptized September 3; born August 15, 1815.
Littleton Waller, son of Littleton Waller and Anne Stratton Tazewell.
Baptized September 18; born August 22, 1815.
Harriott Anne, daughter of Thomas R. and Anne P. Swift.
Baptized November 7; born August 25, 1815.
William James, son of Peter and Maria Louisa Kerrison.
Baptized November 24; born December 13, 1814.
Elizabeth Anne, daughter of Thomas and Anne Gatewood.
Baptized November 24; born April 30, 1815.
Benjamin Parsons, son of Nathaniel and Mary Murphy.
Baptized December 3; born July 17, 1813.
Mary Eleanor, daughter of Nathaniel and Mary Murphy.
Baptized December 3; born November 3, 1815.
Mary Anne, daughter of Edward and Mary W. Frith.
Baptized December 11; born March 30, 1809.
Kiturah Goodson, daughter of Edward and Mary W. Frith.
Baptized December 11; born November 12, 1810.
Edward, son of Edward and Mary W. Frith.
Baptized December 11; born September 27, 1815.
Henrietta, daughter of Edward and Mary Catherine Linscoot.
Baptized December 24; born July 7, 1815.
Samuel Bedford Bolling, son of William and Anne Stevens.
Baptized December 27; born September 22, 1815.
Rebecca Bacon, daughter of Edward S. and Sarah E. Waddey.
Baptized December 28; born October 18, 1815.

1816

William, son of William and Pamelia Couper.
Baptized January 1; born August 10, 1814.
Sophia, daughter of Jacques and Margaret Tousard.
Baptized January 20; born November 30, 1815.
Rebecca, daughter of Edward and Sarah Wilson.
Baptized January 25 at Kempsville, Va.; born August, 1805.
William Henry White, son of Henry and Rebecca Cornick.
Baptized Jan. 25 at Kempsville, Va.; born Aug. 13, 1815.
Susan Eliza White, daughter of William and Phillis Jones.
Baptized Jan. 25 at Kampsville, Va.; born July 14, 1815.
Elizabeth Amy Hunter, daughter of James and Mary Moore Nimmo.
Baptized February 15; born December 28, 1813.
Jane, daughter of Robert B. and Ann Taylor.
Baptized March 1; born February 3, 1810.
Thomas, son of George and Courtney Newton.
Baptized March 3; born February 2, 1816.

Robert Tucker, son of William and Hannah Armistead.
Baptized March 3; born March 25, 1816.
Cordelia Anne, daughter of William and Hannah Armistead.
Baptized March 3; born October 22, 1802.
Catherine, daughter of James and Maria Graves.
Baptized March 27; born September 2, 1808.
Cornelia Indiana, daughter of William and Mary MacRea.
Baptized March 27; born March 1, 1816.
Mary Eliza, daughter of William and Mary MacRea.
Baptized March 27; born March 5, 1816.
Sarah, daughter of George and Elizabeth Balfour.
Baptized March 1; born September 1, 1815.
Mary Walker, daughter of William and Sarah C. Pannell.
Baptized April 4; born September 13, 1815.
Jacob Moore, son of Jobel and Eliza M. Valentine.
Baptized April 15; born March 26, 1816.
Jeanette Graves, daughter of Charles and Eliza Donaldson.
Baptized April 15; born March 21, 1816.
Angelia Mallory, daughter of William and Angelia M. Dickson.
Baptized April 21; born March 22, 1815.
Virginia Sanders, daughter of William and Peggy Davis.
Baptized April 21; born July 6, 1815.
Mary Elizabeth, daughter of Francis and Anne Smith.
Baptized April 21; born July 9, 1814.
Mary Anne Sarah, daughter of John and Frances P. Southgate.
Baptized April 21; born August 8, 1815.
James Nimmo, son of Charles and Margaret K. Ellis.
Baptized April 25; born December 21, 1815.
Anne Walke, daughter of Thomas and Anne M. M. Williamson.
Baptized May 19; born January 1, 1816.
Peggy Eyre Parker, daughter of Hallary and Sally Stinger.
Baptized May 30; born February 24, 1815.
Charles Cazy, son of John H. and Anne B. Cocke.
Baptized June 7; born January 1, 1814.
James Bennet, son of Mathew Phripp and Mary Taylor Wright.
Baptized June 9; born January 13, 1802.
Mary Frances, daughter of Mathew Phripp and Mary Taylor Wright.
Baptized June 9; born April 4, 1807.
Imogen, daughter of Mathew Phripp and Mary Taylor Wright.
Baptized June 9; born August 18, 1808.
Octavius Augustus, son of Mathew Phripp and Mary Taylor Wright.
Baptized June 9; born January 28, 1812.
William Henry, son of Mathew Phripp and Mary Taylor Wright.
Baptized June 9; born October 30, 1814.
Robert McCandlish, son of James R. and Eliza T. Nimmo.
Baptized July 7; born May 24, 1816.
James Martin, son of Thomas and Rehoboth K. Dickson.
Baptized September 12; born August 15, 1815.

Burial List of the Rev. Robert S. Symes, Rector of Christ P. E. Church

———o———

—1809—

February—John Calvert
March 10—Monsieur Bereau's child
April 28—William Ingram (Mayr)
April 30—Francis McClenahan
May 2—William Raincock
May 3—Mrs. Sarah Oldner
May 4—Capt. Freeman G. Collins.
June 9—Mrs. Frances Thomas
June 26—John Calvert Taylor (son of Richard)
July 29—Mrs. McKay
July 29—L u c y H i l l (niece of Thomas Hill)
August 18—William C. T a y l o r (son of Richd. at 18 mo.)
August 21—Willis McCoy (son of Joshua at 28 yrs.)
August 22—Capt. M a r m a d u k e Wyval
August 23—E. S. Waddy's child
August 23—Adam Boyd
August 23—Hayward
August 30—Mrs. Marr
September 3—Mr. Andre
September 24—William Etheridge.
September 29—Anne Eliza McCandlish
October 4—Mr. Marr's child.
October 16—Mr. Robert Boush
October 24—Mrs. Milhado
October 29—Mr. Reed's child
November 26—Mr. William Street

—1810—

February 22—Mr. Andre
February 25—Mrs. Jerro
March 15—Mr. R o b e r t S m i t h (Princess Anne)
March 18—Major Saunders
March 20—Mr. McDougal
March 23—Mr. A. C. Jordan
March 31—Capt. Soloman Steed
April 4—Mrs. Margaret Kelly
April 19—Captain Hall (N. W. Woods)

April 26—Mr. Hughes
April 30—Mr. George Loyall
May 4—Mrs. C o r n i c k (Princess Anne)
May 6—Col. Josiah Parker (Isle of Wight)
May 12—Thomas H o l s o n (Vermont)
May 14—Mr. J. Southgate's child
May 31—James Noble
June 2—Mr. Proby's child
June 7—Mrs. West
June 17—Mrs. E. Thompson
July 1—L. W. Tazewell's child
July 10—Dr. B. Stark
July 25—T. G a t e w o o d's child (Thos. Whiddon)
July 26—Mr. George White's child, George Anthony
August 3—Mr. Ott's child
August 7—Mr. J. Camp's c h i l d, Susan Emery
August 8—Mr. Hodges' child
August 10—Capt. Bramble's child, John Henry
August 18—Mrs. Theo. Armistead (Martha T.)
August 16—Mr. K e l l y's child, (George)
August 18—Mr. Theo. Armistead's child (a daughter)
August 23—Capt. J o h n Stone's child, Juliana
August 28—Mr. E. H. Moseley Princess Anne)
September 5—Mr. Peter Durant
October 2—Mr. Harrison Allmand, Jr.
October 16—Mr. H. M. Armistead's child
October 22—Mr. J. T. Oldner
November 20—Mr. James Langley
December 11—Captain Dixon
December 17—Mrs. Hunter (Princess Anne)

December 20—Mrs. Gibbons
December 27—Capt. McAllister

—*1811*—

February 24—John Venanden
February 25—Miss Applewaite
March 13—Mr. T. Willock
March 13—Mr. C. Selden's infant
March 15—Mrs. Hayes
May 22—Mrs. Geesling
May 26—Mrs. Bowdoin
May 31—Lieut. Josiah Watson, U. S. N.
June 7—Mrs. Quinn
June 14—Mrs. O'Connor
June 17—Mrs. Maxwell's child
June 21—Mr. Henry Wolf (at Mrs. Heermann's)
July 6—Mr. F. Whittle's child
July 11—Mr. John Nimmo
July 20—Mr. Malachi McCay
July 25—Mr. W i l l i a m Walke's child
July 26—Captain Black's child
July 30—Mrs. E. C. Henop
August 1—Rev. James Price
August 11—Mrs. Eliza Young
August 17—Mr. Jos. Foster's child
August 18—Mrs. Taylor, wife of J. T.
eptember 2—Madame Bouvart
September 6—Mr. F. Kighly
September 24—Mr. Pat. Foster's child
September 24—Mr. Max Herbert's child
September 25—Capt. Strong's child
September 25—Miss L. Lownds
October 1—Mr. George Newton's child
September 28—Mr. G. W. Camp's child
October 4—Mr. P. Harmanson's child
October 7—Mrs. Valentine
October 21—Mr. Jones' child
November 1—Mrs. E. Haynes
November 6—Mrs. Allmand
November 11—Mr. Jordan Marchant

November 14—Capt. Vaughn
November 21—Mrs. Langley
November 23—Mr. S. Moseley's child, Alexander
November 27—Mr. H. Camp
December 1—Capt. Livingston
December 2—Mr. Josh Bagnall
December 18—Dr. Ferte (at 86)
December 23—L. Mercer, U. S. N.

—*1812*—

January 2—John Cooper
January 2—L. Camp
January 11—S. Jourdan
February 9—Lieut. Lee Massey, U. S. Me.
February 10—Peter Jerro
February 14—Madame Barrot
February 22—Genl. Thomas Matthews
February 23—Mr. Wood's child
February 23—Mrs. Peck
March 20—Mr. William Ballard
April 18—Major Lindsey's child, Robert Adam
April 21—Mrs. Vaughn
April 24—Mr. Jerrand (Essex), U. S. N.
May 10—Mrs. E. West
May 10—Mrs. Powell
May 12—Mr. Atkinson
May 13—Mrs. Haughton
May 22—Mr. A. Lee's child
May 26—Mr. D. R. Waddey
June 3—Capt. Thomas Haynes
July 6—Mrs. Mears (Sowells Point)
July 14—Mr. N. Paynter's child
July 28—Mrs. Kighley's child
August 4—Mrs. H. Fisher
August 21—Mr. McIntosh's child, William
August 16—Mr. James Rhodes
September 3—Lydia Ross
September 22—Mr. J. Proudfit
September 28—Mrs. Niemeyer
October 2—Capt. Lemuel Cornick's child, Thos. Jefferson.
October 10—Capt. Thos. Cornick
October 28—Mr. Richard Lawson's child

219

November 22—Mr. Theo. Armistead
November 27—Mrs. M. Moore
December 2—Mr. Richard Odner
December 4—Mr. W. M. Christian
December 8—Mrs. Susan M. Smith
December 15—Mr. Jos. Tatem
December 19—Mrs. S. A. Smith
December 24—Capt. Halliday

—1813—

January 17—Mrs. Sarah Keeling
January 24—Robert Gordon
February 13—Mrs. Juliet Manson
February 18—Capt. Southcomb
March 3—Major Rease
April 10—M. Doyle
April 13—Lieut. Anderson's child, Martha P.
April 19—Abraham*Phillips, Midshipman U. S. F. Constellation
April 23—Joseph L. Biggs, Lieut. U. S. F. Constellation
April 27—Major Lindsay's child
May 6—Julia Tousard
May 10—T. Rhodes (New York)
May 12—Capt. H. M. Allen, U. S. A., (Fort Nelson)
May 15—John Tucker
May 21—Thomas Armistead
May 24—Margaret Sansford (Farmer)
June 7—Mr. M. Peter's child.
June 9—Mrs. Heerman
June 13—C. R. Pollard (Ætat 79)
June 24—Mrs. Morgan (wife of Capt. M.)
June 30—Capt. Fisher's child
July 1—Mrs. J. Camp's child, Virginia
July 3—Capt. S. Vickery's child, Robert Boush
July 8—Mr. Daniel Tracey
July 9—Capt. Magagnos' child, Josephine
July 14—J. B. Vache
July 22—James Moore
August 2—Mr. Niemeyer's child

August 8—Major Maurice's child, Richard Henry
August 10—Mr. Tyler's child, Anne Eliza
August 14—Mr. J. Caton (Ætat 79)
September 2—Mr. Alex. Wilson's child
September 14—Mr. James Cuthbert
September 15—Mr. John L. Cosby
September 19—   Clark's child, (U. S. N.)
September 23—Mr. S. Moseley's child, Burwell B.
September 27—Mr. Wood's child, William Francis
October 4—Mr. Harmanson's child, Anne Thomas
October 7—Mr. Fitz's child.
October 13—Dr. Cowdery's child, Theodoric
October 17—Rev. G. Halson's child, George
October 20—Mrs. Land, wife of Hillary
October 24—Mr. Shiflet (Albemarle Troop)
October 25—Mr. Joshua Herbert's child
October 28—Capt. Maxwell's child, Virginia
October 30—Mr. H. Holt's child
November 30—Mr. Norris (not pub.)
November 12—Dr. Jeffery's child
November 13—Charles Mahon
November 17—Mrs. Anne Hutchings
November 17—Miss Harriott Wilson
November 27—Mr. Klein's child
December 27—Mrs. Talbot, wife of Kader
December 29—Lieut. William T. Olonne (King William County)

—1814—

January 5—Miss Eleanor Kean (Portsmouth)

January 12—Francis Randolph ♥
January 14—Capt. Charles Reade
January 18—Mr. Biddle's child
January 30—Mrs. Elizabeth Cornick (widow of Lemuel Senr)
February 2—Joshua Herbert's child.
March 10—   Hall (Midshipman, U. S. F. Constellation)
March 15—Sarah Williamson (Ætat 70)
March 16—Miss Mary Willoughby (Ætat 30)
March 17—Mr. Williamson's child, Mary Walke
April 1—Miss Eliza Portlock
April 3—Mrs. C. Vickery
April 3—Robert B. Hunter
April 9—Capt. Watson's daughter
April 9—Lieut. Hungerford (Westmoreland County)
April 24—   David (Jew) child, Henry
May 16—John Smith (Kemps.)
May 18—Mrs. Young (widow Rev. George)
June 2—Thomas Newton's child
June 6—John Lovett Senr (Princess Anne County)
June 16—Paul Proby
June 20—Miles King Senr
June 23—Capt. J. Vickery's child (infant)
July 4—William Davis' infant, Edgar Haynes
July 5—Mrs. Willock
July 11—Thos. Vansantts (Navy Yard, Gosport)
July 13—Mrs. Wood's infant, Jane
July 22—Miss Elizabeth Ritter (Dr. Taylor's)
July 25—Max. Herbert's infant, Joshua Nicholson
August 3—Nathaniel McGill
August 5—Mrs. Cordell
August 13—Dr. Hodges' child
August 16—Rev. Anthony Walke
August 22—Charles Donaldson's child, Julia Thomas
August 28—Mrs. Chamberlain
September 13—Mrs. M. Aitcheson

September 25—Mrs. Paynter, wife of Nathaniel
September 28—Mrs. James Herbert
September 29—Capt. Bramble
October 2—Lieut. Keyser (38 Reg. U. S. I.)
October 3—William Nimmo (son of William, grandchild of James, aged 23 mos.)
October 8—Mrs. Calvert (mother of Mrs. Richard Taylor)
October 16—Mr. Miles' son, Robert (Ætat 10)
November 7—Mrs. Land (wife of R.)
November 17—David Milhado's child (infant), Mary
November 20—Mrs. Milhado (wife of David)
November 23—Edward S. Waddey's child (Edward)
November 29—John Tucker Calvert
November 30—Samuel March
December 2—Thos. Armistead's child, at 2 years
December 2—James McDonald, at 17 years
December 27—John Lawrence (Ætat 80)
December 29—William Bishop (Princess Anne)

—1815—

January 4—Sawyer Woodhouse's child
January 11—George Rowland's child, at 5 yrs. and 3 mos.
January 13—Mrs. Mushrow, at 58
January 14—   Dixon (a German)
January 26—Elizabeth Hopkins (spinster)
January 31—James B. Warren
February 4—Peter Foster
February 6—Capt. Galt
February 10—Catherine Hopkins (spinster)
February 22—Lieut. Kirby (35th Reg. Inf.)
March 10—Jacob Birdsaul (Mercht. Service)

March 13—   Polacey
March 18—Mrs. Bramble's child,
        Margaret
March 19—William Hopkins
March 23—Mrs. Moore (Ætat 72)
April 11—Capt. Jno. Brown (Ætat
        56)
April 25—Nicholas Wilkinson
        (Ætat 70)
May 1—David A. Wallace
May 7—Capt. Joseph Canby
June 9—Mrs. M. Farmer (Ætat 69)
June 28—Lt. Phillipe (a sailor from
        Pensance, England)
July 5—Mrs. Woodhouse (wife of
        W. D.)
July 7—Miss Eyre (Eastern Shore)
July 26—Miss Fanny Archer
August 9—Mr. William Nimmo's
        child, Mary Anne, at 3
        years
August 15—D. Sandford's child,
        Daniel, aged 2 mos.
September 16—Lieut. Kennedy's
        (U. S. N.) child, aged 16
        mos.
September 25—Mrs. Love
September 26—Capt. Magagnos'
        child, Francis, aged 16.
        mos.
September 27—Max. Herbert's
        child, Sarah Virginia
October 1—J. Haywood's child
October 20—William Ellegood
October 23—Miss Godfrey, aged 22
October 31—Capt. Gardner
November 1—P.... Wilson, aged 82

November 10—Mrs. Moseley (wife
        of B. B.)
November 15—Madame Claudine
        Borin, aged 86
November 21—Madame Laland,
        aged 78
November 21—Grenoble en Dau-
        phince
November 25—Mrs. P. Harman-
        son's child, Frances Susan
November 27—Henry Woodhouse,
        age 16 (Princess Anne)
December 16—Col. Lindsay's child
December 20—Mr. Frith's infant,
        Edward, aged 2 mos.

—1816—

January 2—Mrs. Hagnes (widow)
January 10—Capt. John Paulsen
January 18—Thomas Dickson's
        child, aged 6 yrs.
January 25—Edward Roberts
February 14—Mrs. Keeling
February 15—Mrs. Colley
February 18—Mrs. Bradley (An-
        tigua)
May 12—Mrs. Edney, aged 87
        (Camden County, N. C.)
May 17—Monsieur Fause, aged 60
June 6—Capt. Robert Walker
        (Capt. Baltimore Packet)
June 7—John Saunders
July 7—Genl. Taylor's infant
August 24—Lewis Bernard
August 25—Mrs. Keeling (widow
        of Revd. Jacob)

INDEX

BARKER, Eliza A., 189, Ebenezer, 119, Mrs. Mary Ann, 140.
BARKWELL, Mary Ann H., 109, Louisa C., 126.
BARLOW, Jane, 179, Ruel V., 170.
BARNABY, Rebecca, 26.
BARNS, Mrs. Anna, 10, John, 1, 2, 10, 15.
BARNES, Amy M., 149, Anthony L., 195, Caroline A., 168, Edward A., 135, Elizabeth Ann, 173, Griffin, 116, John, 62, John J., 149, Lucy Ann, 144, Otway C., 187, William C., 149, 161, 173.
BARNET, James, 18.
BARNETT, James, 70, John, 197.
BARNEY, Julia Ann, 104, Mrs. Mary, 19.
BARRAUD, Anne B., 16, D. C., 101, Daniel Cary, 83, Lelia A., 101, Philip, 16, 25, 28, 71, 73, 101.
BARRET, Robert, 57.
BARRETT, Elizabeth, 27, Henry, 162, John, 5, 6, 112, 135, Nancy, 5, Robert, 67, Robert S., 194, William H., 145, 177.
BARRINGTON, Mrs. Elizabeth, 20.
BARROM, Benjamin A., 199, George A., 147, 168, 176, 199.
BARRON, Bardon, 131, David, 141, Jane E., 94, Margaretta, 98, Mary, 109, Mary Augusta, 94, Robert, 7, 13, Samuel, 145, Lieutenant Samuel, 129, Mrs. Sarah, 26, Susan V., 109, Susanna, 13, William C., 177.
BARROTT (Barrot), Ann V., 109, Ellen, 130, Elie, 69, 102, Madame, 219, Paul, 4, Peter, 24, Robert, 95, Robert J., 155, Samuel Thomas, 99.
BARROWS, George, 154.
BARRY, Ann Eliza, 141, Garret, 90, James, 79, 108, 140, 141.
BARSTOW, Peleg, 46.
BARTEE, Andree, 108, John, 67, 178, Mary, 197, Mrs. Pamelia, 62, Virginia, 171.
BARTHOLOMEW, Joseph, 78.
BARTLETT, Mrs. Martha Ann, 119.
BARTLET, Patrick, 86.
BARTLEY, George W., 197, Joseph, 11.
BARTON, Jeremiah, 15, John 127, Sheldon T., 180.
BASTIAN, Elizabeth, 99, 109.
BASSETT, John 71, Sarah Ann, 154, Mrs. Sarah, 131.
BASS, Willis, 178.
BATH, William, 109.
BATISTA, Josef, 82.
BATISTE, John, 161.
BATISCE, Mrs. Parmelia, 82.
BATTEN, Caleb, 36, Martha, 62.
BATTERSON, Mrs. Ann, 40.
BATTLEY, Joseph F., 165.
BUXTON, James, 65, Stephen G., 65.
BAYLEY, Isaac R., 75.
BAYLOR, Baynham, 135, Richard, 121, Richard G., 121, 156, Thomas G., 156.

BAYNE, Charles, 2, Eliza Jane, 177, Lilly, 177.
BAYNES, George, 25, Kitty, 28, Mrs. Mary, 15, Mrs. Nancy, 48.
BAYTO (Baito), 171, Joaquin, 180, 194.
BAUGH, Richard W., 44.
BAUM, Nathan, 199.
BAZIN, Ann, 100.
BEACHAM, Mrs. Anne, 45, John, 118.
BEADLES, Ann, 79.
BEAKLEY, William, 55.
BEAL, William, 24.
BEALE, Catherine C., 184, Charles, 17, Charles H., 151, 167, Charles L., 20, 98, John E., 19, 97, 86, 92, Margaret W., 159, Mary Eliza, 184, William C., 107.
BEAN, Martha Ann, 165.
BEANE, William, 154, 161, 172.
BEASY, Francisca, 30.
BEAT, Louisa, 118.
BEATON, Thomas B., 137.
BEAUCHAMP, Mrs. Louisa, 160.
BAUCLAIR, Nicholas, 158, 182.
BEAUMONT, Mark, 156.
BEAZLEY, Mrs. Sarah Ann, 200.
BECDELIVRE, Mrs. Marie Victoire, 11.
BEDOUT, Bennet, 134.
BECKLEY, Margaret, 177, Marion, 177.
BEDELL, Richard, 102, Benjamin W., 142.
BEEN, James, 127.
BEGG, Anne, 24.
BEGGY, Mrs. Peggy, 35.
BEHENNA (Behanna), Adair, 207, Elizabeth Melson, 207, Henry, 12, 207.
BELMINA (or Balmina), Mary, 87.
BELL, Alexander, 44, Alexander, Jr., 133, Ann, 37, David, 115, 125, 135, 153, Jacques, 23, Jenny, 196, John, 44, 50, John H., 81, Mary, 48, Mrs. Mary Ann, 114, Mary Jane, 168, Richard H., 64, Russell, 160, Sarah, 196.
BELLAMY, Robert, 171.
BELLIFELT, Mrs. Mary, 131.
BELOTE, Ann, 193, Mrs. Elizabeth, 202, Emily, 156, George E., 172, James L., 195, 199, P. L., 198, Susan, 132, 154, Virginia Ann, 195.
BELTO, James L., 177.
BENEDICT, William, 77.
BENFIELD, Eliza, 83.
BENFORD. 57.
BENNETT, Catherine, 200, George, 43, James, 200, Mrs. Mary M., 26, Thomas, 92, William, 12, 18, 20.
BENNITS, Mary Ann, 84.
BENSON, Alley, 91, Ann, 26, Benjamin, 156, Elias, 58, 72, Grace, 11, John, 200, Joseph, 12, Lyas, 55, Margaret, 128, Theodore, 93.
BENSTAN, Elizabeth, 23, John, 23.
BENSTON, John, 120, 152, Thomas, 143, 159.
BENTACURT, Michael, 31.

172, John, 135, Jonathan, 172, Moses, 105, 140, Nathan, 61, Mrs. Sarah, 169.
BONSAL, Caleb, 53, 107, 142, Ellen, 142, John 172, Mary E., 189.
BOOKER, Ann, 177, Armistead, 206, Elizabeth, 206, Elizabeth W., 206, Mrs. Elizabeth W., 41, George, 206, John Sclater, 206, Richard, 206.
BOON, David, 166.
BOOS (Booz, Booze), Catherine, 9, Charlotte, 107, Frances, 58, Mary, 107, Nicholas, 9, 10, Philip, 6, 46, 56, 80, William, 107, 166, 196.
BOOTH, Eliza Ann, 140.
BOOTHBY, Thomas Freeman, 145.
BORDEN, James, 155.
BORDWINE, James, 83.
BORGES, Manuel, 167.
BORIN, Madame Claudine, 222.
BORN, Michael, 163.
BORUM, John H., 177, Samuel R., 202, William F., 123.
BOSS, Charlotte, 86, Elizabeth, 89, Nancy, 163.
BOSSIDNICK, Mrs. Margaret, 107.
BOSWELL, Thomas H., 108, William R., 126.
BOSWORTH, Ebenezer C., 132.
BOTSFORD, S. N., 167.
BOTTIRELL, George, 152.
BOUCHER, Henry, 50.
BOUGHAN, James G., 94.
BOULT, Thomas, 188.
BOURDAIN, Bernard, 21.
BOURK, Ann M., 105, Catherine, 115, Redmond, 105, 115, 141, Sarah, 141.
BOUSOUMAT, Frances, 24, Jane, 15, Marianne Revel, 15.
BOUTIN, Celestina Lamasurier, 98, John Charles Mary Louis, 27, Lewis, 208, Margaret, 208, Rose Lemasurier Celestine, 208.
BOUTWELL, Edward, 38.
BOUSH, Ann, 2, Mrs. Ann, 58, Ann Eliza, 134, Ann M. (or N.), 69, Catherine B., 40, Charles S., 2, 37, 66, Eliza Amy, 55, Mrs. Elizabeth, 38, Fanny, 42, Mrs. Frances, 22, Frances E., 100, Frances M., 98, Frances S., 141, Joseph, Jr., 196, Mary, 11, Mrs., Mary L., 83, Nathaniel, 11, 16, 100, 205, Polly, 203, Robert, 3, 40, 37, 218, Susan E., 162, Susanna, 105, Terry, 197, Thomas, 4, William Frederick Wilson, 73, Wilson, 32, 108.
BOUVART, Madame, 219.
BOWDEN, Richard, 17, Robert W., 125.
BOWDOIN, Mrs., 219, Sally E. Courtney, 137, Mrs. Sarah, 53.
BOWEN, Joseph, 11.
BOWER, John F., 91.
BOWKER, Charles J., 165.
BOWLER, Bettsy, 6, Washington, 132.
BOWLES, John, 143.

BOWMAN, Benjamin Franklin, 207, Elizabeth McClauchan, 207, Samuel A., 111, Thadeus, 207.
BOWYER, James H., 174.
BOWZER, George, 192.
BOYD, Adam, 218, Mrs. Ann, 135, Mrs. Elizabeth, 6, 51, George, 6, John, 17, Joseph K., 61, 97, Sarah, 93, T., 80, Thomas, 95.
BOYCE, Mrs. Sarah, 42.
BOYNTON, Jeremiah, 128.
BRAITHWAITE, Thomas, 143.
BRADFORD, Edmund, 187, Sarah, 12.
BRADY, Bartholomew, 168, Barbara, 137.
BRAIDFORD, Walter, 135.
BRADLEY, Mrs., 222, William, 79.
BRAGG, Frances, 51, George, 99, Talbot, 51.
BRAYWELL, Ann, 5.
BRAINE, John H., 77, Robert R., 77.
BRAMBLE, Captain, 221, George, 119, 125, 159, John, 21, 22, 206, 214, John Henry, 206, 218, Margaret, 206, 214, 222, Margaret Ellis, 214.
BRANDA, Mrs. Ann R., 105, Charles, 83, Augustus, 11, 176, 200.
BRANDON, Mary, 9.
BRANDT, Nicholas, 32, Louisa, 201.
BRANIGAN, Jane, 19.
BRANT, Soloman, 47.
BRAY, Caleb W., 125, Sophia, 191.
BRAZIL, Mary, 34.
BREKENRIDGE, Henry, 57.
BREMEN, Maximilian, 169.
BREMOND, Mrs. Ann, 128, Dennis, 109, 128, Salvani, 109.
BRENEMAN, Rudolph, 38.
BRENT, Mrs. Sarah, 49.
BRETTE, Florentinus, 43, 50, Jules Florintin Boulleaton, 80, Paul Jules, 87.
BRESHOOD, Thomas, 4.
BREWER, Charlotte 44, William, 198.
BREVILLE, Louis, 73.
BRIAN, Daniel, 12.
BRICE, Andrew, 184, Jacob, 192.
BRIDGEFORD, Maria, 96.
BRIDGERS, Nancy, 1.
BRIDGET, 33.
BRIGGS, James, 16, Mrs. Martha, 101.
BRIGHT, Henry, 155, Martha, 157.
BRIMLINE, Henrietta, 193.
BRINSON, Mrs. Elizabeth, 62.
BRITAIN, Charles, 65.
BRITE, Hamilton C., 194.
BRITT, Nancy, 194, Benamin F., 179.
BRITTON, Amelia (Mrs.), 106.
BRITTAM, Robert, 119.
BRIQUET, Ann, 65, David, 93, Claudius, 28, 33, 34, 40, 65.
BROADRICK, Anna Jane, 192, Jeremiah, 124, Margaret, 85.
BROADERS, Bartholomew, 10.
BROCK, Edward, 29, Henry, 152, John, 29, William, 80, 175.

BROCKETT, Edgar L., 202.
BRODIE, Martha, 42, Charles D., 36, Lodowick, 42.
BROKENBROUGH, John, 2, Mary, 2.
BROOKE, Edmund, 87, George E., 137, John M., 198, Rosalin, 108, Susan, 104, Walter T., 135.
BROOKS, Mrs. Amanda, 155, Caleb, 118, David, 44, Eliza S., 176, James, 34, James M., 133, Mary Eliza, 176, Samuel, 5, Thomas, 181, William, 200, William A., 131, William J., 196.
BROWN, Abraham, 89, Ann, 206, Mrs. Ann, 118, Ann Elizabeth, 69, Ann W., 106, Mrs. Amelia, 106, Benjamin, 7, 191, Beverly, 77, Charles, 169, 177, Daniel, 119, David, 61, 80, Evelina, 96, Elizabeth, 144, Mrs. Fanny, 28, Francis H., 130, Francis Henry, 206, George, 206, Hannah E., 21, Jeremiah S., 88, John, 3, 121, John D., 155, John G., 22, 54, 82, John Godinicus, 1, Mrs. John G., 41, Joseph, 2, 34, Capt. John, 221, Joshua, 3, Lancaster, 87, Mrs. Mary, 6, 75, Mary, 114, Mary E., 89, Mary P., 91, Margaret, 39, Mrs. Margaret, 137, Nancy, 191, Nathaniel, 7, Peter, 18, 160, Peter William, 4, Philip Nicholas, 9, Richard D., 71, 74, Robert, 112, 147, 158, Samuel, 140, Samuel W., 96, Susan E., 89, Thomas, 137, Virginia, 121, William, 149, 189, William B., 18, William Hamilton, 91.
BROWNE, Anne, 213, Eliza Anne, 213, Francis H., 159, 169, Hannah Edwards, 213, Henry, 213, Anne Eliza, 213, Margaret, 213, Mary Susan, 213, Mrs. Julia A., 180, Thomas Henry, 213, George A., 213, William, 178, William Hamilton, 122.
BROWNLEY, Jesse, 146.
BROWNLOW, Mrs. Elioner, 17.
BROUGH, Robert, 9, 15, 17, 32, 71, 76, 80, 93.
BROUGHTON, Annis, 2, Eliza Bell, 188, George, 2, 72, Mrs. Jeanett, 177, Martha E., 175, Mary L., 152, Nancy, 126, Thomas G., 37, 48, 126, Thomas G., Jr., 148, William, 201, 182, 197.
BRUCE, Charles Lewis, 137, Capt. Henry, 27.
BRUER, John, 1, Mrs. Sarah, 1.
BRUMAUD, Roc, 10.
BRUMFIELD, George, 33.
BRUNET, Henry, 30, S. E E., 184, Sarah W., 143, Mrs. Sarah, 45.
BRUNDELL, Philip G., 116.
BRYSON, Gilbert H., 162.
BRYANT, Mrs. Mary, 128, Mary A., 141, Samuel, 138, William, 101.
BRUSHWOOD, Thomas, 27, 97.
BRYAN, Benjamin, 54, 213, Catherine, 12, Eliza Ann, 114, James, 114, 117, 191, Loyd Jones, 213, Margaret, 213, Mary

E., 191, Maria P., 117, Samuel, 137, William, 9.
BUCHANAN, James, 171.
BUCKLEY, John, 125, Margaret, 177, Marion, 177, William, 96.
BUCKNAM, Eliza Ann, 144, Joses, 90, 118, 152, 144, 177, Eliza S., 118, William H., 146, Sarah Jane, 177.
BUCK, Mary, 69, William H., 198.
BUDD, Polly, 80.
BULLIFUNT, Mrs. Mary, 151.
BULLOCK, Amanda M. F., 142, George, 98, Joseph M., 132, 142, Mary, 84, Mrs. Mary A., 132, 177.
BUNKLEY, Joseph, 152.
BUNTIN, Catherine, 27, Eliza, 99, Esther, 26, Joshua, 25, 26.
BUNTING, Mary Ann, 84, Martha, 72, Thomas, 25.
BURCHELL, Mary, 88, 167.
BURCHER, John, 10, 53, Lewis, 130, Miles P., 161, Smith, 104.
BURCHETT, William G., 201.
BURCHILL, Mrs. Jane, 108, John, 98.
BURDICK, Mrs. Hannah P., 114.
BURDICK, Maria, 163.
BURK, Edmund, 75, M., 142, Margaret, 169, William, 75.
BURKE, Mrs. Bridget, 138, John, 184, Margaret, 3, 8, Martin, 130, Richard, 9.
BURKETT, Abby, 3, Nancy, 3.
BURKET, John, 1.
BURMOT, Mrs. Ann, 18.
BURNE, Sophia Lisburne, 21, William, 21.
BURNS, Eliza Ann, 155, James B., 156, 165, 202, James R., 165, John, 111, John, Jr., 171, Lelia A., 111, William, 122, William R., 107.
BURGEN, William, 98.
BURGESS, Ann, 112, Charles Thomas, 188, Elizabeth, 117, Henry, 179, James, 198, John, 50, 83, 86, 87, 100, 167, 168, 176, 192, Nathaniel, 25, 30, 46, William, 80.
BURNHAM, Ann E. R., 160, Richard, 84, William B., 181, William P., 152, 187.
BURROW, Bardon, 172.
BURRUS, Charles, 161, 169, Richard D., 147, 171, 161.
BURROUGHS, Elzy, 63, 70, 76, 87, John J., 83, Sarah Ann, 76, Thomas C., 187, 195, Thomas G., 199.
BURT, C. D., 45, Eliza E., 200, John M., 98, 102, Mary Antoinette, 169.
BURTON, John, 16, Robert, 133, Robert H., 156.
BURWELL, Fitch, 170.
BUSBY, Mary A., 150.
BUSHNELL, Charles R., 101.
BUSKY (Buskey), Mrs. Mary, 109, Margaret O., 38, Mrs. Rachel, 155, Elizabeth, 158, James, 201, Joshua, 19.
BUSTIN, Benjamin, 114.
BUTCHER, Miles, 149.
BUTE, Wilson, 157.

BUTLER, Eliza Osborne, 63, Mrs. Fanny, 18, James, 141, 194, John, 58, John H., 117, John O., 160, Lawrence, 16, Mathew, 138, Maria, 73, 79, Doctor Peter, 15, Robert, 101, Thomas, 119, 152, Tristram (Tristrim), 18, 27, 63.
BUTMAN, William, 11.
BUTT, Ann, 44, Camilla, 73, Cary W., 78, Dorcas, 62, 73, Edwin, 166, Eliza, 149, 201, Elizabeth, 124, Mrs. Elizabeth, 20, 178, Fanny, 6, Mrs. Frances, 26, Frances C., 62, Francis, Sr., 128, Francis, 37, 38, 44, Francis, Jr., 113, 151, 156, 194, Hillary, 22, James B., 44, John J., 194, John N., 84, John W., 78, Martha, 29, Martha Ann, 178, Martha Pricilla, 194, Mary, 13, Mary Ann, 174, Mary Eliza, 199, Margaret, 99, Mrs., Margaret, 77, 133, Polly, 29, Samuel, 106, 121, 96, Mrs. Sarah, 122, Susan, 48, Wilson, 157, William, 26, 27, 29, Willoughby, 98, 118, 138.
BUTTS, George W., 171.
BUXTON, Frances, 82.
BYRNE, Ann, 7, Peggy, 7.
BYRD, Mrs. Carolina Virginia, 159, George J., 117, 129, John, 19, Oran, 20, Mary, 83.

C

CADENHEAD, William, 26.
CADDIS, David, 126, 144.
CADORE, Vincent, 4.
CADY, Hiram, 110.
CAFFIE, Charles, 166, Jesse M., 168, 194.
CAFFREY, Isabella, 37.
CAIN, Robert, 157, Samuel, 129.
CAKE, Hannah Frances, 157, Mary Jane, 161, William, 56.
CALBERT, Chloe, 30, Sally, 30.
CALBIAC, William, 5.
CALCUTT, Charles James, 185.
CALLAMBER, Elizabeth, 189, Elizabeth B., 189.
CALLENY, Francis, 91.
CALLIS, Frances, 201, Joel, 65, 96, 99, John, 139, Joyce, 195.
CALVERT, John, 218, John Tucker, 221, Mrs., 221, Mary E., 137, Rebecca, 23, Samuel, 56.
CALVIN, James M., 62.
CAMERON, William, 36.
CAMM, Mrs. 142, Robert, 115.
CAMMACK, William, 8, 69.
CAMPBELL, Mrs. Alice, 5, Amey (Mrs.), 6, Ann, 23, 71, Mr. Ann, 8, 95, Mrs. Ann C., 50, Archibald B., 42, Charles, 21, 39, Jane, 111, John, 27, 98, John J., 54, 90, Lucy, 52, Mary Ann, 42, Philadelphia, 133, Sarah M., 73, William B., 140, William, 6, 133.
CAMPER, Sarah, 9.
CAMP, Ann, 36, 42, 46, 209, Anne, 205, 211, Boswell T., 200, Eliza, 208, Frances,

208, 214, G. W., 209, 214, 219, George W., 24, 43, 145, 155, George Washington, 214, Mr. H., 219, Mr. J., 218, Mrs. J., 220, John, 4, 78, 103, 205, 209, John James, 114, L., 219, Rebecca Frances Begg, 117, 211, Sarah M., 103, Susan Emery, 205, Susan Emery, 218, Virginia, 209, 220, Washington, 211, William C., 122, William G., 24, 117, 211, William S., 157, 189.
CAMPOS, Francis Silva, 141, 144.
CANBY, Jane, 110, Capt. Joseph, 222.
CANFIELD, William B., 181.
CANNON, Charlotte, 186, James, 146, 177, John J., 191, Henry, 102.
CANN, Sarah.
CAPAMAGY, 43.
CAPEHART, Mary, 202.
CAPHART, John, 171.
CAPPS, Andrew J., 181, 184, Betsy Ann, 143, Caleb, 188, Didemma, 188, Elizabeth, 49, Erasamus, 106, Lydia, 52, Joseph, 138, Prudence, 174, Ryland, 157, 188, Smith, 144, 151, William, 111.
CAPRON, John, 62, Richard, 84.
CARBRY, Thomas, 97.
CARDONA, Francisco, 174.
CAREY, David, 114.
CARGILL, Lainia, 185.
CARIBO, Henry, 82.
CARLINE, Charles, 5, 10, Elizabeth, 81, James, 5, Mrs. Margaret, 46, Mary, 10.
CARLOTTE, Virginia, 151.
CARLON, John, 155, 198.
CARMICHAEL, Dr. Edward H., 83.
CARNAL, Robert, 161.
CARNES, Josephine V., 199, Joseph, 199.
CARPENTER, Edward W., 176.
CARR, Dale, 26, Elizabeth, 164, Julia A. B., 202, Mary J., 164.
CARROWAY (Carraway), Emmy, 90, George T., 146, John, 47, Mrs. Martha C., 106.
CARRIER, Soloman, 30.
CAROLL, Maria, 181.
CARROLL, Rebecca, 48.
CARSON, David, 98, Eliza Ann, 88, John, 98, 100, William, 11, 31.
CARTER, Charles G., 100, Edward, 103, Elenor, 1, Mrs. Eliza, 5, Elizabeth, 43, George, 125, 127, Mary Ann, 85, Nancy, 24, Robert A., 95, 104, 118, Susan, 12, Thomas, 162, Winney, 127.
CASSEN, Mrs. Mary, 29.
CASEY, Graham, 201, Mary Jane, 210.
CASTEEN, James, 67, 76, 91.
CASTER, Sarah, 106.
CASTIGNET, Jean Baptiste, 56.
CASLIN, Hannah, 13.
CARY, David, 149, Isaac, 5, Mrs. Mary G., 174, Miles, 159, Obed, 81, Susannah, 5, Thomas, 140, Thomas H., 169, William, 42, 46.

CASON, Mrs. Elizabeth, 128, John, 102, Joseph, 185, Sarah Ann, 185, Willougby, 42.
CASSADY, John, 109.
CASSIN, Mrs. Mary Ann, 71, John, 53, 97.
CASTINE, Mrs. Elizabeth, 102.
CATT, Mrs. Nancy, 67.
CATHERINE (negro), 158.
CATON, Mr. J., 220.
CAUTHORN, Robert, 147.
CAVEN, Henry, 16.
CAVENDER, Margaret, 72.
CAWSON, William, 10.
CAYS, Robert L., 138.
CECELIA (negro), 166.
CHABANET, Peter, 24, 39.
CHAMBERS, James, 114, Mrs. Susan, 106, William, 7, 9.
CHAMBERLIN, Edward Jr., 137.
CHAMBERLIN, Edward, 212, Capt. Edward, 13, James, 192, Louisa J., 192, Mrs., 221, Maria, 212.
CHAMBERLAINE, Edward 47, George, 44.
CHANDLER, Georgianna M., 195, Hartwell J., 151, John A., 73, 76, 83, Mary L., 73.
CHARLES, John S., 150.
CHANEY, Thomas, 152.
CHANNICKS, Mary, 11.
CHAPMAN, Ann, 9, Anna Maria, 170, J., 75, Lucy, 170, Mary Anna, 108, Robert, 11, 29, 99, 108, 134, Samuel B., 167, Susan F., 134, William J., 138.
CHAPPELL, Edward, 82.
CHARCON, Pablo, 96.
CHARLTON, John F., 124, John T., 112, 113, 114, 121, 125, 133, Mrs. Margaret, 141.
CHARNICK, Bridget, 24, Rosannah, 26.
CHASE, Increase, 92, Lothrop, 6, 11, Mary A., 157, Moses B., 87, 92, Richard, 157.
CHASTELIER, Sairaphine, 28.
CHAUDRON, Laurede, 67, Paul Emile, 70.
CHAWNING, William, 106.
CHAZEUX, Louis, 88.
CHEATHAM, Asa B., 140.

CHERRY, Alexander, 31, Drucilla, 195, Gowsadey, 102, James, 109, 140, 199, Josiah, 102, 121, Judith, 66, Lozetta, 109, Lydia M., 128, Mary, 187, Mrs. Patience, 80, Polly, 54, Silas, 129, Thomas, 79, Willis, 31, Wright, 102, Wright W., 133.
CHESRAE, Hester, 8, George, 8.
CHESRUE, Hester, 8, George, 8.
CHEVERS, Mark L., 99.
CHILDERS, Isabella H., 67.
CHILDRY, Robert, 178.
CHILDS, Harriet, 129, Jane M., 146, Timothy, 122, William W., 146, 187, 189, 190.

CHISMAN, Edward, 55.
CHIVES, Rachel, 159.
CHOLAS, Jean Pierre, 65, 68.
CHOWNING, William, 105.
CHRISTIAN, Elizabeth Jane, 206, Martha Jones Rivery, 208, Susanna, 206, 208, Mr. W. M., 220, William, 206, 208.
CHRISTIE, Charlotte, 108, James, 55.
CHROWHORN, Mrs. Mary Ann, 106.
CHURCH, Elizabeth, 55, William, 184.
CHURCHWARD, George, 110.
CLAMMITT, William, 91.
CLARICO (Clerico), Joseph, 10, 12, 45, 56, 74, 95, 108, Sarah Ann S., 124, Virginia, 170.
CLARK, Alexander, 17, 52, 84, Andrew, 94, Mrs. Ann, 16, Catherine, 52, Charles, 74, Elizabeth, 22, Mrs. Eliza, 101, George, 34, 53, 97, Jane, 21, John K., 48, John Thompson, 208, Jonathan, 70, Joshua, 11, Mrs. Margaret, 73, Mary, 208, Molly, 22, Philmer, 67, Quintin, 10, William, 208.
CLARKE, Alexander, 104, Alexander Sr., 144, Chauncey, 79, 98, 102, 118, 123, Edward, 106, Edwards, 117, Mrs. Eleanor, 40, Mrs. Elizabeth, 89, Elizabeth H., 144, Ellen Anna, 180, Fanny, 155, Mrs. Gertrude, 101, James, 65, James A. S., 161, John, 46, John J., 117, Lemuel B., 53, Mary C., 152, Mathias, 170, Matilda, 194, Mr. (child of), 220, Robert, 189, Samuel B., 185, Thomas, 116, Mrs. Troy, 66, Virginia, 154, William, 42, 51, 79, William E., 158.
CLARKSON, Peggy, 31.
CLAYTON, Mary, 41, Thomas G., 152.
CLEGG, William H., 170.
CLEANER, Mrs. Beky, 82.
CLEARWATER, Mrs. Charlotte, 166, Edward, 164, 165.
CLEARY, Nicholas, 161.
CLEAVER, Grace Turner, 53, John, 53.
CLEMENT, Louisa Henrietta Leydier, 41.
CLEMENTS, John, 161.
CLEMMITT, Ann, 127, Robert, 127, 119, 191.
CLIFT, Josiah, 181.
CLINE, William H., 173.
CLINGMEN, George, 29.
CLINTON, Thomas G., 151.
CLOIT, Clarissa, 89.
CLOWES, Isaac, 118, 131.
CLUBB, Samuel, 83.
CLUFF, Mathew, 18, 58, 110, 142.
COADY, Catherine, 79.
COATES, Mrs. Nancy, 3.
COBBETT, James, 171.
COHEN, Philip J., 104.
COCHETEL, James, 67, 68, 72, John, 28, 29.
COCHRAN, Mary, 19.
COCK, Jennett 2, John, 2.
COCKBURN, Charles, 23.

230

COCKE, Anne B., 217, Anne Blaws, 211, Anne Blaws Barraud, 211, Buller, 104, Charles Cazy, 217, Charles L., 104, John H., 90, 217, John Hartwell, 211, Mary D. T., 173, Mary P., 202, Philip St. George, 137, Thomas J., 173.
CODD, John E., 108.
CODDLE, Mary, 55.
CODWISE, George W., 159.
CODY, Hannah, 31.
COFIELD, Sampson, 28.
COFFIELD, William, 119.
COFFIN, Mrs. Mary, 65, Reuben, 1, 20, 26, 29, William, 93.
COFFMAN, Richard, 89.
COGAN, James, 92, 110, 126.
COGHELER, Mary Ann, 93.
COKER, William A., 198, William Henry, 197, 198.
COLE, John H., 148, Josiah, 32, 57, Mrs. Lucretia, 79.
COLES, Isaac A., 94.
COLEGATE, Esther, 47.
COLEMAN, Elizabeth, 15, Henry, 188, Samuel, 2, 13, 15, William, 89.
COLIER, George W., 152.
COLLIER, Valentine John, 17.
COLLS, Mrs. Eliza Ann, 129, Mrs. Martha, 52.
COLLEY, Harriot H., 79, John G., 107, 118, 140, Leonora, 208, Mrs., 222, Mary Willoughby, 208, Nancy, 207, Nathaniel, 207, Nathaniel W., 118, Salter, 207, 208, Sarah, 64, William, 79.
COLLINS, Alice, 57, Catherine, 88, 138, Elizabeth C., 192, Capt. Freeman G., 218, James, 162, Jane, 72, John, 129, 165, 190, John B., 166, 190, 193, Margaret, 130, 165, Samuel R., 85, William, 110, 120.
COMBS, William, 8.
COMSTOCK, John W., 181.
CONE, Elizabeth, 174, Hillary, 162, James, 162, Martha, 162.
CONELLY, Mrs. Jannet, 3.
CONLY, Barney, 2.
CONNDLY, Mrs. Mary, 53.
CONNELL, Charles, 88.
CONNEL, John, 78, 88.
CONNER, Peter, 185, Thomas, 137.
CONNOR, Benjamin F., 137, Margaret R., 57.
CONNOWAY, John, 30.
CONRAD, John, 180.
CONSOLVO, Charles, 129, Elizabeth, 65, Mary Eliza, 140, William, 2, 121.
CONSTABLE, Frances, 8, Mary J., 149, Thomas, 8, 64, 65, 67, 98, 167.
CONWELL, George C., 118.
COODY, Elizabeth, 26.
COOK, Godfrey, 59, 60, 119, Godt Frederich, 31, David, 90, Isaiah, 68, John A., 181, Richard H., 44, William, 95.

COOKE, Ally, 119, Armistead T. M., 172, 174, 186, Dr. Armistead T. M., 156, Augustus B., 186, Charles, 180, Elizabeth, 48, 201, Elizabeth S., 95, George, 196, Giles B., 66, 91, 95, 156, Isaiah, 23, 59, 69, James, 75, John H., 16, Jonathan, 9, Mary Ann, 108, Margaret E., 156, Mordecai Jr., 156, 174, Rebecca, 68, Richard H., 33, Sarah, 195, William A., 123.
COOLING, Mrs. Lucy, 84.
COOLEY, Mrs. Margaret, 201.
COOPER, Ann Pierce Parker, 208, Ann R., 104, Arthur, 55, 63, 134, 142, 147, 179, Mrs. Catherine, 69, Copeland Leopold Parker, 208, David, 16, 24, 35, Eliza, 140, 155, Elizabeth, 117, Elijah, 106, George, 149, Gilley, 2, James, 70, Jane, 151, John, 28 39, 109, 218, 79, Margaret, 93, Martha, 168, 176, Martha Ann, 35, Mary, 30, Mary Ann, 93, 109, Mrs. Mary, 36, 39, Nancy, 82, Randolph, 114, Richard, 118, Samuel, 200, Sarah, 32, William, 4, 20, 63, 76, 208, Willis, 2.
COPES, Elizabeth, 179, Rachel Parker, 179.
CORBY, Ebenezer, 142, Thomas M., 44.
CORBEY, George, 165.
CORBELL, Sarah, 170.
CORBIN, Richard R., 109.
CORDELL, Mrs., 221.
CORDIS, John B., 12.
CORDONA, Michael, 187.
CORE, Margaret, 177.
CORI, Margaret, 177.
CORNALET, Henry, 24.
CORNICK, Adam, 209, Anne E., 111, Ann H., 62, Andrew Jackson, 215, Benjamin Franklin, 209, Mrs. Elizabeth, 221, Elizabeth F., 172, Elizabeth K., 118, Henry, 33, 216, Horatio, 103, 144, John, 104, 41, Margaret F., 180, Mary, 25, 209, 215, 214, James, 78, 130, 131, 144, 155, 172, 180, James Madison, 214, Joel, 9, Lemuel, 209, 214, 215, Capt. Lemuel, 219, Lemuel Senr., 220, Mrs., 218, Mary Ann Miller, 209, Nancy, 9, Peggy, 40, Rebecca, 216, Sarah P., 192, Thomas J., 180, 176, Thomas Jefferson, 210, 219, William Henry White, 216.
CORNWALL, John J., 26.
CORRAN, John T., 137, William B., 137, John, T., 137.
CORSEY, James, 39.
CORY, Nelson, 139.
COSBY, John L., 32, 220.
COSGROVE, Thomas, 102.
COSTER, Joseph, 147.
COSTIN, Bowdoin, 106, Louisa, 110.
COTTELL, Aaron, 9.
COTTEN, Henry, 189, 198, Frances A., 192.

COTTON, John, 177, Mary F., 197, Nathaniel, 177, Polly, 73, William, 71.
COTREL, Mrs. Nancy, 18.
COTTRILL, John, 13.
COUCH, Mrs. Ann, 8.
COULTON, Samuel, 116.
COUNSELS, Mrs. Mary Ann, 202.
COUPER, Eliza, 211, Parmelia, 211, 216, William, 19, 40, 63, 73, 84, 211, 216,
COURRECH, J., 68.
COURRECK, Joseph Francois Henri, 67.
COURTNEY, Mrs. Lydia, 149, Richard, 138.
COWAN, Mrs. Mary, 70, William B., 149.
COWDAN, John, 2.
COWDEN, John, 3.
COWDERY (Cowdry), Cornelia W., 126, Esther, 32, George W., 158, 197, Jonathan, 35, 91, 126, Mahala B., 100, Savage B., 32, Theodoric, 219.
COWLES, Ira, 60, Mrs. Jane,, 200.
COWLING, Benjamin, 36, Louisa A., 115.
COWNE, Sarah Maria Whiting, 206, Sarah, 206, Robert, 206.
COWPER, Abraham, 37, John, 13.
COX, Ann P., 50, Barbara, 44, Fadamy, 174, Godfrey, 14, 43, 44, J., 53, James, 39, 46, Mrs. Louisa, 121, Miles S., 132, 145, 191, Nancy, 24, Susanna, 63, William, 11.
COXELL, Agnes H., 186, Anne E., 137, Catherine H. D., 136, Eliza M., 136, Mrs. Elizabeth M., 143, Robert, 54.
CRAB, Jane, 28.
CRAGER, Elizabeth, 26, Peter, 13, 16, 20.
CRANDELL, Bethia, 120, Dudley, 9, 18.
CRANDLE, Mathew Boney, 144.
CRANE, Margaret R., 211, Thomas, 103, 100, William A., 139, William M., 84.
CRASMUCK, Michael, 19.
CRAVEN, Ann Maria, 180.
CRAWFORD, Mary Ann, 43, Mrs. Sarah, 17.
CRAWLEY, Ann E., 6, John, 128.
CRAY, Patrick, 90.
CREEKMORE (Creekmure), Ann W., 111, Ballance, 110, 96, Ephram B., 110, Mary, 123, Virginia, 198.
CREIGHTON, Mrs. Catherine, 57, William; 164.
CRETIA, Mrs. Pennie, 154.
CREW, Elizabeth, 173.
CRICKMORE, Margaret, 125.
CRIPS, Anthony, 25.
CRISWELL, Mrs. Ann, 121.
CRITCHET, Sarah, 13.
CRITTMORE, Mrs. Mourning, 101.
CROCKER, Actous, 96, David, 183, Mary, 46.
CROEL, John, 81, Sarah C., 184.
CROMMELIN, James, 62.
CROSBIE, Mrs. Hannah, 82.
CROSBY, Mary Frances, 155.

CROSSLEY, Mrs. Helena, 154, Mary Ann, 150.
CROSSGROVE, Mrs. Mary Ann, 110.
CROSGROVE, Mrs. Ruth, 111.
CROSSLEY, Susan, 147, Thomas, 36.
CROSSLAND, Mrs. Catherine, 79.
CROSMUCK, Michael, 73, 78, 84.
CROSS, Cornelius C., 62, George, 159, 176, 180, Nancy, 39, William, 39.
CROUCH, Elizabeth, 18, Emily, 130, Margaret, 5.
CROWDER, Thomas Jr., 127.
CROWELL, Elizabeth, 113.
CROWN, Mary, 23.
CROW, Archibald, 97, George L., 187, 197, Robert M., 76, Thomas, 58, 102.
CROZIER, Eliza, 197.
CRUES, Sarah, 7.
CRUISE, Catherine, 4.
CRUMP, Richard Jr., 118.
CRUSE, Rachael, 16.
CULL, David, 92, 127, 138, 181.
CULLANY, Ann, 106.
CULLEN, William, 118.
CULNEY, William, 81.
CULPEPPER, Daniel, 90, Jesse, 109, Mrs. Margaret, 184.
CUMMINGS, Henry, 89, Margaret, 10, 171.
CUNNINGHAM, Alexander, 27, 34, 121, 122, 135, 88, 108, Alexander M., 142, Ann, 23, Ann J., 162, Daniel, 115, Eliza, 23, 135, Eliza T. B., 92, Eleonor, 121, James Alexander, 12, James, 209, James B., 23, 60, 78, Joseph F., 56, 162, John, 18, 74, Mary, 7, Mary Ann, 122, Mary Louisa, 141, Patrick, 52, Penelope, 209, Robert B., 119, 169, Samuel, 199, Mrs., Sarah Ann, 170, William E., 129, 141, 150, 157, 158, 189, William Edmund, 209.
CURLE, Catherine, 29, Eliza Kello, 9, Mary, 9.
CURRAN, William, 19.
CURRIER, Mary Jane, 200, Nathaniel, 85, 113, 114, 129, 150, 151, 173, 176, 184, 191, 200, Robert A., 191.
CURTIS, Abel, 42, Ann, 185, Drayton M., 41, Mrs. Isabella, 148, Leno, 92, 120, Mrs. Lydia, 108, Morris, 120, Richard Henry, 116, Samuel, 75.
CUSTER, Sarah, 106.
CUSTIS, John W., 120.
CUTCHIN, Joseph, 38, Patrick H., 200.
CUTERELL, James, 42.
CUTHBERT, Frances, 213, James, 51, 220, 213, James Henrietta Francis, 213, Mary Susan, 70.
CUTHERELL, Anne, 186, Elie, 164, 186, Harriet, 176, Jemima, 187.
CUTHERILL, Sarah, 187, Harriet, 196.
CUTHRILE, Elizabeth, 20, John, 20.
CUTHRILL, Elizabeth, 196.
CUTREL, Elijah, 61, Mrs. Susan, 86.

DOUGHERTY, Anne, 66, John, 2, Hugh, 51, William, 195.
DOUGLAS, Alexander, 57, Ann, 3, Miss H. F., 151, William E., 151.
DOVE, Richard, 55, 120.
DOWDY, Godfrey, 144.
DOWENS, Mrs. Nancy, 97.
DOWLY, Mrs. Elizabeth, 37, John, 37.
DOWNES, Henry, 181.
DOWS, Josiah, 116.
DOWTY, Littleton, 22.
DOXEY, Mrs. Rebecca F., 186.
DOYLE, Ann, 125, Daniel S., 124, Eliza, 65, Elizabeth, 163, George, 65, 99, John E., 154, 161, 163, M., 220, Marcus L., 118, Martin, 4, Martin A., 123, Richard, 154, 164, 170, Walter James, 174, William, 184.
DOZIER, A. S., 182, 189, Cader, 181, Cloe, 7, Mrs. Emily, 106, Emily Jane, 162, Huldah E., 191, John, 136, Lydia, 191, Margaret, 121, Mrs. Peggy, 12, Virginia, 181, William A., 186.
DRAGHTON, Mrs. Ann, 89.
DRAKE, Ethelbert, 74, Francis, 3, 33, 41.
DRAPER, Margaret, 21.
DRAYTON, Thomas, 106, 123.
DREDGE, Dolly, 173.
DREENAN, John, 21, 43.
DREWRY, Margaret D., 164, Mathias, 164.
DREW, Martha C., 98.
DREWER, John, 152.
DREAMER, Mrs. Polly, 119.
DREMER, Isaac, 109.
DRINANE (Drinan), Anne, 63, Eleonore, 26, John, 1.
DRISCOLL, Mrs. Catherine, 1.
DRISDALE, Henry B., 206.
DRIVER, Mrs. Dolly, 12.
DRUMMOND, Anne, 211, Augustine, 89, Charles H., 172, Eleanor, 147, 150, Mrs. Eleanor, 153, Eliza A. F. B., 120, Eliza Ann Frances Bayley, 211, Elishea A. F., 131, Mrs. H. A., 161, James, 134, Jane C., 161, Richard, 34, 211, 120, Samuel, 121, Sarah, 34, Stephen H., 34, Spencer, 86, William S., 134.
DRURY, Horace, 172, Thomas, 4.
DRYDEN, Charlotte, 136, Eliza A., 136, James, 60.
DUBOURG, Andre, 68.
DUCHAMPS, John B., 59.
DUDLEY, Ambrose, 117, Ann S., 6, Caleb, 180, 187, Charles, 119, Mrs. Frances, 201, Jesse, 191, 196, John, 108, Johnson, 180, Joseph, 201, Loveman, 85, Mary A. M., 124.
DUDGEN, Christian, 19.
DUESBERRY, Elizabeth, 102, George H., 124, George W., 113, 118, Henry, 95, 101, Sarah E., 176, Thomas, 105, 176.
DUEON, John, 107.

DUFORT, John, 50, Joseph Antoine, 10, 29, 39, 41, 49.
DUFFY, James, 171.
DUGAN, Anna, 181.
DUKE, David, 198, Rachael G., 84.
DUKES, Joseph J., 180.
DULTON, Ann, 209, Ann Augusta, 209, Eliza, 75, Thomas, 209, William, 63.
DUNBAR, James, 111, 121, John, 131, John T., 200, Laura Jane, 199, Sarah E., 200, Thomas, 141, 145, 199, William D., 122, 199.
DUNCAN, David, 87, 97, J. E., 152, James, 48, James F., 134, William, 97.
DUNFORD, Emanuel, 202.
DUNLAVY, John, 44, 58.
DUNN, Anthony, 92, Cuddy, 7, Edward, 107, Edward T., 148, 163, 168, John, 3, 23, 34, 59, Lelia Ann, 58, Mary F., 101, Pleasant H., 195, Robert, 72, Sarah, 92, Sarah W., 59, Sulphia, 110, Valentine, 7, William, 10.
DUNOVIN, James, 82.
DUNIVAN, John, 11.
DUNSTON, Jacob B., 153, John, 38, 80, 90, 120, 153, 162, 168.
DUNTON, Catherine, 128, Henry G., 117, Mrs. Nancy, 83, William, 56.
DUPERU, J. M., 94.
DEPUY, John, 93.
DURAND, Elie, 103.
DURANT, Hannah, 48, Henry, 5, 7, Peter, 218.
DURFEY, Harriet, 152, Pricilla, 156, William, 200.
DUTTON, Lewis, 151.
DUVAL, Mary Frances, 197.
DUVEL, Ann, 118.
DUXEY, Jesse W., 151.
DYE, Catherine, 82, Margaret C., 144, William, 33, 118.
DYER, Isham, 58, James B., 196.
DYSON, Fanny, 35, Mrs. Frances, 142, George, 141, James, 35, 58, James Jr., 28, John, 121, Jonathan, 35, Manner, 4, Mary, 67.
DWIGHT, Ellen F., 191.
DWYER, William, 49.

E

EAGER, Mrs. Eliza Ann, 91.
EARLE, Edward, 173.
EASTWOOD, Mathias, 10.
EATON, John, 27, Susan, 90.
EATT, Sarah Esperance, 18.
EBERLE, George, 46, 58, 60.
ECCLES, James, 67, 110, Thomas, 132, 149, 142, 162, 161, 171, 177, 192, 193.
ECHEVARRIA, Houstet, Arnand, 33.
EDDENS, Mary Eliza, 121, Robert, 121, Samuel, 101.
EDDINS, Robert E., 109, Susan, 153.

EDMONDS, Francis B., 169, George, 99, John W., 197, Joseph, 198, Robert L., 54, William, 47.
EDDY, Peter, 7, Mrs. Sarah, 19.
EDMONDSTON, Eliza Washington, 65.
EDNEY, Mrs. 222.
EDWARD (Negro), 66.
EDWARDS, Elizabeth, 43, Frances Virginia Ann, 170, Giles, 98, Indiana, 201, Isabella, 126, Jane, 167, John A., 154, Joseph J., 195, Lucy L., 144, Margaret, 146, Nancy, 198, Oney, 53, Oscar E., 170, Overton W., 142, Samuel, · 19, Susan W., 142, Thomas, 13, William, 126, William H., 156, 170, William Lee, 144.
EGAN, Lydia, 135, Margaret, 135.
EGGLESTON, Pamelia, 62.
EHRBECK, John, 174.
ELCOCK, John, 24.
ELDER, Francis, 23.
ELDRIDGE, Thomas, 156, William, 110.
ELLEGOOD, Rebecca A., 59, William, 222.
ELLEN, Ann, 132.
ELLERS, John, 148.
ELLIOTT, Eliza, 33, Mrs. Elizabeth, 10, Elizabeth J., 202, Gabriel, 5, Lieut., Jesse D., U. S. N., 50, John, 62, 120, Peggy, 30, Peter, 33, Polly, 106, Robert, 5, Samuel C., 186, William, 52, 102.
ELLIS, Charles, 55, 217, George, 115, Gibson P., 161, James Nimmo, 217, Joseph, 140, Margaret K., 217, Nancy, 66, Otis, 123, 100, Zachus (Zacheus), 48, 49, 50, 51, 66.
ELSTOB, Edward, 50, 53.
ELTON, James, 34.
EMMERSON (Emerson), Benjamin, 99, 181, James, 102, Mary Anne, 193, William F., 193.
EMERY,. Frances, 205, John, 205, Join Jordan, 205.
ENGLISH, George, 25, Peggy, 40.
ENNIS, James, 88, 91, William, 47.
ERICKSON, Gertrude, 119.
ERSKINE, Mrs. Catherine, 168, Samuel, 157.
ERVIN, Mrs. Jane, 126.
ESHER, Louisa Ann, 127, Louisa G., 195, Sarah Ann, 162.
ETHERIDGE (Etheredge), Ann, 158, Ann F., 184, Anne, 205, Mrs. Ann, 22, 97, David, 90, Delilah, 58, Elijah L., 201, Frances, 185, Henry, 24, 97,, 122, John E., 187, Mrs. Margaret, 55, Richard, 69, 105, Thomas, 151, William, 205, 218, Willima Oldner, 205.
ETHERTON, William, 12.
ETTING, Samuel, 104.
EUSTIS, James, 169.
EVANS, Charles, 145,, 151, Edward, 24, Eleanor, 46, Elizabeth, 190, George, 46, Joshua, 22, Keziah, 85, Mary, 75,

Richard, 156, Sally, 22, Thomas, 169.
EVANSTALL, Mrs. Amelia, 161.
EVEREDGE, Mary, 27.
EVERETT, Agnes Elizabeth, 198, Nancy, 198.
EVERTS, Egbert, 6.
EWELL, Elizabeth, 46, 64, James C., 157. Jesse, 64, Jesse T., 200, John, 24.
EWIN, Mrs. Jane, 126.
EYER, Amy, 93, Emily Ann, 120, Miss, 221.

F

FABRE, Maria C., 52, Peter, 52.
FACE, Elizabeth Van Dalia, 200, Mrs. Jane, 35, William H., 200.
FAIR, Charles, 35.
FAIRCHILD, Marcus A., 174, William, 80, 82.
FALVEY, Aug., 78, John, 78.
FALCONER, John, 178.
FALLON, George, 189.
FALMARK, William, 169.
FARANT, George W., 129.
FARINHOLT, Jesse, 12.
FARMER, James, 145, John, 42, 149, 168, Mrs. M., 222, Robert, 91.
FARR, William C., 18, 25, 37, 44, 63.
FARRAGUT, David Glasgo, 99, 130, 172.
FARRELL, Philip, 87.
FARRALL, Thomas, 84.
FARRIER, John, 25.
FARRINGTON, George, 10.
FARRIS, Mrs. Penelope, 170.
FARTHERNY, John, 87.
FATHERLY, Ann, 160, Elizabeth A., 160, John, 68, Samuel, 92, Sarah, 70, Thomas, 160.
FAUCHER, John, 22.
FAULDER, Hannah, 1.
FAULKNER, William R. S., 201.
FAUQUIER, Ann, 127, Elizabeth G., 127, John, 40, Sarah, 99, William 40, William M., 99.
FAUSE, Monsieur, 222.
FAWN, John, 40.
FEAR, Mary, 86.
FEARING, Isaiah, 54.
FALTHOUSE, George, 164.
FENESSY, Catherine, 75.
FENTRESS, Ann, 120, Barbara Frances, 196, Cary, 151, 158, 181, Eliza, 139, Harriet, 183, Harriet M., 181, Hillary W., 74, Jeremiah, 196, 202, Joshua, 93, Lemuel, 144, 149, 182, Lovitt, 75,_158, Mary E. C., 182, Mary F., 169, Mary R., 158, Reuben, 62, 70, 120, 176.
FEREBE, Elizabeth, 155.
FEREBEE, Enoch, 137, Frances Ann, 76, Mary Ann, 137, Sarah Frances, 144.
FEREBER, Frances, 29.
FERET, Alexandre, 136, 140.
FERGUSON, Ann, 96, Catherine, 113, Finlay, 17, Finlay F., 150, Henry, 101,

236

James, 138, Mary, 152, Margaret, 92, Peter, 40, 48, Rebecca, 79, Robert S., 80, Susan, 59, Thomas, 141, 147, William, 193, William G., 196, William H., 171, 178.
FERNANDES, A. O., 67, Joseph P., 150.
FERRARR, Elizabeth, 202.
FERRALL, Thomas, 108.
FERRAT, Joseph, 152.
FERRIS, Edwin L., 154, James, 122, 181, John, 90, 99, 134, Sarah H., 175.
FERRY, Mrs. Mary, 36.
FERTE, Antonio, 61, Dr., 219.
FERTSON, James, 96.
FESSLER, Mary, 202.
FIELD, James E., 199, Mary, 32.
FIELDS, Mrs. Sarah, 101, William, 93.
FIETT, Peter, 105.
FIGELEY, Mrs. Elizabeth, 131.
FIGEROUX, Raymond Jr., 13.
FILLEY, Etta Emeline, 123.
FILMARK, Mrs. Maria, 174.
FINCH, Elizabeth, 80, George, 17, 69, 80.
FINLEY, Ann, 135, Thomas, 187.
FINN, Stephen, 109, Elizabeth, 131.
FINNEY, Crawley, 73.
FISHER, Mrs. Ann, 10, Caleb, 100, Capt. (child of), 220, Charlotte Butler, 212, Elliana, 85, Eliza, 93, Eliza B., 139, Elizabeth, 160, Frances, 26, Mrs. H., 219, James D., 123, John, 144, 164, 202, John A., 156, John J., 173, Joseph, 8, Keziah, 109, Lucy, 212, Mrs. Mahalia B., 126, Mary L., 134, Mrs. Mary, 60, Mrs. Rachael, 34, Richard, 212, Richard B., 160, Richard W., 193, Reuben, 134, Stephen, 138, 183, Susan, 87, Thomas, 154, William, 56.
FISK, Martin, 6, 7, 45, Mary Ann, 89.
FITNAM, Ann, 123, Christopher, 123, Mary, 119.
FITTON, Mary Ann, 139.
FITZ, Mr. (child of), 220, Lydia, 137, Nathaniel, 36, Sarah A., 137, Virginia, 173.
FITZGERALD, Henry B., 3, 5, Mathew, 28, Thomas, 11, Mary, 143, Mary J., 163, Mrs., 158.
FITZGERALD, Edward, 143, Henry, 200.
FITZGIBBON, Edward, 169.
FITZHUGH, Eliza Virginia, 128, John, 16, 30, 151, Margaret P., 139, Nancy, 16.
FITZPATRICK, Michael, 77, Mrs. Peggy 3.
FIVEASH, Fanny, 76, John W., 96, 129.
FLAC, Rose Celestine, 21.
FLAGG, Mrs. Elizabeth, 3.
FLAHAVAN, Mrs. Catherine, 10.
FLANAGAN, Benjamin F., 164, 179, Caroline Virginia, 179, Emily, 164, Frances, 155, Mrs. Frances, 199, Lydia L., 155, Peter M., 141, Stacey, 174, 179, Tully, 197, Wallace, 111.
FLANEY, Semon, 72.
FLEER, Thomas, 123, 164.

FLEMING, Ann H., 27, John, 89, Mrs. Sarah, 139, William A. T., 158.
FLETCHER, E., 198, Eliza, 192, Mrs. Elizabeth, 13, William H., 200.
FLINN, James, 75.
FLINTHAM, William, 43.
FLOOD, Eleanor, 31.
FLORIE, Simon, 89.
FLOWERS, James, 25, John, 13, 97.
FLOYD, Frances W., 63, Peggy, 17, Thomas C., 139, William R., 156.
FLYNN, Catherine, 159, James, 171, 176, Mary, 124.
FOLLEN, C. Johan, 199, Catherine, 188.
FOLLAN, C. Topan, 199.
FOLLER, C. Johan, 199.
FOLER, S. J., 140.
FOLTZ, Abby, 1.
FONTAIN, Thomas, 24.
FONTAINE, Francis C., 50.
FONTIER, Joseph, 146.
FONTO, Peter, 178.
FORBES, Cornelius, 171, Helen, 17, Rosetta, 179, Samuel A., 126.
FORD, Edward, 105, William, 39.
FOREMAN, Christian A. R., 152, Sarah, 118.
FORREST (Forest), Anne, 135, Anne L., 183, Ellen, 135, Eliza, 135, Elizabeth, 36, James, 45, John, 36, 135, Mary, 135, Samuel, 175, 183, William, 135, 190, William S., 149.
FOSDICK, John H., 47, 48.
FORT, Lewis, 15.
FOSTER, Ann T., 134, Charity, 72, Desdemona, 102, Edmund, 160, 166, Elizabeth, 76, Elizabeth E., 150, Francis, 2, 3, 4, 7, 25, 46, Mrs. Hannah, 60, James, 189, John B., 202, John H., 90, John M., 181, Mr. (child of), 219, Lucy, 210, Margaret R., 211, Martha Ann, 187, Mr. Pat. (child of), 219, Peter, 39, 52, 221, Sarah, 97, Sarah Beddinger, 211, Seth B., 211, William F., 66, 120, 150, William Miles, 210, William P., 40, William Part., 210.
FOULON, Elizabeth, 23, 26, Jean Baptiste, 22, Mrs., 56.
FOURNIQUET, Louis J., 120.
FOY, Terentius, 19.
FRANCIS, Daniel, 195, Eliza, 173, James, 153, John, 13, 82, Michael, 85, Rebecca, 87, Salah, 93, Wells, 50, William, 140, 58, William Jr., 173.
FRANCOIS (negro), 82.
FRANCOIS, Jean, 39, 65, John, 54.
FRAETAS, Lorea, 44.
FRANK, Anthony, 31, Rosa, 170, Rose, 155.
FRANKLAND, Henry W,, 145.
FRANKLIN, Thomas, 69, 134, 144, 154, William, 15.
FRASER, Upton S., 89.

FRAZER, David, 39, Elizabeth, 43, John, 23, 45, Maria, 40.
FRAZIER, James, 6, John, 13, Margaret, 13, Upton S., 130.
FREDERICK, Henry A, 113, Michael, 125.
FREE, Mrs. Catherine, 164.
FREEMAN, Edward, 174, John, 19, 24, 58, 63, Joseph, 74, Joseph A., 99, Lucy, 74, Virginia, 179, William G., 179, William Grigsby, 40.
FRENCH, Daniel D., 150, Euphemia, 176, John, 18, 76, 83, 130, 139.
FRENOI, Joseph, 127.
FRESHWATER, Edward, 192.
FRIGELEY, Mrs. Elizabeth, 131.
FRITH, Kitturah G., 117, Kiturah Goodson, 216, Edward, 216, 222, Mary Anne, 216, Mary Ann L., 143, Mary W., 216.
FRITSON, Mrs. Patsey, 114.
FRITTS, George, 30, 38, 52.
FRIZZEL, Jesse, 116, Willoughby, 116.
FROMENT, Peter, 21.
FROST, Benjamin, 48, Lucy L., 160, Mary E., 175, Peter E., 199, Robert, 184, Samuel, 167.
FROUD, Ann, 22.
FRUTIER, Mrs. Mary, 103.
FRY, Christopher, 7.
FRYER, Richard, 7, 38.
FUGITT, William, 144, William B., 158.
FULGERON, Elizabeth, 84.
FULLER, Affrica, 88, Isaac, 78, 99, Jeremiah, 161, John, 1, 73, 152, 180, 191, 198, Mary, 7, Nancy, 152, Peter, 152, William, 77.
FULLERTON, Charles S., 34.
FULLINGTON, Jacob, 177.
FULTER, Susan, 64.
FULTON, William, 26.

G

GABRIEL, Joseph, 17.
GAGE, George W., 165.
GAINS, Susan, 71.
GALAGHER, Henry, 168, Patrick, 126, 168.
GALEVIN, Lewis, 60.
GALT, Alexander, 69, 84, 180, Capt., 220, Dickie, 89, John M., 132, Sarah T., 84.
GALVIN, Dr., 80.
GAMBLE, Mrs. Kitty A., 54, Thomas, 15, 17.
GAMMON, Ann H, 87, James, 117, Joel, 87.
GANGS, Margaret, 98.
GANTZ, Francis, 93.
GARBER, Albert J., 112.
GARCIA, Barneto, 171.
GARDNER, Mrs. Ann Eliza, 157, Capt., 222, Eliza, 128, Elizabeth, 44, Frances T., 116, Henry, 122, Isaac O., 185, John, 144, Joseph, 44, Mary, 169, Mary Ann, 99, Mrs. Mary, 35, William, 23, 73, 86,

William H., 99, Lieut. William Henry, 94.
GARNETT, Charlotte O., 157, Elizabeth S., 198, Louisa, 148, William, 148, 154, William H., 157, 198, William Henry, 162.
GARRET, Sarah, 108.
GARRIS, John, 51.
GARRISON, James S., 87, Joshua, 102, Louisa C. M., 102, Pricilla, 4.
GARROW, Mrs. Ann, 127, Mrs. Dorothea, 135, Mrs. Jane, 60, John, 127, William, 68, 96.
GARSENT, Mary Victoria, 18.
GARVAIS, Mrs. Sylvia, 167.
GARY, George Cuthbert, 131.
GASKINS, Mrs. Annis, 3 , James S., 183, James W., 192, Job, 2, Spencer, 30.
GATEWOOD, Anne, 206, 216, Elizabeth A., 137, Elizabeth Anne, 216, Philemon, 89, Richard, 92, T., 218, Thomas, 23, 13, 217, Thomas Whiddon, 206, 218.
GAUTIER, Benjamin, 52.
GAY, John, 60, Sarah, 21, Mrs. Sarah, 20.
GAYLARD, John, 158.
GAYNER, Thomas, 19, 20.
GEAY, Catherine, 152, Felicete, 135, Peter, 135, 152.
GEBOO, Peter, 108.
GEE, Mrs. Ann, 62, Edward, 53, John H., 104.
GEESLING, Mrs., 219.
GEHART, Mary, 80.
GEOFFROY, J. P., 103, John P., 153.
GEORGE (negro), 147.
GEORGE, Edward, 178, John, 3, 9, John H., 70, John Lewis, 23, Malana W., 70, Nancy Willis, 19, Polly, 61, Pinckney, 98.
GERALD, Joseph, 200.
GERHART, Jacob, 54.
GERKIN, Charles H., 191.
GERMAIN, Peter, 38, 39, Rochas, 80.
GERVAIS, Augustus, 207, Jerke, 105, John Amedee, 208, Sophia, 208, Mrs. Sylvia, 167, Raymond, 109, 207, Redmund, 27.
GHISELIN (Gheselin), Ann R., 92, John D., 67, 111, 113, 125, 150, John D. Jr., 194.
GHISEMAN, Elizabeth, 133.
GIBBONS, Henry, 193, James W., 159, John N., 71, Mrs., 219, Richard, 8, Sarah Archer, 41, Susan, 117, Thomas, 41, 114.
GIBBS, Mrs. Hellen H., 118, John, 162, 171.
GIBSON, Elizabeth, 150, Hannah, 77, Jenny, 3, Luther R., 178.
GIDDENS, Killey, 25.
GIFFORD, John, 55.
GILBERT, Catherine, 107, Eliza, 7, 47, 90, Elizabeth, 183, George W., 65, James, 42, 77, 90, 158, James W., 198, Kitty, 110, Maria, 27, Mary Ann, 77, Mary F.,

183, Mathew, 83, Reymon, 7, 27, Susanna H., 45, Thomas W., 198.
GILDEN, John, 40.
GILFILLAN, Georgianna Hand Stuart, 96.
GILLY, Nancy, 101.
GILMAN, John, 27, 29.
GILMORE, Henry, 89.
GINES, Juliann, 102.
GIST, C. H. Jr., 116.
GIVENS, Eliza, 200, James, 169.
GLASS, Rebecca, 132, 157.
GLEASON, Ellen, 108, James, 75, John, 90, Mrs. Mary Ann, 125, Mrs. Saka, 99, William, 105.
GI EESON, James, 83, Sophia, 48.
GLENN, Eliza, 87, Louisa C., 56, Mathew, 93, 87, Mathew Jr., 102, Mathew C., 118, Matilda, 93, Thomas, 26, 56, 73, 96.
GLENNAN, Michael, 188, William, 177, 180.
GLISAN, James, 64.
GLISSON, Midshipman Olier S., 140.
GODFRED, Amelia, 65.
GODFREY, Eliza, 122, 181, Mrs. Eliza, 93, Elizabeth, 93, Mary, 105, Miss, 222, Sarah, 124, William, 107, 170, 202, 200.
GODIN, Mrs. Marie, 76.
GODWIN, Ann, 3, James, 21, Lewis, 75, Mrs. Patsy, 75, Mrs. Dolly, 31.
GOFF, Ann, 31.
GOLDEN, Mary Ann, 96.
GOLDING, Hetty, 61, Mrs. Hetty, 44, Sophia, 94.
GOLDSBOROUGH, James N., 163.
GOLDSMITH, Aaron A., 199.
GOLLADAY, Frederick, 57.
GORMAN, Mrs. Hannar, 91.
GOOD, James, 100, Richard, 10, 11, 18, 16, 19, 35, 40, 41, 42, 45, William, 9, 24.
GOODALL, Ann, 105, Mrs. Elizabeth, 107, Park, 64.
GOODMAN, Anna Maria, 75, James, 74.
GOODRIDGE, Elijah, 95, Sewall, 167, 183.
GOODSON, Elizabeth, 195, Rebecca, 34, William H., 190.
GOODWIN, James, 2, 9, William N., 200.
GORDAN, John D., 105, 192, William, 114.
GORDEN, Joseph, 82, Mrs. Nancy, 53.
GORDON, Ann, 5, Cornelius T., 176, Mrs. Elizabeth, 52, James Jr., 147, 153, John, 37, Joseph, 56, 58, Louisa, 33, Read, 172, Robert, 128, 220, Virginia Jackson, 128, William, 5, 64, 69, 90.
GORE, Richard, 40, Jonathan, 190.
GORLIER, Francis, 15, 38, Francoise, 39, J., 80, Jn., 76.
GORMLY, George, 12, John, 119.
GORMLEY, Bryan, 24, 48, Dennis, 192.
GORNTO, Ann Eliza, 202, James, 202.
GOULD, Elizabeth, 130, Thomas, 171.

GOULDEN, Daniel, 1, 34, Pamela Ann, 1, Lucinda Ann, 174.
GOULDER, Susan, 156.
GOULDING, Margaret, 123.
GOURLEY, David, 12, 28, 34, 81, 85.
GOVE, Jonathan, 190.
GOW, Ann, 3.
GOWAN, John, 38.
GOZELIN, John, 9.
GRAENACHER, Louis, 159.
GRAHAM, Agnes, 127, Mrs. Elizabeth J., 122, Charles, 170, 171, Charles H., 174, James A., 106, June, 162, John, 127, Mrs. Maria, 108, Tildsey, 36, 41, 44, 60, 94, Thomas, 181, William, 181, 195, 202.
GRANBERRY (Granbery), Augusta E., 102, Eliza, 44, Elizabeth, 135, Henry A. T., 113, John, 44, 210, John Stowe Hastings, 210, Lewis, 69, 134, 135, Mary Ann, 134, Mary Louisa, 113, Susanna B., 210, William H., 202.
GRANIER, Joseph, 24.
GRANT, John, 31, Nancy, 31, Mrs. Nancy, 52, Susan, 168.
GRANLING, George, 171.
GRANVILLE, Jane, 113.
GRATIOT, Charles, 98.
GROVES, Caleb, 176.
GRAVES, Catherine, 217, Eliza, 129, James, 66, 217, Julia, 54, Maria, 66, 217, Mrs. Maria, 169.
GRAY, Alice G., 106, Benjamin C., 184, Edward, 122, Elizabeth, 99, Ellen, 90, James, 122, 143, John, 3, 42, 110, Mrs. Mary, 54, Nelson R., 202, Mrs. Sally, 95, Sarah, 122, Thomas R., 199, William, 85, William F., 72.
GRAYSON, Spence, 6, 7.
GREAR, Livy, 18.
GREAVES, James, 11.
GREEN, Joel, 106, John, 24, 43, John W., 158, Joseph, 103, Mary G., 74, Neil, 82, Richard L., 31, 42, 74, 108, Mrs. Sarah, 110, Susan A., 113, Timothy, 194, William, 79, 119, Lieut. William, 112.
GREENSHIELDS, Thomas, 12.
GREENWOOD, C. F., 191, George, 139, Margaret, 171, Martin, 171, William, 184, 194, 197.
GREGORY, Elizabeth, 202, 205, Henry Poindexter, 205, Isaac, 197, 202, Lemuel, 178, Mary Ann, 200, Nehemiah, 205, Martha Jane, 197, Dr. Nehemiah, 21, William, 33, William W., 188.
GRANDALL, Tabitha, 136.
GRICE, Charles A., 88, Josh., 77.
GRIEVE, William, 201.
GRIFFIN, George, 105, Hester, 81, John, 191, John T., 185, Margaret, 108, Martha, 11, Mary Elizabeth, 191, Michael, 97, 111, 172, 144, Sarah, 81, Thomas, 21, 93, 113, 138, 146, Thomas

HARDING, Mrs. Anna, 16, Eliza, 47, 61, 87, Henry F., 118, John, 160, Thomas, 61, William, 122.

HARDISON, Charles W., 135, Edward W., 138, Henry C., 191, 194, Isabella, 145, John B., 162, 191, Stacy, 177, Thomas A., 124, 135, W. J., 123, William J., 124.

HARGEAN, Elizabeth, 90.

HARGROVE, Mrs. Mary, 88, Robert W., 168, Susan, 114.

HARMAN, Mrs. Catherine, 73, Margaret, 157, Susan, 125.

HARMANSON, Anne, 212, 213, Anne Thomas, 212, 220, Edward Lewis, 213, Frances Susan, 213, 222, Mr. P. (child of), 219, Mrs. P., 222, Patrick, 11, 212, 213, Virginia, 213.

HARMON, Ann, 127, Shadrack, 36, 52.

HARMEN, Elizabeth, 92, William, 25.

HARNETT, Mrs. Aphia, 40.

HARPER, Ann, 23, Arthur T., 198, 199, John, 124, Zebedee, 191.

HARRINGTON, George, 176.

HARRIS, Adeline, 138, Benjamin, 147, Charles, 112, Charles F., 138, Elizabeth, 55, 158, Elias, 197, Henry, 152, Mrs. Esther, 2, Hannah, 28, John, 187, Mary Elizabeth, 112, Nancy, 197, Polly, 197, Richard, 6, Sarah, 124, Mrs. Sarah E., 175, Statia, 76, William J., 196.

HARRISON, Alexander, 122, Mrs. Anne, 6, Benjamin, 10, Catherine, 149, Charles, 17, Elizabeth, 172, 192, George, 89, Henry S., 202, James, 76, 186, James P., 162, James R., 192, John, 6, Mathew, 10, Nancy, 152, Pamela, 61, Sarah, 202, Temperance Ann, 149, William H., 125.

HARSHAW, Charles, 69, Eliza, 121.

HART, Honoria, 91, James, 119, John, 23.

HARTMAN, William, 184.

HARTNETT, Richard, 99.

HARTSHORN, Amelia D., 182, Mary, 144, Samuel W., 104, 112, Sylvanus, 112, 144, 182, 186, Virginia, 186.

HARVEY, Ann, 102, Francis, 10, G., 145, George, 109, James, 65, 61, 86, 111, John, 19, 22, 141, William, 130.

HARWOOD, Elizabeth B., 107, Evelina, 167, Harlow, 50, John R., 45, 89, 107, John W., 201, Maria, 151, Samuel, 145, 162, Sarah, 162, Susan Gilbert, 157, Susan H., 167, Virginia, 143.

HASKELL, John H., 181.

HASKINS, J. H., 133, Jane, 159.

HASKINGS, Mrs. Elizabeth, 3.

HASSET, William, 13.

HASSON, Edward H., 7, 8.

HASTER, Lorentz, 68.

HASTIE, Henry, 209, Margaret, 209, Mrs. Margaret, 87, Elanda Cattell, 209.

HASTINGS, Eliza, 212, George, 113, John Granberry, 212, Jonas, 44, 212.

HATCHER, Charles, 125, John, 86.

HATFIELD, William, 97, 98.

HATHAWAY, Benjamin, 10, 18, David, 159, David M., 172, Ephraim (Ephriam), 33, 172, James L., 159, John R., 185, Jethro, 16, Mrs. Mary, 197.

HATTER, John, 188.

HATTON, Benjamin, 79, 92, Esther, 142, Mrs. Esther, 159, Goodrich, 17, 35, John, 81, John G. H., 140, Mary, 55, Capt. Robert, 5, Thomas F., 122.

HAUGHTON, Mrs., 219, Thomas, 153, Willaim, 7.

HAVAN, John, 3.

HAWARD, Mrs. Charlotte, 149.

HAWES, William, 108.

HAWK, Mrs. Elizabeth, 106.

HAWKE, Lewis, 54, Margaret, 120.

HAWKINS, Ann, 103, Eliza Ann, 157, Elizabeth Jane, 199, John, 103, 131, Mary Ann, 131, Rebecca, 122, Thomas W., 46, William, 169.

HAWTHORN, Mathew, 13, Thomas, 15, 191, William J., 191.

HAY, Elizabeth, 145, James, 24, 27, Jane, 191, William J., 191.

HAYER, Francis H., 18.

HAYDEN, Ann, 95, Mrs. Ann, 97, Uriah, 66.

HAYES, Harvey H., 124, Laurence, 82, Christian, 133, Robert, 180, Mrs., 219.

HAYMAN, Christian Elizabeth, 199, John, 195, Rosetta, 199, John, 196, Erasmus T., 183, John Randall, 182.

HAYNES, Mrs. Catherine D., 167, Mrs. Elizabeth, 87, Frances, 38, George, 4, Jonathan, 58, Margaret A. T., 146, Margaret Anne Tyler, 206, Mary D., 161, Mary F., 187, Mrs., 222, Margaret O., 54, 206, Mrs. Rebecca, 173, Capt. Thomas, 219, Thomas, 8, 10, Miss Sally, 10, Thomas J., 38, 206, William, 137, 146, 161, William B., 181.

Sally, 10, Thomas J., 38, 206, William, 137, 146, 161, William B., 181.

HAYNOR, Mary, 134.

HAYS, Christian, 139, George, 139, James, 199, William, 122, 133, 137.

HAYWARD, 218, Alexander, 28.

HAYWOOD, Alexander, 45, 51, 54, Ann, 64, Mrs. Ann, 71, Mrs. Diana, 88, Elizabeth, 45, J. (child of), 222, John, 111, Nancy, 54, Mrs. Rebecca, 63.

HEATH, Ann, 168, Elizabeth Ann, 193, Elizabeth J., 198, Emma, 180, George, 100, James, 153, John, 22, Mrs. Margaret K., 179, Susannah, 12, Tabitha, 78, 100.

HEAREY, Mathew, 3.

HEBDEN, Eliza, 157.

HEBDON, Charles, 135, Mrs. Lucy Ann, 171.

HEDMAN, Mary Ann, 156

HEDDRICK, Elizabeth, 105.

HEDRICK, Hetty, 52, John, 50, John C., 13, Susan, 54.

HOGG, Mrs. Jane, 199.
HOGGARD, Eliza Ann, 108, James, 24, Margaret, 156, Susanna, 4, Thurmer, 172.
HOGGART, Susanna, 4.
HOGGES, Matilda, 19.
HOGWOOD, Mrs. Eliza Ann, 119, William, 136.
HOLDEN, Julia, 128, Life, 128, Thomas, 35.
HOLINSCLATER, Catherine Lowly, 206, M., 206, William Sheldon, 206.
HOLLAN, James, 184.
HOLLAND, James, 173, 195, 198, Mary Ann, 198, Nehemiah, 78, Peter, 8.
HOLLIER,, Ann, 207, Harriot C., 94, Harriot Curl, 207, ulia Armistead, 207, Simon, 207.
HOLLOWAY, Lewis,182, Julianna, 46, Polly, 202.
HOLLOWELL, Betsy, 168, Salira, 180.
HOLM, Charles, 114, 125, 128, Charles L., 151, Charles S., 140, 142, 139.
HOLMES, Ann Eliza, 183, Elizabeth, 103, Mrs. Elizabeth S., 190, George, 109, Captain James, 142, John, 175, John S., 154, John W., 139, Lemuel K., 169, Mrs. Louisa, 90, Lydia, 183, Mary Ann, 63, Nicholas, 17, Dr. Robert, 35, William, 21, William C., 112, William J., 136, 171, 196.
HOLMS, William, 121.
HOLSON, Thomas, 218.
HOLSTEAD, Richard, 76.
HOLT, Ann Belfield, 209, Ann R., 113, Anne S., 212, Catherine, 151, Clara,, 133, 209, Frances Louisa, 133, Mr. H. (child of), 220, Henry, 15, John E., 16, 81, 103, 209, Dr. Henry C., 170, Mary E., 157, Mary Eloisa, 103, Mary C. E., 124, Randolph D., 168, Mrs. Rebecca, 92, Samuel, 16, Sarah Anne Lewis, 212, William, 9, 151, 157, William C., 50, 59, 212, Willis, 90.
HONSEN, George, 84.
HOOD, William, 13.
HOLTON, Mrs. Elizabeth, 103.
HOOPS, William, 96.
HOPE, Christopher C., 193, John, 158, 166, John C., 103, Virginia, 158, William, 139.
HOPKINS, Abigail, 28, Amanda T., 160, Ann, 94, Catherine, 221, Elizabeth, 221, Elizabeth A., 202, Elizabeth H., 202, Henry, 105, John, 113, Mary, 79, William, 222, William Fenn, 134, Stephen, 30.
HORNER, Mrs. Hannah, 20, Louder, 18.
HORNSBY, Mrs. Alice, 55.
HOSIER, David, 165, Nathaniel, 138, Robert, 196.
HOUSAUR, Eliza, 97.
HOUSE, Mrs. Elizabeth, 125, James, 147, 148, 169, 183, John, 92.

HOUSEMAN, John, 174, 177, 179.
HOUGH, John M., 161.
HOUGHTON, Mary P., 87, John, 36, Timothy, 67, William M., 124.
HOWARD, Calthorpe, 192, Mrs. Charlotte, 149, Henry, 192, Levi, 200, Reubin A., 173, Robert D., 170, Mrs. Sally, 46, Samuel, 16, William, 139, 185.
HOWE, William H., 189.
HOWELL, Mrs. Elizabeth, 129, 193, Elizabeth S., 185, Mary, 185, Mary Ann, 187, Mrs. Pricilla, 75, Robert B. C., 127, William, 35, 48.
HOWES, James, 146, Mary, 16.
HOWLETT, Mary Frances, 173.
HOWSER, Mrs. Louisa, 98.
HOZIER, Eliza, 134, Robert, 134.
HOYER, Mrs. Letitia, 124.
HOYT, Mrs. Susan M., 174.
HUGHBURG, Joshua, 11, 13.
HUBBARD, Christopher, 137, Diana, 83, Elizabeth, 9, Mary, 15, Mathew, 9, 15. 35, Mathew Jr., 53.
HUBBERD, John, 85.
HUDDLE, Mrs. Sarah, 110.
HUDGEN, Gabriel, 113, Moses, 198.
HUDGIN, Nancy J., 136.
HUDGINS, Joanna, 171, Joshua, 22.
HUDSON, Edward, 16, 76, Mrs. Margaret, 34, William, 22.
HUGHES, Ann, 97, Christopher, 82, Elias, 97, Elizabeth, 83, John, 11, 112, 176, Mr., 218, Mann P., 88, Mary, 115, Mrs. Mary, 147, William, 20, 114.
HUGES, Ellena, 179.
HUGHLET, Thomas, 144.
HULL, Jacob, 72, Joseph, 16, 27.
HULINGS, Ellen E., 178.
HUME, Mrs. Ruth, 64, Thomas, 42.
HUMMINS, Nancy, 51.
HUMPHREY, Lewis, 25.
HUMPHREYS, Margaret, 2, Thomas, 101.
HUNGERFORD, Lieut., 221.
HUNLEY, LATSHA, 18.
HUNT, Charles H., 84, Henry, 26, John B., 162, Joseph, 37, Marharet, 37, Mary A. E., 187, Prudence, 112.
HUNTER, Ann, 39, Catherine, 29, Catherine H., 68, Eliza W. B., 144, Frederick Milcah, 208, Henrietta, 208, 215, Henrietta L., 213, James, 29, 44, 66, 68, 81, James F., 145, 161, James Francis, 213, Jacob, 164, Josiah, 211, Josiah Wilson, 33, 211, Mrs., 218, Margaret, 211, Margaretta, 115, Martha, 70, Mary Ann, 145, Robert B., 221, Sarah Gray, 81, William, 29, 90, 91, 94, William H., 148, William F., 213, 66, William Henry, 215, William T., 44, 208, 215, William W., 125.
HUNTINGTON, Jeremiah M., 102.
HUNTLEY, John, 41, 61.

Catherine C., 99, David, 51, 53, Edward, 49, Eleanor, 45, Eliza, 53, 58, 132, Elizabeth, 133, 144, 77, Mrs. Elizabeth, 185, Elizabeth T., 195, Erasmus, 175, Frances, 19, Frederick W., 148, George, 168, George H., 132, Henry, 161, James, 185, James H., 123, 124, 170, 175, 183, 190, Jane J., 143, Dr. Jerome B., 185, Jesse, 136, 154, Joel, 62, 70, 77, 78, John, 156, 160, 194, John C., 98, Josiah T., 169, Keziah C., 116, Lewis, 116, 156, 170, Lucy F. R., 175, Malachi, 83, Martha A. T., 125, Mary, 137, 205, Mrs. Mary, 19, Mary E., 175, Mr. (child of), 219, Nancy W., 197, Nathaniel R., 163, Noah, 83, Paul G. C., 26, Pemma, 187, Phillis, 216, Richard, 142, 161, 162, Robert, 101, 102, 194, Rowland, 91, Susan, 114, Susan Eliza White, 216, Tabitha, 7, Thomas, 58, 83, Thomas T., 78, 116, 125, Walter F., 97, 104, William, 5, 19, 32, 167, 205, 216.
JORDAN, Mr. A. C., 218, Mrs. Abby, 98, Alexander, 16, 83, Arlethia L., 192, Augustus C., 16, Charles, 149, 192, Eliza, 39, 157, Francis, 200, James, 183, James C., 117, Jamima, 192, John A., 117, Josiah, 108, Josiah W., 117, Lewis C., 149, Marcus T. C., 48, Mrs. Martha S. F. S., 73, Margaret, 99, Mary, 133, M. T. C., 69, Willoughby, 23.
JOSEPH, Thomas, 72.
JOURDAN, S., 219.
JOYCE, Asam, 61, John J., 164.
JUNIOR, Ann.
JURO, Peter, 13.
JUSTINE, 54.

K

KAHO, Frances Ann, 118
KANE, Richard, 42.
KARCHER, Jacob, 194.
KARNS, John, 60.
KAVANAUGH, Thomas, 201, Mary, 201.
KAYE, George, 100.
KAYTON, Abraham, 201, Bernard, 201, Henry, 196.
KAYS, Mrs. Catherine E., 169.
KEAN, Ann, 30, Eleanor, 219, Robert, 195.
KEANE, Daniel, 84, Michael, 86, 89, 90.
KEATING, James R., 134.
KEATON, Frances B., 67, Thomas C., 67.
KEEFE (Keef, Keefee), Catherine, 127, Mrs. Catherine, 157, Mrs. Mary Ann, 140, Michael, 124, Thomas, 127.
KEELE (Keel, Keell), Mrs. Elizabeth F., 108, Henry, 36, 47, R., 25, Virginia, 143, Virginia A., 167.
KEELING, Catherine, 189, David F., 187, 190, Eliza, 209, Mrs. Eliza M., 132, Elizabeth, 74, Elizabeth A., 177, Elizabeth Grayson, 209, Frances, 91, Mrs. Harriet, 140, Henry, 8, 51, 122, 132, Revd. Jacob, 222, Mrs. Jacob, 222, Mrs.

Jaca, 140, John, 62, John T., 210, John W., 150, 184, Margaret, 91, Mary, 33, Mary Ann, 122, Mary G., 53, Mary Grayson, 210, Mrs., 222, Nathaniel D., 62, Mrs. Patsy, 77, Ralph P., 105, Robert, 102, 122, Sarah, 53, Mrs. Sarah, 220, Thomas Jr., 127, Thomas W., 104, William, 116, William E., 104, William Langley, 209, William Moseley, 208, William S., 71, 91, 112, 102.
KEEMER,, Mary Ann, 122.
KEENAN, James, 43, 59, Patrick, 31, 59, Sarah, 107, Terentius, 31, 21, 59, William, 31, 43, Mrs. Jane, 75.
KEHOE, Joseph, 169, 170.
KEHLMELLE, Eliza, 45.
KEIGER, Hugh, 157.
KEIN, Ann, 35, Eleonor, 35.
KEINS, William K., 8.
KEITCH, George, 125.
KELFREN, Mildred, 25.
KELLAR, Susanna, 9.
KELLER, Maxey, 24.
KELLINGER, Lucy, 53.
KELLS (or Kello), George, 35.
KELLUM, John C., 45, Major, 64, Mary S., 125, Pricilla, 18, Samuel, 49, Severn, 10, 13, 18, Thomas, 141, Mrs. Margaret, 74.
KELLY, Mrs. Elenor, 11, Elizabeth, 162, George, 39, 43, 59, 206, 218, James, 159, John, 147, Joseph, 141, 150, 174, 171, 145, Mrs. Margaret, 218, Mary Ann, 89, Mrs. Maxey, 6, Munroe, 183, Susan, 115, Mrs. Elizabeth, 159, Margaret, 206.
KELSICK, James, 46.
KEMPE (Kemp), Anzoletta, 145, Frank, 189, Hannah, 96, James, 198, Mrs. Mary, 156, Mathew W., 174, Sarah, 202.
KEMPTON, Ephram, 5.
KENAN, Ellen, 93.
KENNEDY (or Canniday), James, 13.
KENNEDY, Charles Henry Allen Harvey, 213, Edmund Archer Champlin Fawn, 213, Edmund (or Edward) P., 213, Lieut. Edmund P., 42, Edmund Pendleton, 163, Edward, 162, Eliza, 13, Mrs. Elizabeth, 51, Nicholas, 46, Peggy, 4, Mrs. Sarah, 48, Mrs. Sarah Ann, 57, Lieut. (child of), 222, Martha, 213, Mary E., 163, Dennis, 213, Ebenezer, 75.
KENNON, George T., 69, 79, 102, 109, 116, Dr. George T., 59.
KER, James, 1.
KERR, George B., 32, John, 77.
KERBY, George, 158.
KERRIGAN, Martin, 126.
KERRISON, Louisa Maria, 212, Maria Louisa, 216, Peter, 212, 216, William Peter, 212, William James, 216.
KERRY, Richard, 122.
KEVILL, Thomas, 201, 197.
KEYS, John, 189.
KEYSER, Lieut., 221.

246

ophilus, 197, William, 100, 106, 96, 118, 137.
MILLERSON, Sarah, 200, Ward, 193.
MILLINER, William Y., 139.
MILLISON, John S., 122, Mrs. Mary, 36, William, 100.
MILLOW, Martha, 50.
MILLS, Ann, 73, Betsy, 9, Edward, 115, Ephraim, 93, George T., 202, Job B., 35, 37, Polly, 25, Robert, 20, Sally, 105, Mrs. Susan, 171.
MILLSON, William, 30, 125.
MINAHIN, Morris, 21, 22.
MINER, Edward, 48.
MINERS, Virginia, 141.
MINGO, Lydia, 201.
MINTER, John F., 202, Martha, 179.
MINTON (Minten), Harrison, 163, Joseph B., 160, 165, 178, 184, Julia Ann, 162.
MITCHELL, Alexander, 19, Benjamin, 168, George M., 21, George W., 138, Hannah, 119, James, 33, 35, 37, 42, 51, 73, 85, 94, 104, 116, 120, 123, 124, 134, 139, 147, Jane E., 139, John, 5, John M., 148, Joseph, 15, Margaret, 42, Mary, 56, 164, Mary Ann A., 144, Robert, 53, 94, Sherman, 95.
MOFFITT (Moffatt, Moffit), Anne, 56, Anthony, 32, Mrs. Esther, 57, James, 156, William, 11.
MOHAN, Margaret, 17.
MOIR, Isabella, 169.
MOIZEAU, Luke Peter, 18.
MONGER, William, 85.
MONIER, Arsene, 72, Euphrosine Sumonavril (Mrs.), 5, Orphise Mariane, 21.
MONIHAN, Francis, 85.
MONTAGUE, Robert V., 184, W. V., 184, William V., 159.
MONTELANT, Eugene de, 98.
MONTGOMERY, James, 151, Mrs. Jane, 47, Jane Alice, 80, John, 11, Robert, 90, 94, 196, Virginia, 196, William, 100, 80.
MOODY, Alexis Julius Jr., 17, Ishmael, 91, Reubene B., 151, Thomas, 11, Willis J. C., 175.
MOON, Hiram, 156, C. Hiram, 156, Edward, 9.
MOONEY, William G., 192.
MOORE, Amos, 110, Ann Belson, 90, Anna Maria, 152, Ann, 175, 210, Augustine, 210, Bartlet, 199, David, 20, Edward, 9, Edward W., 149, Elizabeth J., 201, Elizabeth L., 129, Francis, 36, Franklin G., 181, Gershan, 48, 96, Henry, 49, 153, Horatio, 175, Isaac, 121, 136, James, 220, John, 26, 36, 37, John O., 185, Joshua, 34, 48, 78, 104, 113, 75, 137, 165, Mrs. Mary Ann, 114, 104, Mary Ann Frances, 96, Mary Eliza, 199, Mrs., 222, Mrs. M., 220, Nancy, 17, Nathaniel, 55, Nathan, 55, Peter, 160, 163, 201, Sarah, 125, Susan, 83, Susan

Almira, 100, Thomas, 55, 84, Thomas C., 152, Virginia Thomas, 210, William, 81, 128, William J., 193, 194, Mary Ann, 163.
MORAN, Catherine, 142, Catherine A. D., 154, Elizabeth, 56, Erin C., 153, Jasper (Gasper), 30, 56, 32, John, 56, Joseph, 30, Mary, 142, Michael, 151, Robert, 79, Susan, 142, Thomas, 4.
MORAO, J. C. de Figaniere e, 96.
MORCIN, John H., 137.
MORECAI, Isaac, 201.
MOREL, Pierre, 18.
MORELAND, John, 12.
MOREY, Eliza, 151.
MORGAN, Capt., 220, Mrs. Catherine, 30, Eliza, 46, Micajah, 196, Mrs., 220, Nancy, 126, Wilson B., 139, William G., 105.
MORJO, Marie Perede, 80.
MORONEY, Edmund, 85.
MORRESAY, Mathew, 177.
MORRIS (Morriss), Ann, 25, 96, 130, Benjamin, 195, Benjamin A., 173, 174, 185, 190, Mrs. Elizabeth, 116, Esther, 38, Jack, 170, John, 153, Kader, 85, Lucinda, 171, Mary A., 172, Mary Ann, 113, Michael, 82, Mrs. Nancy, 31, Robert, 122, 130, Sally, 85, Sara, 41, Susan, 53, Thomas, 99, William 91, 98, 113, William T., 172.
MORRISETTE, William, 89.
MORRISON, Allan, 197.
MORSE, Charles, 195, Jacob B., 159, Jesse, 195, Joel, 55, Lydia Frances, 195.
MORTON, Crowther, 144.
MOSELEY, Alexander, 204, 219, Amy, 122, Ann S., 139, Burwell B., 69, 220, Burwell Bassett, 55, Mrs. B. B., 222, Catherine B., 130, Charles, 85, 122, Clarissa, 16, Edward, 2, 9, Elenor, 12, Mr. E. H., 218, Frances B., 97, Hannah B., 209, Hillary, 8, 16, Mrs. Jennett, 9, John, 86, Martha, 138, Mary B., 48, Mary E., 122, Mary Walke, 82, Nancy, 8, S., 220, Mrs. S., 219, Samuel, 70, 97, 209, Samuel Jr., 89, Susan A., 138, William, 7, 70, 154, Phoebe Ann, 140.
MOSS, Martha Ann, 144, Nancy, 77.
MOSSMAN, Archibald, 84.
MOURNING, 78.
MOURTON, Ebenezer, 5.
MULLAN, John O., 6.
MULLHOLLAN, Bernard, 59, 148, Sarah Jane, 148.
MULLAN, Mrs. Helen B., 88.
MULLIN, Mrs. Catherine, 136.
MUNCHAM, Thadeus, 35.
MUNDOWNY, Keziah, 59.
MUNN, Mrs. Ann, 136, Reuben, 2.
MUNROE, Mary 3, Elizabeth, 60.
MUNSON, George W., 154, Henry W., 137.

PARKER, Ann, 11, Copeland, 52, 98, 100,
140, 159, 192, Diana Robinson Hall,
140, 159, Eliza S., 98, Elizabeth T., 192,
George, 17, James H., 123, John 9, 74,
153, Josiah, 111, Col. Josiah, 218, Mrs.
Margaret, 82, Martha Everard, 159,
Mary Ann, 100, Mrs. Nancy, 15,
Nicholas Wilson, 100, 111, 132, 140,
159, 172, 192, Pamelia A. T., 140, Rose,
6, Samuel, 76, 132, 149, Sarah, 24, Mrs.
Sarah, 118, Thomas, 63, Thomas H., 32,
William, 162.
PARKERSON (or Perkerson), Mrs. Ade-
line, 28.
PARKERSON, William, 183.
PARLATO (Parlatto) Vincent (Vincen-
tius), 29, 43, 80, Eliza Vincent, 71,
Emily Vincent, 80.
PARR, Mrs. Jane, 202, Joel, 140, Joel E.,
168, Lydia, 178.
PEAKE, John G., 198.
PECK, Isaac O., 129, 131, Mrs., 219,
Simeon, 2, 15, 19, Thomas, 175.
PEDAMUS, John, 55.
PEED, Mrs. Elizabeth, 35, Frances, 23,
Joel, 98, Lemuel, 23, 141, 176, Mary,
85, Nathaniel B., 150, Mrs. Polly, 20,
Robert, 107, William B., 111.
PEEK, John, 62.
PEEL, Mrs. Mary, 140.
PEET, Harriet Ann, 194, William, 194.
PEGLER, Henry, 188.
PEGRAM, Edward S., 123, 169, 199, 180.
PELON (probably Peillon), Mrs. Anne
Justine, 41.
PEILLON (Pellion), Stephen, 59, 62.
PEMBLETON, Mary, 4.
PENDLETON, Elisha, 125.
PENDRED, Charlotte, 115, Eliza Ann,
156, John, 56, Mrs. Mary, 59, Mary
Ann, 114.
PENDEGRAST, Lieut. Garret J., 109.
PENNOCK, Alexander Moseley, 215, Alex-
ander M., 170, 182, 183, Ann, 28,
Courtney, 51, Elizabeth, 215, Maria, 25,
Sarah C., 60, William, 21, 25, 28, 37,
51, 215.
PENNYWELL, Ann, 105.
PENNY, Thomas ,157, 192, 173.
PEPPER, Wilson S., 186.
PERBOTH, Anna, 22.
PERGUSON, Mary, 152.
PERIN, Elizabeth, 52, Mary, 35, Patrick,
35, 51, 70, Patrick V., 82.
PERKINS, John, 166, 183, Joseph, 46, Dr.
Richard C., 182, Valentine, 200.
PARRINGTON, William, 37.
PARRY, John, 127.
PARSHLEY, Susan, 125.
PARSONS, Elihu, 95, Mrs. Elizabeth, 156,
Gabriella C. W., 123, Lorenzo, 159, 198,
Ralph G., 157, Sarah, 12.
PASCAULT, Hardy Aime, 22.
PASCAL, Paul olycarp, 41.

PATE, James, 55.
PATER, Stephen, Andrew, 46.
PATTERSON, Ann, 37, David, 18, 37,
Edward, 189, Mrs. Elizabeth, 71, James,
16, Jane, 113, Jannet, 32, John, 63, 93,
Mariah, 3, Mary, 56, Nancy, 93, Re-
becca, 90.
PATTON, George, 6, Thomas, 201.
PAUL (Paull), D'Arcy, 95, Edward Alex-
ander, 178, James, 79, Samuel W., 158.
PAULSEN, Capt. John, 222.
PAULSON, George O., 129.
PAYNE, Edward, 165, Elizabeth, 55, 180,
Helen Maria, 87, John, 58, Livy, 56,
Mary, 87, Richard, 23.
PAYNTER, Mrs. Nathaniel, 221, Mr.
(child of), 219, N. W., 200.
PEACHAM, John, 31.
PEACHY, Thomas G., 73.
PEAR, Mary, 6.
PEARCE, Catherine, 130, Elizabeth (Mrs.),
4, James A. H., 170, 188, Walter, 124.
PEARMAN, Carter L., 156.
PEARSON, Elisha T., 175, Obediah B.,
125.
PEBWORTH, Anne, 185, Elizabeth, 8,
Mrs. Esther, 55, Martha, 47, Mary, 60,
William B., 92.
PERRIER, Francis A., 80, Mrs. Jane C.,
122.
PERROW, Samuel, 58.
PERRY, Amelia, 182, Jane, 97, Juliana,
37, Mary Jane, 137, William H., 169.
PETERS, Ann W., 46, Mrs. Ann, 4, Eliza-
beth, 209, Hannah, 11, Henrietta, 46,
James, 34, John, 147, 148, 166, Judson
R., 201, Lewis, 171, Mary C., 36, Milnor
W., 43, 66, 209, Mr. M. (child of), 220,
Sarah Ann, 123, 209, Thomas, 8.
PETERSON, John, 45, Rebecca, 137.
PETITT, Sarah, 55.
PETRIE (Petree), Alexander, 5, James, 72,
John Jr., 122, 137.
PETTY, John, 155.
PHILBRICK, Jane, 136, Patton S., 62.
PHILLLIPE, Lt., 222.
PHILLIPS (Philips), Abraham, 220, Ann,
30, Charles, 180, Elizabeth, 26, Enoch,
198, John, 124, 126, Mrs. Nancy, 176,
Samuel, 112, 124, Susan, 113, Thomas B.,
138, William, 127, William J., 180.
PICHOT, Frederick, 76, 81.
PICOT, Giles, 32.
PICKARDICK, Samuel, 110.
PECKERELL, Adolphus H., 171, Esau,
179.
PICKET, Machen, 139.
PIEMONT, Amanda, 97, An nEliza, 169,
Eliza A., 113, John, 93, Margaret, 169.
PIERCE, Amanda W., 202, Mrs. Ann, 95,
David, 42, Elizabeth, 124, Elizabeth F.,
202, Mrs. Fanny, 25, George H., 155,
John, 46, Margaret, 215, Maria Harriet,
89, Rebecca M., 135, Rice B., 106,

Samuel, 51, Thomas, 51, 215, Wentworth Willis, 215, William W., 89, Wilson, 112.
PIERSON, Nicholas M., 202.
PIERCY, James, 16, 21, James L., 81, L. L., 66.
PIGEON, Corine, 141, E., 141, Francois Marie, 5.
PIGG, Mary Jane P., 188.
PINES, Susan, 165.
PINKERTON, Ann, 79, William, 79.
PINKHAM, Henry, 73.
PINN, Benjamin, 13, Joanna, 13.
PINNER, Catherine, 169.
PIPER, Jonathan, 45.
PITT, Mrs. Ann H., 132, Benjamin, 49, John R., 45, Martha Smith, 49.
PITTS, John R., 58.
PLUME, Ann, 3, William, 3.
PLUMMER, Willis, 192.
PLUNKET, Achilles, 24.
POINDEXTER, Carter Braxton, 21, 22, 171.
POINER, Mrs. Mary, 144.
POINTIER (Pontier), Honore, 67, 68, 83, Mary Augustine Evelina, 67, Mary Francoise, 83, Marie Heloise, 68, Mary Sicilia, 134.
POINTER, Isaac, 55.
POKE, Mary Ann, 116, Rebecca Jane, 121.
POLLACY, Lawrence, 212, Sally, 212.
POLLACY, Lawrence, 212, Sally, 212, ----------------, 222.
POLDING, Mary, 47.
POLLARD, Benjamin, 3, 43, 107, 161, 158, C. R., 220, Elizabeth, 194, Lewis R., 77, 92, Margaret E., 59, 161, Rebecca, 202, William P., 11, 45.
PONCE, Francis, 149.
POOL, Elizabeth, 100, William, 150.
POOLE, Howard, 94, Mrs. Margaret, 27, Martha, 36, Mary, 8.
POPE, Charles T., 171.
PORTELETTE (Portlet), Medara, 46, 69, 72.
PORTER, Mrs. Ellen, 83, Elizabeth, 24, Elizabeth Myers, 17, John J. B., 117, Sarah, 135., Sem, 119, William H., 130.
PORTLOCK, Catherine, 148, Eliza, 221, John, 36.
PORTNET, William, 61.
POST, Mrs. Louisa, 120.
POTTS, Bartley, 64, Benjamin, 6, Mrs. Elizabeth, 101, John, 28, Pricilla, 115, Robert, 71.
POWELL, Alexander, 202, Mrs. Ann D., 201, Elizabeth, 46, 201, Henry, 171, James H., 202, John T., 194, Mrs., 219, Margaret, 96, Mrs. Matilda, 116, Merit, 191, Nancy, 106, Peter, 181, Sarah, 46, William, 194, William K., 201, 186, William S., 120.
POWER, John, 85, 165.
POWERS, Betsey, 74, Lewis A., 200, John,

155, Mrs. Nancy, 196, Pricilla, 35.
POYNER, Lydia W., 138, Mary, 138, William, 92.
PRADERES, Thomas, 25.
PRATT, Margaret Susan, 193.
PRAY, John, 32, Mary H., 153.
PREBLE, Henry, 114.
PRECIOUS, Mary, 34, Matthias, 34, William P., 48.
PREESCHERN, Elizabeth, 194.
PRENTIS, Eliza B., 78.
PRESCOTT, Charlotte, 65, Mrs. Charlotte, 68.
PRESCOTT, Charlotte, 65, Mrs. Charlotte, PRESEOREZ, Mary, 22.
PRETLOVE, John, 20.
PRESSON, William, 6.
PRESTON, James P., 13, Robert G., 186, William, 77.
PRICE, Asa, 85, Charles, 77, Francis E., 199, 195, James, 192, Rev. James, 219, John, 27, John B., 167, John T., 114, Mrs. Peggy, 4, Sally, 2, Seth, 1, Stephen, 1, Thomas, 2, William, 174, William Evans, 15, 23, 30.
PRIME, William S., 139.
PRIMROSE, Edward, 20.
PRINCE, Mrs. Elizabeth, 67.
PRIN (Laurent, Lawrence), Luc Laurent, 29, 32, 49, 56.
PINN, Benjamin, 34.
PRIOR, Leon, 165.
PRITCHARD, Edward, 100, Henry, 4, Noah, 6, Robert C., 133, Mrs. Sarah Ann, 176, Susan P., 133.
PRITCHET, William, 165.
PROBY, Helen, 68, Mr. (child of), 218, Paul, 221, Sophia S., 126.
PROESCHER, Mary, 202.
PROPER, Elizabeth, 104, Evalina M., 74.
PROUDFIT, Mr. J., 219.
PRYSOUGH, George, 185.
PUGH, Joseph W., 191.
PULLEN, Elizabeth, 78, John M., 157.
PURCELL, John, 170.
PURDIE, John E., 190.
PURDY, Elizabeth, 51.
PUSEY (Puzey), Abby, 48, Mary, 35, Martha R., 69, Pamelia, 154.
PUTEGNAT, J. P., 149.

Q

QUARLES, Moses, 195, Roger, 86.
QUICK, Bennett, 172, William, 183.
QUINN, Ann, 164, Daniel, 138, John, 38, 57, 173, 155, 196, Mary, 154, Mrs., 219, Patrick, 13, William H., 192.
QUIRK, Thomas, 173.

R

RADCLIFF, Mary Anne, 188.
RAE, William Iron, 20.
RAILLON, Octavus Augustus Valentine Bowen George Washington Warren Lewis Jr., 17.

RITTER, Charlotte, 19, Elizabeth, 19, Mrs. Elizabeth, 221, Margaret, 19, Mary, 5.
RIVALAIN, Lewis M., 22.
RHEA, Daniel Sr., 155, Daniel Jr., 155, Elizabeth Ann, 173, Mary Ann, 155, Robert, 173.
RHODES, Jacob R., 25, T., 220, James, 219.
ROACH, Thomas W., 132, William L., 181.
ROBERT, Benjamin, 88.
ROBERTS, Anna Eliza, 161, Ann T., 95, Mrs. Catherine, 91, David, 82, 86, 88, Edward, 16, 222, Mrs. Frances, 51, James, 30, 113, John, 20, 42, 128, 152, John A., 140, John H., 122, 142, 174, Julianna Dunston, 199, Lemuel, 93, Martha, 67, N. G., 187, Sally, 93, Sarah, 168, Mrs. Sarah, 47, Thomas, 30, William, 137, 145, 155, 197, William D., 49, 98, 106, 161, 163, 164, 168, William, 199.
ROBERTSON, Alexander, 139, Ann, 13, Anne Elizabeth, 154, Duncan, 200, Mrs. Elizabeth, 107, Elizabeth C., 190, Francis O., 150, Harrison, 190, Helen, 154, James, 75, 130, Joseph, 109, Joseph H., 111, 146, 154, 175, Maria, 47, Mary, 27, Mary F., 154, Moses P., 179, 194, 195, Richard L., 86, Robert, 29, 76, 140, Thomas L., 68, 71, 126, 146, William V., 155, William, 137.
ROBINS (Robbins), Alice, 136, George, 172, John, 30, 55, 67.
ROBINSON, Ann Hartwell, 208, E. C., 191, Edmund C., 140, Elizabeth, 184, George, 135, Henry, 98, James, 74, 86, 109, 200, John E., 200, John T., 116, Jordan, 141, Joseph, 141, Merritt Moore, 208, Robert S., 176, Sarah, 159, Thomas, 147, William, 149, 159, 202.
ROBLIN, William, 110.
ROMBOUGH, Ann M., 109.
ROBSON, William, 95.
ROCHFORD, Patrick, 90.
ROCKWELL, A. M., 149.
RODGERS, Ellen A., 134, John, 34.
ROGERS, Aaron, 57, Abraham, 52, A. A., 141, Catherine, 117, Elizabeth B., 114, Mrs. Ellen, 120, 124, Mrs. Hanna, 107, Harriet, 80, 173, James B., 126, Jane, 62, John, 64, 86, John C., 186, John R., 88, Jonathan, 37, Lewis E., 136, Mary, Richard J., 198, Rufus K., 115, Mrs. Sally, 111, Sarah Jane, 166, William, 12, 75, 84, 93, 98, William Jr., 166. 104, Mary Ann, 190, Mary Ann D., 98, ROGERSON, Jane, 40.
ROHAN (Rowan), Richard, 154, 155, Mrs. Margaret, 168, William, 130.
ROLLINS, Mary, 46.
ROLPH, Elizabeth, 142.
ROMAIN, Mrs. Ursula, 81.
ROOK (Rooke), Thomas, 138, 165, John

B., 169, Martha, 165.
RONEY, F. P., 91, Mary Catherine, 189.
ROPER, George, 78.
ROQUIE (Roque), Francis, 202.
ROSE, Ann, 4, Archibald, 26, 79, 82, 87, Catherine M., 83, Isaac, 145, James, 57, John, 85, Mrs. Katy, 184, Mr. Mary, 82, Robert M., 91, Dr. Robert W., 192, Stephen P., 41.
ROSER, Mrs. Ann D., 69, William, 17.
ROSS, Andrew, 123, Mrs. Elizabeth, 27, George, 67, James, 174, Mrs. Jane, 112, John G., 108, Jonathan F., 93, Lydia, 219, Mrs. Lydia, 2, Mrs. Mary, 24, 79, Thomas, 19, 64, Walter, 20, 35.
ROSSON, William, 174, John C., 62, Willis, 69.
ROTHERY, Emanuel, 20.
ROUG, Adelaine, 24.
ROUNDEY, Thomas F., 182.
ROURK, Francis, 202, John, 5.
ROUSE, Sarah, 99.
ROUX, Bernard, 73, 100, 118, 137, Capt., 56, John, 39, 50, Marie Antoinette Pamela, 50.
ROWAN (Rohan), Richard, 154, 155, Mrs. Margaret, 168, William, 130.
ROWE, Mrs. Ann, 37, Anne Eliza, 71, Catherine, 188, John, 165, Mary, 28, Thomas, 19, Virginia, 179, William, 71, 173.
ROWLAND, Ann, 205, 207, 212, Charles Henry, 212, Charles H., 155, Emily, 178, George, 36, 95, 129, 205, 207, 212, (child of), 221, George William, 207, John Hambleton, 205, John H., 129, William, 95.
ROWSAY, John Tabb, 11.
ROYE, Mrs. Susanna, 10.
RUDD, Fanny, 21.
RUDDER, Elizabeth, 177, Henry, 177, Mrs. Hester, 165, Jonathan K., 180, Sarah, 186.
RUDOLPH, Titan, 127.
RUFFIN, Thomas, 79, 86, 87, 89, 90, 97, 96, Philip, 195.
RUGGLES, Mrs. Frances, 37.
RULON, Job, 185, 186, Samuel, 178.
RUSSELL, Benjamin, 62, Catherine, 127, Eliza Ann, 148, Michael, 107, Nancy, 48, John, 140, John W., 111, 120, Jonathan, 137, Patrick, 127, 143, Penuel, 19, 62, Sarah, 76, Stephen S., 121, Thomas, 76.
RUSH, John, 11.
RUTH, MOSES, 29.
RUTLEDGE, Mrs. Elizabeth, 21.
RUY, Edward, 8.
RYAN, Alexander, 148, Catherine, 29, Mrs. Elizabeth Stansbury, 142, Capt. James C., 183, James, 124, Lawrence, 52, Mary Ann, 100, Mrs. Martha, 70, Patrick, 1, 13, 21, 16, 32, 47, William, 22, William C., 114.

SHEA, Michael, 81, Nancy, 81.
SHEARLOT, Mrs. Polly, 81.
SHEERMAN, Mrs. Fanny, 102.
SHEBORN, Hubberd, 64.
SHEFFIELD, George W., 188.
SHEILD (Shield, Sheilds, Shields), Ann
W., 182, Augusta Lavinia, 201, Mrs.
Catherine, 56, Charles H., 83, 158,
Elizabeth N., 202, Hamilton, 80, 92,
Henry, 30, Henry H., 83, James H., 162,
Martha, 182, Martha M., 182, Mary C.
H., 162, Richard H., 182, William, 107,
William C., 80.
SHELAR, Mrs. Mary, 82.
SHELTON, Mrs. Elizabeth, 2, Mrs. Sarah,
120.
SHENTON, John, 99.
SHEPHERD, Ann B., 74, Mrs. Ann, 32,
Edmund, 197, Elizabeth, 15, 17, 45, 205,
Elizabeth O., 139, Frances, 17, John,
205, John C., 126, John Cornick, 205,
Lewis, 110, Sarah M. C., 181, Smith,
103, Soloman, 15, 17, Thomas S., 139,
Virginia, 181, William, 123, 139, Wil-
liam L., 193.
SHERMADINE, Francis, 196.
SHERMAN, Elizabeth, 67, Herbert, 67,
William, 200.
SHERWOOD, Iaac, 87, Stephen, 109.
SHETTLE, Henry, 99.
SHIBLEY, John, 66, 85.
SHIFLET, Mr., 220, William, 55.
SHIBLEY, John, 66, 85.
SHIPP, Mrs. Ann Eliza, 138, Eliza Ann,
166, Frances, 166, John, 98, 165, 192,
Mary, 32, Moses, 155, Sally, 11, Samuel,
11, Sarah, 98, Sarah Ann, 192, Sarah E.,
178.
SHIPWASH, Dinah, 80, Jemima, 39, 80,
Julia, 23, Mason, 90.
SHIRLEY, Ambrose, 18, Ann D., 87,
Martha, 87.
SHORT, Mrs. Anna Jenkins, 63, Fanny, 7,
Mary, 155.
SHORE, Mary Ann, 165.
SHORTER, Eliza Jane, 180, Peter, 180,
182, Sarah Ann, 182.
SHRAEDER, Ann E., 164.
SHROEDER, Ann, 126, Margaret, 156.
SHREIVES, Sarah Ann, 160.
SHRIVES, John L., 162.
SHUSTER, George, 27, Jacob, 58, Jacob
Jr., 35.
SHUTE, Mrs. Elizabeth, 131.
SHUTTLE, Ann Maria, 197.
SIBLEY, F. A., 174, 183, John G., 192.
SICKLES, Elizabeth, 160, Margaret, 160.
SIDDONS, Benjamin C., 115.
SIKES, Augustus, 138, Jesse H., 202, John,
168.
SILVERTHORN, George, 28.
SILVIA, Antonio, 156.
SIMCOE, Horrace H., 173, 170.
SIMMINGTON (Simington), Maria, 78,

Robert, 24, 29, 28, 37, 78, 134, Mrs.
Sarah, 97, William, 15, 24, 41, 44, 52,
84, William C., 172.
SIMMONS, Andrew, 109, 184, Ann, 202,
Daniel D., 194, D. D., 140, Dr., 158,
Mrs. Dorothy, 16, Eliza Anne, 214,
Elizabeth, 214, Mrs. Elizabeth, 63, John,
84, Margaret, 109, 151, Simon H., 114,
Thomas, 58, 71, William, 214, Willis, 33.
SIMMS, Jerusha, 181, Mary Elizabeth, 185,
William D., 129.
SIMONET, Marie Roalie, 32.
SIMON, John, 39, Nicholas, 39, Simon,
199.
SIMONS, Sidney, 165.
SIMPKINS, Joseph, 118.
SIMKINS, Mima, 3. .
SIMPSON, Elizabeth Ann, 159, Elizabeth
Terrant, 41, Mrs. Elizabeth, 190, George,
193, James, 94, John, 117, John E., 158,
159, Lucretia, 152, Philip H., 166, Mrs.
Rebecca, 65.
SINCLAIR, Ann, 192, Arthur, 140, 170,
George Terry, 170 ,Dr. William B., 175.
SINGLETON, Mrs. Amy, 58, Eliza, 30,
Henry, 66, John, 17, 30, 69, 99, Mary
D., 99, Nancy D., 17.
SIVELY, Mary A., 158.
SKIDMORE, Mrs. Jane, 86.
SKILMAN, Sophia, 148.
SKINNER, Charles W., 86, Mrs. Hannah,
189, Mrs. Martha, 194, Matilda, 172,
Sarah J., 201, Thomas, 76.
SKIPTON, William, 8.
SKIPWITH, Humberston, 79, 94, Pliny,
17.
SLACK, Mary Ann, 67, 120, Sarah, 29,
Sarah Ann, 74, Susan F., 95.
SLAGHILL, Maria, 95.
SLATE, John, 119.
SLATER, John T., 191.
SLAUGHTER, 108.
SLIDER, Nancy, 79.
SLOAN, James B., 105, 125, 126.
SLOANE, Davis, 102.
SLY, Elizabeth, 5, Margaret, 1.
SMALL, Amy, 196, Arthur, 90, Arthur A.,
196, Elizabeth, 159, Mrs. Elizabeth, 100,
Joseph R., 200, Sarah E., 196, Mrs.
Susan, 79, William, 20.
SMAW, Mrs. Eliza, 114, Henry, 70, Heze-
kiah, 104.
SMELLY, Mrs. Nancy, 90, William, 160.
SMELT, Mrs. Ann, 92, Miles, 37.
SMILEY, Francis, 93, James, 144, 180, 92,
174, 194, Jane, 93.
SMITCHEN, Mrs. Sally, 65.
SMITH (Smithe), Alexander P., 97, An-
drew, 194, Ann, 209, Ann F., 168, Ann
Sophia, 210, Anne, 211, 214, 217, Archi-
bald, 188, 196, Caleb, 103, 104, Charles,
82, 182, Charles H., 127, Charlotte, 125,
157, 165, Caroline, 159, Mrs. Caroline
Augusta, 202, Catherine Horseley, 207,

188, Mary Bassett, 175, Matty, 215, 213, Matty Lindsey, 215, Robert B., 50, 114, 123, 119, 141, 169, 121, 215, William, 82, William E., 150.
STARR, John, 152, William H., 185.
STARRETTE (Starette), Frances, 125, Mary Ann, 105.
STASBOROUGH, John, 83.
STAVRO, Hannah Cecelia, 197, George, 198, George W., 190, Gertrude F., 147, John, 56, 89, 101, 113, John B., 189, Mary, 147.
STAYLER, George Jr., 198.
STAYTEN, Sarah J., 196.
STEADY, William H., 174.
STEED, Ann, 78, Fanny, 206, 213, George Washington, 213, Margaret, 28, Robert E., 12, 205, 68, 111, 213, Soloman, 25, 40, Capt. Soloman, 218, Virginia Frances, 146, William, 206.
STEELE (Steel), Jane, 149, William, 186, William R., 190.
STENT, Anna, 63.
STEPHENS, Absolom, 46, E. F., 164, Elzie F., 165, Walter, 19, William, 31.
STEPHENSON, Charles, 119, Ferdinand, 8, Henry, 102, 113, Sarah, 97.
STERLING, Eliabeth, 88.
STERRETT, Susannah, 126.
STERVANT, Mrs. Nelly, 18.
STETSON, Mrs. Eliza, 4.
STEVEN, Anne, 206, Martha Eliza, 206, William, 206.
STEVENS, Absolom, 9, Andrew, 139, 171, Ann, 208, Anne, 79, 214, 216, Cadjo, 125, Elizabeth, 101, 129, Jane, 68, John Cowell, 214, Margaret, 79, Richard Archer, 208, Richard Harris, 118, Samuel Bedford, 216, William, 214, 32, 160, 208, 216.
STEVENSON, Ann Eliza, 188, Charles, 114, Mrs. Elizabeth, 125, Eliza S., 202, Esther, 114, Henry, 102, Polly, 61, Turner, 15.
STEWARD, Ann, 113, Christy, 10, John, 102, 86.
STEWART, Abia, 82, Ann, 57, 80, Athel, 72, Edward Henry, 53, George, 107, John, 99, 118, 126, Lydia, 168, Pleasant, 46, Robert, 135, Mrs. Sarah, 165, Sarah Jane, 202, Unice, 47, William, 37, 47, 101, William H., 139.
STIGER, Ruth, 42.
STILLMAN, Eleazar, 153, 1661, 194.
STINGER, Hallary, 217, Peggy Eyre, 217, Sally, 217.
STIRON, William, 129.
STOKER, Peter, 29.
STOCKLEY, Sally, 5.
STOESER, Leo, 167.
STOKARD, Mrs. Marie Cassin, 107.
STOKES, Andrew, 186, David M., 133, Elizabeth, 214, Exun, 114, Polly, 147, Thomas, 186, 187, 200, William, 214.

STOLP, Christian, 122. 132.
STONE, Daniel, 7, 50, 106, 131, Eliza, 96, 208, Elizabeth, 96, 134, 104, 214, 215, Ellen, 181, Fanny, 131, Frances, 146, 181, Mrs. Frances, 160, John, 131, 208, 214, 215, Capt. John, 218, John Phripp Reid, 206, Johnson, 206, Juliana, 118, 205, 208, 218 Lelianne, 215, Louisa, 139, Mrs. Maria, 62, Mitty Richards, 72, Sarah, 206, Simon, 155, 189, Virginia, 134, 214, William C., 178, 186, William F., 28, William T., 26.
STORRS (Storse, Storz), Andrew, 174, Mrs. Elizabeth, 35, John, 10, William, 34.
STOTT, Timothy B., 179, Virginia, 174, William, 113.
STOUT, Mrs. Eliza, 137, John H., 184, John J., 61, Thomas, 158, 192.
STOW, Cyrus, 66.
STOWE, Willis R., 44.
ST. PIERRE, Mrs. Jennette, 90.
STRAND, Nancy, 62.
STRATTON, John, 26, Margaret, 26.
STREET, Martha, 58, Mr. William, 218.
STRIBLING, Cornelius K., 87, 154.
STRINGER, Smith, 35.
STRIPE (Stripes), Joseph, 41, 46, 97, Mrs. Mary, 113.
STRONG, Capt. (child of), 219, Harriet, 144, Nathan, 12, Nathaniel, 208, Sarah, 208.
STROUD, Ann, 47, John, 20, 87, 109, Mrs. Susan, 151.
STRUTHERS, James, 2,4, 10.
STUBBS, Jabez S., 125, Simon, 139.
STUBLIN (Stubling), John, 26, 52.
STURGES (Sturgis), Jacob, 142, William, 48,
STURTEVANT, Earl, 53, Martha Jane, 166, William P., 168, William, 166.
STUTSON, Mrs. Elizabeth, 62, Samuel, 45.
STYLES, Richard, 95, Wilson, 49.
STYRON, Elizabeth, 172, Nancy, 172.
SUGGS, Dorothy, 96, Elizabeth, 34, Mrs. Elizabeth, 35, George, 3, 7, 23, 34, 47, 87, 96, Marha Canby, 47, Rebecca, 81, William B., 23.
SUMMERS (Sumers), Mrs. Ann, 116, Ezra, 103, Ezra T., 184, Francis, 90, 106, Helen, 98, Jane, 106, Mary, 61, Mary Frances, 184, Minty, 91, William, 81, Mrs. Sarah Ann, 75, Tildsley, 102, 81, 122.
SUMMERSON, Mrs. Louisa, 191.
SUMTER, Mary Ann, 141.
SUTHERLAND, Mrs. Lavinia, 170.
SUTTON, Capt., 142, John, 166, Lemuel, 117, 134, 138, Samuel, 117, William, 188.
SULLIDEN, Mary Eliza, 58.
SULIVAN (Sullivan), Delphe, 2, Jeremiah, 138, Joanna, 2, Thomas, 83.

SULLY, Chester, 38.
SWAB, Barbara, 29.
SWAIN, Benjamin, 48, Charles, 40, 48, Charlotte C., 183, Harriet, 48, Joshua B., 151, Thomas, 75.
SWANK, Eliabeth, 77, Catherine, 95, 132, John, 95, 132, 77, Mary Ann, 132.
SWAN (Swann), James, 88, Thomas, 114.
SWEENEY, Andrew, 202, James, 160, 186, Johanna, 84.
SWIFT, Anne 211, Ann P., 216, Harriott Anne, 216, Lydia Riche, 211, Lieut. Thomas R., 50, Thomas R., 57, 211, 216,
SWINDELLS, James H., 83.
SWOOBE, Sarah, 85.
SWORDS, John T., 94.
SYKES, Ann, 198, Augustus, 139, 173, 174, Harriet A., 159, Henrietta, 173, Jane, 187, John, 179, Lovey Ann, 179, Machriste, 170, Slaughter, 191, William E., 199, 202, Zachariah, 175.
SYLLIVAN, Joanna, 2.
SYMES, Charlotte, 207, 210, 214, Mary Sharp, 210, Robert Reade, 207, Robert S., 66, 207, 210, 214, William Leigh, 214.

T

TABB, Charlotte A., 122, Edward P., 154, Henry, 135, John, 74, 131, 122, Philip E., 90, Philip Edward, 96, Mary A. O., 149, Mary W., 16, Martha M., 145, Thomas C., 144, 145, 146.
TALBOT, Constane, 13, Diana, 186, Isaac, 64, 116, 146, Kader, 12, 214, Mrs. Kader, 220, Margaret Ann M., 116, Margaret Anne Miriam, 214, Mary, 91, Mary D., 146, Mary Tabb, 138, Mrs. Mariam, 13, Miriam, 214, Sarah Ann, 195, Virginia, 186, Sarah W., 66, Mrs. Ann, 135.
TALCOTT, Andrew, 127.
TALLEY, Mrs. Ann, 86.
TALLY, Thomas, 82.
TANEY, Louisa A., 86.
TANGUIRE, William M., 42.
TANGUY, Margaret Helen, 10.
TAPLEY, Bernard, 86.
TARMAN, Joseph, 57.
TARRANT, Carter, 39, Jane, 65, William C., 188.
TART, Lydia, 27.
TATE, Mrs. Eliza, 25, Nancy, 57.
TATEM (Tatum), Ann Elizabeth Loller, 129, Diana, 74, James, 28, 101, 184, Mr. Jos., 220, Joseph, 151, Maria, 75, Prudence, 28, Robert H., 92, Sarah, 101, Sarah C., 141, William, 154.
TAULSON, Margaret, 85.
TAYLOR, Alexander P., 169, 173, Alley, 91, Ann, 13, 210, 216, Anne, 205, Archibald, 95, Arthur, 17, 71, 129, 214, Arthur Jr., 112, Babel, 179, Benamin J., 137, Caroline V., 117, Eliza, 208, Eliza

Calvert, 163, Elizabeth, 1, 107, 207, Edmund, 168, Francis S., 2, 83, 100, 210, Genl. (child of), 222, George W., 113, Georgiana A., 129, Georgiana Alexander, 214, James, 3, 19, 205, 211, James Jr., 9, 13, 41, Jane, 216 John, 16, 31, 95, 166, John Carr Calvert, 208, John Calvert, 218, John O., 122, John S., 200, Joseph, 91, 161, 192, Mrs. J. T., 219, Louisiana, 182, Major, 24, Margaret, 28, Mary, 214, 215, Mary Eliza, 97, Mary Emmott, 214, Mary P., 194, Matty, 130, Miles D., 171, 178, Nathaniel, 194, Rachael, 31, Reese, 170, Richard, 2, 97, 144, 163, 207, 208, 215, 218, Mrs. Richard, 221, Robert, 13, Robert B., 16, 90, 205, 216, Robert E., 120, 130, Dr. Robert E., 111, Sarah, 205, 209, 211, Sarah Alexina, 163, Sarah Lindsay, 83, Mrs. Susan, 173, 191, Tazewell, 140, 183, 205, 211, Virginia Elizabeth, 210, Virginia F. G., 146, Virginia Frances Gilliat, 215, Walter H., 126, 195, Walter Herron, 159, 163, 207, William A., 193, William Augustine, 209, William B., 136, William C., 218, William Edmund, 210, William Eyre, 205, William, 78, 92, 136, 185, 209.
TAZEWELL, Ann E., 187, Ann Stratton, 211, 216, Littleton Waller, 15, 21, 211, 216 (child of), 218, Littleton Waller Jr., 175, Mary, 190, Sarah Ann, 211.
TEBO, William, 182, William L. M., 125.
TECLEOD, William, 83.
TELFAIR, Mrs. Sarah, 6.
TEMPLE, Stephen L., 146.
TERRIER, Peter, 21.
TERRILL, Doct. George, 120.
TETREVILLE, Peter Germain, 39.
THAYER, Collin, 190, C., 181, Margaret, 190, Susan A., 181.
THELABALL, Elizabeth D., 24, Richmond, 24.
THOM, Jacob, 165.
THOMAS, Benjamin, 95, Ebenezer, 3, Mrs. Frances, 218, James Jr., 53, John, 10, 90, 136, 158, John W., 173, 195, 196, Joseph, 69, Josiah, 95, 130, Lucy, 187, Mrs. Mary, 133, Thomas, 109, William, 30, 70, 117, William B., 127, 162.
THOMPKINS, John J., 152, 188, 195, 199.
THOMPSON, Ebenezer, 154, Edmund, 171, Mrs. E., 218, George M., 123, Henry, 183, Henry F., 183, 187, Herbert C., 78, James, 12, 31, 39, 55, 77, Jane B., 196, Jesse, 85, Mary, 57, 170, Maria, 71, Mrs. Mary, 173, Nicholas O., 144, 165, Robert B., 152, Sareina, 98, William, 9, 20, 139, 143, 165, William H., 170.
THOMSON, Eliza, 83, 206, Smallwood, 206, William, 206.

VAIL, Mrs. Elizabeth, 150, Julia Ann Hester, 169.
VALENTINE, Benjamin, 13, Edward, 71, 145, Eliza M., 217, Jacob, 53, 208, Jacob Moore, 217, Jobel, 217, Mary Frances, 208, Mrs., 219, Rachel, 44, Sarah, 208.
VALERTIN, Maria Magdalaine, 76.
VALERY, William, 57, 77.
VALLANCE, Isaac, 91.
VANDERSLICE, Adam, 56, 65.
VANDERBERRY, Richard, 49.
VAN GOVER (Vangover), Elizabeth F., 179, John, 141.
VANHOLT, Mrs. Elizabeth, 85.
VAN KALTHEN, Mrs. Rosina, 22.
VAN LEVAN, Moses, 106.
VANOSOSTE, Guilliaume (William), 11, 13.
VANSANT (Vansantts), Frances (Francinsi), 26, Thomas, 221.
VAUGHN, Augustus M., 186, Capt., 219, Elizabeth, 13, Frances, 50, Isaac, 9, James B., 73, 212, Jane, 7, John S., 184, John W., 177, Mrs. 219, Mrs. Mary, 18, Mrs. Mary G., 140, Sarah H., 143, Susanna H., 212, Thomas, 60, William, 7, 141, 178, 212.
VEAL (Veale), Samuel, 150, Mrs., 158, William C., 147, 174, 177.
VENTERS (Ventis), Elizabeth, 23.
VENTUS, John, 7, 18.
VERNANDEN, John, 219.
VERMILION, Dennis, 140.
VERNON, John, 47.
VERONIQUE (Sally), 68.
VICKERS, John, 20, Mrs. Mary Eleanor, 45.
VICKERY, Ann W., 153, Catherine, 210, Eli, 10, Mrs. Eliza B., 158, Capt. J. (child of), 221, Jacob Jr., 164, Margaret, 10, Robert Boush, 210, 220, Samuel, 78, 210, Capt. Samuel, 40, Capt. S., 220.
VICKHOUSE, Elizabeth S., 200.
VILET, Peggy, 20.
VINCENT, Mrs. Ann, 136, Frances M., 158, Francis, 51, 68, Frederick, 71, John, 115, John P., 97, John S., 166, 167, Sampson Clement, 68, William P., 116, F..........., 80.
VIOLEAU, Arnaud, 29, Jerome, 39, John Augustus, 39, Marie Magdaline, 29, Rene Charles, 29.
VIZONEAU (Vizonneau, Vizeneau), Mrs. Orphise Marie Ann, 37, Peter, 18, 20, 21.
VOINARD, Otelia, 101.
VOSS, William, 187, William Thomas, 159.
VOYART, John, 110, L'amy, 38.

W

WADDY (Waddey), Daniel R., 37, Mr. D. R., 219, Edward S., 26, 53, 78, 213, 221, 216, (child of), 218, Edward, 207, 213, 221, Louisanna, 207, Margaret, 207,

Rebecca B., 131, Rebecca Brown, 216, Sarah, 213, 207, Sarah E., 131, 216.
WADE, Elizabeth, 10, Zebulon, 76.
WADLINGTON, Elias, 98.
WADSWORTH, Daniel, 199.
WAGAN, David, 146.
WAGGONER, William, 82.
WAGNER, Peter, 155.
WAITE, Abel, 81.
WAKE, Flamstead, 5.
WAKEFIELD, George, 39, Mrs. Sarah, 98.
WAKEMAN, James, 44.
WALDEN, Elizabeth, 43.
WALDIE, James, 12.
WALES, Asaph, 63, James, 38, John, 51, 54, Nancy, 9.
WALKE, Anne, 40, Rev. Anthony, 221, Anthony Jr., 17, 46, Calvert, 194, Jane Eliza, 133, John N., 122, Lucinda, 171, Mary, 41, Richard, 146, Susan M., 133, William, 148, Mr. William (child of), 219.
WALKER, America, 76, 90, Aliph, 109, Mrs. Ann, 113, Dempsey, 109, Mrs. Dinah, 9, Edward, 179, Elizabeth, 13, 92, Ellen, 90, George, 28, Henry B., 80, Henry B. C., 138, James, 15, John, 75, 86, 146, 180, Joseph, 117, Lilly, 20, Levi, 121, Mary, 193, Mary Ann, 193, Margaret, 10, Margaret Ann, 142, Nathaniel S., 202, Capt. Robert, 222, Mrs. Susan, 102, Thomas, 32, 185, Thomas R., 100, William, 96, William S., 92, Wilson, 87, 89, 109, 111.
WALAC (or Walace), Anthony, 1.
WALLACE, Mrs. Aphia, 7, David A., 222, Edward, 198, Eliza Frances, 148, Mrs. Elizabeth, 4, Elizabeth C., 43, Fanny, 22, Mrs. Kezia, 36, Mathew, 39, Mrs. Nancy, 3, Owen, 123, Samuel, 150, Soloman, 140, Thomas D., 185, 195, William, 201.
WATERFIELD, John, 186.
WATERMAN, John, 98.
WATTERS (Waters, Watirs), Fanna, 43, James, 150, 185, 199, Mary, 185, Margaret, 130, Mrs. Margaret, 182.
WATHALL, Virginia T., 191.
WATKINS, Mrs. Elizabeth S., 172, Howard, 147, 171, Mrs. Jennet, 36, Mary, 94, Mary E., 171, Martha, 19, Robert, 9, Virginia, 202.
WATLINGTON, James, 89, 84, Louisa, 84, Nathaniel, 68, Nathaniel Jr., 49.
WATSON, Anne Carr, 212, Capt. (daughter of), 221, David, 48, Edward, 125, 187, 205, 212, Elizabeth Gordon, 212, George, 145, James, 81, 106, J. M., 175, John, 138, Lieut. Josiah (U.S.N.), 219, Margaret, 15, Mary D., 158, Mrs. Mary, 35, Mrs. Nancy, 149, Richard, 133, 138, 205, Sarah Carr, 212, Sax., 205, Severn, 36, Seven, 24, William, 15, William H., 86.
WATTINGTON, James, 88.

WATTLES, Andrew D., 153.
WATTS, Ann, 77, Bartlett (Bertlett, Bartley), 149, 168, 173, Elizabeth Ann, 187, Emeline, 181, Euphan, 38, John, 181, 186, 187, John M., 89, 105, 164, Mrs. Lucretia, 70, Mary Frances, 186, Samuel, 162, Sarah Ann, 164, Winchester, 162.
WAYLAND, John, 60, 170.
WAYNE, William A., 163.
WEAVER, John, 127, Mary R., 188, Patsey, 18, Mrs. Mary Ann, 67.
WEBB, Delia A., 197, Edward, 115, Eliza, 160, Fanny, 138, Harriet, 154, Isabella, 15, John, 82, 101, John M., 198, Martha M., 170, Mary C., 98, Richard, 61, Sally, 72, Thomas F., 152, Thomas T., 170, Virginia, 152, William, 9, 20, 72, 81, 96, William B., 118, 130, William G., 115.
WEBSTER, John, 136, 137, 161.
WEIDEMEYER, William, 151.
WEITHMAN, James, 191.
WALLER, Littleton, Tazewell, 115, Littleton T., 190, Mathew P., 187, 190, Orfa, 134.
WALLET, John H., 135.
WALLIS, James, 18.
WALSH, Margaret, 142, Margaret M., 142, Roger, 28, 33, William, 1.
WALSOND, Maria, 37.
WALTERS, B. B., 147, Mrs. Fanny, 72, George, 174, James, 139, Sarah Elizabeth, 147.
WALTHALL, Henry, 58.
WANGNER, Elizabeth, 72.
WARBURTON, Mrs. Mary, 145.
WARD, Ann, 124, 130, Anthony, 108, Bryan, 12, Elizabeth, 32, Mrs. Eliza G. C., 51, Francis A., 94, James, 4, 54, 103, 106, Jane E., 130, Mary Ann, 146, Rebecca, 193, Sarah, 24, 44, Dr. S., 51, William, 6, 24, 27, 32, 43, 130, 124, 201.
WARDERMAN, George, 93.
WARDEN, Martha Ann, 195.
WARE, Samuel, 112.
WARING, Annet M., 91.
WARNER, George, 156, John, 3.
WARREN, Ada, 138, Ann, 92, 189, Ann Eliza, 141, Elizabeth, 23, Mrs. Elizabeth, 6, 107, Elizabeth F., 122, Ellen, 111, Frances, 25, Isaac, 153, 159, Jacomine N., 76, James, 140, James B., 221, John, 25, 26, 189, John Jr., 35, Lyndia, 66, Maria, 4, Mary A., 104, Mary Ann, 119, 142, Mrs. Polly, 80, Rosini, 111, Thomas, 21.
WARRINER, Edmund, 1, 5.
WARRINGTON, Lewis, 70.
WARTHALL, Amelia Ann, 169.
WARWICK, Benjamin, 106, 108, 111.
WASHINGTON, Mathew, 81.
WELCH (Welsh), Catherine, 18, Mrs.

Hannah, 35, 40, John, 101, Mary, 12, Mark J., 128, Rebecca, 186, Sarah, 186.
WELD, Edward, 19, 31, 35.
WELDEN, Rebecca, 121.
WELKER, John R., 93.
WELLONS, Thomas H., 149.
WELLS, Elijah Gardner, 165, George, 50, Henry, 59, Mrs. Jane, 54, Mary, 115, Mrs. Patsey, 57, William H., 159.
WELTEN, Susan, 61.
WELTON, Henry, 166, 175.
WENDELL, Oliver, 61.
WERCKMULLER, Anna, 158, Hellena M., 153, H. T., 150, Simon B., 76, 120, Victoria, 171.
WESCOT, Mrs. Ann, 34, Major, 34.
WESSON, William, 79.
WEST, Adeline, 208, Ann Cornick, 179, Beverly, 89, Mrs. E., 219, Eady, 33, Emeline, 115, Mrs. Hannah, 173, Harriot, 4, James, 4, 73, James C., 133, John, 2. 7, 20, 26, 33, 55, 58, 174, 178, 208, John R., 76, John W., 124, 125, Mary, 1, 152, Mary Harris, 25, Mrs., 218, Olivia S., 135, Robert, 178, 190, Thomas B., 135, 163, 179, Thomas Wade, 4, William, 18.
WESTON, John C., 172, John W., 159, Lilly, 190, Nancy, 82, Noah, 15, Robert J., 143, Stephen C., 144.
WESTRAY, Levi, 169.
WESTWOOD, Jane Stith, 70, Zedee, 197.
WEYLAND, John, 171.
WEYMOUTH, Elizabeth A., 202, Rebecca, 198.
WHALEY, John, 48.
WHEELER, Mrs. Ann Eliza, 144, Carleton, 30, Charles, 180, Eliza, 162, Guy C., 75, Luke, 28, Samuel, 145, Samuel J., 152, Susan, 28.
WHETON, Anthony H., 74.
WHIGGLETON, Mrs. Mary, 47.
WHILLOCK, Mrs. Hannah, 112.
WHITAKER, William, 101.
WHITE, Ackey, 196, Amelia, 155, 206, Amy, 90, Ann, 22, 110, Benjamin, 18, 27, Ceder W., 122, Charles, 170, Daniel, 76, David, 196, Edward, 172, Elisha C., 90, Elizabeth, 123, 128, Elizabeth T., 135, Mrs. Elizabeth, 112, George, 10, 207, 219, George Anthony, 207, 219, George Washington, 18, Gideon, 140, Harriet, 155, James G., 125, 115, John, 69, 125, John K., 110, John S., 188, Joseph, 82, Mariam, 78, Mary, 32, 46, 146, 165, Mary Ann, 161, Mrs. Mary J., 18, Patsy, 74, Paulina, 96, Rachael, 196, Richard, 16, 165, Robert, 82, Samuel, 56, 63, 128, Sarah, 89, Mrs. Sarah, 43, 47, Susan, 145, Thomas, 154, 165, Thomas B., 145, Thomas C., 89, 90, William, 100, William D., 82, William T., 185.

George, 221, James, 60, John J., 174, Dr. John P., 105, Margaret, 209, Mary, 183, Mary Ann Dandridge, 209, Mary Louisa, 191, Thomas O., 164, Virginia Ann, 140, John, 68, Jane H., 66, Christianna, 120, Georgiana, 177, Mrs. Sally, 4, William D., 107, Elizabeth, 68.

Z

ZAAL, Hendrick, 29.
ZABRISKIE, Horsburgh, 186.
ZEILIN, Jacob, 179.
ZWISSLER, Otto, 202.

www.ingramcontent.com/pod-product-compliance
Lightning Source LLC
Chambersburg PA
CBHW071847270326
41929CB00013B/2130

*9 7 8 0 8 0 6 3 5 1 1 5 5 *